A Southern Rebel

The Fred W. Morrison Series
in Southern Studies

John Salmond

A Southern Rebel

The Life and Times of Aubrey Willis Williams

1890–1965

The University of North Carolina Press

Chapel Hill

© 1983 The University of North Carolina Press

Manufactured in the United States of America

Library of Congress Cataloging in Publication Data

Salmond, John A.
A southern rebel.

(The Fred W. Morrison series in Southern studies)
Bibliography: p.
Includes index.
1. Williams, Aubrey Willis, 1890–1965. 2. United
States—Economic policy—1933–1945. 3. United States—
Politics and government—1933–1945. 4. Afro-Americans—
Civil rights—Southern States. 5. Politicians—United
States—Biography. I. Title. II. Series.
E748.W685S24   361.6'092'4 [B]   81-23087
ISBN 0-8078-1521-7   AACR2

This book is dedicated to my children,
Kerry, Nicola, Paul, and Mark

Contents

Acknowledgments

This book began as a study of the National Youth Administration, until my interest in its head took over from my interest in the agency itself. It has been ten years in the making, and during that time I have accumulated a substantial array of debts. I must now try to acknowledge some of them.

Writing United States history from the other side of the world is not easy. It would be quite impossible without the generous financial support of various institutions and groups. This book could not have been written without the assistance of the American Council of Learned Societies, the Eleanor Roosevelt Foundation, the Australian Research Grants Committee, and the Research Committee of La Trobe University. Publication assistance was provided by the Eleanor Roosevelt Foundation and the La Trobe University Publications Committee. My most sincere thanks to them all.

Then, I must thank the members of the Williams family and those friends who took time and trouble to share their remembrances with me. I am particularly indebted to the late Mrs. Anita Williams, Professor Aubrey Williams, Jr., Mrs. Virginia Durr, and Mr. E. D. Nixon. I hope this book in some small way helps repay their kindness and generosity.

As is true for the works of all historians, librarians and archivists own part of this book. It owes much to the assistance and forebearance of a score or more of such people from the Franklin Delano Roosevelt Library, the Harry S. Truman Library, the National Archives, the Wisconsin State Historical Society, the Tuskegee Institute, the University of North Carolina Library, the Duke University Library, and the Memphis Public Library, to name but a few. My thanks to all those who helped me in this way.

Many colleagues both at La Trobe University and at other institutions have shared in the making of this book, by talking about problems, by reading drafts, and by providing support in a multitude of ways. I wish particularly to thank Susan Poynton, who helped as my research assistant at a critical time in the book's life, my La Trobe colleague Dr. William Breen, whose many valuable suggestions have substantially improved the work, my mentor at Duke University, Dr. Richard L. Watson, Jr., and Professor Bruce Clayton, of Allegheny College, Meadville, Pennsylvania, whose wise counsel was crucially important at a vital stage in its development. Mrs. Barbara Sayers of La Trobe University has typed and retyped the manuscript until she practically knows it by heart, as well as being a generous and supportive friend. David Perry at the University of North Carolina Press has substantially improved the manuscript through his careful editing. My gratitude to all these people named, and to those too numerous to list who have also helped in similar ways.

Parts of this book first appeared, in modified form, in the *Journal of American History*, the *South Atlantic Quarterly, Historian*, and a collection of essays on the New Deal published by the Ohio State University Press in 1975. I am grateful for the permission of their various editorial boards to reproduce some of that material here.

Finally, I wish to mention a group of people whose friendship and concern have, in a real sense, made this book possible: Peter Tomory, Lucy Frost, Derick Marsh, Carrah Clayton, Ralph Gallagher, Tony and Hilary Barta, Grant Wason, my colleagues in the La Trobe University Department of History, and, in so many ways, David Jolley and Karin Liedke. My humblest thanks to them all, including of course those to whom this book is dedicated.

Everyone mentioned above has helped in shaping whatever merit may be found in this work. I alone am responsible for any deficiencies.

JOHN SALMOND
Melbourne, 1981

A Southern Rebel

1

Boyhood in Birmingham

Springville, in north-central Alabama's St. Clair County, twenty miles northeast of Birmingham, thirty-five miles southwest of Gadsden, county seat of neighboring Etowah County, is today, as it always has been, a small town of less than a thousand people, little more than a stop on the highway north. Northern Alabama has historically been a region of small farms rather than large plantations; its broken, rolling, pine-wooded, dry, and sometimes mountainous terrain was ill-suited to large-scale agriculture. Before the Civil War few slaves were held there. Small subsistence farms predominated, and that pattern continued after 1865. The people who settled northern Alabama, too, differed from those who came to the bottom half of the state, where the large plantations were located. Central and southern Alabama folk came overwhelmingly from South Carolina, Georgia, and Virginia; those who peopled the north were predominantly from the hills of North Carolina and Tennessee.

Alabama politics has always been molded by tension between the small farmers of the north and the planters of the central and southern regions. The relatively higher concentration of blacks in the southern and central parts of the state resulted in differences in attitudes to race, which exacerbated the economic differences between the two regions. Northern Alabama was where, in the 1890s, Populist strength was greatest, while in the twentieth century what passed for progressivism in the state Democratic party generally had its roots in the northern and north-central counties. It was in Springville, then, in the heart of this region, "sometime between darkness and daylight" on August 23, 1890, that Aubrey Willis Williams was born, the third child in a family of five sons and two daughters.[1]

His mother's family was fairly typical of the folk who peopled northern Alabama. Of Scotch-Irish origin, the Taylors had moved from Virginia in the early nineteenth century, settling at Claytons Cove, sixteen miles north of Birmingham. Nonslaveholding, God fearing, the family epitomized the small farming folk of the region. His father's people were rather different. Of Welsh extraction, they had moved to Alabama from North Carolina through the Cumberland Gap in 1819, but had gone to the southeastern part of the state to Dale County, where his great-grandfather had soon acquired extensive holdings, including a number of slaves. Williams's father, therefore, was born on a plantation. His grandfather, however, was deeply troubled by the morality of slave ownership and in 1855 successfully petitioned for permission to free some of his people. Both grandfathers served in the Civil War, and both families were devastated by it. For the former planter, however, the consequences were worse. His wife, permanently unhinged by the collapse of her world, could never admit that the struggle had been lost. It was partly for her sake, partly in the hope that a change of location would drive away the memories, that Williams's grandfather moved his family north during Reconstruction, settling in Springville, but four miles from Claytons Cove. Charles Williams and Eva Taylor eventually met, fell in love, and married.[2]

Aubrey Williams often used to speak of his father, Charles, as someone, who though far too young to fight in the Civil War, had nevertheless been ruined by it. He "never got over the feeling of having his roots cut from under him and being adrift," he once wrote, and though he was a skilled blacksmith and carriage builder, who won awards at exhibitions in both Paris and St. Louis for vehicles that he had built, he never succeeded in providing for his family, in large part because of his "ruinous habit of drinking." Williams remembered his childhood "as one of living in many places and many houses, moving around, looking for a cheaper place to live." The first of these moves took place when he was but a six-month-old baby. Hoping that there would be good money for blacksmiths in the booming new industrial city of Birmingham, Charles Williams moved his family there in the fall of 1890. Birmingham, therefore, was the town in which young Aubrey was formed.[3]

Born, as C. Vann Woodward says, "in an old cornfield in 1871 of the union of a land company and a railroad," Birmingham was by 1890 a booming, bustling industrial city of nearly thirty thousand people, a town of great contrasts, of conspicuous opulence and of foulness and squalor. It was a town, however, where fortunes could be made.[4]

For Charles Williams, however, the fortune, and the attendant opulence, never came. He quickly drank away what little money his smithing made. By the time Aubrey was ten, the Williams family had lived in about twenty houses, all in the "backside of Birmingham," as he later described it. Indeed, so poor was the family that the children were all forced to leave school at a very early age to supplement the family budget, though it nearly broke Eva's heart that they had to do this. For Aubrey, the end of his formal education came in his seventh year, after only one full year at school. After having attended "for three months in the fall," he was taken away and put to work as a delivery boy on a laundry wagon, for which he was paid one dollar weekly. He did not have the job for long. "I was always hungry in those days," he later wrote, and to fill out his meager diet, he began stealing the change from the pocket of the man that he worked for, "to buy bananas." He was found out and sacked. Fortunately, his mother found him a position as a cash boy in the growing department store of Loveman, Joseph, and Loeb. His job was to move change, as required, to the various parts of the store. For this he received $1.50 weekly. Of that he kept ten cents to pay for his Saturday night's supper, and gave the rest to his mother.[5]

Thus, much earlier than most people, Aubrey Williams left a large part of childhood behind and began to earn a living. He learned early, too, about tragedy. When he was about eight his younger brother, Roby, left unattended in an outhouse, found some matches, lit them, and set fire to the building. Shockingly burned, he lingered for four days, his father constantly at his bedside, before death came. Then, too, Williams learned early from a number of sources about the complexities of race relations in the South. Mary, the black woman who helped his mother, always called young Aubrey "Judge." It was through her, he later wrote, that he first came "to look upon Negroes as persons." She would talk to him about the harshness of black life, and he would react with outrage. One of his father's friends married a black woman. From then on he was ostracized in white society and forced to conform to the developing Jim Crow laws. Yet, as a cash boy at Loveman, Joseph, and Loeb's, he later related, he had plenty of opportunity to observe the mulatto mistresses of the town's leading citizens as they shopped for fineries in the store, their bills conveniently taken care of. The inconsistency struck him sharply. "There were the big men, the men whom everybody admired," the pillars of the local churches, doing "all the things we had been taught were sins, drinking, gambling, dancing, whoring, and with colored women." It was a puzzle to the young cash boy.[6]

Life was hard in many ways, but not unrelievedly so. His mother was a deeply religious woman, a devout Presbyterian whose faith sustained her through the various adversities of her life. Aubrey was devoted to her, and generally went with her to services—sometimes as many as six a Sunday—revival meetings, and church socials. Quite early, the church became the center of his social life. Then there were the normal pranks and delights of boyhood, raiding watermelon patches on warm summer evenings, fishing in the streams and ponds of the city, playing baseball with the neighborhood children. The Williamses were gregarious folk, and whenever they moved, they usually made friends with the people next door. One such neighbor, a plumber named Martin, used to double as the local dentist, pulling children's teeth with his plumbing pliers. Mrs. Williams never allowed him to touch her brood, however, much to Aubrey's relief.

The family often visited back to Springville and Claytons Cove for family reunions. Although at the end of his life he was to write that "the men who burned the busses and kicked the Freedom Riders almost to death looked exactly like the ruined people I used to know as a boy in Claytons Cove," at the time he eagerly looked forward to those visits, especially if it meant a chance to see his cousin John. "He was an example of how close we were to the Old Frontier," he once wrote. "He not only raised everything he ate or practically all, and made everything he used, he was his own blacksmith, wagon builder, wheel wright and he shoed his own horses. We boys thought he was the perfect man, that he could and did do anything and he just about could."

He liked to visit his Aunt Joe, too, his father's sister who lived in Birmingham, because she was pretty and kind and lived in such a splendid apartment. He was rarely taken there, however, and always over his mother's obvious disapproval. Indeed, once Eva flatly refused to let him go to his aunt's for Sunday dinner, saying that "she is not a good woman." Aunt Joe was never invited to the Williams home. Only later did he find out the reason: She was a "kept woman." Early childhood passed, not carefree, often puzzling, but not totally without its lighter side.[7]

Williams's interrupted formal education continued—after a fashion—through his church connections. He became a familiar figure at the Fifth Avenue Cumberland Presbyterian Church, where he was befriended by the pastor, Dr. I. D. Steele, and his young and beautiful wife. Mrs. Steele took a particular interest in the young lad, and soon Aubrey was visiting her every Tuesday and Thursday evening. She taught him how to read and write and introduced him to the world of books. Williams, for his part, adored her. Soon he found a way to repay her for her kindness and concern. Mrs. Steele loved the theater, but as the pastor's wife, she could little afford to be seen at performances. Her husband's parishioners would have been scandalized. Aubrey, however, was able to attend. Moreover, he had ready access to theater tickets. The department store had a huge billboard attached to one of the exterior walls on which the theater companies advertised their various performances. In return, a number of tickets were always available for store employees. Whenever he could, the young Williams would secure one of these, attend the performance, often fighting to stay awake, and then tell Mrs. Steele all about it. She "saw" the plays, therefore, through him, and he delighted in it. Mother Eva's considerable qualms were quietened somewhat by his argument that he was only "doing it for Mrs. Steele."[8]

Others were attracted to the boy not only because they felt sorry for him but also because they were impressed by his capacity for hard work, his serious and Christian attitudes, and his genuine desire to learn. The manager of his department at Loveman, Joseph, and Loeb's offered to adopt him when he was ten or eleven, and a year or so later the principal of a local primary school, whom Williams had met in the store—"a wonderful fella," he later described him—regularly devoted his lunch hour to giving the youth personal tuition. He eventually persuaded him to attend night classes, and this he did whenever he could afford it. Thus, in piecemeal fashion, he picked up the rudiments of a formal education.

By that time he had left the department store, where by the age of twelve he had been placed in charge of wrappings for the entire

store—for $3.50 weekly. This gave him enough money to spend
something on himself. Years later, he recalled the thrill of buying
some "very expensive clothes," using the store discount.[9] However,
other stores offered even more money. He next worked for J. Black
and Sons, where he ran the wrapping department, before being
promoted to the hat department when he was sixteen. His particular responsibility was to wait on foreigners and Negroes. Then he
moved to Joe and Lee Slaughter's, where he sold men's suits, and
from 1907 until he left Birmingham he was employed by the Somers
Tailoring Company, where he became assistant manager of men's
furnishings at $21 a week. The young man was beginning to make a
career for himself in the department store business.[10]

But other interests and concerns were claiming him. The church
was still important to him, though he was beginning to have doubts
about some of its teachings. During his adolescence two men, both
connected with the church, had a profound effect upon him, helping to shape in important ways his thinking on both social and
theological questions. One was "Dad" Bridges, the assistant pastor
at Fifth Avenue Cumberland Presbyterian; the other was a Presbyterian minister known in Birmingham as Rev. "Brother Bryan."[11]

Both these men, in one way or another, taught him something of
the social dimensions of his faith, helping him to see that there was
much more to Christianity than simply the pursuit of personal salvation. Rev. Bridges, the church's "troubleshooter," was no social
gospeler, but he did convince the young Williams that sin had to be
looked at in more than strictly theological terms. For him, sin and
socioeconomic conditions were closely intertwined. The failings of
an individual were often the result of his economic situation, he
believed. Alleviate that, end his poverty and degradation, and his
"sin" often withered away. That point of view eventually cost him
his job at Fifth Avenue Cumberland, the parishioners generally
being much less receptive than Aubrey to any suggestion that the
church had a social role to play. For Williams, on the other hand, it
opened the possibility of working actively for social change within
the framework of institutionalized Christianity.

Rev. Bryan took him a long way further down that road. Bryan
himself was even less of a social Christian than Bridges. The message he preached was an intensely personal one, but he preached it
to a different group. Bryan's mission was to the outcasts, those on

the bottom rung, the folk who would never be found in the pews of
Fifth Avenue Cumberland. Every weekend this man, who, Williams
later wrote, "used to give away his clothes to people in need,"
brought the Christian message to the drunks and deadbeats of the
city, the poor, exploited cotton mill workers of the Avondale district on its outskirts, and, most important, to the prisoners, either in
the jails or leased to work in the surrounding mines. Aubrey normally went with him.[12]

The convict lease system began in the South in the years immediately following the Civil War. Lacking money for penitentiaries and
faced with a mounting convict problem due to the harshness of the
legal system and the extreme privation that often forced men to
steal in order to live, the impoverished state governments hit on a
novel means of making a virtue out of a necessity. Hired out to
work, convicted criminals became not a drain on the public purse
but a means of augmenting it. In the late nineteenth century, most
southern states adopted some variant of this practice.

The system was iniquitous in conception and vile in execution.
The possibilities for corruption were endless, as the convicts were
often leased and subleased until the line between state and individual contractor was hopelessly broken. Inspection was at best per-
functory, and often ignored. The convicts were worked shockingly
hard in the swamps, forests, and mines of the South and barbarously
treated, often kept on the verge of starvation and brutally flogged
for the slightest misdemeanor. In the Alabama mines, for example,
convicts were often forced to work knee-deep in water, without
shoes, winter and summer. They usually worked under the task
system, adapted from slavery days, which meant that the men had
to mine a certain stated amount of coal each day. If they failed to
reach the target, the whole squad was flogged. Small wonder that
the annual death rate for these unfortunates ranged between 10 and
20 percent. Both black and white convicts were leased, and it was
generally conceded that the treatment of the blacks was even more
cruel than that meted out to the whites.[13]

To such convicts, those leased to the mine owners of Birmingham
and its environs, Brother Bryan brought his message of hope and
salvation. Sunday after Sunday he tramped or rode to their camps,
holding services, praying with them, caring for the sick, comforting
the dying. He showed the same compassion for them all, black and

white. Aubrey accompanied him whenever he could, assisting him
in whatever way possible. The experience stayed with him for the
whole of his life. More than fifty years later, he could still recall
vividly the horror of it all, the "bestiality and brutality" of the
guards, the "horrible methods of punishment" which were com-
monplace, the degradation and despair of the prisoners. Though
Williams eventually came to doubt the relevance of Brother Bryan's
message of personal salvation, the minister's selfless devotion to the
underprivileged was always a model for him. It was through these
two clergymen that Williams was introduced to the possibilities of
social action. His Christianity led him to work among the poor and
outcast.[14]

By the time he was sixteen, he was doing such work on his own.
He still went to the coal mines, but he moved into other areas of
need as well. At Avondale the young man who himself had had almost no formal schooling now taught those who had been similarly
deprived. Every Sunday afternoon he taught basic literary skills to a
class of around fifty mill workers, usually in their late teens, youngsters like himself whom economic privation had forced from the
classroom. Later, when he was eighteen, he organized a boys club at
the Birmingham YMCA. Each week he and about thirty ten year
olds, often from the poorest homes, would meet, work in the gym,
eat a "10 to 15 cent dinner," and generally have a good time. Williams once described this involvement as "the sweetest experience
of my life."[15]

As he worked with the poor and the hungry, he became less and
less satisfied with the conventional approach to Christianity. Largely
as a result of the inequalities he had seen, and also because of the
double standards he had observed in the lives of the so-called "pillars of his church," he began very seriously to question the point of
trying to save souls. At about the age of sixteen, he later stated, he
stopped being "an eager-beaver in the ranks of those who worked
in the Army of the Lord," gave up "Hell and the Devil," and began
to stress the disparities that he saw between the example of Jesus
and those who now spoke in his name. That attitude got him in
some trouble at Fifth Avenue Cumberland. Asked by the new assistant pastor, the Reverend J. M. Broady, a man whom Williams
considered to be "nothing more than a Tennessee horse-dealer," to
take the pulpit one Sunday in recognition of his efforts with the

boys club, he denounced those who "unashamedly had turned it [the church] into a money making scheme," challenging his listeners to show some social responsibility. Rev. Broady, visibly angry, later told the congregation that had he known what the young man's message was to be, he would not have afforded him the privilege of the pulpit. Thus, even in his teens, Williams displayed a passionate concern for the poor and a proclivity to say exactly what he thought, no matter what the occasion. Both traits would stay with him the whole of his life.[16]

At the time, therefore, when many young people were occupied primarily with the familiar personal concerns of adolescence and burgeoning adulthood, Williams was unusual in his early commitment to helping those less fortunate than he. He was, he said, an intense, "pretty morbid youngster," who, when praying, often asked for "something hard to do."

But not everything about his teenage years was serious. Though, he later admitted, he normally walked to work in the morning "thinking about the plight of people," he strolled home in the evening, more often than not, "daydreaming about girls." The tall, handsome youth had his normal share of adolescent affairs of the heart. He first fell in love when he was thirteen and a wrapper boy at J. Black's. He could see the object of his affection only before Sunday school and had to content himself with letters the other six days of the week. All went well until she found out his address. Realizing that he was from the wrong side of the tracks, she dropped him immediately. Economic circumstance caused another romance to fail four years later. The young lady that time was "the spit and image of the then reigning beauty of the American stage, Maxine Elliot; black eyed, black haired and just blossoming into a beautiful woman." He had met this vision at a church picnic, where she had tenderly nursed a hand that he had hurt while playing baseball. He adored her, but she gave him up when he could not afford a box or carriage for the local horse show. Desolated, he buried himself in his social service work.[17]

By the time that he turned twenty-one, the young Williams had achieved a measure of success for himself as a department store salesman. His reliability, capacity for hard work, and experience had virtually ensured a departmental managership for him in the near future. Moreover there was much more to hold him in Birm ingham than the job. His family, particularly its strength, his mother Eva, to whom he was devoted, was there, as were his friends, his church, and, of course, his voluntary social service work.

However, he still had his dreams. One of those had long been to go to college, there to get the formal education he had so far been denied and to train for the ministry. Although he had increasing doubts about the institutional church and quarreled with certain theological perspectives, he had no such doubts about Jesus. There seemed no better way to serve one's fellow man than through him. Given his lack of formal schooling, college seemed an impossible dream. "Dad" Bridges, however, told him of a school in the Tennessee mountains, Maryville College, which was tailor-made for people like Williams. It accepted students who had not had a high school education, gave them that in a modified form, and then let them move into an undergraduate program. This was exactly what he wanted. Eva was similarly enthusiastic, and he began to save.

By 1911, at the age of twenty-one, he had put enough aside to finance his first year. He applied, therefore, and was accepted for admission in the fall semester. His family and friends gave him a grand send-off, putting together a trunk full of things for him which they presented ceremoniously at a huge going-away party. Williams himself provided the food at that affair. For some time he had been operating a small chicken business, putting the profits into his Maryville fund. With his departure, it had to be closed up. At the party, therefore, they had a great chicken fry, which "liquidated that night, the chicken business entirely." Nearly three hundred people feasted, sang, and bade him farewell. The next morning, Aubrey Williams, well fed on chicken and with his new trunk, his collection of *Punch*, *Redbook*, and *Atlantic Monthly* magazines, and his dreams, kissed his family good-bye and set off for the mountains of Tennessee and the next phase of his life.[18]

2

"Over There"–And Other Places

The Tennessee town of Maryville, sixteen miles from Knoxville, is set in one of the most beautiful areas of the United States—the foothills of the Great Smoky Mountains. The countryside is green, wooded, rolling or hilly, and beautiful all year round—spectacularly so in the fall. Set on top of a hill and surrounded by its own woods, Maryville College looks out on a thoroughly pleasing natural prospect.

The college was founded in 1819 by the Presbyterian church, making it one of the oldest in the region. Evangelical Christian emphasis has always been paramount. As late as 1965 the prospectus stated that "the only teachers and officers appointed are those who gave clear evidence that they possess a genuine Christian faith and life program and are actively related to an evangelical church." Chapel and religious teaching were still compulsory, drinking was entirely prohibited, and heavy restrictions were placed on smoking. When Williams went there in 1911, the evangelical influence was even more pronounced. The president was Dr. Samuel Tyndal Wilson, a man so narrowly devout that he would not even travel by public transport on Sunday. Once, when inadvertently delayed, he alighted from a train at midnight on Saturday and walked the rest of the way home, rather than contravene his principles, and he set the tone for the college. In time, Williams became disenchanted with his rigidity, but initially it did not bother the young man, who was thoroughly entranced with the prospect of relief for the first time in thirteen years from the responsibilities of being a breadwinner. He began his studies in an almost euphoric state of mind.[1]

The course work at Maryville was routine and, as one would expect at a school where many of the students were drawn to the ministry, heavily and evangelically Christian in tone. Few of the teachers made much of an impression on Williams. One who did was Arthur W. Calhoun, a professor of Greek. Williams was thrilled by the breadth and sweep of his courses. "We were all grasping for the truth," he wrote later, "and he was a man who was bringing some order into this dark, unintelligible mass of contradictions."

Calhoun was too liberal, too broad, for Maryville, however. After a lecture on the family in which he presented human development in a way that contradicted the biblical account of the Creation, he was summarily dismissed. Williams was deeply shocked, as were many of his fellow students. He led a deputation of three to discuss the dismissal with other faculty members, but it was to no avail. Dr. Wilson was adamant. Calhoun was out of step with Maryville's religious thinking. Moreover, he had, it was disclosed, once been a member of the American Socialist party, and if this were generally known some of the college's benefactors might well be sufficiently outraged to stop their contributions. So Calhoun left, preaching a dramatic sermon in the chapel just before he went on a text from Matthew, chapter 23, in which Christ repeatedly cries, "Woe unto you, scribes and Pharisees, hypocrites."

Williams was profoundly disturbed by the firing. "To have this man dismissed in such a fashion," he wrote subsequently, "struck us as a great injustice and for me left a permanent scar." He maintained contact with Calhoun all his life and often corresponded with him, while his attitude toward the college's president was permanently altered. Even though he "loved Dr. Wilson so much that I named one of my sons after him, Winston Tyndall," he "could never forgive him" for this action. It was one of the reasons why after four years, having finished high school and completed his freshman year there, he decided to leave Maryville, and it reinforced what was already becoming a passionate commitment to freedom of speech and belief, for which he was to be a fighter all of his life.[2]

Though Williams described life at Maryville as in some ways "a second childhood," only in his first year there was he able to attend as a full-time student. That year he lived on money that he had saved in Birmingham, but that was not possible thereafter, partly because an attack of typhoid in the summer of 1912 ended any chance of vacation earnings. Like many of the other students, he was forced to find work in the town in order to keep himself afloat. Fortunately, a trade he had learned as a sideline in Birmingham now stood him in good stead. He found regular work as a window trimmer and sign writer for a local firm, for which he was paid $3 weekly. As board at the college was only $1.85 a week, he had money left over for clothes and, above all, for books. Williams read avidly throughout his Maryville years.[3]

When he was free from study or work, Williams was more often than not involved with church work. Despite his growing doubts about institutional Christianity, he was still thinking of the ministry as his vocation. During his stay in Maryville he did a lot of preaching, usually in remote mountain hamlets that did not have regular pastors. A number of these villages were "moonshine towns"; in some, vicious and prolonged blood feuds still raged, and in most the residents were highly suspicious of strangers. At times the terrain was so rugged and its inhabitants so inhospitable that Williams needed the assistance of the local marshal even to reach his destination. Yet the simple piety of these people and their unaffected friendliness once he had their confidence profoundly impressed him and ameliorated at least some of his doubts.

Not so his involvement in the religious life of the college itself. Frequent revivals were part of Maryville's program, and in 1914, Williams became chairman of the committee charged with arranging these. Troubled by what seemed to be an untoward emphasis on emotionalism—"I always associated sex with revivals and I think I was right," he was to assert later—he approached Dr. Wilson to see if a more low-key approach could be tried, one that involved a modicum of social Christianity. Once again, Dr. Wilson was unbending, and Williams resigned his position.[4]

But not all of his Maryville experience was serious and frustrating. Far from it. He made many lasting friends among the students. One of these, Wiley Rutledge, was later appointed to the Supreme Court by Franklin Roosevelt, and the two Maryville boys lunched regularly together when they were both in Washington.[5]

With another friend, Charles E. ("Turkey") Smith, he found a way of combining fun and profit. They developed a "comic debating team" act. Solemnly arguing such propositions as "whether it was easier for a chicken to roost on a round or a square limb," they toured the East Tennessee mountains, where they were enormously popular with church groups and a much-sought-after act at church socials. For those efforts they received three to four dollars nightly —and a good meal. It was a thoroughly painless way of making money.

His college experience included the usual pranks, dormitory raids, and the like, one of which landed him in court. A number of students, Williams among them, climbed the county courthouse steeple and painted the hands of the clock in their class colors. Apprehended and brought to judgment, they were found guilty and fined one dollar by the judge, "with a great smile on his face." (Ironically, that incident was raised years later by political enemies in Wisconsin, who used it as the basis of an assertion that Williams had a police record in Tennessee.) So even at a church college there was time for horseplay and college fun. Williams later said that it was the Maryville experience that first moderated the solemnness of demeanor that he had developed during his early adolescence.[6]

There was also time for further affairs of the heart. The tall, good-looking Alabamian with the soft drawl was highly sought after by the Maryville girls, as is attested by the number of former classmates who wrote to him later when he became a public figure to ask which one of them he had married.[7] Williams enjoyed the company of attractive women then, as he was to do all his life. One such involvement, however, caused him much pain and remorse. He vaguely talked of marriage to one young and lovely girl. She took him to be proposing and eagerly accepted. He knew he could not marry her, but put off telling her so until there was no other way out. The memory of her shock and grief, and the hurt anger of her father, stayed with him for decades. He always recalled the incident as one of the most shameful things he had ever done. More than twenty years later, when he was a New Deal official and was making a speech in New York, he caught sight of her in the audience waving a white handkerchief at him. After the meeting he looked for her, but she had vanished in the crowd. In a way he was glad. Two decades had not erased the shame, and he did not really know what to say to her. Williams never forgot such instances in his life when he failed to live up to his self-imposed standards.[8]

Williams left Maryville College at the end of the spring semester in 1915 after successfully completing his freshman year. Despite its rigidity, the college had given him his first sustained taste of formal education, and he had reveled in it. He wanted to continue his studies, but still had doubts about the ministry, doubts that the Maryville experience had in some ways reinforced. Yet no other career seemed to him to be as personally satisfying or to afford a similar chance to help the less fortunate in life, and he wanted to do that. Further study was necessary, but that would take money, something he had very little of. He resolved, therefore, to defer entering another college for a year, while he tried to earn sufficient to pay for his education to continue. The need for finances became even more urgent when, just a day or two before he was to leave Maryville, his room was gutted by fire, and most of his possessions were lost. He left, therefore, as he put it, "with a reference from Dr. Wilson which described me as honest and indomitable," but with little else.[9]

Fortunately, he had a job to go to, one which Dr. Wilson's reference may have helped him get. He was hired as an advance man for the Redpath Chautauqua organization, one of the biggest and most successful in the region. His task was to go to the areas where lectures had been scheduled a few days in advance and take care of all the local arrangements. His initial assignment was to arrange a series of lectures in the heavily Cajun counties of southern Louisiana, the first time he had been in that fascinating and colorful area. "I had the exhilerating [sic] feeling of being in another country," he wrote of the experience. The Cajun girls, too, deeply impressed him. Once, on a train, "the most beautiful creature I had ever laid eyes upon,"—a young Cajun lass—walked by him. He simply rose from his seat and followed her through the rows of carriages until she arrived at her seat—with her five stalwart brothers. They made it clear to Williams that they did not relish the attention that he was paying their sister, and he beat a very hasty retreat.[10] After Maryville, he found the itinerant life of a Chautauqua organizer tremendously refreshing.

He was also good at it. Early in 1916 he was promoted to superintendent. In his new post he had to ensure that the speakers' arrangements were all taken care of, to collect their guaranteed fees and pay them at the appropriate times, and, normally, to introduce the speakers to the audience. One of the lecturers whose affairs Williams had to handle was William Jennings Bryan, who always resolutely refused to take the podium until the guarantee was safely in his pocket. At times this posed problems that Williams had to resolve, even if it meant frantic trips to banks to try to borrow money. Such intransigent behavior did little to endear the Great Commoner to the young superintendent.[11]

By the fall of 1916, Williams had put aside enough through his Chautauqua work to resume his studies. He applied to a number of institutions, and was accepted by a few. One which did so was the University of Cincinnati, a school which had particular appeal because not only could he complete his bachelor's degree, having been given a year's credit for his Maryville studies, but he could also take courses at nearby Lane Theological Seminary. Therefore, he went to Cincinnati, the first time he had moved outside his native region.

Cincinnati, "cradled," as Zane Miller put it, "in the gentle Southern bend of the Ohio River," was a city of about 370,000 in 1916, having grown from about 260,000 in 1890. Formerly known as the "Queen City of the West," it had lost its crown after the Civil War to such rapidly developing metropolises as Chicago and Detroit. At the time that Williams moved there, it had just gone through a period of thoroughgoing municipal reform under the direction of Progressive "boss" mayor George B. Cox.

One of the agents for reform was the University of Cincinnati, which had become, under the presidency of Charles W. Dabney, an active force in the city. Dabney's aim was to make the institution a true "university of the city," the brain behind the reform impulse. To that end he had introduced new programs and greatly expanded old ones, especially in the liberal arts, programs specifically geared to urban problems. In 1912 the first courses in philanthropy and sociology were offered, under teachers recruited from city institutions and private social work agencies. These were the areas that Williams decided to study.[12]

He found it hard to settle down. Though he enjoyed his studies, he missed his native region and his Maryville friends. Moreover, he was increasingly unsure about his purposes in continuing to prepare for a religious vocation, for his belief in a personal God was becoming less and less firm. He was also bothered by what he conceived to be the irrelevance of studying the grand sweep of Western civilization while in Europe men were dying in the tens of thousands to preserve Western ideals. Like many young Americans, Williams tended to see World War I in Manichaean terms as a struggle between the forces of light, the Allies, and those of darkness, the kaiser and his cohorts. If the Allies fell, he believed, so fell Western civilization. As a believer in the values supposedly reposited in the

Western tradition, he wondered if he should not be more actively involved in trying to preserve them. Finally, he had money worries, for his savings were not going as far as he had hoped. For all these reasons he abruptly left the university in the spring term of 1917 and returned to the Redpath Chautauqua, again as an advance man. There he found company and assistance in the advice of an older co-worker, O. W. Thomas, who helped him decide what course to follow. He went back to Cincinnati in the middle of June 1917 and applied to go to Europe with the YMCA as an ambulance driver. He was accepted and almost immediately sent overseas—presumably to the battlefields of France.[13]

Though he had hoped to drive ambulances, Williams was sent first to Paris to work as a recreation official in the YMCA headquarters there. Paris in 1917, even after three years of bloody war, had not totally lost either its gaiety or its wickedness. For Williams, son of the small-town Protestant South, the shock of Parisian culture was profound. The YMCA hostel where he was billeted was relatively luxurious; the officials living there permanently even had maids assigned to them. The young woman detailed to look after Williams presumed that as part of her duties she would be required to scrub his back when he bathed. Very quickly, he informed her that that service would not be needed.

Gradually, he adjusted to the alien environment. Moreover, he thoroughly enjoyed his work with the YMCA, especially among the French soldiers, from whom he quickly picked up a smattering of the language. Listening to their stories of the front, to their accounts of privation and horror, he wondered whether, sitting safe in Paris, he was doing enough in the battle to save Western civilization. By November 1917 he had decided that he was not, and he enlisted in the French Foreign Legion as an infantryman.

This was a vastly different war from the one he had known in Paris. The legion in 1917 was involved in some of the bloodiest shock-troop fighting on the Western Front. In the Battle of Chemin des Dames, more than half of Williams's company was killed. He survived the slaughter, though its effect on him was such that, like many another soldier, he very rarely chose to talk about it in later years.[14] Moreover, the futility of the struggle, the mindlessness of it all, filled him with despair. During lulls in hostilities the legionnaires and their enemies used to fraternize, bantering with each other about girls and occasionally swapping cigarettes, before recommencing to kill each other. The statesmen of the world had a profound duty, he believed, to so order international affairs that decent human beings would not be required to murder each other again in this mad way.

The American First Division reached France early in 1918. Williams enlisted at the first opportunity, and was posted as a private to the Fifth Field Artillery on February 13, 1918. Again, he survived heavy fighting, remaining with the Fifth Field until after the Battle of Soissons in April. He was then plucked out of the ranks and sent to train as an officer at the U.S. Army's artillery school at Samur. For him the shooting war had effectively ended.

His career as an officer trainee was scarcely distinguished. Unable to master the mathematics involved, he was always near the bottom of the class. But Samur for him was much more than study. Indeed, that was almost irrelevant. It was a chance to relax, to try and forget the horrors of the front. It was a time of frequent visits to Paris, lovely in the spring and early summer. "We had many pleasant experiences there," he later recalled, "and got an insight into French life and wine and horses and horse riding and good eating. I seldom have ever had such a similarly happy period in my lifetime."[15]

The lures of the older, more worldly culture were modifying the value system of the young southern Protestant who still had thoughts of becoming a minister. Indeed, Williams's lifelong passion for horse racing dates from his days at Samur, when he first tasted the delights of the track, especially the thrill of backing a winner at long odds. Betting on outsiders was a habit that stayed with him all his life and affected much more than merely his habits at the race track. As shall be discussed, Williams was often drawn to "get-rich-quick" schemes, most of which cost him, rather than made, money. But there was in them the element of beating the odds, something he first experienced on the racetracks of Paris, an environment quite different from that in which he had been formed, but which clearly had great attraction.

Despite his lack of aptitude and application, however, he did manage to scrape through the officer trainee course, and was commissioned as a second lieutenant in the Fifth Field Artillery on August 1, 1918, as an instructor and stationed far from the front. He was transferred on September 8 to the 131st Field Artillery, again as an instructor, with the headquarters company. He saw no further action.[16]

With the armistice came indecision. He could return home, or he could take advantage of an offer from a grateful French government to those who had fought for the legion to remain in France and study at a French university. He chose the latter course; securing a furlough from the army, he entered the University of Bordeaux to study philosophy. Academically, the experience was of little value. Neither his language skills nor his academic background was remotely adequate to cope with the rigorous demands of the elitist French system of higher education. Quickly abandoning plans to take out a doctorate, he enrolled instead for the diplôme d'études supérieure, in itself a course of some rigor, which required the presentation of a thesis in French, English, and Greek. With the generous assistance of a Professor Ryessen, who befriended him, he managed to put together a thesis on Royce's Monism that was of sufficient quality to enable him to present it for defense. The defense, of course, took the traditional oral form and, in Williams's words, was "disastrous." About fifty people were present, and he was very nervous indeed. As he could not understand the questions being put to him in rapid-fire French, his halting answers could hardly have been satisfactory. Professor Ryessen, however, came to his rescue. Taking over the questioning, he talked slowly, drawing Williams out on general philosophical questions, enabling him to make a sufficient impression to be awarded the diploma "with the lowest mark possible"—and without having gained much from the experience.

In other ways, however, the Bordeaux sojourn was important and enjoyable. Williams roomed there with an all-American football player, with whom he became firm friends. Eventually, Williams was best man at his wedding to a beautiful French girl, whom he was later to make a supervisor on an NYA homecraft project. Williams himself had a French girlfriend, and the four of them delighted in exploring the old town, eating in the cafes, drinking the wine. Also, through Professor Ryessen, who was secretary of the Workers General Federation of Europe, Williams was able to meet trade union leaders from all over the Continent and sit in on some of their discussions. For the first time he confronted doctrinaire socialism, and it added a new dimension to his own emerging social and political philosophy. And, of course, 1919 was when President Woodrow Wilson was in Paris, and Williams was never prouder of his country than at that time, when, alone, Wilson seemed to be fighting the battles of humanity everywhere. "I cried like a baby" when Wilson arrived, he later wrote. "We were proud of being the greatest democracy. The Statue of Liberty was our symbol. I loved the Stars and Stripes." Of course, this faith, this optimism, was transient, but for the young Williams, it made France in the spring of 1919 a wonderful place to be.[17]

Williams returned to the United States on August 12, 1919, having formally received his Bordeaux diploma at a graduation ceremony which he described as "very splendid." He was never to go abroad again. He was honorably discharged from the army at Camp Gordon, Georgia, on August 30, and proceeded immediately to Birmingham to see his family. The city was "booming and roistering," and he found himself rather "a stranger in my own country," so great had been the changes of the past two years. He was baffled in many ways by the America that he found, particularly by the attitude of people toward the war. As a result of his experiences, he had developed a passionate hostility toward war and a determination to ensure that it did not happen again, and he was disturbed that his fellow citizens did not seem to share his commitment. Moreover, the spirit of intolerance that showed itself in the Red Scare of 1919 bothered him profoundly. Still, not all the changes were to be deplored. He approved of the new knee-length skirts. "The freeing of women from corsets and underskirts, the plunging and stomping of the Charleston, was probably the one positive good that was to come out of World War I so far as Western civilization was concerned," he was to write later.[18]

The sense of bewilderment at the changes in society in part reflected his own personal confusions. The war and Bordeaux had meant a postponement of thoughts about the future, but that was now no longer possible. He decided to return to Cincinnati to complete his degree; yet increasingly his choice of the ministry as a career seemed a mistake. By this time, he had "no belief in a personal God, no belief in the efficacy of prayer except the effect on the person who prayed, holding religion to be a control arrangement devised by ancient rulers who needed something to regiment their people."

And yet he still thought of the pulpit as a great teaching medium, and one that he was well able to use. Not long after his return to Cincinnati he once again found himself occupying one. A small Lutheran church in nearby Dayton, Kentucky, with whom he had had connections before the war, asked him to serve as pastor on a part-time basis. He badly needed the money, so he agreed despite his lack of belief, which he covered up by preaching about aspects of contemporary society or on historical themes. One such series of sermons, "The Ten Great Religions of the World," was extraordinarily popular, and many people came across the river from Cincinnati to hear him. This encouraged him to schedule a further series, this time entitled "Capital and Labor," and to advertise it in the Cincinnati press. Retribution was swift. The Kentucky Lutheran Synod insisted that Williams be dismissed forthwith and threatened revocation of the church's charter if the demand was not complied with. The local church board of deacons was disposed to resist, but Williams, acutely conscious of the fact that his career almost certainly lay elsewhere, resigned his position.[19]

Fortunately he was able to find another one almost immediately, as assistant director of the Cincinnati Community Service Association, with particular responsibility for public recreation, work that he enjoyed immensely. Moreover, his studies were going well, and partly as a result of them he was finally thinking his way through the confusions and doubts that had beset him for years. No one helped more than Dr. Ernest Talbert, professor of social psychology at the university. Recognizing the potential in the young southerner, he took a close personal interest in him, which eventually developed into a lifelong friendship. Talbert, Williams said, "gave me something to hold on to. . . . Never advising me, never telling me what to do, but suggesting papers and books that bore on what I was trying to do that he thought would be helpful. Bless this good and great person; would that the world but more, that the universities, had more of Ernest Talberts."[20]

Talbert's friendship and help, together with that of William K. Reeves, his employer in the Community Service Association, enabled Williams to work his way through his vocational and personal worries. He approached his studies with vigor and, with the aid of summer schools and generous credit provisions, was able to complete his bachelor's degree in 1920.

Despite the demands of study and employment, however, he still found time for fun. He took part in the senior class play in 1920, a farce by A. E. Thomas called "Her Husband's Wife." Aubrey played one of the leading roles, that of John Belden, described in the program as "the genial uncle of Irene and Richard." And he still had lady friends aplenty. A poem, "The Piteous Plaint of a Pursued Preacher," written by a number of his female classmates and dedicated to him, indicated that he was as attractive as ever to the girls. It poked gentle fun at his southern accent, among other things.[21]

Increasingly, however, one girl occupied his attentions. Williams had met Anita Schreck, a local physical education teacher and swimming instructor, in 1919. Of Mexican and German descent, she had a dark-eyed beauty and a lively personality that completely captivated him. He thought her the most beautiful girl that he had ever seen, and by April 1920 he was describing himself as "Anita-centered." "The world," he wrote, "is a duplex affair, and all lives center in us not them." "Madly in love," he borrowed money, and they were married on December 18, 1920. On the day of their wedding he wrote to her to say that, having met her, he could not think of going through life alone.[22]

Williams continued full-time with the Community Service Association in 1921, working mainly in recreation. He still enjoyed the job, but knew that it was stopgap employment only. In the first place, it simply did not pay enough. Anita was soon pregnant, and more money was going to be needed. Second, the church and the ministry still pulled at him. After the Dayton experience he had thought that prospect had gone for good. However, in 1921 he joined the Cincinnati branch of the Unitarian church. He found the Unitarian creed, with its nonevangelical, nondoctrinal emphasis, thoroughly congenial. Once again, the ministry, for so long his chosen career, briefly beckoned.

In the spring of 1921 he applied for entrance and scholarship assistance to Harvard University Divinity School. He also applied for the assistant pastor's job at a Boston Unitarian church. The congregation invited him to conduct worship, he did so, and they offered him the position. For some weeks he tried to make up his mind. The proposed stipend was attractive, and the money was needed more than ever with the arrival of his first son, Winston Tyndall Williams. Friends, family, and acquaintances urged him to accept. Even the Reverend J. M. Broady, whom Williams had so antagonized in Birmingham, was friendly and encouraging. "My dear children," he wrote, "I am sure you will never find yourself in the largest possible way until you address yourself to the task for which you originally went into training." Moreover, Harvard Divinity School accepted him and even offered a small scholarship. The possibilities were tempting.[23]

In the end, however, Williams turned down both the scholarship and the job offer and, in so doing, permanently decided against the church as a career. His faith was just not strong enough. He decided to stay in Cincinnati and hope that something else would turn up. Something did, and sooner than he expected. The Wisconsin Conference of Social Work was looking for an executive secretary. Reeves had influence with the body and warmly promoted Williams's abilities and potential. To Aubrey's surprise he was offered the job, and so, in mid-1922—knowing "practically nothing of the technicalities of social work," but very willing to learn—Williams, along with Anita and baby Winston, left Cincinnati for Madison, Wisconsin, and a new life.[24]

Learning the Trade

In 1926 the Wisconsin Conference of Social Work described itself as "an organization of private citizens which devotes its entire time to the prevention of delinquency and crime, the eradication of poverty, and the development of ways and means in local communities and in the state at large which will humanely care for dependent and neglected children. Its aim is the gradual providing of the best possible group of opportunities, through education, health, city planning and recreation, for the children, and the men and women in our communities throughout Wisconsin."

Somewhat more tersely, Williams was to describe it later as a "watchdog." Supported by private funds, it sought to obtain better standards of work by public agencies in areas of social policy. Organized in 1881 as the Wisconsin Conference of Charities and Corrections, it was initially little more than an annual discussion group for private individuals interested in the provision of welfare measures for the poor and the insane, but partly as a result of the surge of reform that occurred in Wisconsin during the La Follette years, when the state became a social laboratory for the nation, it greatly expanded its activities in the second decade of the twentieth century. Its name was changed in 1918 to the Wisconsin Conference of Social Work, and in 1920 the first full-time executive secretary, Edward D. Lynde, Williams's predecessor, was appointed. Under Lynde and its energetic president, Mrs. Isaac P. Witter, the conference greatly expanded its day-to-day activities and the sphere of its operations and for the first time attempted to organize on a county basis. By 1922, 1220 persons and two hundred organizations had affiliated with it; it had formed an unofficial but strong connection with the famous Extension Division of the University of Wisconsin, which provided office space, postage, full-time stenographic service, and part of the executive secretary's salary; and it had established itself as the premier such organization in the United States.

Its membership was overwhelmingly wealthy and upper class, with a significant number of academics and, more important, women involved. Thus it epitomized one of the crucial way stations in the transition of social welfare work from something essentially private and charitable to a clearly defined profession, with its own organization and sets of standards, a procedure which Roy Lubove has so ably described. It was into this developing institution, in a political and social climate quite foreign to that in which he had been formed, that Williams went in the middle of 1922.[1]

Williams was warmly welcomed at the first conference board meeting he attended as "just the right man for the place" and praised for his "earnestness and ability." Yet he had scarcely occupied his office before some of the conference's directors were wondering if they had made the right choice. In his maiden speech to the 1922 annual meeting he vigorously attacked Wisconsin's, or, rather, the present state administration's, policy toward Indians. Reacting to this, the *Milwaukee State Journal* inquired as to the background of "the upstart . . . who had come to the state from Alabama" and the board convened a hasty meeting to review the question of his appointment. By a majority vote the board decided to stand by him. This was the first of several occasions during his ten-year stay in Madison in which his tendency to pull no public punches got him into political hot water.[2]

For a while, though, all went smoothly. After an initial unhappy period in a dirty rented apartment with "several chairs with no bottoms, frayed rugs and beds which when you got into them made as much noise as a crane in a scrap-yard," the young couple scraped together the down payment for a white wooden house in the suburb of Nakoma, where they lived throughout their Wisconsin sojourn. There Anita settled happily into the role of housewife and mother—the Williamses' three younger sons, Aubrey, Jr., Morrison, and Jere were all born during their first years in Wisconsin—while Aubrey got a grasp on his new job and tried to shape it to suit him.[3] He moved swiftly. His report to the board of directors of May 31, 1923, indicated that he had already taken the conference into new areas, particularly the building up of local organizations. Moreover, he was already working on what was to be his first major project for the conference—and his first success.

This was the "better cities" contest. Wisconsin cities that entered the contest were judged under certain criteria to determine which had "the most ideal environment for the raising of children."[4] Cities were evaluated in the following areas: city planning, industry, education, health and physical development, social welfare, recreation, public library, public administration, religion, and town and country relations. Developing scoring schedules, publicizing the contest, and dealing with the complexities of judging occupied nearly two years of fairly intensive endeavor. By the end of 1925 the contest was over, and the winners were the cities of Kenosha and Chippewa Falls. The effort involved had been considerable. In 1924 alone, Williams made well over two hundred visits to Wisconsin communities in order to stimulate interest in the contest. But the attendant favorable publicity and the extent of community involvement made it all worthwhile. Moreover—and this was probably the main reason for its promotion—the contest revealed many weaknesses in Wisconsin's cities, numerous areas where urgent community action was needed. Having identified such soft spots, the task of the conference was to apply pressure to have them eradicated, and Williams worked hard at doing that in the years after 1925. In the organization of this program, Williams had revealed the capacity for swift administrative decision, the power of exhortation, and the ability to work for incredibly long hours, often including a good deal of tiring travel. These were traits that would characterize him for the whole of his working life.[5]

One area of weakness in several cities that the contest had revealed was child care, and it was to this problem that Williams next turned his and the conference's attention. The conference became a leader in the fight to establish a children's code for the state. The long struggle over this issue is a perfect example of the way that the conference went about its business. Having decided to investigate the problem of child abuse, it made its first task the securing of accurate information of its extent. A Children's Code Committee was therefore formed under the chairmanship of Mrs. J. William Gross and with a full-time director, Mrs. C. W. Areson, with whom Williams maintained a close liaison. Between 1926 and 1928 this committee's primary charge was to secure accurate information on "the exact status of destitute, abandoned, illegitimate and delinquent children" in Wisconsin and to examine existing laws pertaining to them. Furthermore, it made an intensive study in ten selected counties of a whole range of child-related social problems, including illegitimacy, adoption practices, delinquency, and destitution, and built up a body of fact on which to base recommendations for change.[6]

The second task was publicity, and in this Williams played a vital role. In 1927 and 1928 he crisscrossed the state, giving scores of speeches to church groups, civic groups, fraternal societies, and labor unions on the need to provide a better deal for the unfortunate children of Wisconsin. To illustrate his argument he used information and examples unearthed by the Children's Code Committee. He told, for example, of the eleven-year-old girl who, having given birth, simply gave the child away. He talked of the "baby farms currently operating throughout the state." He told the story of "Janet," a pregnant, feeble-minded fifteen year old who had been sent to work for a forty-year-old widower and who was being held in virtual servitude by him, but whose plight could not be alleviated because there was no state department or agency under whose jurisdiction she could be placed. Williams spoke about the problems from the public platform; he kept the newspapers supplied with material illustrating the problems and attesting to the inadequacy of Wisconsin's mechanisms for dealing with the situation; and he applied pressure on friendly legislators. In this last effort he was assisted by Mrs. Witter and Marie Kohler, president of the conference from 1927. Miss Kohler was a member of a socially prominent Wisconsin industrial family and the sister of Walter Kohler, who was elected governor of the state in 1928. Through Miss Kohler, to whom Williams was devoted, the conference had a very close friend in court. During this fight, then, Williams played a vital role, coordinating the work, publicizing the problem, and stimulating morale. This was the sort of tireless activity that once caused Judge Marvin B. Rosenberry, a longtime friend of the conference and its president in 1926, to remark, "I regard him as one of the ablest men in this field in the country. He is not only well trained but thorough, dependable, industrious, practical and constructive. He is able to arouse interest and stimulate people to constructive social work."[7]

By mid-1928 the gathering of information had been largely completed, and the next step was to draft legislation for introduction in the legislature. This was done by a small team under the direction of Edith "Jane" Foster, who had replaced Mrs. Areson as the execu-

tive director of the Children's Code Committee and whose friendship with Williams was to last the rest of his life. Essentially, the
proposed legislation codified existing laws relative to neglected,
dependent, delinquent, and illegitimate children. But more important, it greatly modified court procedures that applied to children,
virtually rewriting the existing statutes and completely changing the
juvenile court system toward one of flexibility and humanity. The
Children's Code Bill was introduced into the Wisconsin legislature
early in 1929, and though there were some objections, principally
from conservative members of the legal profession, passage was
swift. Williams was able to report to the annual meeting of the
conference on October 7, 1929, that the Children's Code was "now
the law of the State." There was, however, still work to be done,
mainly in publicizing the provisions of the code and in constructing
machinery to ensure that it worked at the local level. Regional
conferences were organized throughout 1930, and the conference
maintained a close watch on its operation thereafter. The fight,
however, had proved an unqualified success. Present-day Wisconsin
legislation on dependent and neglected children is still based largely
on the Wisconsin Children's Code of 1929.[8]

The first years in Wisconsin were years of endeavor and fulfillment. The job kept him busy, and although he at times mused on
the incongruity of working on behalf of the less fortunate through
an agency basically controlled by those whom fortune had favored,
this did not bother him unduly at this stage. His relations with those
who led the conference—Witter, Judge Rosenberry, and Kohler—
were genuinely good. Indeed, he later wrote of Mrs. Witter as "a
very beautiful woman, a gifted person, the wife of one of the State's
largest paper-mill owners, and a hard man who brooked no differences with what he thought was right yet she contrived to be an
idealist and a person of good will in her own right. I confess I loved
her, not passionately." He found kindred spirits among the staff and
others in the social work profession—like Jane Foster. Moreover,
he greatly enjoyed the close connection between the conference
and the university. Located as it was in the Extension Division, it
could not help but become involved in campus intellectual life.
Williams soon found friends among the academics of his own age
and counselors and teachers among those who were older. Before
long, Anita and he became part of a group that made regular pil-

grimages to the home of the august John R. Commons, where they took tea and listened to the great man talk and where, after the sage had retired, they removed their shoes and danced to the latest tunes in the economist's living room. There were problems, of course. Like all young couples with growing families, they always had money worries. Moreover, Anita was not always happy at the frequent absences from home that the job necessitated. But, basically, the first years in Wisconsin were happy ones.[9]

However, this was to change, as did so much else, in the years after 1929. Life in Wisconsin, like that everywhere, became less pleasant. Williams began to feel increasing dissatisfaction with the job that he was doing and the people with whom he was working. He experienced more and more the constrictions of working within a privately funded agency and of having to moderate his responses to suit the tastes of his essentially wealthy, moderate board of directors at a time when, to him, strong statements and decisive, committed action were required. The urgency of the problems created by the Depression, he believed, demanded it. The early years of the Depression were crucial ones for Williams. His attitudes toward human distress and the role of the state in alleviating it sharpened, and he became more outspoken, less able to compromise. Predictably, his relationship with his board of directors suffered as a result.

One source of frustration was, of course, a shrinking budget. The conference was almost totally dependent on private subscriptions and donations for its revenue, and by 1931 those were fast drying up. Furthermore, the Extension Division, itself hit by sharply reduced university finances, was forced to withdraw its contribution, and not enough money was left to maintain existing operations, let alone expand them. In desperation, Williams proposed in October 1931 that his salary be cut from $4,800 to $3,700, but that was not agreed to at that time, though less than six months later all employees were forced to take a 10-percent cut in salary. Lack of money was greatly restricting the conference's operations at a time when, as Williams perceived it, they were needed more urgently than ever.[10]

Increasingly, Williams was concerned with the situation of the unemployed. Joblessness, and its attendant misery, was no less of a problem in Wisconsin than in the rest of the United States in the years after 1929, and Williams wanted the conference to concentrate its activities in that area. Bringing the organization into the area of transient workers, he had it help defray the expenses of the Reverend Paul McKinney, a Madison minister who was attempting to provide some measure of shelter for the city's homeless men, and he advocated the extension of McKinney's ideas to other communities. In addition, he successfully persuaded the conference's executive committee to commit some of its limited budget to the publication of a handbook on the administration of relief in times of unemployment for the use of local relief officials. But by far his most important effort on behalf of the unemployed was to throw the conference firmly behind the fight for a decent public relief bill for Wisconsin. In all of his activities for the unemployed, Williams was unflinching on one basic principle: by far the best form of relief, in his view, was work relief. The dole was expensive, inefficient, and socially wasteful. "Wherever possible," he told his executive committee in 1931, "relief shall be in the form of wages for work done." That fundamental perspective was one from which he never departed. It characterized his approach to relief policy throughout the New Deal period.

In this insistence on the provision of work relief as being both morally and economically the only acceptable course for governments to follow, Williams was coming down firmly on one side of the debate over public relief policy that had sputtered intermittently in social work circles throughout the 1920s, that was given both urgency and a wider canvas by the economic collapse, and that was to continue into the New Deal era. Some who favored work relief, such as the economists William Trufant Foster and Waddill Catchings, pointed less to the morale-boosting effect of keeping men at work than to its economic benefit. They argued that the extensive use of well-planned public works projects, together with progressive tax policies, could boost economic recovery. Others, like Paul Douglas, who was later to become a senator, agreed with this, but emphasized the social effects, pointing out that the use of relief labor on public housing development, for example, improved the quality of people's lives, as well as providing economic stimulus.

Those who opposed work relief concentrated their arguments on its cost, which would always be more than a simple dole. Some, however, like Leo Wolman, also pointed out that the use of public works projects to provide emergency unemployment relief could also be inefficient, in that the skills of the unemployed were often not used to best advantage. By 1931 the focus of the debate tended to be on the economics of work relief. At least in liberal circles, as Clarke A. Chambers has pointed out, a consensus had been reached by then that, economic considerations aside, work relief was better for morale than cash relief, which in turn was better than relief in kind. The debate would not finally be resolved, as far as federal policy was concerned, until 1935 with the creation of the WPA, but for Williams it was already an issue on which he would never willingly compromise.[11]

The strategy adopted to try to influence public relief policy in Wisconsin was similar to that used in the successful fight over the Children's Code: establish need, draft a bill, and then apply pressure for its passage. During 1930 the conference surveyed as best it could the relief situation in the state, and on the basis of that survey and information from other parts of the country, Jane Foster, by then the conference's assistant executive director, prepared draft legislation. (Aubrey's general secretary at this time was a highly capable and faithful lady named Rose Nathanson, whom he had acquired through the Extension Division.) The draft bill's prime intent was to revise existing legislation to equalize the administration of relief across counties, but it also called for an additional relief appropriation of $5,554,000, to be raised by a surtax on annual incomes of more than $6,000 and to be spent principally on work relief. After some revisions, Williams arranged to have the draft bill introduced into the state legislature.[12]

The problem was he had not quite cleared his actions with his executive committee before going ahead. Not all were happy at some of the legislation's provisions. The surtax, in particular, caused considerable concern among committee members, almost all of whom were earning well over the suggested figure. Although the executive committee eventually decided to support his action, it did so only after much debate, and the committee gave its executive director a rap over the knuckles for his precipitate approach. Yet that precipitousness was perhaps an indication of a growing dissatisfaction with the way he had to work, with the limitations placed upon him in a time, as he perceived it, of great national urgency.[13]

The bill had a hard time in the legislature, where it not only had to face the predictable hostility of entrenched conservatism but had

to compete with a plethora of rival relief proposals. Eventually, it
passed the senate, but was finally defeated in the house of assembly.
While the bill was under consideration, Williams was a ceaseless
lobbyist on its behalf. One such action caused further trouble with
the board. The conference had been allotted fifteen minutes of
radio time on a local station each Sunday to discuss aspects of its
work. In 1931, Williams used one of those spots to advocate passionately the passage of the relief bill. There was a strong reaction,
particularly from the Milwaukee County Community Fund, a charitable organization which had been a longtime conference contribu-
tor and on which the conference was now dependent for half of
Williams's salary. The fund's president, Irving Seaman, expressed
great regret that Williams had taken such a committed position,
pointed out that many members of the fund, including "a large
number of substantial donors," certainly did not agree with him, and
declared that the fund might have to reconsider its support of the
conference. Williams's characterization of people earning more than
six thousand dollars as selfish and socially irresponsible had particularly offended some members. Williams's own board met in
emergency session, and though they made no formal censure, they
expressed a considerable degree of unhappiness with his performance. He was, however, unrepentant. He pushed ahead with proposals for more public relief legislation and advocated a further
approach to the Milwaukee fund for cash, but the incident increased
his dissatisfaction with the job he was doing and, in particular, with
the incongruity, as he saw it, of working for a group of essentially
wealthy people at a time of total social distress.[14]

   He had had other disagreements, too, both with his board and
with the state political authorities. He and the conference had gotten into trouble with the state Board of Control, an agency whose
function was to supervise the administration of all the state's penal,
correctional, and hospital institutions. In his endeavors on behalf of
the Children's Code, Williams had exposed some Dickensian situations in certain institutions: young lads in orphanages forced to
stand still for upwards of forty-five minutes for minor disciplinary
infractions; the supervisor of a school for blind girls who sexually
molested his charges; the wholesale use of the strap, an iron collar
and tongue clamp which made it impossible for the wearer to make
a sound, drink, or eat, as a punishment device in the Waupun state

prison. Such matters were well ventilated in the press, and the Board of Control came in for heavy criticism. Thus, Williams found himself regarded in political circles as a meddler. Even Governor Kohler, with his strong conference connections, warned him in 1930 to moderate his criticism of the state's correctional institutions and those who ran them, something, of course, which he was not disposed to do. It was during this controversy, incidentally, that the question of his so-called "police record" in Tennessee was raised, which indicates how thoroughly his past had been investigated by those whom he had angered.[15]

Other reasons contributed to his growing dissatisfaction with the Madison situation. Marie Kohler had given up the WCSW presidency in 1930. She had been an inspiration to him, and he found it very hard to adjust to her absence. Financially, with four growing boys and a mortgage, he desperately needed more money than the modest salary that the conference could afford to pay him. From time to time he attempted to remedy that situation, with "get-rich-quick" schemes, as he was to do, from time to time, throughout his life, but generally such projects only exacerbated his financial problems. One such scheme, an attempt from 1929 to 1933 to make a quick killing by farming leased minks and foxes, cost him particularly dear. Those were bad years. Later he would describe the period from 1929 to 1932 as "years I prefer to forget, as a matter of fact I recall very little that happened. I think I was mostly baffled by the business world."[16]

From 1931 he was looking hard for another position, and not necessarily in social work, though that was his preference. Expressing his interest "in the development and formation of public policy in the general field of social work," he negotiated with the Texas State Council of Social Agencies for a job that was similar to his Wisconsin post, but nothing came of that effort. An offer of a position on the field staff of President Hoover's Committee on Public Relief was withdrawn after he roundly criticized federal relief policy at a conference of social workers. He thought, too, of upgrading his academic qualifications and perhaps teaching social work at the university. Thus, he was delighted when he was offered a position as lecturer in sociology without salary for the first semester of the 1932–33 academic year to teach a course on American community development. Enthusiastically, he began to plan his lectures and reading lists—which included Stuart Chase, the Lynds, Walter Lippmann, Veblen, and Norman Thomas—for he hoped that experience might lead to a permanent position. Then, if he could not leave Madison, at least he might be able to get away from the conference. He was never to teach the course, however, for the chance to experience fresh fields came much sooner than he had dared hope.[17]

Of all things, a dead automobile battery helped Williams to move out of the increasingly unhappy Madison situation. One morning in September 1932 he had planned to drive to nearby Wausau to try to raise funds for the ailing conference, but the battery problem prevented him from doing so. While he was waiting impatiently for it to be charged, he received a telephone call from Frank Bane of the American Public Welfare Association offering him a position for up to a year, provided the conference would grant him leave. Given the tension between the organization and its backers over Williams's activities, the conference was glad to do this. Accordingly, he reported to Bane in Chicago in early October, after having hastily arranged for someone to cover his teaching at the university. The capable Rose Nathanson was left in charge of the conference office.[18]

The job that Bane had for him was a daunting one. Congressional pressure and the exigencies of human suffering had forced a reluctant President Hoover to move the federal government into the field of public relief. On July 21, 1932, he signed the revised Emergency Relief and Construction Act, one of the provisions of which enabled the Reconstruction Finance Corporation (RFC) to lend money to the states for relief purposes. Williams's task was to persuade state governors in the midwestern and southern regions to make use of this money, to assist them in organizing its disbursement, and to review the arrangements already made for its use. For this purpose, he was appointed as a consultant to the RFC Relief Loans Division, headed by Frederick H. Croxton, who had replaced Walter S. Gifford as chairman of the President's Unemployment Relief Organization in August 1932.[19] Here was a chance for him to put into practice the views on work relief that he developed while in Wisconsin—and which he had recently advocated so passionately.

First stop was North Dakota. Here Governor Schafer, a thoroughgoing individualist, pronounced himself quite unconvinced that conditions were sufficiently perilous in his food-providing state to justify an application for RFC money. He was strongly of the opinion that such an application would be a denigration of cherished ideals of self-reliance and local self-help. Williams tried hard to convince him otherwise, but to no avail. Eventually, however, he persuaded the governor to visit eleven homes with him, all occupied by farm people, to see the extent of the poverty there. Williams had visited the homes previously, so in a sense they had been selected for maximum possible effect; yet they were at the same time reasonably typical of poverty in the Plains states. Governor Schafer was appalled at what he saw, and was particularly moved at the plight of one gaunt, sad-eyed woman, who took him to the cellar in which she customarily stored the fruit that she preserved. Silently, she pointed to the rows of preserving jars around the walls. All of them were empty. The governor thanked Williams for what he had done and immediately applied for a loan, even though, as Williams later stated, "it meant that he was throwing overboard one of his most cherished principles and accepting something that all his life he had regarded as beneath what he held to be manly. Self-reliance was the cornerstone of his life. . . . I admired him for his stubborn adherence to his principles." Williams's initial foray into the field of federal policy had been successful.[20]

After brief, and similarly successful, stops in Montana, Idaho, and South Dakota, Williams arrived in Jackson, Mississippi, in early November. He was to spend the next three months in that state. The governor had needed no urging to apply for RFC money, for conditions in Mississippi had reached such a desperate state that food riots and looting were an almost daily occurrence. Williams was required to set up a structure through which the money could be distributed, and for that he was given a free hand. He went to work with a will, for it provided him the opportunity to apply his ideas.

First, he organized relief distribution on a decentralized basis, with the county as the main administrative unit. Within four weeks he had chosen a county director for each of Mississippi's eighty-two counties, generally selected by the "long walk" principle. When interviewing applicants, Williams would sit at a desk at one end of a long room, so that the candidates would have to walk fifty feet toward him. He considered this to be a stern test of character. If a candidate met his eyes the whole of the way, he passed the test; if not, he was dubious about hiring him.

Secondly, he arranged it so that relief was provided in return for useful community work, at the rate of three dollars worth of work per family head per week. There was to be no dole. He adhered firmly to this principle then, as he was to do throughout his New Deal career.

Third, he made the administration of the scheme quite independent of private welfare agencies, another principle from which he never deviated and one which would become an issue in the first months of the New Deal. In this case, it provoked a bitter fight with the Mississippi Red Cross, which wanted to control both the certification of those eligible and the disbursement of the money, but with the governor's backing, he held firm.

Finally, he realized that it was not enough simply to set up the structure. He had to keep it constantly under scrutiny, and to that end he made frequent forays into the field to see how the county directors were shaping up, again presaging an administrative style that he was to develop later. It was during these trips that he learned a valuable lesson. Initially, he had hoped to hold regular meetings with the unemployed in order to discuss policies with them. His first attempts to do so, however, in Tupelo, Cleveland, Greenwood, and Laurel, all ended in uproar and near riot, and he abandoned his plans for more. The situation was far too volatile, he decided, to bring the unemployed together even for the best of purposes.[21]

Williams's activities were not universally applauded. He faced constant abuse from Jackson editor Fred Sullens, who called him "this fellow who was sent in here by Hoover," while many planters violently objected to his distributing free vegetable seeds to relief clients. As one of their number said, "They did not want their niggers planting gardens." He insisted, however, and the governor supported him.

He got his way, too, on another issue, and in so doing once more previewed what was to become a constant theme. Williams decided that he wanted to employ some Negro caseworkers in the administration of the scheme, given that so many of the recipients were black. The governor was aghast at the idea, but Williams won him round with the expedient argument that "only a Negro could get the truth out of another Negro" and that the employment of a few blacks might very well prevent welfare cheating. Thus, from the beginning of his federal career, Williams showed his concern to bring blacks into the relief machinery. Williams later wrote that he

"learnt a lot" through the experience in Mississippi, and certainly
much of his experimentation there was later to become general
policy. When he moved on, he left behind a functioning, relatively
efficient, statewide relief organization. He had done his work exceedingly well.[22]

The next brief stop was in his native Alabama, where, like Governor Shafer of North Dakota, Governor B. M. Miller, oblivious to
the suffering around him, was loudly invoking traditional verities to
justify his refusal to apply for loan money. Williams got nowhere
with him, until the Alabama director of public welfare recalled the
governor's great admiration for Mississippi's arch-segregationist
sage and former senator John Sharp Williams. In conversation with
the governor the next day, Williams casually alluded to a totally
fictitious kin relationship with the great man. The lie had the desired effect. Governor Miller softened his attitude and duly applied
for the loan. This was "letting even the devil help you across the
bridge," Williams later asserted. No doubt Governor Miller soon
discovered that he had been tricked, but by then Williams had again
moved on, to the Texas of Governor "Ma" and Jim Ferguson, where
he was to spend the next three months.[23]

The Fergusons were a colorful pair. James E. Ferguson was first
elected governor of Texas in 1914 as a "progressive demagogue."
Easily winning reelection in 1916, he was removed from the gov-
ernorship the following year and banned from holding office again
after disclosures that he had appropriated state funds for his own
use. He managed, however, to wield the substance of power, though
denied the trappings, through his wife, Miriam, or "Ma," as she was
almost always called. "Ma" was twice elected governor, in 1924 and
1932, but Jim made the decisions. They were newly in charge when
Williams arrived in Austin.[24]

He got on well with them, as he generally did with people in
whom he perceived a populist heritage, for whom he was often
willing to make excuses. "Jim Ferguson was no paragon of virtue,"
he wrote later, "but he ran with the small rancher, the farmer that
farmed his own land, the small banker and the town merchant," and
not with the men of wealth, power, and influence. Moreover, the
problem confronting him in Texas was not of the Fergusons' making, but of the previous administration's. RFC money had been
sent to Texas late in 1932 and had been channeled through three

regional chambers of commerce, in the course of which it had been scandalously mismanaged. Williams's first task was to try and find out what had happened to the loan. That proved impossible to do. He tried to get an audit made, but found that as no records of the disposition of the money existed, that was not feasible. The strong suspicion, however, was that much of it had gone to private pockets. Williams then requested permission to appear before the Texas State Senate and report on what he had been able to find out about the activities of the chambers of commerce, but he was refused. Frustrated, he could do no more. "The scandal was like so many which came to the surface the last days of the Hoover administration," he complained, "buried in the hurricane."

Unable to investigate the scandal, Williams's next job was to set up a structure that would prevent a similar occurrence in the future. Extracting a promise from Jim Ferguson that there would be no attempt to influence appointments, he decided to apply as far as possible the Mississippi model. Relief was to be provided in return for work, and was to be organized on a decentralized basis, each county having its own administrator. Texas has 252 counties, and Williams soon decided that no stranger could select so many "honest and capable" men for the job in a state that size. Thus, he turned to a Texan, the flamboyant Colonel Lawrence Westbrook, engineer, agriculturist, politician, bon vivant, and ladies' man, a character who, when in Washington, "liked nothing better than to go about . . . with grey gloves and his riding crop." This was the first time the two men had met. They were soon to become colleagues in the Federal Emergency Relief Administration (FERA) and lifelong friends. Working together, they managed by the end of March 1933 to put together a working relief program, based on the principles of decentralization and work relief, its administration firmly in the hands of public officials, not private welfare agencies or commercial organizations.[25]

Texas was to be his last stop, and Williams prepared to return to Madison. He had been away from Anita and the boys for more than six months, and he missed them. Moreover, the work of the conference was in disarray, despite Rose Nathanson's best efforts to keep things going, and he had much to attend to there. Finally, he had to mend his fences at the university. The course that he had been scheduled to teach had gone ahead during his absence, but with a set of substitute lecturers, and that had caused much concern among the administration. Indeed, Professor John L. Gillin, newly elected president of the conference and a member of the university's sociology faculty, warned him that "hell may be raised" soon if he did not come back and tidy up those academic loose ends.

So he prepared to return home, planning on the way to attend a regional conference of social workers in Waldemar, Texas, where he was to report on his RFC activities. While his desire to be with the family again was strong, the few months just past had been exciting and creative, free from the frustrations of the last years in Madison. He had had the opportunity to put his ideas on work relief into practice under conditions that he controlled. He had become even more conscious of the immensity of the need for a thoroughgoing federal relief policy, and he had enjoyed very much being part of the RFC effort. Thus, he did not relish the thought of giving it all up and returning to the conference.[26]

He did not have to. Williams had been so busy over the past few months that he had taken little account of what had been happening on the national scene or of the changes beginning to take place. He had voted, not for Franklin Roosevelt in 1932, but for the Socialist candidate, Norman Thomas, for he considered Roosevelt to be little different from Hoover in the inadequacies of his proposed solutions to Depression problems, and subsequent events had given him no reason to change his mind. He had not heard of the people whose names were beginning to become household words—like Harry Hopkins, the man whom Roosevelt had chosen to direct the federal government's initiatives in the field of public relief.

However, Hopkins had heard of him and of his work in Mississippi and Texas, and he wanted him to join the organization that he was in the process of building. While at the Waldemar conference, Williams received a telegram asking him to come to Washington for an interview on May 1, 1933. There, Hopkins took him to lunch, and the two men talked about relief problems and policies. Hopkins told him a little of his plans for his infant agency and of his broader dreams, then asked Williams to join his staff and offered him the position of director of FERA activities for transients. Williams asked for time to think it over, and Hopkins agreed. He had, he explained, to check Williams's credentials with the Wisconsin politicians before anything could be settled. He would be in Detroit in a week's time, he said, and the two of them could meet again there and discuss the matter further. Williams then went back to Wisconsin.

A week later he and Hopkins met in Detroit. Hopkins had a number of questions about urgent problems facing him, the most important concerning the disbursement of relief funds. He could not decide what role private agencies should have in that task. The private agencies and charities, the traditional disbursers of relief in less troubled times, were lobbying hard for the job, and a decision could not long be postponed. Hopkins was disinclined to compromise on this issue, being firmly of the opinion that the federal government, the chief provider of funds, should also have the largest measure of control over their distribution. Others in the new administration, however, were of different mind.

Williams had no doubts at all. Drawing on his recent experiences, he argued that Hopkins had no choice but to retain control of the money himself. Hopkins expressed agreement and said he would soon be in touch, though this time there was no talk about a specific position for Williams. Williams returned to Madison a little worried, wondering if Hopkins had changed his mind or, more likely, if his political enemies had managed to have his proposed appointment quashed.

Hopkins had changed his mind, in fact, but only concerning the task that he wanted Williams to perform. A week later the relief administrator called to offer Williams, not the job of director of transient activities, but the post of regional director for the southwest region. Williams needed no urging. He had seen enough of Hopkins already to know that with him he had the chance to do the sort of job that he had dreamed about. He accepted, and so began a relationship that was to change his life.[27]

4

The New Deal Arrives

When he came to Washington in the heady first one hundred days of the new administration, Williams was one of thousands of professional people—lawyers, social workers, doctors, engineers, architects—who were to staff the greatly expanded and newly created instrumentalities of the federal government. Already President Roosevelt had moved the government into many areas hitherto considered not its concern, as he waged a dramatic war against the worst ravages of the Depression. The Federal Emergency Relief Act, which created the Federal Emergency Relief Administration (FERA), was a prime example of this. Passed on May 12, 1933, its implementation began on May 22 with the swearing in of Harry Hopkins, director of relief work in New York state, as head of the federal relief effort. He had $500 million to disburse, and within a day he had spent $5 million of that, irrefutable evidence that delay and temporizing in the relief area were things of the past. Within days the restless, intense Hopkins had selected a central office staff, had called on state governors to form state relief organizations, which he termed a prerequisite for qualifying for federal relief, and had begun to select field staff to oversee the operations in the various localities where the money would be spent by local relief agencies.

The provisions of the act made it clear that the states, and through them the localities, were to be deeply involved in the disbursement of the money. The first $250 million was to be given to them on a matching basis, one federal dollar for every three state dollars appropriated and used for relief. The other $250 million was for direct grants to states that were able to show that they had no more state money available for matching grants. Hopkins had decided unequivocally that the money should be distributed through public, not private, agencies and that the federal government should exercise as much control over the operation as was possible under such a grant-in-aid system, which left the detailed administration in the hands of local relief organizations. It was essential, therefore, that the FERA be staffed at the field level by men tough enough to stand up to state governors and relief boards and to local authorities in order to ensure that proper procedures were followed and that federal guidelines were complied with and to see that Hopkins's insistence that politics be separated from relief was adhered to as closely as possible, taking account of local conditions and circumstances. They also had to be able to make quick decisions, often in areas where evolving federal procedures had not yet caught up with the reality of particular situations. That was Williams's new job, field representative in the southwestern region.[1]

First, however, his Wisconsin affairs had to be cleared up. The conference directors had not been altogether happy about his prolonged absences in 1932, and early in the new year they had told him that he had to make up his mind: Either he committed himself totally to the American Public Welfare Association or he came back to Madison at the end of the task that he was then doing. That was the situation when the FERA offer came through, and the conference did not stand in his way. The tributes accorded him were generous, though they contained some hints of the various controversies that he had caused. Judge Rosenberry, for example, stated that "the fact that antagonisms had been aroused by various activities of the Executive did not matter, that when you build you cannot help but make antagonisms. . . . Mr. Williams had given his time and service to the Conference unstintingly for many years, and that now he had an opportunity to carry on his work on a much larger national scale, and therefore we ought to release him for that opportunity." A minute of the board read in part, "One can almost say his leadership has made the conference what it is today. His tireless and devoted service merits the heartfelt appreciation of this Board. His devotion, courage, vision have been a constant inspiration. . . . We do not feel we can hold him here in this hour of the Nation's need." Even allowing for the normal tendency to exaggerate in such situations, these tributes indicate that, despite the tension he had caused from time to time, he left Madison well regarded by those with whom he had worked.[2]

Anita and the boys, the Williamses had decided, would remain in the white wooden house in Nakoma, at least for the time being.

The new job would require constant traveling, and if Aubrey was going to be away from home most of the time, it seemed cruel to insist that the family be uprooted. The prospect of another long separation from his family was the only damper on his enthusiasm as he left to join the New Deal.[3]

The stretch of territory over which he had been given jurisdiction was vast; the southwestern region comprised Alabama, Louisiana, Mississippi, Arkansas, Oklahoma, and Texas. It was a region of want. The Depression there had cruelly accentuated the general situation of southern backwardness and deprivation. It was also a region with a sturdy tradition of independence and a distrust, among its politicians at least, of the heavy hand of Washington. Finally, it was a region in which political patronage was a normal condition of affairs, and where some of the most colorful and corrupt politicians in the nation resided. Williams had to go into that area to make sure that adequate state relief structures were set up, that federal money was being disbursed according to agreed guidelines, that there was no discrimination according to race, and that "politics" was kept out of the FERA. It was a tough first assignment.

Williams scarcely had time to familiarize himself with the basics of the FERA operation before he was off on his first tour of duty. That trip, which included extensive travel through every state in his region, was one in which at times he seemed to be doing nothing but firing people and getting into trouble with politicians, one in which he had all sorts of bizarre adventures, but one, also, which so impressed Hopkins that he marked the new man down for early promotion. It was perhaps the most important learning experience in Williams's public life.

First stop was Louisiana. There he found that the state relief commission was being run by the local president of the Bell Telephone Company out of a suite of offices in the heart of the city, with five highly paid lawyers on his staff. He also found that more relief money had been lent to insolvent banks than had been disbursed to the unemployed. After three days of investigation, Williams fired the state's relief administration, demanded that the relief commission be replaced—"including the lawyers"—and then sat back to await the wrath of the only politician that mattered in the state, Senator Huey Pierce Long. It did not come. Long made a decision that he "was a thousand times better off having nothing to do with it" (the administration of relief in Louisiana) and that it would save him a whole lot of time and political trouble if he kept right out of the relief picture, and on that he was consistent for the rest of his life. As he characteristically told Williams, "I am through with this whole goddam fucking business. Hereafter its your sucking bastard, and I'll be giving you and Hopkins and that fucker in the White House unshirted hell every day from now on."

But he never did so, on relief matters at least, and it was partly for that reason that Williams never really shared the malevolent view of the Kingfish that so many other New Dealers held. A second reason was more deep rooted. As he had the Fergusons in Texas, or even Governor Murray in Oklahoma, he always considered Long to be on the side of the ordinary people, someone with roots ultimately in the populist tradition. He could excuse, therefore, much of Long's erratic and undemocratic behavior. Without Long to worry about, Williams was able to fashion a working operation relatively quickly. It was during his first stay in Louisiana, too, that he adopted a practice that he continued throughout his period in government. He began mingling incognito with the people on relief, or likely to be so, visiting depots and dockyards, flop-houses and missions, listening to their talk, sharing their silences. In New Orleans he regularly used to "get up at five or six in the morning and go down to the river front and get a bowl of blue beans and sowbelly and a cup of coffee for 15 cents. There I met transients, dockworkers, night serenaders, street-walkers, pimps, whores and all sorts of people. Most had nothing to say, they ate their beans and sowbelly and drank their coffee in silence."[4]

After the initial flurry of firings, Louisiana posed relatively few problems. That was not the case with his next stop, Arkansas. There he found the situation "desperately bad"; every appointment was "political" and "filled with persons with little or no fitness for the work." There was no investigation of applications for relief—indeed, one caseworker had been fired for so doing—and need was less of a qualification for receiving assistance than close adherence to the state Democratic machine.

Williams began to clean things up, demanding as a first step the sacking of the incompetent state relief director. There he ran into the opposition of the governor, J. Marion Futrell—"who always had a large quid of tobacco in his jaw, it stuck out like a birds egg," and whose proud boast it was that he owned only one pair of underpants—and, more important, the state's senior senator, the redoubtable "Joe" Robinson. When, as he was fated to do all his life, Williams made an indiscreet public statement at a most inappropriate time, this one praising the action of the Arkansas cotton pickers who were currently on strike, Robinson wrote to Roosevelt demanding that he be dismissed.

Hopkins immediately recalled him to Washington, and Williams thought his career in government was already over. Far from it. Having received Robinson's complaint, President Roosevelt had expressed an interest in Williams. A White House dinner for state relief administrators had already been arranged, and he was asked to join the party. So off he went, "frozen with fear," to meet the man whom he was to come to love so profoundly. Roosevelt was the essence of cordiality, he later recalled. The president called him Aubrey and talked cheerily with him about his work, but he himself behaved "rather stupidly," for he was very nervous. He was by no means the only person so affected. Asked by Roosevelt how things were in her state, Gay Shepparson, newly appointed relief director for Georgia, replied, according to Williams, "Georgia is all right, Mr. President," in a voice so high pitched it was almost a scream. Still, despite the nervousness it was a great occasion for them all, for the president managed to convey to each one of them the feeling that he cared about them and the people that they worked with. For Williams, it was "one of the greatest moments that I had ever lived."[5]

Reinforced by Hopkins's adjuration to do everything necessary to clean up the mess there and not to worry unduly about Senator Robinson, he went back to Arkansas, where he found the situation in a turmoil. In some counties desperate people seemed ready to march on relief depots to seize for themselves the aid that the system was denying them. Governor Futrell implored Williams to help, which he agreed to do once the relief director had been dismissed. Reluctantly, Futrell complied. Williams then set about establishing a reasonable operation, and by early August the situation was much better. The governor was "not overly happy," but was going along with it all, and Senator Robinson was also cooperating, busying "himself just enough to give a show of protecting some fellow" who was marked for dismissal, but not really taking it seriously. A new state director had been appointed, and most of the political appointees had gone. Funds were being disbursed on criteria of need, not political coloration. Hopkins was impressed with what Williams had accomplished, and told him so.

It had been hard work, but nevertheless there had been some time for relaxation. Once, at a dinner party in Little Rock, Williams found himself besieged by a most attractive collection of southern belles, all anxious for what they termed "private lessons." He had not the slightest idea what they meant, and it was not for some time that he realized that he had been mistaken for the famous psychiatrist and sex therapist Frankwood E. Williams. The meaning then became obvious.[6]

From Arkansas he went to Mississippi. There he found the organization that he had established while he was with the American Public Welfare Association largely intact, but the situation was in a turmoil nonetheless over wage rates. The planters, anxious about their labor, objected furiously to the minimum wage rate paid by the FERA for what work relief was available. Low as it was at thirty cents an hour, it was more than they paid their blacks. Fearful of losing their cheap labor supply to government projects, they brought so much pressure for changes in the FERA wage structure that the governor was threatening to stop relief payments altogether unless Washington complied. Williams told him that "they would have to take full responsibility for any such move," and that he, Williams, "would be forced to state publicly that the Federal Government was no party to such a move and stood ready to grant aid to Mississippi when so requested." After two days the governor backed down, and by August, Williams could write that he felt "better about Mississippi than I have for some time." Again, he had displayed firmness and a refusal to compromise under pressure. That was the only confrontation that he had in those early days with a distinctly racial overtone.[7]

Next stop was Alabama, where he found a patchy operation. The field staff was good, but there was confusion and dissension at the top, owing mainly to a violent personality conflict between the state relief director, Thad Holt, and the director of social services, a Mrs. Tunstall. Each accused the other of usurping authority. Holt had a tendency to "make drastic departures with respect to policy in respective counties without consulting" Tunstall, while she, often countermanding his directions, was "the cause of constant disturbances so far as the state and field staff were concerned." Both demanded that Williams do something about the situation. He drew up a set of rules that clearly defined their respective functions, which he hoped "would iron out some of the difficulties," but it did not work. By October, Tunstall had left the organization, to be replaced by Loula Dunn, who was to become one of Williams's most trusted allies and who was also a personal friend of Holt's. Despite this initial strife, however, the Alabama organization caused him relatively little trouble. The field staff, mainly child welfare association workers taken over by the FERA, was easily the best in his region.[8]

Oklahoma, his next port of call, was a very different story, for that was "Alfalfa Bill" Murray's territory. The governor was a remarkable person, a classicist, a man who, dissatisfied with the textbooks used in the state's agricultural colleges, had ordered them scrapped and then written his own, but a man who dressed like a tramp, who ruled his state like a personal fiefdom, and who regarded any intrusion into his domain by the federal government with the deepest distrust. Williams had been warned about "Alfalfa Bill," but as he later wrote, "Everything I had heard did not prepare me to find what I did."

Their first interview was a disaster. The governor was seated with his feet on the desk, his hat on, his unkempt hair flopping over his eyes. Behind him stood the huge, silent Indian who accompanied him everywhere. Williams was seated in a chair that had a chain attached to one leg. The chair jerked back violently if one tried to move forward, as Murray did not like people to sit too close to him. He offered Williams mate tea, and drinking that brew was an act, he later said, "which required more patriotism than any I was ever called to perform for my country," for the governor strained it through a handkerchief "that looked like it hadn't been washed in six months." After that, however, the pleasantries were ended. Murray furiously denounced Roosevelt, that "syphilitic son of a bitch who has sent you down here to police me and my state," threatened Williams with arrest, and vowed total noncooperation. Williams abruptly walked out of the interview, returned to his hotel, and called Hopkins, who told him he had done the right thing. Murray eventually telephoned Williams to offer a grudging apology, but that was by no means the end of his troubles in Oklahoma. That he managed to set up a reasonably efficient organization in that state at all is a tribute to his tenacity of purpose, while the fact that he ended up developing a real regard for the old governor attests both to his generosity of spirit and, again, to his tendency to romanticize those whom he considered to be of the people, for the governor obstructed him every step of the way.

Williams found the relief organization in the state to be a corrupt shambles. The director, Sam Banks, who was a Murray lackey, had an office in a bank vault and knew nothing about relief work. The county directors were all political appointees and had a free hand in their areas. With no oversight they were, Williams suspected, often helping themselves to the public till. Williams demanded that he be allowed to tour the counties. Murray said no. When Williams went anyway, the governor telephoned Roosevelt in a futile attempt to have him stopped. Williams completed his tour and, appalled at what he found, the scale of suffering and the corruption of those charged with relieving it, decided on drastic action. He went straight to the governor's mansion on his return and demanded that the thirty county relief directors be immediately replaced. Murray, who was lying on his bed, a place from which he often did business, and dressed "in a pair of grey woollen drawers," surprisingly agreed, but immediately substituted a new set of cronies. After more pressure was applied, Williams began to construct a working organization. The state relief director was replaced—by a woman, and again only in the face of furious resistance from the governor.

Nevertheless, Aubrey got to like him and would sometimes go about with him and watch in awed fascination as the business of the state of Oklahoma was done. He recognized that the world of the Murrays was past. "We were trying to digest," he later wrote, "too many men like Governor Murray, . . . colorful and picturesque, but out of place and out of time, with little comprehension of what was going on in the world." Yet, the governor eventually cooperated, at least to an extent that by September Williams was able to report that the Oklahoma program, which was now being handled completely on a work basis, was "more respectable than I have found anywhere else. We have reorganized Oklahoma," he said, "from everything under the Governor. I wouldn't attempt to reorganize him. I have a great deal of admiration for that man and a high regard." But it had been very hard work indeed, and again he had needed all his reserves of toughness and determination. Moreover, the time that he had been forced to spend in Oklahoma had placed him behind schedule. Hopkins called a conference of all FERA workers for early September, presuming that field-workers would have finished their first tours of duty by then. Williams, however, had been able to spend only a short time in his last, and in some ways most difficult, state, Texas. He left for the conference reluctantly, knowing that a lot of work remained to be done there before he could feel satisfied that his region was in good working order.[9]

The September FERA conference proved to be very important to Williams. At the time he thought he was an odd man out. His views on what could and should be provided by the federal government under the guise of relief seemed much more far reaching, much more radical, than those of his colleagues. Moreover, his insistence that the only really acceptable form of assistance was work relief again seemed to set him apart. Not from Hopkins, however. The administrator praised Williams's activities as "the kind of field work I want."

Then, as he prepared to leave for Texas, Hopkins asked him "to stay around Washington" for a few more days. He was allotted temporary office space with a fellow worker who, he recollected, "had a strong perfume," but he was given no particular tasks to do. Hopkins introduced him around to various people of importance— they spent one long evening with senators La Follette, Costigan, and Wagner, for example—and he and Williams had long conversations about every aspect of the FERA's operation.

Hopkins was particularly interested in Williams's commitment to work relief and the way he had acted on that commitment whenever he could in the states under his jurisdiction. Hopkins was also a strong advocate of work relief and wondered about the possibilities of instituting a generalized federal work relief scheme relatively quickly. The time, he believed, was right. The debate over work relief as against direct relief was coming to a head. Time, structure, and circumstance worked to force the FERA to operate mainly on a direct basis, but those administering it were becoming convinced that only the provision of work could preserve both the skills and morale of the unemployed.

The locally based pre-1929 relief systems had mainly been concerned with assisting the unemployables, those in the community who through physical or mental infirmity were incapable of keeping themselves. That system had collapsed because it had been unable to cope with the scale of the problems caused by the Depression. In the changed context, when the overwhelming majority of those seeking relief were not unemployable but able-bodied casualties of economic disaster, the need for the state to provide the employment that the straitened private sector was unable to furnish became more and more insistent. Furthermore, those who, like Williams, had been frustrated by the inefficiencies of working within the competing jurisdictions of federal and state authorities saw in the adoption of a work relief approach the chance to develop a truly national program. A sense of urgency derived from the disturbingly obvious perception that the FERA was not providing relief on a scale sufficient to get the country through the winter. Moreover, there were ominous rumblings among the unemployed themselves, who were demanding work, not the dole. Something else was required, and a federal work relief plan seemed the answer. Several people were contributing ideas, but nothing definite had emerged, and Hopkins asked Williams to put his mind to the proposal. Delighted, he said he would. Shortly afterwards he returned to the field, after having had a brief discussion with Jerome Frank and Rexford Tugwell about a work scheme. He was unaware that Hopkins had probably already marked him out as his deputy.[10]

Williams went directly to Texas, where he found a situation of a gravity sufficient to keep him from any serious thoughts on long-term planning for several weeks. Ma and Pa Ferguson had tried to maintain the organization developed by Williams earlier in the year, and under Colonel Westbrook, the flamboyant but highly efficient state director, and his deputy Marie Dresden, a fine operation had been developed. Westbrook had quickly established proper procedures for the distribution of funds and had also accepted the proposition that trained social workers should be employed in FERA positions wherever possible. In many ways Texas was looking as good an FERA operation as there was in the nation. However, anxious to control the relief organization as a means of reducing the governor's power, anti-Ferguson forces were attacking Westbrook constantly and accusing him of everything from corruption to Communism, and the strain was beginning to show. He desperately needed unequivocal federal support if he was to survive.

This Williams gave him, and publicly. The Fergusons arranged for Williams to address a joint session of the Texas legislature on September 20, 1933. Stating that he was "not here to instruct the legislature on what the State of Texas should do," he nevertheless proceeded to do just that. He refuted in short order the charges of corruption and inefficiency laid at Westbrook's door. Rather, he said, Westbrook was honest, efficient, and "unusually free from political influence and is living up to the strict rules of the Federal Administration." Under him, he argued, Texas had developed about the "best organization in the Union," and he stated that Washington would continue to use his agency for the disbursement of FERA funds despite the allegations against him. Indeed, he said, if Westbrook were driven from office, it would be regarded so seriously at the federal level that the flow of funds might dry up. "I went on to say unequivocally," he concluded, "that the administration of funds under the . . . directorship of Mr. Westbrook has been and is eminently satisfactory to the Federal Government."[11]

The strong statement of support was instrumental in moderating the attacks on Westbrook. Relief funds in the fall of 1933 were too important to be put at risk for short-term political gain. There was grumbling among some sections of the legislature, but nothing more. One state senator at a barbecue jumped on Williams for "dictating with the flag around [him]," but most expressed their private support for his position. By November, Williams was able to report that Westbrook's position seemed secure and that relief matters in Texas were working smoothly. Yet again, his ability to withstand political pressure had been convincingly demonstrated. Williams had obviously been a successful field representative in a difficult region.

The FERA always had two basic problems to contend with: insufficient money and the clash of jurisdiction between federal, state, and local authorities. There was little that anyone could do about the first of these, given the competing claims on the federal purse, while the second could be approached in one of two ways—either by letting local and state authorities have their head or by imposing as large a measure of federal control as possible. In opting always for the second alternative, Williams demonstrated his conviction that the relief effort should be a national one and that the federal government should have ultimate control over it. Increasingly, this was the view that the majority of those involved were coming to adopt, and though it was still strongly opposed in 1933 by some who thought that the local communities should take care of their own in their own way, with minimal federal involvement, there was little indication that the states and counties were either willing or able to accept the task. In such a context continued centralization of the relief effort was inevitable.[12]

Having secured matters in Texas, Williams moved eastward to see how his other states were doing. Inevitably, a number of local problems had to be ironed out, but basically, they were working well. That being the case, he was freer to think about the discussions that he had had with Hopkins and others in Washington about work relief. He wrote to his chief in mid-October saying that he had been working on "the plan I discussed with you, Tugwell and Jerome Frank," that he had modified it somewhat, and that he would let him have a draft soon.[13] Shortly afterward, he wrote a long letter to Hopkins criticizing the operation of the FERA and enclosing a detailed draft of a scheme to provide only work relief. His plan, which would be wholly federally financed, would replace direct relief with a "system of employment in which men would be paid a daily wage for performing work" and turn the unemployables back on the states. "Our treatment of the unemployed," he concluded, "at the present is untenable. Our program of relief is unacceptable to millions of the best people that we have got and those we are helping are being reduced by our methods and the amount of our grants to a status of chronic destitution."[14]

Hopkins responded quickly. He had after all been talking and thinking along those lines for several weeks, and Williams's proposal was probably but one of several similar schemes around. But it was the most detailed, and yet the simplest, advocating as it did the use of FERA county units for its administration. It could, literally, be brought into operation in days.

Nevertheless, one major problem remained to be surmounted. Organized labor had long been opposed to any program of government jobs that competed with union labor, and President Roosevelt was bound to listen to their views. Williams said he thought his old Wisconsin acquaintance John R. Commons could help on that point. Certainly it would be worth a try. He made a hurried trip to Madison, and there the old economist provided the answer. Digging around in his study, he came up with an 1899 issue of the American Federation of Labor's publication the *Federationist* in which Samuel Gompers had argued for a government employment scheme strikingly similar to the one now being proposed. Excitedly, Williams phoned Hopkins to tell him the news. That was all the administrator wanted. The president was always impressed by arguments from history. A few days later, on November 6, 1933, he lunched with Roosevelt and outlined a proposal to put four million men to work on fully federally funded projects. A day later the president agreed, and the Civil Works Administration was born.[15]

It is rarely possible to trace the origins of an institution like the CWA to see who, if anyone, can clearly be held responsible for its conception. Usually, many have had a part in it, and that is the case in this instance. The proposal had been thrashed out over weeks, with a number of people contributing. Yet a case can be made for arguing that Williams's contribution was much greater than that which historians have generally given him credit for—resolving the doubts about organized labor's support. First, he and Hopkins had discussed the idea at length in Washington in September and had corresponded thereafter about a specific plan. That process had culminated in Williams's detailed document of late October, a document which resembled very closely the structure of the CWA. Second, the fact that Hopkins telephoned Williams to tell him of the president's agreement and insisted that he interrupt a speech in order to take the call lends credence to the view that his contribution was much more than a minor one. Third, there is the evidence of Williams himself. He at least was in no doubt as to where credit should lie. Cabling Anita, who was still in Madison, after Hopkins's call, he stated elatedly, "President today ordered my plan put into effect. Watch for announcement afternoon papers. I of course will not be mentioned but I am too happy to care very much about that."[16]

Finally, the action of Hopkins himself confirms the important part that Williams played in the creation of the CWA. On November 8 he telegraphed him saying that he wanted him to come to Washington to help in the planning of the new agency. When Aubrey arrived, Hopkins confirmed that this was to be more than a temporary shift. He needed a deputy, someone who shared his perspectives on relief matters, who was a fighter, and yet who had demonstrated an ability to get on personally with a wide range of people, including the politicians with whom he often had to differ in the public arena. Above all, he needed someone whose sympathies, whose commitment, were with the unemployed and whom he could trust implicitly. He had decided that Aubrey Williams was that man.[17]

5

The CWA—And After

Williams hardly had time to reflect on his rapid elevation, for, with Hopkins, Frank Bane, and Corrington Gill, the man in charge of the FERA's statistical side, he was quickly engulfed in detailed planning for the new agency. Working feverishly to meet a November 15 deadline, when the details would be announced at a conference of state governors and mayors of the larger cities, they completed the task only a few hours ahead of schedule.

Essentially, the outlines of the program that Hopkins announced were these. Pointing out that the principle of work relief had already been firmly established through FERA practice, he said that the president had simply decided to extend that, at least temporarily. Roosevelt had decided to put four million men to work, by December 15, on public work projects throughout the country. They would be paid at reasonable wage rates, with margins for skill and regional variations built in—southern workers would receive approximately 20 percent less than their northeastern counterparts, for example—and could work a maximum of thirty hours weekly. At least half the people employed by the CWA were to be selected from relief rolls; the rest were to come from the unemployed, those certified as such by the United States Employment Service and not necessarily on relief. The operation was to be kept as decentralized as possible. Acting under broad general guidelines, local and regional officials, in most cases FERA employees wearing an extra hat, would take primary responsibility for initiating projects and employing workers. These projects were to be self-liquidating and of the sort that could be completed within three to four months, which ruled out large-scale construction projects, for example. That type of job remained the province of Harold Ickes's Public Works Administration (PWA). Neither "politics" nor discrimination on racial grounds was to be a consideration in the disbursement of CWA funds. The program was to cost just under one billion dollars.

Of that, $400 million was transferred from the PWA, nearly $90 million came from unused FERA grants to the states, and $345 million came from a special congressional appropriation. About 10 percent came from state and local government sources.[1]

The response to the new agency was enthusiastic, and local, state, and central officials were soon overwhelmed with applications for projects, as the effort to meet the December 15 deadline began. Local projects had to receive merely the approval of state CWA officials. Only those projects receiving specific federal sponsorship were checked in Washington. Given the speed at which the operation was forced to develop, it is hardly surprising that many of those applications went virtually unchecked. The types of projects approved were immensely varied, ranging from remedial education to the construction of airports. About 80 percent, however, had to do with the improvement of public property—street repair, sewer development, small public construction jobs, and the development of recreational facilities. By any standards, the speed with which the plan became reality was impressive. Though Hopkins exaggerated when he told Roosevelt that the goal of having four million men at work by December 15 would be achieved, he was not too far off. By mid-January, in fact, well over that number were on the job.[2]

It was inevitable, given the extreme haste of its inception and the inexperience of thousands of the people charged with administering it, that the CWA would have its problems, and that proved to be the case. The problem of the wage scale was never satisfactorily settled, and, indeed, wage rates were reduced three times in the agency's short life, as costs mounted far more rapidly than anticipated. Nevertheless, in the South, even allowing for those reductions, thousands of people received more money than they had ever seen in their lives before, itself a reason for bitter criticism of the program from some quarters. Without doubt, many projects were inadequately checked, and a number were of very little value. Political influence did enter into decisions about the locations of certain projects and in the choice of men to run them. There was misuse of funds, and there was graft. Yet, again, given the scale of the operation, the looseness of its structure, and the fact that the overworked officials administering it were also trying to operate the FERA, what is surprising is that such problems were relatively limited. There were, after all, nearly 190,000 separate CWA projects, yet despite detailed investigations only 240 charges of serious irregularity were ever proved. Hopkins was correct in his insistence that it was a remarkably clean operation.[3]

Moreover, it undoubtedly succeeded in its primary purpose. It got the country through what proved to be a very severe winter. CWA workers and their families, who might otherwise have starved and suffered intense privation from cold, did not. Most CWA paychecks were expended on such mundane but crucial things as food, clothing, heating, and shelter. For its employees, many of whom were working for the first time in years, they provided self-respect as well. Searle F. Charles is correct when he writes that "the lift in morale cannot be measured. C.W.A. improved the lives of over sixteen million Americans for a period of time."[4]

Within the CWA administration, Williams, like the other members of the Washington staff, handled all manner of tasks. With no time to develop clearly defined administrative structures, Hopkins farmed out jobs to his assistants as needs arose. Inevitably, however, certain parts of the operation became the particular preserves of one or other of the assistant administrators. Williams soon became responsible for maintaining relationships with state administrators and consulting with them about the everyday problems of administration. He advised them on such matters as wage rates, purchasing problems, and selection policies and relieved Hopkins of much of the detailed administrative work.

Williams also checked out complaints. For example, when Congressman John F. Dockweiler, a California Democrat, wrote to Hopkins alleging that the CWA organization in Glenwood, California, was firmly in Republican hands, the matter was immediately turned over to Aubrey.[5] In January 1934 he flew to Denver to investigate an alleged illegality in the use of funds there. Finding the allegation to be true, he recommended the immediate dismissal of the state administrator. Hopkins agreed and acted within minutes of receiving Williams's phone call.[6] In February he was in Alabama to investigate a series of complaints that CWA officials there discriminated against union labor in their hiring policies.

Williams toured the states regularly on Hopkins's behalf, drafted letters for presidential signature on various policy matters at Hopkins's request, and wrote soothing letters to congressmen and senators whose feathers had been ruffled by some CWA action or another. He assured Representative Lister Hill of Alabama, for example, that Jane Foster, his successor as southwestern regional field representative and whom he had deputed to investigate certain alleged hiring irregularities in Alabama, was, although a woman, nevertheless a tough-minded individual who would "get the facts in connection with the investigation in Alabama if they are to be gotten. I know of no person I have more confidence in, and I shall send you a copy of her report in a day or two." In short, he relieved his chief of a whole range of administrative tasks, as well as becoming Hopkins's closest colleague and advisor. Based from the beginning on mutual respect, their relationship was already developing into one of friendship.[7]

One area that Hopkins asked Williams to handle completely on his own was that of race relations. Black Americans had not expected much from Roosevelt and the new administration. Indeed, a majority of those able to vote in 1932 had supported President Hoover, despite their parlous economic position and the Republican record of inaction and unconcern on racial issues throughout the 1920s. Yet it was not long before some black leaders began to express cautious optimism about the administration's attitude toward blacks, to wonder if perhaps they had been wrong in their cynicism about the Democrats, and to hope that the promised New Deal might indeed be extended to them.

A prime reason for that change was that among those who came to Washington to man the augmented federal bureaus and agencies were a few who were genuinely committed to the cause of black equality and who intended to use their positions of relative power to act on that commitment whenever they could. Those men and women believed that the components of the liberal approach were indivisible and that extending black rights was an essential part of liberal reform. John B. Kirby has called them "race liberals," and the name is apt. Perhaps the first, and certainly the most important, to be so identified was Secretary of the Interior Harold L. Ickes, but there were others, including Will Alexander of the Farm Security Administration, Gardner Jackson of the Department of Agriculture, Harry Hopkins, and Aubrey Williams. In time, Mrs. Roosevelt became closely identified with the cause of black rights and its leading spokeswoman.

Together, this group worked constantly throughout the era to make the promise of American life a reality for American blacks, and, as Harvard Sitkoff and Kirby have recently shown, what painful and partial progress was made toward racial equality during the decade owed much to their efforts. They fulfilled their commitment in various ways: they appointed blacks to their staffs, often, but not always, to deal specifically with "black issues" as they affected a particular bureau or agency, and tried to ensure that those working with and under them treated blacks fairly. Most of the New Deal's administrative creations included a clause in the acts authorizing them or in subsequent regulations which specified equality of treatment for all Americans under its provisions. In many cases, as with the Civilian Conservation Corps, for example, little attempt was made to honor such a covenant fully, and the requirement remained purely a paper one. However, in those programs where race liberals had influence, a genuine attempt was made to make equality of treatment a reality.[8]

The CWA was specifically enjoined not to discriminate in its hiring policies for reasons of race, and Williams was asked to see that, as far as possible, that policy was complied with. It was his first attempt to cope with the problem to which at a later stage in his life he would dedicate his whole activity. There was plenty for him to attend to. Complaints of discrimination against blacks, especially in the South, in both employment and wage rates, began to reach the Washington office within days of the agency's commencing operations. As far as he could, Williams dealt with them firmly and uncompromisingly. To the Mississippi CWA, for example, he wrote, "We must insist that . . . our administration boards, state and local, make their position very clear that these jobs are given out without regard to race or color. Your position should be made public." Handling charges of discrimination brought against the CWA by prominent Negro citizens, he painstakingly reviewed each allegation and insisted that any injustices be promptly rectified, as far as was possible. Of course there was discrimination in the CWA, despite the official strictures against it. Given its size, the speed of its mobilization, and the prevailing attitudes on race, that was inevitable. However, the extent to which it was moderated by the central agency, and the degree to which the nondiscriminatory policy was enforced, was in large part the result of the diligence of Williams.[9]

One of the products of his concern to get the Negro a fair deal within the relief structures, and in keeping with the general views of the New Deal's race liberals, was the creation early in 1934 of a special office of Negro affairs in the FERA and the appointment of a black to head it. Williams urged the creation of such an office on Hopkins, and was charged with finding the right man for the job. After consulting with a number of black and civil rights leaders, he appointed Forrester B. Washington, dean of the Atlanta School of Social Work, to the position, largely on the recommendation of Will Alexander, head of the Atlanta-based Commission on Interracial Cooperation. Williams took a great interest in Washington's work and was most unhappy when he resigned in August, after only six months in the job, frustrated at his inability to influence policy and concerned that he was serving as "merely window dressing" for the New Deal.[10]

Williams had no illusions about the way that blacks were often treated by the relief agencies. Writing to Mrs. Roosevelt early in 1934 in one of his first contacts with her, he stated starkly, "The negroes don't get a fair deal. I don't know how to secure one for them. I do think we should take every means to correct discrimination where we have a bill of particulars and maintain thereby a strong and vigorous policy that this Administration will not knowingly tolerate the deliberate depriving of Negroes of the benefits of relief."[11] Trying to get fairness for American blacks became one of his most urgent concerns both throughout his period of government service and beyond, and also one of his most important contributions to the New Deal. Few public administrators of the time were better respected and trusted by the black community, and he was often to prove an invaluable link between blacks and the administration.

Roosevelt began to dismantle the CWA as the warmer weather returned, in the South first and then progressively throughout the rest of the country. By April it was all over. It had by then built and repaired over forty thousand schools, 255,000 miles of roads and streets, and hundreds of airports, post offices, and other public buildings. It had employed fifty thousand primary and secondary teachers and pioneered in adult education. Not all the work done was first class, far from it, yet Charles is again correct when he states that "despite these weaknesses, C.W.A. stands out in all American history as one of the greatest peace time administrative feats ever completed. For this Hopkins and his staff must be given credit."[12] Those who ran it were certainly proud of it. More important, they had shown, if only for a short time and in far from the best conditions, the immense possibilities inherent in a thoroughgoing, federally organized, work relief program. They would certainly look for the chance to try again.

Williams was bitterly disappointed by the president's decision to terminate the CWA. He had a proprietary interest in the agency, of course. But beyond that, he was convinced that, despite its cost, the only morally legitimate form of relief was the provision of work and that to return to the "dole" system that had characterized the FERA in 1933 would be a disastrously backward step.[13]

His concern was at least partially mollifed by the knowledge that Hopkins planned to increase greatly the work component of the FERA's activities as part of a general restructuring of the agency's operation, now that the first frenetic months were behind it. Indeed, it was Williams who broke the news of this restructuring—at Hopkins's request, of course. In a long *New York Times* article entitled "The New Relief Program: Three Great Aims," he revealed that the hand-to-mouth program of 1933 was in the course of being replaced by a permanent one. Pointing out that neither Hopkins nor Roosevelt liked direct relief, but that it had at least "kept breath in bodies that under the policies of the previous Winter, would have given up the ghost," he stated that the CWA, "that colossal enterprise of government," had indicated the direction in which the administration intended to move. Relief policy up until then, he said, had been based on the assumption that the nation was a homogeneous one and that a "national blanket policy" could easily be adopted, and that was clearly not the case. The need to recognize both geographical and economic divergence was evident, and the FERA was proceeding to do just that.

Relief policies would be tailored to fit the needs of three great and differing groups—rural people, stranded people, and urban people. For the debt-ridden farmers still on their own land, the relief effort would concentrate on providing cash to help ease the debt situation, seed and stock to enable them to use their land more efficiently, and education to aid them in coping with an increasingly complex society. For the stranded marginal men locked in a cycle of poverty, relief would attempt to provide both relocation and retraining. That could take the form of assisting landless persons to acquire land of their own or of resettling those that lived on poor or worn-out land on better soil. For the urban dweller, the job of government would be to provide "means of keeping alive, and, if possible more than merely alive, the people who legitimately belong to the industrial organization until that organization is functioning properly," and there the new work program would have a crucial role. Finally, Williams argued for the removal from the labor market of "very considerable numbers of those people between the ages of 18 and 24 or 25" and their placement in educational institutions, for a federally run social security scheme, and for the return of responsibility for the care of unemployables to the states and localities in which they incurred their dependency.[14]

This article is worth extended comment for two reasons. First, Williams would hardly have been flying a personal kite in an article of such importance, but, rather, would have been making public developing administration policy. The article, therefore, indicated that the battle for work relief, as opposed to direct relief, was nearly over. In its discussion of a broad work scheme, of rural rehabilitation programs, of expanded aid to farmers generally, and of programs geared specifically to the needs of young people, it provided an accurate preview of what were to become some of the cardinal features of the Works Progress Administration and the National Youth Administration. Planning for those agencies, therefore, was clearly well advanced in the early months of 1934. Those who advocated a diminution of the federal government's involvement in relief and the retention of direct relief for economic reasons had been placed on the defensive. Second, it was significant that Williams was detailed to present the program, for that reinforced for the public what was already becoming clear within the organization, that Williams, although not yet formally so designated, was in fact the second in command.

The young social worker was taking easily to the administrative role. Within the FERA structure he had several specific tasks. As head of the Division of Relations with the States, he was responsible for the day-to-day contact with the state FERA offices, for advising them as to policy, for answering their questions, for dealing with their complaints, and, at times, for making sure that in a conflict between a state and the agency the federal will prevailed. The regional representatives reported directly to him, and the politicians were constantly in contact with him.

Williams quickly learned when to compromise and when to be tough; he also found that, to do his job well, he had to be on top of the operational details, something that Hopkins did not have to concern himself with. When the southwestern field representative, for example, asked for advice regarding a specific situation in Pulaski County, Arkansas, Williams had to know enough of the context to make his advice relevant. As a result, he rapidly acquired a working knowledge of the whole of the FERA's activities, something no one else in the institution had.[15]

As well as heading the Division for Relations with the States, Williams was responsible for FERA transient activities, for some aspects of the rural rehabilitation program, and for the scheme to assist college students, one of the strands that eventually came together in the NYA. He also provided support and companionship for his chief. The relationship between Hopkins and Williams soon ripened into a firm friendship. Different in many ways, they shared, as well as a love of horse-racing, a commitment to helping the unemployed, a common vision as to how that could be done, and an impatience with bureaucratic procedures that stood in the way of realizing their vision.

At time, strains entered their relationship, none more so, from Williams's point of view, than when Hopkins developed political ambitions and began to work for the 1940 Democratic presidential nomination. Williams was opposed to his running, mainly because of his conviction that "people in relief should stay out of politics." Moreover, Joseph P. Kennedy, the Boston financier whom Roosevelt had appointed the first chairman of the Securities Exchange Commission and of whom Williams always had a very low opinion, was favorable to a Hopkins candidacy. Williams told Hopkins of his opposition, said he hated to see him "mixed up with people like Joe Kennedy," and refused to attend meetings of his unofficial campaign committee. For this, he said, he got the "absent treatment" for two weeks. Then, too, Williams did not share an enthusiasm for some aspects of Hopkins's life-style—his enjoyment of Long Island society, for example. Hopkins, for his part, as shall be discussed later, was occasionally seriously embarrassed and more often exasperated by Williams's increasingly frequent verbal indiscretions. Nevertheless, the two men had enough respect and affection for each other that they were able to accommodate these and other differences. They were indeed a team.[16]

In July and August 1934, Williams found himself in sole charge of the FERA. Concerned with Hopkins's indifferent health, Roosevelt had sent him to Europe for two months, ostensibly to investigate housing and social insurance schemes there, but really to have a rest. Initially, Williams found some aspects of the task a bit daunting, particularly dealing with the press, but he was soon taking most matters in his stride. He attempted to keep Hopkins informed about what he was doing, but, inevitably, was forced to act on his own from time to time. For example, when the president wanted quick advice on how the FERA could best be used in assisting the victims of drought in the Southwest, he did not have time to consult his chief. He had to work out a plan of his own. Similarly, it was Williams who broke the news to the press that the administration was planning a new work relief program similar to the CWA, which would soon be submitted to Roosevelt for his approval. Williams enjoyed very much holding the fort for Hopkins, and was gratified that people thought he was doing the job well. Writing to his chief, he told of the ultimate compliment that he had received. "Mac [Marvin McIntyre] paid me a very high compliment," he said. "He told Hull [Cordell Hull] 'Williams acts in situations just like Harry Hopkins.'" The evidence indicates that the compliment was justified. He had, at least, already so impressed George S. Wilson, the retiring director of public welfare for the District of Columbia, that he was offered Wilson's position.[17]

One result of his temporary stewardship of the top FERA office was that it enabled him to improve his contacts with New Dealers outside the relief ambit. As an assistant administrator, he already sat on one or two minor policymaking bodies and had chaired the subcommittee of the Committee on Economic Security which dealt with public employment and public assistance. Substituting for Hopkins, he not only attended meetings of the full committee but sat in on cabinet meetings as well. And, of course, he was asked from time to time to brief the president himself on relief matters.[18]

By mid-1934, Williams was well settled into the heady life of New Deal Washington. Anita and the boys had joined him in November 1933, he had leased a pleasant, large house with lots of yard in Arlington, and he had finally sold his Wisconsin home. His salary was almost twice what he had earned in Madison, and for the first time in their married life money was not a consuming concern. Anita and he were beginning to make friends among the New Deal crowd, for there were many like them, young, idealistic, vaguely leftist, and newcomers to the city and to government service. They worked hard, but also partied a lot. Though Aubrey was never much of a drinker, he and Anita both liked to dance, and conversation was always plentiful. It was at such a party that they first met Clifford and Virginia Durr from Montgomery, Alabama, he a lawyer with the RFC, she a well-connected southern lady of decidedly liberal inclinations. They would remain friends for the rest of their lives.[19]

Williams, too, was learning something about the people he worked with, both his colleagues at FERA and those in other agencies and departments. Never a man to check a judgment, he had already formed strong opinions about many of them. He liked and felt politically close to his FERA colleagues Corrington Gill, Jacob Baker, Lawrence Westbrook, Robert Kelso, and the beautiful and brilliant Elizabeth Wickenden, later to become his trusted aide and devoted friend. One exception, however, was Pierce Williams, a former RFC representative whom Hopkins had appointed as a field representative and who considered Williams to have the "sloppiest mind in the outfit." There was never any love lost between the two men.

His friendship with Hopkins, as has already been mentioned, had firmed by mid-1934. They spent a lot of time in each other's company, both at work and at the race track, where Hopkins found Aubrey's proclivity for betting on long shots amusing—and his tendency to win on those amazing. Other people he had come to admire were senators La Follette, Hugo Black, Costigan, and Wagner, with whom he often socialized but who, he said, never once tried to use the relationship to political advantage, and Justice Brandeis. Early in his Washington career, the old justice invited the Williamses to dinner. They dressed up to the hilt, expecting formality. Instead they were received by Mrs. Brandeis in her carpet slippers. Nevertheless, the evening went off very well.[20]

If there were many people both within and without government whom Williams had already come to respect and to identify with, there were others whom he had already come to dislike profoundly. From his earliest days in Washington, he later wrote, he was puzzled by the fact that the president seemed to have around him "some of the worst horses arses . . . I have ever met," and the explanation that politics necessitated their presence only partially satisfied him. Among the early qualifiers for that appellation were Sumner Welles, an assistant secretary of state, John Studebaker, the commissioner of education, and Jesse Jones of the RFC, whom Williams once described as "about as crooked as a snake" and "as sympathetic to the aims and purposes of the New Deal as a dog is to a cat that has just given him a bloody eye." Williams identified Jones as one of a group of people who were ostensibly working for the New Deal but who were in reality hostile to the president. Vice-President Garner, he said, was their leader, but Jones was "the brains of the group." In Williams's view he was "a pretty unsavory character," without the remotest sense of, or interest in, the potential for reform of the agencies he administered. Williams was never able to come to terms with such people. They had, he believed, no business being part of a liberal movement, and served only to strangle some of its aspects. Jones, he pointed out, insisted that all loans made by the RFC's Small Loan Corporation had to be financially sound. That defeated one of the corporation's purposes, which was to help people considered too risky by the private banks. For Williams, the only true New Dealers were the liberals.

By mid-1934, Williams had identified other distinct groups in the New Deal constellation. The nature of that identification, the differences he discerned between their groups, throws some light on the diversity both of the movement as a whole and of the people involved in it, as well as on Williams's perception of himself and his own place in the framework. First, he said, was the group that had Harold Ickes as its center. Williams admired Ickes in many ways, in particular his honesty and his tenacious commitment to principle, but he also recognized his eccentricities and his enormous vanity. Moreover, coming as he did from a progressive Republican tradition, "and having led reform movements in Chicago before most of the New Dealers were out of knee britches," Ickes had trouble working with many of the younger reformers. "He never really succeeded in fitting into the President's team," Williams thought. He was of "another generation than Hopkins, Tugwell, Berle and even F.D.R." Ickes was the leader of the Bull Moose group; these were people with a Progressive heritage who were in general sympathy with the New Deal's objectives but who were not always able to relate to the people involved in it. Senators Hiram Johnson and Burton K. Wheeler, he said, were closely associated with Ickes.

Cordell Hull headed a group in the State Department that had some connections with the Garner faction. This group was in constant disagreement with the foreign policy advisers in the White House. Williams said that "there was something awry between Hull and Roosevelt"; he thought that something might have derived from Hull's resentment at having been passed over for the Democratic nomination in 1932. Whatever the reason, Williams thought, the State Department group was not unreservedly loyal to the New Deal.

Of the liberal groups, two were of particular importance. One was centered around Frances Perkins, the secretary of labor. Its members, he said, were technocrats, who brought crucial organizational and administrative expertise to many of the most important social programs. Arthur Altmeyer of the Cabinet Committee on Economic Security and Louis Brownlow were dominant figures in that group.

The other important liberal group was that clustered around Hopkins, the group to which Williams himself belonged. Less concerned with administration than was the Perkins group, and more with policy, this faction comprised, in Williams's view, "most of the real New Dealers." By mid-1934, he said, Hopkins was the leader of the most liberal wing of the New Deal and had gathered about him a diverse group, including Henry Wallace, secretary of agriculture, Rexford Tugwell, "brilliant youngsters" like Elizabeth Wickenden, and, of course, people like Aubrey Williams. They found in Hopkins a person who both shared their ideals and who had the confidence of the president. For Williams, this group was the liberal core of the New Deal.[21]

Of course, some people defied easy categorization. One such person was Louis Howe, the president's political mentor, whom Williams got to know early and whom to his surprise he liked very much. Initially repulsed by his physical appearance, "crouched over his small desk in the White House, with a skin which seemed full of pot holes, coughing up phlegm in a most nauseating manner," Wil-

liams came both to value his political sense and to welcome his
company, sometimes with Hopkins, at racetracks. Indeed, Williams
later wrote that, after Mrs. Roosevelt's, Howe's advice was consistently the best he was ever given while in Washington.[22]

It was during 1934, in fact, that Williams first began to realize
what a singular woman Mrs. Roosevelt was, although their relationship then was far from the close one it would become in the later
years of the New Deal. He had met her initially in 1933 and had not
been particularly impressed partly because of reports that she had
deliberately snubbed "Ma" Ferguson at a Dallas reception. His next
encounter with her, however, changed his mind. Early in 1934,
Hopkins delegated him to meet with a group of women who were
involved with serving lunches to the transients of the District.
Mrs. Roosevelt, apparently, had been bothered by some aspects of
the operation and wanted it investigated. One of this group was
"Cissy" Patterson of the McCormick-Patterson newspaper clan,
whose *Washington Herald* was bitterly anti–New Deal. The others
were, as Williams described them, "dowagers of Washington." Mrs.
Roosevelt, it seems, thought that these good ladies were treating
their lunchtime duties as a social outing, arriving in chauffeured
limousines to do their stint, with little concern for the people they
were supposed to be serving.

Eventually, Williams, George Allen, then one of the capital's
commissioners, Mrs. Roosevelt, and Cissy Patterson met in Hopkins's office. As Williams described it, "Mrs. Roosevelt took over,
she began by describing the meager quantity of what was being
served the men. Then she moved on to the costs of the whole
project showing that each meal served was costing what should
have bought a bountiful meal, and wound up by saying 'This is
simply not good business' with a rising crescendo." Even the redoubtable Mrs. Patterson was silenced, so forceful was the first lady.
Allen conveniently remembered another appointment, and Williams was left to deal with the ladies on his own. He could not recall
the outcome of the meeting, but did "remember that at least one
person in those present was very much impressed by the First Lady
of the Land." That attitude was to deepen and grow as the years
went by.

His direct dealings with the president during this time were intermittent, confined mainly to the weeks he ran the FERA for

Hopkins. The awe that he had felt at his initial meeting in 1933 still persisted, the fact that he should be discussing policy with the president of the United States amazed him. But, too, he had a growing conviction that Roosevelt was a man who, like him, "suffered greatly for those that are hungry and ragged" and that under his leadership great things were possible. One of the first of those could be the ending of direct relief.[23]

Active and detailed planning to put the whole federal relief operation on a work basis had begun even before the CWA was terminated. Indeed, Williams's lengthy *New York Times* article of April 1, as has already been mentioned, clearly indicated the direction of FERA thinking. Throughout the spring and summer blueprints were produced, broad suggestions were honed down into policy, alternatives were canvassed, and the whole enterprise was costed out thoroughly. When Williams told the press on August 10, 1934, that a plan for a thoroughgoing work program would soon be submitted to the president, its details were so far advanced that he was able to describe in outline, for example, what was later to become the federal arts projects, as well as to discuss the range of professional projects envisaged. The WPA was not created in a hurry, but was the result of months of detailed planning by FERA staff, drawing on both the CWA experience and FERA experimentation. Williams was fully involved in all that activity.[24]

The production of blueprints, no matter how well drafted, was one thing; persuading Roosevelt to adopt them was another. Increasingly sympathetic to the work relief approach, he was nevertheless conscious of its projected cost and aware that it would inevitably provoke congressional opposition. He was slow to commit himself, therefore, to such a basic change in the federal relief structure. Indeed, although relief was often discussed in the 1934 off-year election campaigns, no indication was given that major structural alterations were planned.

Nevertheless, support for the work relief approach was slowly growing. At a conference in August the mayors of a number of major cities strongly supported the development of more federal public works programs, with the states and communities assuming responsibility only for the unemployables. Fiorello La Guardia, the influential mayor of New York, was particularly vocal on the issue. Moreover the administration's efforts to promote economic recovery were faltering by the fall. Private industry offered no employment for the millions on relief. Moreover, the pump-priming effect of the CWA had been obvious. The pressure to repeat and extend it was considerable.[25]

What finally convinced the president to go ahead with not only the works program but a host of other reform legislation was the sweeping Democratic victory in the 1934 congressional elections. Instead of suffering the expected off-year losses, the administration made substantial gains in both houses. Shortly afterward, while driving to the Laurel Race Track, Hopkins turned to Williams and others and, in perhaps his most quoted utterance, exclaimed, "Boys, this is our hour. We've got to get everything we want—a works program, social security, wages and hours, everything—now or never. Get your minds to work on developing a complete ticket to provide for security, for all the folks of this country up and down and across the board."[26]

For Hopkins, Williams, and the other FERA people, committed as they were to developing a massive work program, "getting everything" meant tidying up the plans that they had already laboriously pieced together and then convincing the president to adopt them. This they did in November, amid growing press speculation that the president was considering the feasibility of ending FERA and setting up in its place a work relief program on a scale which would dwarf the CWA, and at a cost of eight to nine billions of dollars. Such speculation was largely correct. In early December, Hopkins and Roosevelt discussed the details of the scheme, and Williams and Leon Henderson and Beardsley Ruml, two economists, worked on the fine print. The president took little persuading, once the cost estimates had been revised downward. The plan was quickly accepted. When Hopkins phoned Williams with the news, he rejoiced. He had lately grown even unhappier with the FERA structure, and now it was all to be changed, and according to his most deeply held ideas. He could not have wished for a better Christmas present.[27]

Planning for what was to become the WPA had occupied much of Williams's time in the last months of 1934, but it was not the only such activity in which he had become involved. In May 1934, speaking of the effects of the Depression on youth, Mrs. Roosevelt had confessed to "moments of real terror" when she thought that "we may be losing this generation. We have got to bring these young people into the active life of the community," she argued, "and make them feel that they are necessary."[28] Responding to such expressions of concern and to the realization that the government's initial response to the problem of young people in the Depression, the Civilian Conservation Corps (CCC), was a stopgap measure only, the FERA had developed programs throughout 1934 specifically geared to the needs of America's deprived youth.

The problem was a crucial one. Accurate statistics on unemployment levels during the Depression decade are difficult to obtain, and those for youth have a far greater margin for error than those for the adult unemployed; most of the latter, having already worked, were more readily traceable. Many surveys were made, however, and although they were based on incomplete evidence, they all point to a problem of frightening dimensions. George P. Rawick, who has made the fullest scholarly analysis of the available statistical material, believes that it is a reasonable assumption that at any time during the 1930s at least 20 to 30 percent of those between the ages of sixteen and twenty-four were unemployed. Youth were among the worst casualties of economic collapse.[29]

The social effect of those statistics was what gave Mrs. Roosevelt and many like her their moments of terror. Denied work, youths were denied their chance to live normally, to grow in independence and maturity, to have fun, to marry, to become adults. Maxine Davis believed that "fear . . . is making old people out of young ones." She talked of "a generation robbed of time and opportunity just as the Great War left the world its heritage of a lost generation." Some warned of the breeding ground for revolution that this new lost generation would certainly become—denied the chance to function within the prevailing social system, they would almost certainly attempt to overturn it. Others stressed the deadening, rather than the disruptive, effect of the large-scale deprivation of youth. The United States was in danger of producing a whole generation of apathetic misfits, who lacked confidence in themselves and their society, who were unskilled, untrained, utterly unable to become the productive adults upon whom social and economic recovery and growth would depend. The long-term effects would be disastrous. As Bruce Melvin put it, "Never before in the history of this country has America been faced with a problem as grave as the present youth problem."[30]

The Roosevelt administration had moved quickly to check the problem. On March 31, 1933, less than a month after his inauguration, the president had signed the CCC into law. Within weeks thousands of young men between the ages of eighteen and twenty-five were at work all over the nation, planting trees, checking soil erosion, blazing trails, and developing parks. They lived in camps or companies of two hundred men, under military control. The CCC had quickly become the "glamour agency" of the New Deal, but neither that nor the real accomplishments in the field of conservation masked the reality that it was no answer to the problems of youth in a depressed economy. It offered no real job training, it toughened bodies but gave no new skills, and it catered to the most desperate cases only. At its peak in 1935, it enrolled about five hundred thousand young men. Usually no more than two hundred and fifty thousand were in camp at any one time. Furthermore, about 50 percent of the young people in need were female. It was no use to them. Thus, for a congeries of reasons—sex, educational and vocational aspirations, physical condition, family responsibilities, motivation, disinclination to accept military control—the CCC was irrelevant to the needs of most young Americans. Indeed the administration itself quickly recognized that more was needed, and during 1933 and 1934, usually under FERA auspices, further youth programs were launched, over which Williams was given a general control.[31]

A group particularly hard hit by the Depression was college students. The twin problems of reduced parental income and the lack of part-time or vacation employment meant that thousands of them simply did not have the money to complete or even begin their tertiary education. Suffering the consequences of shrinking endowments and constricted state and local budgets, the colleges were quite unable to bridge the gap between resources and needs through increased scholarship assistance. As a result, college enrollments dropped 10 percent between 1932 and 1934.

In the summer of 1933 an FERA-sponsored conference of educators discussed the problem and agreed that an experimental program of student aid should be tested at the University of Minnesota. For the fall semester of that year, selected students were supported partly by FERA money and partly by a state matching grant. In return, they performed various jobs around the campus. That scheme was extended to all non-profit-making, tax-exempt colleges in the spring of 1934 after a delegation of college presidents had persuaded Roosevelt that the need was desperate. About 10 percent of enrolled students were paid fifteen to twenty dollars monthly during the school year, again in return for work. College presidents were responsible for selecting the students to receive the aid, but were expected to employ only those who would otherwise have been forced to quit school. By the end of 1934 about seventy-five thousand college youth had been assisted in this way.[32]

The FERA, too, had begun to help those youth who were both out of school and out of work and who were unable or unwilling to join the CCC. The transient aid program, established in May 1933 and, since he had moved to Washington, one of Williams's responsibilities, paid some attention to the physical needs of transient youth by developing shelters, residence centers, and a few work camps especially for them. Those were supplemented in the summer of 1934 by the creation of a small number of resident camps for young women, known in FERA circles as the "she, she, she." Groups of up to one hundred women from twenty to twenty-five years of age spent eight weeks to four months in these camps, where they did simple work such as bandage rolling and received instruction in home economics, hygiene, and certain of the creative arts. Administered by the women's division of the FERA, these camps proved expensive to operate and never involved more than three thousand women at any one time.[33]

In cooperation with the Federal Board of Vocational Education, the FERA attempted to stimulate activity in that area also. It provided funds to employ teachers, to create new programs and to develop existing ones, and, occasionally, to build vocational education classrooms. In 1934, through the newly created Federal Committee on Apprentice Training, the FERA tried to develop apprenticeship training programs in private industry, again through the provision of funds.[34]

Thus, by the end of 1934, the administration had taken initiatives toward dealing with the plight of youth beyond the creation of the CCC, and Williams had in some way been connected with most of those. He was glad of this, for his own childhood had been deprived, and he welcomed the chance to try to alleviate such deprivation in others. But he realized that what had been done was not nearly enough. The college aid program barely scratched the surface of need; those for out-of-school youth did not do even that. Those programs were uncoordinated and badly planned and served only to palliate. Youth and its spokesmen were beginning to demand much more. In October 1934, John A. Lang, president of the National Student Federation, submitted to the president a proposal for "a new movement to salvage youth," envisaging the establishment of a Federal Youth Service to provide a wide-ranging program of relief and training. In a series of *New York Times* articles, Eunice Fuller Barnard attacked the inadequacies of existing schemes and called for a much more committed and integrated attack on the problem. The pressures were mounting.[35]

Hopkins was both sensitive to these pressures and sympathetic to the urgency and real need behind them. In October 1934 he wrote to all state FERA directors urging that they "do all they can to help young people" through the provision of jobs, education, and recreational activities. This increased aid, he stated, had to be financed from ordinary relief funds, but special staff could be hired to develop it. As far as possible, such staff were to be chosen from those already on relief. More important, he asked Williams, as a matter of urgency, to review the FERA schemes already in operation, to consider public and private criticism of them, and to prepare a draft proposal for a federal youth program that would both coordinate those existing schemes and make recommendations for their expansion.[36]

Williams went to work with a will and came up with a plan early in November. Drawing heavily on the ideas of several friends in the Office of Education, he recommended that for those still in school the college aid program should simply be expanded. For those young people who had left school, however, a much more sophisticated approach should be undertaken. They should be given work and education, and, indeed, both job and training should be "intimately" connected. "Thus the job," he argued, "will first of all be a broadening of the educational program for each one and will at the same time render some socially valuable service to the community which justifies remuneration from the public treasury." Recreation would also be a crucial element in the program. Administration, Williams proposed, should be kept as decentralized as possible, with an army of local directors, aided by community advisory councils, running the scheme, wherever feasible, through existing schools and colleges. Central direction should be kept to a minimum, and its educational, rather than relief, purpose should be constantly stressed.

Williams's blueprint was circulated widely for comment and criticism, not all of which was favorable. For example, Fred J. Kelly, chief of the Division of Higher Education of the Office of Education, thought it would cost far too much and that it was too "school-oriented." Most comment, however, was encouraging. Other minds were to be influential in the development of the administration's youth program and much planning remained to be done, yet Williams's November discussion paper contained in it much that would later be incorporated into the structure of the National Youth Administration, the agency with which he was to be most closely associated.[37]

Thus, the year 1934 closed out full of optimism for Williams. The substitution of work for direct relief seemed imminent, a youth program was a strong possibility, he was becoming established as a man of some consequence in the whirligig of New Deal Washington, he was finding politically congenial colleagues and friends, and, most important of all, he was able to help "the hungry and the ragged." Despite his feelings for the suffering of the poor and unemployed, which so moved him, the new life was a deeply satisfying one.

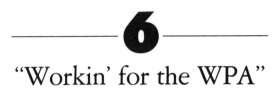

6

"Workin' for the WPA"

On January 4, 1935, President Roosevelt told an attentive Congress that "the Federal Government must and shall quit this business of relief. . . . I am not willing," he declared, "that the vitality of our people be further sapped by the giving of cash, of market baskets, of a few hours of weekly work cutting grass, raking leaves, and picking up papers in public parks." The American people deserved better than that.

What the president proposed to replace the FERA was, as had already been predicted, a vast work program, one which would employ more than three and a half million people. The states would be responsible for those who were unable to work. "It is my thought," said the president, "that with the exception of certain of the normal public building operations of the Government, all emergency public works shall be united in a single new and greatly enlarged plan. With the establishment of this new system we can supersede the Federal Emergency Relief Administration with a co-ordinated authority which will be charged with the orderly liquidation of our present relief activities and the substitution of a national chart for the giving of work."[1]

The announcement was widely supported, but it also provoked some debate and dissension. There was opposition in Congress to the scheme, and there was argument within the administration over who should control the nearly $5 billion—$4 billion for the new program, plus $880 million to continue the FERA during the change-over—which came with it.

Congressional objections were centered in the Senate. Conservatives, predictably, were concerned at the philosophy behind the measure, its costs, and the wide discretionary powers that it gave the administration, but the more serious opposition came from the left, from a group of senators who, in William Leuchtenburg's words, "thought the President was not asking enough." Roosevelt

had advocated a wage rate for workers on relief programs of about
fifty dollars a month—"a security wage," he called it—which was
about twice what they would have received under the FERA but
was of course less than prevailing wage rates. Liberal senators like
New York's Robert Wagner and Alabama's Hugo Black, particularly those with labor connections, argued instead for the payment
of prevailing wage rates, even though the number who could be
employed under the scheme would therefore be reduced. They
were joined by a motley crew of Republicans and antiadministra-
tion Democrats such as Pat McCarran of Nevada and the Louisiana
Kingfish, Huey Long.

Their opposition delayed final passage of the bill for some weeks,
but on April 8, Roosevelt signed a bill which had passed Congress
with its basic provisions intact, but with one or two amendments
added, mainly to sweeten the pill in the Senate. One such amendment was a patronage provision. Under the new law any administrator receiving a salary of five thousand dollars or more was to "be
appointed by the President by and with the advice and consent of
the Senate." Politics was thus built into the structure of the new
program from the outset, and despite the efforts of Hopkins and
Williams to minimize its influence, the works program, much more
than the FERA, always had to operate within certain political pa-
rameters. Indeed, Williams was later to write that "at this point we
lost control of the WPA."[2]

Even before the Senate had approved the appropriation, a bitter
fight had developed within the administration as to who would
administer the new program. The protagonists were Secretary of
the Interior Ickes, who wanted the money for his Public Works
Administration, and, of course, Hopkins, who believed, with some
justice, that since he originated the scheme, he should have the job
of implementing it. Moreover, he was convinced that Ickes's approach, to use the money on projects involving heavy capital expenditures, would be too slow and would certainly not have the
effect of putting large numbers of men quickly to work. He favored
limiting drastically the amount of money to be spent on anything
other than wages, thus narrowing the scope of the works that could
be undertaken but maximizing the number who could be employed.

The infighting was bitter and the lobbying intense as for several
weeks the president masked his intentions. The solution he even-

tually arrived at was, in Williams's words, the creation of "an administrative monstrosity." A troika of Hopkins, Ickes, and the genial
former chairman of the National Emergency Council, Frank Walker,
was to run the program, under the nominal headship of the president. The structure set up to implement this was so complicated
that it took four press conferences to explain it to newsmen. Walker
was to head a Division of Applications and Information, which
would receive proposals for government spending from all sources
and give them preliminary evaluations before passing them on to an
Advisory Committee on Allotments, headed by Ickes, which had
the task of recommending projects to the president. Hopkins's job
was to head a Works Progress Division which at first glance seemed
to have few functions not covered by the other two divisions except
to regulate certain procedures and to certify the availability of labor
in areas where projects were being carefully considered. Workers
were to be either those on relief rolls or those out of work, for no
project under the new scheme was to compete for labor with the
private sector.

That seemed a relatively minor role for Hopkins, and there was
some press speculation that he had been shunted aside. However, a
second function, little noticed at the time, was delegated to Hopkins's division. He was "given the authority to recommend and
carry on small useful projects designed to assure a maximum of
employment in all localities." In other words, he could initiate and
carry out small work projects entirely on his own, without reference to anyone else. That was all the authority he needed. Quickly
renaming his division the Works Progress Administration, he immediately started to invite applications and to authorize low-cost,
labor-intensive projects. Ickes fought a bitter rearguard action, but
by the end of the summer even he knew he was beaten. Despite its
cumbersome administrative structure, Hopkins had come to dominate the new works program. Henceforth its activities would be
synonymous with the division he headed, the WPA.[3]

Williams was not a bystander in the various battles attendant to
the creation of the WPA—he accompanied Hopkins to the White
House on several occasions to back up his chief in putting his point
of view—and he was of course an enthusiastic supporter of the new
approach. But he was not closely involved with the detailed negotiations. While Hopkins was almost totally preoccupied with the

administrative wrangling, Williams's job was to look after the day-to-day operations of the FERA and to superintend the transfer from one program to another. He had to taper off allotments for direct relief as work projects were begun, arrange the transfer of personnel and materials, and attend to numberless minor details in a complicated situation.

Although the phasing out of the FERA took longer and cost $300 million more than the $800 million originally budgeted, that was owing entirely to the delay in getting the works program underway, and not to any administrative sloppiness on Williams's part. He did the job efficiently, even though in the latter part of 1935 he often had to act as WPA administrator as well during Hopkins's frequent absences from Washington, either because of illness or presidential summons.[4]

The designing of a new youth program was also occupying much of Williams's time. Early in 1935, however, the production of blueprints for a youth program passed outside the FERA ambit. In January, Senator David I. Walsh (Democrat, Massachusetts), chairman of the Senate Committee on Labor and Education, introduced into the Senate a resolution asking Secretary of Labor Frances Perkins to prepare and submit to the Senate a plan which would deal with youth unemployment. Well aware of the thinking already going on in the FERA, the secretary immediately contacted Hopkins, who sent her a number of documents, including Williams's draft. She turned these over to Katharine Lenroot, head of the department's Children's Bureau, and asked her to do something about Walsh's request.

Lenroot came up with a scheme in early April which advocated the expansion of scholarship aid at the college level and its extension to high schools and the establishment of a work relief program for those between eighteen and twenty-four years of age who were out of school, out of work, and in need. She also proposed that the Committee on Apprentice Training be extended, along with the CCC and the girls' camp program. Moveover, a junior division of the United States Employment Service should be created to facilitate vocational guidance and placement. The administration of the educational aspects of the program, she argued, should go to the Office of Education, and all other functions should be carried out by a division of the new works program, assisted by an advisory committee of community leaders. The cost would be $96 million, and the program could cover nearly a million young people. Lenroot's scheme went to the Senate on April 5. Hopkins sent a copy with his and Williams's comments to the president a few days later.[5]

Next to get involved was the federal commissioner of education, John W. Studebaker, who had become most concerned at what he believed to be the removal of youth matters from the hands of educators. In a radio address on April 30 he unveiled his office's answer to the Lenroot proposals, in which he proposed the creation of a vast federally financed education program (he called it a Community Youth Program) essentially run through community councils in cooperation with state and local boards of education. The Office of Education would provide what central administration was necessary, but essentially that would involve the disbursement of funds to local educators. He vigorously opposed the creation of any new federal agencies to work with youth and estimated that though, at $288 million, his scheme would cost more than that of the Labor Department, it could involve at least two million young people, more than twice as many as the other plan.[6]

Commenting on the Studebaker program, Perkins drew attention to the crucial difference over administration. She agreed that the educational aspects should be placed under the control of educators, but not the proposed work relief or employment program. She believed that this difference had to be reconciled before the youth program could be further advanced and suggested that a committee of Studebaker, Lenroot, and someone designated by Hopkins be set up to try and iron things out.[7]

No such conference was held. Instead the president turned the various blueprints over to a private group, which he had encouraged to talk about youth matters, for their comments. Unofficial chairman of the group was Charles W. Taussig, president of the American Molasses Company and a man on the fringe of the famous preinauguration "Brain Trust." Taussig had a long interest in youth programs and also had the considerable advantage of knowing Mrs. Roosevelt. In April he invited to his New York home a group of prominent citizens, including the first lady, Owen D. Young, chairman of General Electric, and David Sarnoff of RCA, to discuss a youth program, the first of several such meetings to be held over the next fortnight. This group considered the Williams, Perkins, and Studebaker proposals before eventually coming up with one of its own. That plan drew from all three but was probably closest to the Perkins model. After discussing the proposal with Williams, Taussig formally submitted it to the president in mid-May.[8]

Thus, by the end of May, the president, who was already probably committed to the establishment of a youth program, was in possession of several blueprints on how that could best be accomplished, some features of which were contradictory. His response was familiar. He turned them all over to Hopkins and asked him to produce a program incorporating the best features of them all, although he warned that the cost of the Studebaker scheme was obviously prohibitive. Hopkins, in turn, delegated the job to Williams.

By June 5, Williams had submitted a proposal to the president which contained within it all the elements of what would become the National Youth Administration (NYA). Williams advocated the establishment of a "national youth division" within the WPA, to be administered by a director in conjunction with a national advisory committee. There would be state and local directors and state and local advisory committees; the whole emphasis was on decentralization. The new division would absorb all existing youth programs except for the CCC. It would provide aid both for young people in school and for those out of school and out of work. The cost would be about $60 million annually, and no part of its administration would involve the Office of Education, as the primary function of the new agency was to be the provision of relief.[9]

The president turned the Williams-Hopkins plan over to Studebaker for comment. Predictably, he protested violently. The purpose, scope, and plans for administration of the proposal, he complained to Hopkins, "are very different from the program advocated by the Office of Education which I know has been given consideration. I doubt the wisdom of announcing . . . a National Youth Program and setting up a new administration to operate it." Studebaker sent a copy of this letter to the president. From then on, he was to be a vigorous and increasingly bitter opponent of the NYA and those connected with it, especially Williams.[10]

Williams and Hopkins, for their part, discussed the proposal with Mrs. Roosevelt. They did this partly out of courtesy, partly because she was the most august member of the "Taussig group," and partly because they valued her good judgment. She herself reported that she subsequently talked about the scheme to the president. From this report has come the notion that she "sold" the NYA to a reluctant Roosevelt, that the agency came about more as a result of her powers of persuasion than through her husband's inclination to make any further attacks on the youth problem. Writing long after the event, Williams himself said that "it is only proper to state that the president did what he did largely because of the insistence of the 'missus' as he called Mrs. Roosevelt."

This overstates the situation. No doubt Mrs. Roosevelt was important in educating her husband on the dimensions of youth distress, yet by the time that the final Williams-Hopkins blueprint had been approved, he had long been persuaded of the need to expand activities in that area. By June 1935, to have advocated this to him would have been preaching to the converted. Moreover, by asking Hopkins to prepare the final draft of the proposal the president had virtually closed the door on any further discussion as to who should administer it. He knew very well where the sympathies of Hopkins and Williams lay. Studebaker continued to protest, of course, but to no avail.[11]

Nothing more remained except to tidy up their proposal a little. The word *division* in the suggested title was changed to *administration*, and the cost was cut from $60 to $50 million, but essentially the structure remained intact. Ickes, in whose bailiwick the Office of Education lay, was informed of the decision not to vest any control of the new agency there, and he concurred. Various press releases were drawn up, and on June 26 the president signed an executive order creating the NYA as a division of the WPA and setting aside $50 million from the work relief appropriation as its budget. Williams was named its executive director, hardly a surprising choice given his involvement in its creation.[12]

What was more surprising was that, with his commitment to the work relief program, he agreed to take the position, which was intended to be a full-time one. However, Williams himself claimed that he had had no hesitation in accepting it, so deeply did he feel for disadvantaged young people. It was agreed, therefore, that after he had completed winding up the activities of the FERA, he would drop out of the work relief picture altogether and devote all his time to the youth agency.

Hopkins, however, was increasingly reluctant to let him go. Late in July when both men happened to be in Chicago at the same time, Hopkins to make a speech, Williams to meet NYA state staff, the latter was persuaded to change his mind. The two men were riding to the railway station together in Mayor Kelly's limousine when Hopkins proposed a compromise. "We don't have much time to talk," Williams recalled him as saying, "but I want you to come back as Deputy Administrator. You can keep the N.Y.A., but get an assistant to handle the details." Williams agreed, and for the first years of NYA's existence he combined his efforts as its executive director with his growing WPA duties. That probably was the best of all possible worlds, as far as he was concerned, but it was not necessarily an arrangement which was in the best interests of the youth agency. Too often, especially in the first crucial months, Williams had to relegate important NYA business to deputies or deal with it perfunctorily in order to take care of WPA business. The WPA was clearly what mattered most to him.[13]

Williams was not the only FERA official to be transferred to the new agency. As Hopkins said in June 1935 when asked who his assistants would be, "I made up my mind that I am going to use our [FERA] people. This crowd here—four or five fellows—have been with me since the beginning and they suit me. I cannot hire any better and if they cannot do it, I cannot get any better to do it." In addition to Williams, "this crowd" comprised Corrington Gill, in charge of research, statistics, and finance, Jacob Baker, head of white-collar work, Ellen S. Woodward, head of the Womens Division, Lawrence Westbrook, Dallas Dort, and David K. Niles. Many of the FERA field-workers, too, including Aubrey's namesake and archenemy, Pierce Williams, were transferred to the agency.

Working feverishly in the hot, overcrowded Walker-Johnson building, this band of dedicated men and women aimed at putting 3.5 million men to work by December 1, while ending the FERA. They failed in that objective and had to continue the FERA into the new year for several reasons. First, the feud between Ickes and Hopkins and Hopkins's absence from the office in late 1935, because of illness, inevitably slowed up proceedings. Also, the conservative comptroller-general, J. J. McCarl, was extremely tardy in approving projects. Finally, there were delays in selecting state administrators and developing state and local administrative structures, and the sheer magnitude of the task of matching 3.5 million men to useful jobs throughout the country was overwhelming. This failure, however, is unimportant. What matters is that, by early 1936, Hopkins and his team had succeeded in making the largest public works project ever seen fully operational. It was a magnificent feat of organization.[14]

As it had been with the FERA, the major operating unit of the WPA was the state, which, in Searle Charles's words, "provided a centralized agency to serve as intermediary between the local district officers of W.P.A. and the Washington office." The choices for state administrator, then, were crucial. As Hopkins once said, "Seventy-five percent of my job is over and finished when I have a good State Administrator in a particular state, and if the State Administrator isn't any good, then my troubles are doubled." Hopkins and Williams, one of whose functions within the agency was to head the division of federal-state relations, were fortunate in being able to appoint many fine state administrators, despite the patronage loophole that required that they be confirmed in their positions by the Senate. Nevertheless, a number of frankly political appointments were forced on them, often to the detriment of the program in that particular state.[15]

Within each state office the federal office established four divisions, which were roughly coincident with those in the main Washington office. These were operations, women's and professional projects, employment, and finance and statistics. A constant flow of information, instruction, and advice poured into these state divisions, where it was digested, shaped into particular policies, and sent on to the localities where WPA work was being done.

Below the state level was the district organization. As Charles has pointed out, the choice of the district, a unit peculiar to the WPA, rather than the county for local operations meant that in theory the WPA could shift the work load more evenly. A large urban county, for example, could contain two or more districts, while in rural areas a number of lightly populated counties could be combined into a single district. Districts were meant to be roughly equal in their potential relief loads, and their boundaries were set by the Washington office. That office decided not to make congressional and WPA districts coincide, in order to decrease the potential for political pressure on WPA staff. District offices varied in their structures, but many tried to model themselves along state office lines, with the same four divisions of work.

Acting as a link between Washington and the states were the regional offices. The whole country was divided into five regions, again according to population, and each region comprised several states. The function of those offices, and especially of the field representatives who worked out of them, was to provide an essential liaison between Washington and the states. It was through the field representative, primarily, that policy became operational at the local level, and it was from him that the bulk of suggestions for change emanated. He interpreted orders, circulars of instruction, and the like to local officials, and he was in constant contact with Washington by telephone or by regular report. He was both troubleshooter and trouble anticipator.

The job of a field representative was an arduous one, comprising endless travel, long nights in cheap hotel rooms, and very little rest, but it was one of crucial importance because it was through the field representatives that Hopkins and the central staff were able to keep their massive operation under reasonable control. Fortunately, one of the strengths of the WPA was always the field staff. Dedicated people such as Ray Branion in Region One, which comprised New York and New England, Robert Hinckley in California, and Jane Foster, Loula Dunn, and, for a time, Lorena Hickok in the South provided the essential linkages that enabled the whole machine to work.[16]

The lineaments of that structure had been developed by early 1936. Changes in details occurred throughout the agency's history, but essentially this was the form that the WPA held throughout the period that Hopkins and Williams were associated with it. There were some changes, too, in the people who worked in the center. For example, one of Williams's conditions for staying with the agency was that the man whom Hopkins had initially put in charge of procedures, Donald Stone, be removed, but essentially the team that Hopkins had brought across from the FERA remained unchanged. Its job was to lay down general policies, to approve projects, to maintain a proper balance between administrative and general costs with a view to spending as much money as possible on those who most needed it—the unemployed—to investigate irregularities, to set and change wage rates and schedules of work, to ensure the maintenance of proper standards, and, generally, to operate as efficiently as possible the largest public work relief program that the world had ever seen.[17]

Moreover, new challenges and further responsibilities were always being found for it. One of these was in the area of disaster relief. In March 1936 huge floods, the result of unseasonably heavy spring rains, devastated most of the Northeast. Communications were cut, as roads, bridges, and highways were washed away, and thousands were left homeless. Into this emergency the president threw the WPA. Fifty thousand WPA workers battled the rising waters, WPA-employed nurses and doctors provided medical care for the victims, WPA workers cooked and distributed food for workers and destitute alike. Once the waters had subsided, the WPA spearheaded the massive clean-up. The speed with which the WPA had been able to put large numbers of men and women quickly to work was impressive, and this accomplishment effectively silenced many of its critics. The evidence that it was far more than a gigantic "boondoggle" was convincing. Henceforth, whenever national disasters occurred—the cruel droughts of 1936, for example, which devastated the Midwest, or the floods of 1937—the WPA was there. Nothing was better for its public image than its work at such times of emergency.[18]

It is hard to reconstruct exactly the administrative structure of the first years of the WPA. Hopkins's style was unique, much of the business was done on the telephone, and relatively few records were kept. Yet it is clear that although his position as deputy administrator was not formalized until early 1936, Williams was second in command right from the agency's creation. As early as August 1935, he had been acting administrator during one of Hopkins's increasingly frequent absences from Washington. He had taken over again in October, while Hopkins was on the celebrated cruise on the destroyer USS *Houston* with the president and Harold Ickes, a cruise which had been supposed to end the rivalry between the secretary and the administrator. It had failed to do so, though probably relationships between the two of them had been somewhat improved. The formality of naming Williams deputy administrator, therefore, simply recognized what had been a fact all along. Williams was clearly second in the WPA hierarchy.[19]

So in addition to looking after the areas specifically under his control, Williams handled as much of the routine work as possible, leaving Hopkins free to develop broad policies and, increasingly, to concern himself with matters far removed from relief. During this time the president's general reliance on Hopkins grew, and his own horizons and ambitions expanded. As early as 1934, Williams recalled, Hopkins was "going to the White House to talk about stuff that had nothing to do with relief," and he increased those visits in 1935 and 1936. Thus, even before Hopkins's own illness and that of his wife took him away from the office for months on end, Williams was doing much of Hopkins's job for him.

Williams relished the opportunity to act as the head of the WPA. Once he had completed the winding-up of the FERA, Williams became the man who handled the day-to-day operation of the new agency, who dealt with the specific problems of administration, who met the press on routine matters, who was the first reference point for complaints, who dealt with the myriad reports from the field representatives, who handled congressmen, both their complaints and their requests for favors, who had to satisfy the probing eye of Mrs. Roosevelt. The only part of the job that he could not stomach was having to manage press conferences. "I couldn't put up with the calm front," he complained, "when some pointed and insinuating question was thrown at me. I would give off answers that were responsive."[20]

It was Williams who met a delegation of WPA arts project workers in 1936 who had come to Washington seeking more money and persuaded them to return home, bluntly telling them that the WPA was more likely to be curtailed than increased. It was Williams who overruled a decision of the New York City administrator, Victor Ridder, and agreed that the Workers Alliance of America, a labor union for the unemployed, should be allowed to represent WPA workers in collective bargaining in New York, in so doing articulating a classic New Deal position when he stated, "Workers have a right to organize and they have a right to be represented by people of their own choosing." It was Williams who announced in July 1936 that he had dismissed seven WPA workers for political activity in Oklahoma's Democratic senatorial primary, adding that "I have instructions from the President to keep this thing out of politics and we are going to do it."[21]

The thankless attempt to do just that occupied an increasing amount of his time, especially in 1938, after a series of widely read articles by Thomas L. Stokes, a syndicated newspaperman of New Deal sympathies, had alleged extensive WPA involvement in the

Kentucky Democratic senatorial primary. A rash of similar charges followed as a result of the publicity, all of which were handed to Williams to investigate. Thus, in October, for example, he probed the complaints of a timekeeper on a California project who had allegedly been dismissed for political reasons; earlier he had exonerated a project superintendent in Blount County, Alabama, from charges of political coercion.[22] A massive investigation of alleged widespread political activity in Pennsylvania led to a report to the Senate's special committee investigating campaign expenditures that "I was unable to establish any political activity on the part of persons connected with the W.P.A. . . . . There was not one scintilla of truth in them so far as W.P.A. employees were concerned."[23]

Williams investigated scores of similar allegations in 1938, most of which he found to be without foundation. Where they were proved, as with Loretta Shurlock, supervisor of a sewing project in Renshaw, Pennsylvania, "who directed her workers how to vote and compelled them to bring their registration cards to the project," he brooked no excuses. Such people were invariably dismissed, often against the wishes of the state and local officials concerned. Williams's stand against politics in the WPA was uncompromising.[24] It is ironic, therefore, that, as shall be discussed later, his own career in the agency was terminated because of allegations of political partiality.

Williams, nevertheless, was not one to ignore politically motivated attacks on the WPA. In 1935, defending the agency's policy of appointing "people sympathetic to F.D.R.'s programs" to administrative positions, he asserted:

> I don't think anybody would expect us to hire people who were calling us vile names. No bank or grocery store would do that. We regard this whole affair as the public's business. Anybody has a right to know anything we do. It is the taxpayer's money and their business. We have no secrets. Everytime I have a telephone conversation it is recorded, and citizens may know what I say if they want to. But newspaper scandal-mongering is a different proposition. Some of the papers have me drawing four different salaries, for instance. As a matter of fact, I'm handling four different jobs and being paid for one.[25]

He was vocal, too, in his defense of the WPA during the 1936 election campaign, vigorously denying Republican claims that it was wasteful and "full of politics." Answering Republican National Committee allegations that some proposed WPA-produced movies would be no more than Democratic party propaganda, and should therefore be stopped, he claimed that the Republicans were afraid that "the eye of the camera will reveal a great army of good, solid American citizens at work in the construction of good solid American improvements for the benefits of all the people." "How cruelly the millions of American unemployed have been maligned," he went on to assert, "by people interested only in selfish political advantage. These motion pictures will be a record for posterity of America's ability to meet an economic crisis great enough to destroy any other nation, and by hard work and commonsense to solve it in the American way."[26]

The WPA had no more committed a defender than Williams. Charges that the work was not worth doing and that politics predominated in the organization always caused him to react violently. No doubt part of the reason for this was that he knew more than most just how much time and energy was spent trying to ensure that the work projects were real ones and that the politicians did not have their way with the WPA.

It is safe to say that all New Deal administrators had at some time or another to confront the issue of political patronage. Starved as they had been for years by Depression constrictions for opportunities to help deserving constituents, politicians saw the vastly expanded federal bureaucracy as a prime source of plunder. The response of administrators was varied. Some, like Robert Fechner at the CCC, capitulated and reserved a certain percentage of their administrative appointments for politicians to use as they liked. Others, like Williams and Hopkins, stood against those pressures as best they could. At times, they found it expedient to compromise— "I used to place the mistresses of powerful Senators in the file room where they could do no harm," Williams once recalled—but in general they held out, and in the process they developed a low view of those who pressured them.

Some of Williams's bitterest barbs, in recollection, were directed against such conservative Democrats as Virginia's Harry Byrd or Senator David Walsh of Massachusetts, men who made such a show "of public morality and rectitude," yet who constantly tried to use the relief agencies, of which they were normally publicly critical, for patronage purposes. Liberals like Senator Joseph Guffey of Pennsylvania, an administration supporter and an unabashed spoilsman, also came in for strong criticism, however. Williams became unpopular with politicians of all shades of political opinion as a result of his resistance to their patronage demands. He had good political friends, like senators Wagner, Black, or La Follette, none of whom, he said, "ever once asked me for a job," and he dealt with many other politicians who respected his integrity, like Senator Josh Lee, who once wrote, "I know I am going to get a fair deal from you and always will." Yet, on balance his refusals to compromise on the issue of politics probably cost him a considerable amount of political support.[27]

One of Williams's main tasks was to maintain contact with the regional field-workers, through reports, telephone calls, and frequent visits. He was their reference point, the man to call with a patronage problem, a union dispute, a personality issue—the problems varied widely. Thus, when more money was urgently required to complete an airport project in Boise, Idaho, it was Williams who authorized it; when the Alabama director exceeded his enrollment quota, it was Williams who directed him to lay off some workers. He authorized changes in district boundaries, he transferred funds from one project to another, he laid down policy instructions to field representatives, which he expected to be followed to the letter.[28] To Ray Branion, for example, who had queried the wisdom of closing certain camp projects, he baldly stated, "It is our policy and intention to liquidate the camp as soon as possible," and told him to get to it right away.[29] He even had views on how minor employees in district offices should comport themselves. Once writing to John Rankin, a Pennsylvania local director, he advised him that he believed it "important that such persons as receptionists have an intelligent and happy approach rather than one of a disgruntled attitude and stubborn personality. I am sure that I need not stress the fact that such persons have an importance beyond the range of their positions." His interests, then, as far as the WPA was concerned, were all-encompassing.[30]

Eventually, it proved impossible for him to read every single field report that came to his office. As the administration grew increasingly complex, and, in particular, as he was forced to substitute for Hopkins more and more frequently, his capable and devoted assistant Elizabeth Wickenden—"Wicky" to her boss and friends—took over many of the routine administrative tasks. Yet throughout his years with the WPA he retained, to a remarkable degree, a knowledge of the details of the operation which indicated not only the level of his administrative ability but also his deep and abiding commitment to assisting the poor and hungry. When Franklin Roosevelt once said to him, "Your first loyalty has never been to me. It has been to the unemployed," a remark which Williams found hurtful, the president was at least acknowledging the totality of Williams's involvement with the job.[31]

Williams became a tough, resourceful administrator. Even close friends such as Mary Anderson Bain, who worked for him for many years, admitted that, unlike the president, he had no hesitation about firing people who were not contributing sufficiently. Regularly putting in twelve- and fourteen-hour days himself, he expected those around him to do so as well. Moreover, he could be uncompromising, despite his sympathy for the unemployed, in his defense of WPA policy, even to representatives of the unemployed themselves. Indeed, members of the Workers Alliance, the union he had recognized as representing WPA workers, once heckled him so much that he was unable to complete a talk to them, so incensed were they by his refusal to accede to their demands on wage rates.

Those who worked with him, though, also talked about his loyalty and inspiration, as well as his toughness. Most of his staff were devoted to him, and he reciprocated. There was always an atmosphere of "togetherness" in his office, Bain recalled. No one was closer to him than Elizabeth Wickenden. He had chosen her to replace Donald Stone in 1935, even though Hopkins was worried about her being "too much to the left," and she was his alter ego throughout his years with the WPA. Indeed, he said that he refused to sign any authorizations at all until she had vetted them and claimed that the surprisingly low incidence of improper use of WPA funds was owing to Wickenden's vigilance, integrity, and honesty. His capacity to give praise and to share both responsibility and credit was a prime reason why his staff responded so warmly to him.[32]

Williams was impatient with much of the bureaucratic structure.

The reason he insisted that Stone be replaced, he claimed, was that Stone believed in "a government by records," while he "believed in a government by commonsense and the co-operation of all who were involved in it." "I had an instinctive antagonism," he once wrote, "against setting up a set of rules *a priori* into which every situation of a particular character must be fitted." There were two attitudes in Washington in the New Deal era, he argued further, on how to run a bureau. One he called "the chart idea." It involved "layers of staff, lots of assistants," tightly drawn, complex lines of authority, a distinct hierarchical structure. The other he named "the personal equation." Here, the lines of authority were simple and overlapping, there was no oppressive hierarchy, and the whole enterprise was run on trust and cooperation, rather than rules, structure, and precedent.

In making that distinction, Williams, though oversimplifying, was nevertheless correct in his identification of differing administrative styles in New Deal Washington. The agencies controlled by the established departments were often much more bureaucratically organized, according to well-established procedures, than those like the WPA, which had been created for a specific purpose and were under the direction of no particular department. In the latter a spirit of experimentation in administrative style as well as in function often prevailed. That spirit explains not only much of the WPA's seeming administrative confusion but also much of its freshness, the dedication of its staff, its adaptability and openness to innovation. The loose administrative style that so characterized the NYA had its antecedents in the WPA. Asked by the president to investigate the NYA's structure, George Miller, of the *Chattanooga Times*, was forced to conclude that "though he could not find a semblance of any organizational plan of operation, . . . in his opinion it was the best run outfit he knew, and the cheapest."[33]

As Williams became more familiar with his job, as his ideas on public relief developed and expanded, and, in particular, as first illness and then presidential demand and higher ambition took Hopkins further and further from the Walker-Johnson building and relief matters, he became a recognizable public figure, at least in the sense that his opinions were considered more and more worthy of public circulation. He appeared before legislative committees and subcommittees, he spoke to citizens' groups, professional associations, and academic assemblies, he wrote articles in the press. He became the relief program's most insistent, and at times controversial, publicist.

His views on public relief, in particular the conviction that work relief was the only morally and socially acceptable form of relief, had been with him for a long time, but not until then had he had the opportunity to disseminate them widely. Enthusiastically, he seized the chance. An article he wrote for the *New York Times* in March 1938 is typical of the many public statements that he made at this time. Entitled "Twelve Million Unemployed, What Can Be Done," the article argued for the creation of a permanent federal work relief program, based on the WPA experience. This proposal embodied a concept that he discerned as "gaining credence" in the United States for the first time, "the right to work." In the article he also indicated his views on what the New Deal had done and where it was going. "For the first time we are giving some thought to the common man," he claimed. "For the first time we are acting for his welfare. . . . We have become a nation more socially minded. We are now talking in terms of people rather than in terms of things. . . . We are trying to make the word 'American' again have a significant meaning." There would have to be some redistribution of income if the goal of a national unemployment policy was to be reached, he admitted, but the stakes were so high that "regardless of the financial cost the game is worth the candle. The well-being of millions of our fellow citizens and democracy itself are the stakes." If it refused to undertake the challenge, the United States would be "sowing the seeds for a dictatorship . . . substituting force and political thuggery for democracy."[34]

Many within and without government thought roughly as Williams did about the purposes of the New Deal and had a similar vision of its future. They represented the New Deal's liberal–left wing, a blending of populism, welfare-statism, and idealism, a vision of America which predated the republic. By the end of 1937, Williams had emerged as the senior spokesman for that perspective within the administration, and, as such, he was beginning to be regarded with grave suspicion in some quarters. A June 1938 speech in which he attacked "the heavy hand of monopoly" in traditional, populist style and blamed it for many of the nation's ills prompted a rumbling from the right, a precursor of things to come. Williams's "shoot-from-the-hip" public style, his liberalism, and the uncompromising manner in which he expressed his views would soon lead him into serious political trouble.[35]

In the meantime, Williams carried on with the running of the WPA. He enjoyed the job, and he was fulfilled by it. Moreover, he was becoming an increasingly influential administrative figure. He saw the president frequently, and his acquaintance with Mrs. Roosevelt was ripening into a warm friendship as she became increasingly involved in NYA affairs. Among his growing circle of friends, he counted Clifford and Virginia Durr, Beardsley Ruml, Rexford Tugwell, Representative Lyndon Johnson, and, of course, Elizabeth Wickenden. Most of these worked for the New Deal and, despite the slowing down of the reform impulse as the decade wore on, were still optimistic about continuing the drive toward a more just and equal society. They talked together and danced and partied together—the Williams's large house was a frequent venue for such events—and Williams thoroughly enjoyed it all. Not a drinker, he was nevertheless a gregarious man and an inveterate story teller in the Alabama drawl he never lost. He enjoyed being the center of attraction at such occasions, his lean frame shaking with laughter at a particularly good joke. Despite the pressure of work, there was occasionally the chance for a visit to the racetrack, usually with Hopkins or George Allen. For economic reasons, he never wagered more than five dollars per race. Therefore, he tended to bet on horses at long odds in order to gain value for money. Despite Hopkins's scorn for his selections, they tended to win. One such steeplechaser called Armageddon, which he backed in a flat race at the Empire Track in New York at odds of a hundred to one, "with Harry's derisive laughter in my ears," provided the two of them with a first-class meal at the St. Regis Hotel that evening and a new coat for Anita upon his return to Washington.

Though, he said, he tried to avoid "the blandishments" of high society, occasionally he weakened, especially when horse racing was involved. He once accepted Governor A. B. "Happy" Chandler's invitation to be his guest at the Kentucky Derby, where he had a marvelous time. Mrs. Chandler was particularly pleasant to him, and it was not until the end of the visit that he realized she was desperate for an invitation to the White House and hoped Williams would intercede with Mrs. Roosevelt on her behalf.

Life, then, had its lighter moments. Anita, too, had settled well in Washington. She enjoyed the life, the comparative security that Aubrey's salary brought, and the company of interesting people. The boys were growing up strong and healthy. Although she sometimes wished that Aubrey could see more of them, she recognized that his commitment to the unemployed through the WPA necessarily placed limits on his time.[36]

That commitment was to come to an abrupt end in 1938. Williams's tendency to talk extempore to groups, rather than read a prepared speech, and his penchant for thinking aloud and for making ill-considered remarks were to catch up with him. Minor public officials can probably get away with such behavior; those who have the press about them can rarely afford to indulge in it, and Williams had become one of those.

On June 27, 1938, Williams addressed a conference of members of the Workers Alliance of America, which was held in the new Interior Department Building. He had agreed to attend partly to help his friend David Lasser, the alliance's president, whose leadership was being challenged by a Communist bloc within the organization. He gave one of his typical freewheeling populist addresses, in which he attacked economic royalists and the press, yet expressed the view that the New Deal had fundamentally changed American society. "I have the feeling," he said, "that you have made something here that nobody can ever destroy. I have the feeling that, as long as you and I live, the government is going to support symphonies. . . . There may be lapses. But I have a feeling that the American people have tasted blood here." Toward the end of the address, speaking in support of the president's current campaign to purge the Democratic party of anti–New Deal legislators by involvement in the primary campaigns, he said, "I don't need to tell you. You know your friends well. Just judge the folk who come and ask for your support by the crowd they run with. Vote to keep our friends in power."[37]

The sentiments were probably unexceptionable—the president, after all, had been saying much the same thing on the campaign trail—but at a time when the Stokes articles mentioned earlier had focused attention on politics within the WPA as a political issue, when the Senate committee on campaign expenditures, usually known as the Sheppard Committee, had just begun to investigate such charges, the remarks were injudicious, to say the least.

A violent political storm broke. The predominantly anti–New Deal press had a field day, as Williams was denounced in editorial after editorial throughout the nation. The *Chicago Tribune* demanded his resignation immediately, calling him "an open-mouthed young Rooseveltian liberal"; the *Washington Post* claimed that his statement was "as good—or as evil—a summarization of the mingling of politics and relief as has been made to date, . . . the very negation of democracy." The "political degeneracy" that the present relief system was bringing to this country, the paper trumpeted, "is more subtle than that which has overtaken Germany, Italy and Russia. . . . A party which endorses the wholesale purchase of votes with public funds is one which in time will bring ruin to the strongest nation. . . . Nothing short of the summary dismissal of this official from his present post could undo the injury that has been done." Even the liberal *St. Louis Post-Dispatch* called the speech "demagogic incitement" and reminded Williams that, of all government officials, "those who handle the huge sums voted by Congress for relief" should appear most clearly to be free of "all suspicion of political motivation." "Employers," said the paper, "who have seemed to crack down on their workers by putting political advice in pay envelopes have been roundly—and properly—denounced. Mr. Williams, in practical effect, has done the same thing."[38]

Under pressure, the Sheppard Committee decided not to investigate Williams's activities, but released a statement nevertheless terming the speech "unfortunate." Hundreds of people wrote letters to him, most a variant of the views of one C. S. Boothby, who, terming the speech "astounding," said that it confirmed in his mind his conviction that "this present New Deal administration is composed of the most unscrupulous crooks ever gathered under one banner, . . . a bunch of nitwit communists." A few, like R. B. Aldridge of Hattiesburg, Mississippi, who found the speech "patriotic," were sympathetic, but the majority were unremittingly hostile.[39]

Williams, for his part, privately regretted his indiscretion and claimed to have been misreported. Then, after stating rather naively that there was "nothing political in what I said, nor were any political implications intended," he kept silent. Meanwhile the political storm raged about him, and well-meaning but politically inept interferences by his friends only compounded the problem. For example, Claude Pepper, the liberal Democrat from Florida who was soon to go to the Senate, asserted that he did not believe "Aubrey Williams said what they say he said, but if he had said it he'd have been right," a statement which the *New York Times* described as "incredible but true." It certainly was no help to Williams.[40] The *Chicago Tribune* and a few other newspapers kept the controversy going for a week or so, using Williams as a means of attacking the whole relief operation, before letting it drop for the moment. He was bitterly ashamed—"I could have killed myself," he later wrote —but the president was relatively unconcerned. Hopkins, for his part, expressed his confidence in his deputy's integrity by directing him to investigate and determine all allegations of politics in the WPA entirely on his own account, without reference to any higher authority.[41]

Nevertheless, the incident did hurt the administration and Williams badly. However unjustly, it lent credence to those who alleged that the WPA was really an arm of the Democratic political machine. It gave to Williams a reputation as a sympathizer with leftist boondogglers, a corrupt vote-buyer, or, at best, a garrulous fool. That reputation was to stick in some minds and could constantly be revived. It was the first sustained national publicity that he had ever had, and it was profoundly unfavorable.

Moreover, Williams was to find that, having once received the attention of the press, he was hard put to shake them off. In the week after the incident at the alliance meeting he was scheduled to give three speeches—to the National Conference of Social Work, to the NAACP, and to the American Youth Congress. These were relatively minor affairs, the sort of thing that he had been doing virtually unnoticed for years, but this time they all received full press coverage. His advocacy to the social work conference of the provision of a national employment scheme as a means of ending unemployment prompted a *New York Times* editorial that, after calling him "irrepressible," ridiculed his economics and claimed that he wanted to "introduce a sort of socialism through the back door." A *Times* columnist also wrote a facetious piece about Williams's penchant for delivering speeches. "If everybody in the country worked as hard as Mr. Williams does," he asked, "could any government possibly find enough work for everybody?" The speech to the NAACP, in which he advised Negroes that it was in their interest

to continue to support the New Deal and to heed the lessons of
Nazi Germany, was vigorously denounced as an incitement to racial
hatred and further proof that "the debauchery of the electorate with
bribes and threats is a settled policy of the administration." His
remarks to the youth congress were also fully reported. There he
deplored the concentrations of corporate wealth, praised the WPA,
and exhorted his young audience to "organize to get power into the
hands of the workers." Asked for his comments, Senator Sheppard
said that since Williams was expressing his own opinion to a general
group, his committee had no interest in the matter. Yet again the
impression of irresponsible radicalism and political involvement
was reinforced.[42]

For much of the rest of 1938, Williams was acting administrator
of the WPA. Hopkins was rarely at the office, as he was spending
most of his working time with the president, testing the water for a
1940 presidential bid, or relaxing with friends as his health returned.
Williams had to handle several problems of politics in relief and did
so reasonably well, despite the unfavorable image that his various
slips of the tongue had brought him. He was particularly effective
in refuting charges by the Sheppard Committee of widespread political coercion in Pennsylvania. His own investigations there had
found that there was "not one scintilla of truth" in them. He ac-
knowledged that WPA truck drivers had received letters from local
Democratic party officials seeking contributions, a practice over
which the WPA had no control, but he had discovered no evidence
at all that they had made any. Gradually the publicity of July was
receding into the background.[43]

Then came another serious indiscretion. In late November he
went to Birmingham, Alabama, his boyhood home, to attend the
first meeting of the Southern Conference for Human Welfare. This
liberal organization, with which he would later become closely involved, aimed at bringing New Deal solutions to the nation's "number one economic problem." Mrs. Roosevelt was there—she refused for a while to obey Birmingham's local segregation laws and
sit on the white side of the tent in which the meetings were being
held—as was Hugo Black, Frank Graham, and Claude Pepper. The
New Deal liberal credentials of most of the participants were
impeccable.

Williams was to speak at the opening session, to be introduced by

W. T. Couch, the director of the University of North Carolina Press. Before he spoke, however, the following incident occurred.

> Somehow [we] got on to the class struggle, so when he came back I said jokingly, class warfare does a lot of good, this sentence was much used as a joke in our family. When we had fish one of us would pipe "fish do a lot of good!" It derived from a remark President Cal Coolidge made when Glenn Frank, then editor of the *Century* [*sic*], one of the reporters asked Frank if he would like to meet the President, "Yes I would, thank you", Frank replied. So when they were introduced Coolidge is reported to have said, "You say your name is Shranks." "No Mr. President, Glenn Frank, editor of the *Century* magazine," and Coolidge said, "Magazines do a lot of good." So we adopted the phrase much as families do. So I said to Couch in almost a whisper as I went forward to speak, "Class warfare does a lot of good."

Unfortunately, a reporter heard the remark, which had been delivered off the cuff and off the record and had no relevance to his talk at all. The press the next day was full of it. The *Chicago Tribune* believed that the remark fitted "neatly into the increasing evidence of the New Dealers' source of inspiration. Class warfare is a sine qua non of the Marxian theory of revolution, and it is natural that Mr. Williams and the other New Dealers who are fellow travellers in the great trek to the Communist Utopia should view it with complacency if not open enthusiasm." Representative Martin Dies, whose House Committee on Un-American Activities was just beginning its investigation into alleged Communist subversion in the United States, saw his task justified by the remark. "It just went to show," Dies said, "that many of those opposing racial and religious hatred are openly advocating class hatred." Once again, Williams had seriously embarrassed the administration by a chance remark, reinforcing the view that the WPA's second man was a dangerous radical who subscribed to alien doctrines.[44]

Heartsick, Williams saw Mrs. Roosevelt and offered to resign. "You will do nothing of the kind," she replied, and immediately called the president, who said that he did not want Williams to leave the administration, "only to quit making speeches." Hopkins immediately sent him to investigate a flood problem in Florida, and there the incident ended—for the meantime. Nevertheless, it added to the reputation that was increasingly making Williams a political liability, a reputation which eventually cost him his job with the WPA.[45]

On December 23, to no one's surprise, President Roosevelt named Hopkins as the new secretary of commerce. A few days earlier, Williams had been summoned to the White House, where he expected to be told that he would be the next head of the WPA. "Joyless was the face of Aubrey Williams when he emerged," *Time Magazine*, no friend of his, stated, for the president had not given him the job. "In simple honest words," Williams later reported, Roosevelt had told him that he was a political liability, and could not be confirmed as WPA administrator, especially given the Republican revival in the 1938 elections. "I can't appoint you to succeed Harry," he said. "The situation on the Hill is such that I can't do it." Instead, the WPA was to go to its chief engineer, Colonel F. C. ("Pinky") Harrington, a career army officer with no political connections or problems. Williams was to move full-time to an expanded, independent NYA.[46]

Williams was bitter at what had happened. The *Washington Post* stated that he left the White House "seemingly distraught, and refusing to give an interview." The *St. Louis Post Dispatch* reported that he "had had practically entire charge of the administration of Federal relief for nearly two years" and that, rather than accept demotion, he would leave the administration entirely. Indeed, he did briefly consider going to work for the new California state administration of Governor Culbert L. Olsen. He attended the swearing-in ceremony for Hopkins on December 24 a very disappointed man. Christmas 1938 brought little joy to him.[47]

There were some critics of the move. David Lasser of the Workers Alliance said he hated the idea of an army man running the WPA. Ernest Lindley called it a "concession to practical politics." He agreed that Williams had made "a few indiscreet remarks—but no more so than have been made by Harry Hopkins"—and claimed that the real reason for his removal was that he had "made himself unpopular with too many favor-seeking politicians." "No one fought harder than Aubrey Williams," wrote Lindley in his newspaper column, "to keep the taint of politics out of the W.P.A. Now he has become in a way, a victim of a situation which would not have developed if his advice had prevailed." Nevertheless, most comments echoed *Time*'s view that the recommendation of "Pinky over Aubrey" was sensible and in accord with political realities. "Hopkins's lanky, idealistic foot-in-mouth friend" had probably got what he deserved.[48]

Williams himself tried to assuage his depression by taking himself and his family out of Washington for a while. It was not a success, for distance compounded his misery, though he was sustained to a degree by the many letters of support. To his father-in-law, Leo Schreck, he wrote, "The thing that I feel in the whole business is that willy nilly, for one cause or another, I have lost the power I formerly had to help a lot of destitute, struggling men, women and children, and while I think the President completely means what he says regarding developing the N.Y.A., I seem unable to walk away from the others without bleeding in my heart. I suppose I am foolish and stupid and that I will get over this."

Still, despite the bitter disappointment, the faith in the New Deal and the president remained. "I am getting to feel all right about this move," he wrote to Jane Foster. "Of course, in many ways something went out of me which I cannot deny. The associations I had formed and the opportunity to do things for great masses of people has been broken up and lost and probably will never again return, but I have only one regret and that is that I didn't handle this thing so that I wasn't unhorsed. . . . Still, the President is still here, Mrs. R. is still here, . . . and fundamentally Hopkins is still here because his influence will still dominate the whole program. . . . It has been a long and difficult ride—swift and hazardous—and probably nobody could expect to maintain his seat over a greater number of months than Harry and I did. . . . The remembrances of this will always center around you and Loula and Hopkins and Florence— and David Lasser and the unemployed."[49]

Williams was away from his office for over six weeks. He called his ailment "flu," but more likely it was a combination of nervous strain and physical exhaustion, exacerbated by the disappointment of December. Gradually, however, he recovered his equanimity and faith. To his sister Myrtice he wrote, "What has begun will never be destroyed. . . . I do not think that ever again, for any long period, will the needy unemployed be subject to the desperate and disgraceful treatment that was characteristic of the poor relief arrangements."[50] Aubrey Williams took quiet pride in his part in effecting this change as he turned his full attention and commitment to another "desperate and disgraceful" situation, the plight of the unemployed young.

Aubrey Williams, 1938. (Library of Congress)

Aubrey Williams in 1942. (Library of Congress)

Williams and his sons relax over a game of chess.
Aubrey, Jr., is on his left. (National Archives)

With Anita Williams and J. C. Kellam,
Texas NYA state administrator. (Personal collection)

NYA girl shop workers thread bolts. (National Archives)

Williams lunches with NYA enrollees. (National Archives)

Williams greets members of the National Youth Orchestra, 1940.
(National Archives)

Williams and the Roosevelts at Hyde Park. (Personal collection)

*Inspecting an NYA tool shop with Fiorello La Guardia,
mayor of New York. (Personal collection)*

At an NYA project for Indians, Santa Fe, New Mexico.
(Personal collection)

At a conference for social workers, Waldemar, Texas,
just before joining the New Deal.
Williams is on the extreme right, front row.
(Personal collection)

Girls with chairs that they made under the war program,
San Augustine, Texas, 1943. (Library of Congress)

"Go Way, You Brats, You Don't Belong with the Quality."
Cartoon by Jerry Doyle, Philadelphia Record.

In the offices of the Southern Farmer.
Williams is on the extreme right.
Next to him is Gould Beech. (Personal collection)

On "The Big Issue," with Governor Talmadge, 1953.
(Personal collection)

7

The National Youth Administration

Writing years afterward, Aubrey Williams admitted that "the National Youth Administration had got off to a very halting hesitant start." To a degree, that had been inevitable. Before the new agency could begin to spend its appropriation, a national office had to be set up, state directors had to be appointed, and an administrative link forged between Washington and the state organizations. Potential state directors were plentiful, but finding the most suitable was complicated by several factors, including the desire of Democratic politicians to influence those choices. As he did the WPA, Williams tried to keep the NYA clear of politics, but he did find it necessary to clear his appointments with the leading Democrats in each state, with resulting delays. Indeed, it was not until mid-August of 1935 that he had made sufficient appointments at both the national and state levels to make possible the holding of a conference of NYA staff at which policy could be discussed. In the meantime, applications for assistance poured in from all over the country.[1]

The men and women selected for NYA's Washington office came from a variety of occupations, but most had had substantial experience in either welfare work or some aspect of education. Williams chose John P. Corson, a young economics professor from the University of Richmond, as his deputy, and when Corson unexpectedly had to return to his university in September, he turned to another educator, Richard R. Brown, of Denver, Colorado. Brown, a public school teacher with a long history of activity in youth work, was to remain with the NYA until 1938. Williams chose Dr. Mary S. Hayes, a psychologist with a particular interest in vocational education, to be director of the important Division of Guidance and Placement.[2]

The state directors, too, came from a number of professions, but the majority had had substantial connections with higher education. The Arkansas director, J. W. Hull, for example, had been president of the Arkansas Polytechnic Institute. Anne Laughlin, of Kansas, had taught for fourteen years, including six at Illinois University. Houston Wright, in Oklahoma, had been a high school principal, and was currently state superintendent of high schools. There were a few whose educational experience had been somewhat briefer. One such was the Texas director, Lyndon Baines Johnson, soon to become Williams's close friend, who had taught for a time in the public schools, but was currently on the staff of Congressman Richard M. Kleberg. In general, though, both the state directors and the regional field representatives, who, as in the WPA, provided the link between national and state offices, were people with solid backgrounds in the field of public education.[3]

While Williams was selecting his administrative staff, Taussig, the newly appointed chairman of the National Advisory Committee, was gathering his committee. Some members were forced on him. Roosevelt insisted that he appoint Bernar McFadden, the publisher and physical culture faddist, in return for political services rendered. Others, like aviatrix Amelia Earhart, athlete Glenn Cunningham, and William Green, president of the American Federation of Labor, were there either for reasons of publicity or expediency. Most appointments, however, were not of that ilk. The bulk of the initial advisory committee members were distinguished citizens from all walks of life, but with a common background of involvement in youth affairs; they included the Reverend Edward R. Moore, a distinguished educator and community worker, Owen D. Young, Dr. David de Sola Pool of the Jewish Welfare Board, and Dr. E. H. Lindley, chancellor of the University of Kansas. Blacks were represented by Mary McLeod Bethune, president of Bethune-Cookman College in Daytona, Florida, and Dr. Mordecai Johnson, president of Howard University.[4]

By August 1935, Williams and Taussig judged that sufficient administrative or advisory appointments had been made for policy discussions to begin, and the first advisory committee meeting was held on August 15. Williams and Hopkins both attended. They indicated to the committee that while the college and reemployment programs had made the transition to the NYA in good shape, little had been done with the high school or out-of-school operations. Both men generated much enthusiasm and a sense of new departures. Hopkins assured them "that the government is looking for ideas, that this program is not fixed and set, that we are not afraid of exploring anything within the law, and we have a lawyer who will declare almost anything you want to be legal." Williams, meanwhile, spoke of "a new order of things" being brought about by the New Deal, of which the NYA was to be a part. Nevertheless, the proceedings of the discussions revealed few concrete proposals beneath the enthusiasm, save a desire to involve blacks fully and to persuade local communities to meet at least part of the costs of the work projects. The committee members probably returned home impressed by some of the rhetoric, but still rather confused as to what the NYA was going to do and what their role was to be.[5]

Meeting five days later, the state directors had a similar experience. They came to Washington expecting specific advice and instruction; instead, they got little more than pep talks from Williams, Hopkins, and Mrs. Roosevelt, who asked them to listen to young people's ideas. Williams was unable to tell them what the NYA wage scales would be or what work enrollees could legally perform. He had no guidelines whatsoever, though he advised them to keep in touch with each other, sharing experiences and suggestions. "We have our back to the wall here," he said, "fighting for this group of people. . . . You people are going to write the ticket." That was all very well, but the new state directors had hoped for some specific insights on how the "ticket" was to be written, given the expectations that the NYA had aroused, and which were now going unrealized for want of money and direction.[6]

The situation worsened over the next few weeks. Inquiries from young people continued to roll in, and the high school program began, but there was no movement at all to get the work program underway. By October a number of state directors were frustrated to the point of resigning. Believing that "the tremendous support in the local communities for the N.Y.A." was being dissipated and deploring the fact that "we are still without any definite word as to the scope of N.Y.A. projects and the procedure in regard to them," Burns Weston of Ohio had "begun to wonder about the need for our existence." If relief was all that was required, the WPA could provide it. Isaac Sutton of Pennsylvania thought that Washington was obstructing progress and complained to Taussig that Williams had become virtually inaccessible to his state directors. Concerned, Taussig turned to Mrs. Roosevelt for assistance, and she arranged a dinner at which both the president and Williams would be present and where the lack of progress would be discussed. To her disappointment, however, Roosevelt was in no mood to talk business that evening, and nothing was accomplished.[7]

Williams, for his part, seemed strangely defeated by the criticism and the seeming immensity of the problem. Admitting that the NYA had got off to "a very bad start" and that he would be fortunate if he emerged from his task with "his shirt on or any character left," he doubted if the agency could do more than temporarily alleviate a few problems faced by a few youth. It could not, he believed, make any substantial attack on their plight. Only "a change in the economic structure" would permit that. By the end of October the new agency, which had promised so much, was thoroughly bogged down. Its director seemed pessimistic about its worth, and preoccupied with his FERA and WPA tasks, he was providing neither leadership nor direction. The state staff, accordingly, were confused and frustrated. It had been a far from impressive first four months, and Williams was substantially to blame for the failure.[8]

The most embarrassing blow to the NYA came in November when the New York state director, Fairfield G. Osborne, Jr., resigned, releasing a statement which attacked Washington for having failed to provide either direction or funds. He was tired, he stated, of having to turn young people away from his office daily because he could do nothing for them and argued that unless some work projects were begun immediately, the enthusiasm still present for the NYA would die. Privately, he explained to Williams the reason for his action. "I have felt very deeply about this thing," he said. "I have been terribly hurt to have as many as fifty or sixty young people in here every day, looking for what they expect and they get nothing. I don't see any clarification in this thing. I have been bothered for many weeks."[9]

In the course of this discussion, Osborne stated squarely what was probably the most important reason for the NYA's poor start. Claiming that Williams was almost impossible to get in touch with, he argued that "I think you have been in an impossible situation. I don't think you have had the time to give to the Youth Act. I think it has been humanly impossible with your other duties." Williams's reply was extraordinarily revealing. "I have given at least a quarter of an hour a day to it [the NYA] for the last month," he protested.

Fifteen minutes daily would have been nowhere near enough at any time; under the circumstances it was ludicrous. The NYA was floundering principally because its head, preoccupied with his first love, the WPA, and the enormous task of putting millions to work under its aegis, had tended to put the youth agency to one side. The rhetoric at the state directors' conference had inspired hopes that could not be followed up on because of his other duties.

The situation was compounded by the lack of a deputy, for Brown had not been able to come to Washington immediately, and by McCarl's typical slowness in authorizing expenditures, but basically it was Williams's inability to give more than a fraction of his time to the program which was the reason for the hiatus. Holding down two jobs was simply proving too much for him. He could not cope.[10] Williams tried to persuade Osborne not to release any statement concerning his resignation to the press, because of the effect it would have on public support for the NYA, but his request was to no avail. The controversy surrounding the resignation was undoubtedly the NYA's and Williams's lowest point in the initial months of the program.

Fortunately, things began to pick up. Mrs. Roosevelt, whose special concern the NYA had already become, began to put pressure on Williams, literally forcing him to devote more time to its activities through her constant demands for progress reports, details of project approvals, and the like. The high school aid program had had a faltering beginning mainly because of tension between Washington and school officials concerned at its implications for local educational autonomy, but it now started to work smoothly. It was decided to implement it along the lines of the existing college aid program; NYA money was provided directly to school principals, who in turn disbursed it to needy students in return for work on the campus. By the end of the year more than two hundred thousand high school students were on NYA rolls, receiving, on the average, six dollars monthly, and the number was growing daily. Finally, Brown arrived and immediately began to sort out the specifics of the work program.

From then until he moved full-time to the agency, Williams's position in relation to Brown was rather like his own relative to Hopkins in the WPA. He concerned himself with broad policy, and he was the agency's principal publicist, but he left the detailed administration to his deputy. It was a sensible and realistic division of labor. By Christmas 1935 NYA wage scales, usually about one-third of the prevailing wage scales in a given area, had been settled, and rough guidelines on project suitability and acceptable levels of community contribution had been agreed upon. In early January 1936 the first NYA project workers reported for duty.[11]

By the beginning of 1936, too, the NYA had made a start on some of its more specialized enterprises. One was its Negro program, and there the personal stamp of Williams's growing commitment to the black cause, seen in his work with the CWA, was again evident. At the first state directors conference he had deplored the fact that, in his view, blacks were not "getting a fair deal on government projects," and he had resolved to make the NYA an exception.

The need was obvious enough. The proportion of blacks on relief rolls was double that of whites; among the young the discrepancy was even greater. Using the 1930 census figures as a base, George Rawick has calculated that 37.8 percent of blacks between the ages of fifteen and twenty-four were out of work in that year. By 1935 the percentage had certainly risen. By any index at all, blacks were the most deprived group in the nation, the one most urgently needing government aid. Under the FERA, CWA, CCC, and other agencies they had received some aid, of course, but simply as part of the general population, not in any way according to need. Furthermore, because FERA aid had been allocated through state and local officials, it had been, as Williams well knew, often very hard to prevent discrimination in its distribution. From its creation, therefore, the NYA paid particular attention to the problems of deprived black youths in an effort to redress at least some of those imbalances.[12]

One of Corson's first jobs in his short-lived career as Williams's deputy was to solicit opinions from a variety of people on how the NYA could best aid black youth. Many of those polled emphasized the importance of the high school and college programs. Pointing out that many blacks were being forced to drop out of school for economic reasons, they urged that NYA aid be concentrated on keeping them in school. That view was reinforced at a conference of Negro leaders held in August 1935 to discuss blacks and the NYA. The immediate result was the establishment of a special Negro education fund to provide aid to needy black students who might not be covered by a particular state's regular quota. Thus, very early on, the NYA, largely at the insistence of its director, specifically recognized the need to treat blacks as a group with special disadvantages.[13]

The conference of Negro leaders also emphasized the need to use blacks within the NYA administrative structure, and especially to involve them at the grass-roots level, if the agency was really serious about its commitment. Others made the same point. Mary McLeod Bethune, one of the two blacks on the National Advisory Committee, wrote to Corson that "I am wondering very seriously if it would not be a fine and helpful thing to have a well-prepared negro in your office and one in that of Mr. Williams. I think such a procedure would mean a great deal to the efficient handling of your program, so far as negroes are concerned."

Williams, Corson, and, after the latter's departure, Brown all agreed. On December 2, 1935, the appointment of Juanita Saddler as administrative assistant in charge of Negro activities was announced. Herself a black, Saddler was a field-worker for the YWCA and had been dean of women at Fisk University. Her job was to coordinate and stimulate NYA work among blacks.[14] Also, both Corson and Brown insisted that state directors involve blacks closely in advisory council work and directed that they all appoint at least one black to their state advisory councils. This requirement was generally complied with, though not always happily. It can be said, therefore, that the NYA very quickly gave substance to Williams's commitment to giving blacks as fair treatment as possible within the agency, even despite the general tardiness of organization.[15]

By the end of 1935 the NYA had also made an impressive start toward implementing its vocational guidance and junior job placement program, working in cooperation with state employment services, and the process of transferring the camps for young women from the FERA to the NYA was also proceeding satisfactorily.

At the same time, the National Advisory Committee was attempting to define what its role should be. The group was too large and its members too busy for regular meetings. Taussig therefore set up a number of subcommittees which would be concerned with particular aspects of the youth problem—education, rural youth, minority groups, and recreation, for example. In this way he hoped that a more effective contribution to the NYA's work could be made by the advisory committee.

Some of the subcommittees proved more energetic than others.

The first to produce a report was the youth survey subcommittee, chaired by Dr. Charles H. Judd, director of the University of Chicago's School of Education. This report was to lead to a further conflict between Williams and Commissioner of Education Studebaker, one which would have lasting implications. The report strongly advocated that the National Advisory Committee organize a thoroughgoing survey of the youth problem to accumulate as much data as possible on the needs of deprived young people and their difficulties in securing employment. The president was not particularly interested in the plan, but, partly owing to his wife's persuasive powers, decided to support it and allotted one hundred thousand dollars of WPA money for the survey.

John Studebaker, however, again saw the dread hand of a relief agency involving itself in something that was properly the concern of his office, and he angrily protested to Taussig and the president. Roosevelt, who regarded the matter as being of minor importance, told them to do the survey together, and eventually they drew up a plan which could only be interpreted as a victory for Studebaker. A Committee to Carry on the Youth Survey was to be appointed by the president. That committee was to include members of the advisory committee, but the administration of the enterprise was to be solely the prerogative of the Office of Education. The results were to be published under the office's imprint, but were to indicate that the advisory committee had had some involvement with it. Studebaker was delighted, and began to plan the spending of the money.[16]

Williams, however, upset the apple cart. He had always thought that the idea was not worth the expense, even before Studebaker's involvement. Now that this had occurred, he resolved to persuade Roosevelt to stop the whole enterprise on the grounds that WPA money could be far better spent elsewhere, and Roosevelt agreed. Studebaker was furious, and Taussig felt hurt and betrayed. The incident, unimportant in itself, did nevertheless point to tensions that were to be troublesome for Williams and the NYA in the future. One was the continuing distrust that the Office of Education had for the agency, now exacerbated by personal animosity between Studebaker and Williams. Indeed, Williams considered him to be perhaps the most bitter enemy he ever made during his years in Washington. The other was a growing degree of friction between the National Advisory Committee and the NYA administration. Williams believed that the committee should have no part in the running of the NYA. Its function, he believed, was to act as a public relations body, not to involve itself in policy decision.

Members of the committee, however, had hoped for a more significant role and were already beginning to chafe at Williams's attitude. As one member, Selma Borchardt, put it, "I quite agree with you that the Advisory Committee of the N.Y.A. should not be merely a 'front.' I know that Mr. Taussig has never wanted it to be merely a front. . . . I regret sincerely that there are those who feel that the Advisory Council should have absolutely nothing to do or say about the administrative policy of the N.Y.A." Such expressions of discontent were to become more insistent in the future, as the agency grew.[17]

Nevertheless, by the middle of 1936, Williams and his staff could point to some impressive achievements, especially in educational aid. Despite the continued resistance of some educational administrators, the high school and college aid programs continued to develop and to win acclaim. Indeed, a WPA report on educational activities stated that "so universal and widespread is its commendation that it is not too much to say that student aid is perhaps the most favorably received aspect of the N.Y.A." Williams felt similarly. Speaking to the National Advisory Committee early in 1936, he admitted that "I have a feeling of being surer that we are getting good progress there [the educational program] than I have anywhere else."[18]

The same could not be said of the out-of-school work program. A WPA report in February 1936 stated that "perhaps the most damaging criticism, undeniable though partly explainable, was that six months after the N.Y.A. was established, its work program was not in operation." Admitting that placements were still proceeding very slowly, the report nevertheless pointed out that at that time nearly one hundred thousand youths were at work either on NYA or WPA projects, that many more projects had been approved, and that the problem should soon be overcome.[19]

However, nearly three months later, Williams would say that he was "far from being what you might call optimistic or confident" about the work program, which he thought was clearly the weakest part of the whole enterprise. The reasons for this were many, including his own neglect of the agency during those crucial first months. Some, such as the slowness of certification and placement and difficulties in finding good supervisory personnel and in attracting suitable cosponsorship, would work themselves out as the organization settled into a regular administrative groove. They were teething troubles only. The fundamental problem concerned the nature of the work program itself, what sorts of tasks NYA enrollees should be doing and what the wider purpose of the program should be. Either it would be simply another relief measure or it would go beyond that, as envisioned in its original charge, to provide training in the skills that economic circumstances and deficient education had so far denied the enrollees. Either it would be merely a junior WPA or it would be much more.[20]

Almost inevitably, given the NYA's slow start and the pressure to get as many young people working as possible, the first work projects were established with very little thought to their training possibilities. Many of them, such as park construction or playground clearing, were indistinguishable from WPA enterprises. The aim was to spend as much of the money as possible on labor costs and to keep capital involved to a minimum. These projects did provide work experience, but it was of a general, nonskilled nature, rather like that provided by the CCC.

The majority of the first projects were in the recreational or service areas. NYA youth not only helped build public parks and playgrounds but serviced them as well. Some worked as aides to public authorities, looking after crippled children, assisting state and local traffic departments on road patrols, repairing books in local libraries, rolling bandages for local hospitals, and collecting, cleaning, and distributing clothing on behalf of various charitable agencies. The activities were both useful and various as far as the community was concerned, but their value to the enrollee was much less obvious, and that was the problem that greatly worried Williams and his staff as the NYA approached its first anniversary. When the state directors met in May 1936, it was the question that concerned them most. The president had decided to continue the NYA for at least another year and to increase its appropriation, evidence that it had done a reasonable job. Yet many of the directors believed that the potential in the agency had barely been tapped. Hopkins talked to them about the agency's popularity. "It is going places," he said. "I am telling you frankly that it is one of the most popular things that the Government is doing. It almost rivals the C.C.C. and I should like to see anybody ever stop the C.C.C."[21]

Hopkins talked, too, about the need to "point the direction of the N.Y.A." more precisely, and this the directors could agree with. The experiences of the past year had convinced most of them that the direction should be away from relief and toward the setting up of a new type of training agency, a second-chance educational scheme that would provide permanent skills for deprived youth which would enable them to fit into the mainstream of their economic and social communities.

But when Hopkins said that it was "their show—you have to make it or break it," he begged the question of direction somewhat, because emphasizing the training function would raise many issues —issues of budgetary policy, of relationships with educational institutions and authorities, of the attitude of organized labor—that could best be dealt with at a national level. Despite the decentralist emphasis of the agency, much more coordination and direction would have to come from the top if these questions were to be coped with satisfactorily, and Williams knew it.

On June 26, 1936, the president wrote to Williams formally advising him that Congress had decided to increase the NYA's appropriation for the 1936–37 fiscal year. In so doing, he praised "the splendid record of the National Youth Administration in helping some 600,000 young men and women from the despair of idleness."[22] There was, indeed, much to be praised. Despite the slow start, the NYA had accomplished a great deal in its first year, with the school work program being the most notable success. But it was still primarily a relief agency, and the first task of Williams, Brown, and those under them was to change that.

They went at it with a will. In his press release announcing the program for 1936–37, Williams stressed that the emphasis in the work projects would henceforth be to give training. The labor-intensive projects such as park maintenance or recreation work were to be scaled down and replaced with more solid skilled activities. That directive was followed up by specific instructions for compliance to state and local administrators and by a closer scrutiny by the central office of the types of project approved. Although Williams had decided on the change in policy, it was Brown who supervised the implementation. To him belongs the bulk of the credit for the strengthening of the out-of-school program.[23]

For strengthened it had quickly become. A report from Colorado, for example, showed that as early as November 1936 NYA youths were involved in heavy construction work and in certain skilled trades, as well as in the more familiar recreation projects. By 1937 that had become the norm, as enrollees were engaged in an infinite variety of projects. In New Haven, West Virginia, NYA youths built a large brick and tile community center, which included an auditorium, a library, a gymnasium, and study rooms. That project provided enrollees with useful training in several construction-related tasks, from bricklaying to joinery. In Smackover, Arkansas, twenty-five NYA boys, seventeen white and eight black, built and finished a wood-frame home economics building for the local high school. In Wimico Church, Virginia, as in hundreds of similar small communities, NYA girls took over the running of the town's school-lunch program, receiving valuable home economics training as they did so. In Milwaukee, two hundred and fifty girls were employed on a machine sewing project to make clothing for distribution to those on relief. The emphasis on learning a skill as well as serving the community was already obvious. Moreover, in cooperation with local adult education authorities, some state directors were supplementing on-the-job learning with "after-work" classes of a more formal nature, which were geared specifically to NYA youths. For example, Chet Lund, in Minnesota, had organized by mid-1937 a full-scale adult education program for his enrollees, which included classes in commerce, business, English, everyday law, literature, and public health. The program was firming up.[24]

A sampling of the NYA's voluminous case-study files gives some indication of the effect in human terms of this shift in emphasis. Louise Brown, a polio victim from North Dakota, believed when she enrolled in the NYA that "she would not be able to compete with the average young person in the business world." The NYA proved otherwise. It trained her as a typist and, through its placement office, found her a job in the county auditor's office. Richard Bell, of Athens, Ohio, son of a WPA worker and trained as a chef by the NYA was managing a night restaurant by May 1938. "J. M.," from Whitetop Mountains in Grayson County, Virginia, where they all "tote guns," learned stonemasonry while working on an NYA construction project. People admired his work and gave him contracts, and there was no need to return to Whitetop Mountains. "Now," said the report, "the ill-dressed, dark eyed boy dresses in white, with a panama hat, and drives his own car." Frances Anne Duffy, a virtual deaf-mute from Wilmington, Delaware, was trained by the NYA as a commercial sewing-machine operator. That training not only enabled her to secure private employment but, incidentally, motivated her to improve her lip reading and speech as well because for the first time in her life she wanted to communicate. Not all the NYA stories were similarly successful; the agency obviously had its failures, too. Yet by the end of 1937 it was finally succeeding in its stated aim of providing training for its enrollees, enabling them to come in from the fringe and fitting them into their communities as useful, contributing members.[25]

Certainly Williams thought so. At the state directors conference in October 1937 he professed himself both "surprised" and "tremendously thrilled" at the way things had gone in the past year. "I think . . . we have improved the work projects very, very greatly," he claimed. "Now I think they were in dire need of improvement. Now I'm not saying that in any critical manner, but we started from scratch in this job, where hundreds and hundreds of people would not believe anything worthwhile could be done on such a range. . . . They thought that this was the most foolish thing that had ever been undertaken in America. Well, we did it." His optimism had been bolstered by a report from the WPA's chief engineer, Colonel Harrington, whose staff had recently appraised ninety-eight NYA construction projects and had found their general standard to be "very good," both in the quality and public value of the work and in the worth of the training that the enrollees were receiving on them. Williams's talk of having made "a grand beginning" seemed justified, and much of the credit was due to Brown, who had had to translate the broad shifts in policy into specific performance, to keep up the pressure on state directors, to concern himself with the details of administration. He was much more involved with the administration of the NYA at this time than was his chief, and he had done his work well.[26]

One policy development, however, with which Williams was closely connected was the decision to establish a system of NYA residence centers. As early as 1936, Williams had become concerned that the agency was not doing enough for rural youth. The type of project that was viable in urban areas, to which the enrollees came each morning from their homes and returned home at night, did not suit rural requirements; some projects would have to be "live-in" ones.

The girls' camp provided one model. The chance to develop a more appealing one occurred in 1936, when a tidal-bay project at Quoddy Village in Maine was abandoned by the army corps of engineers because of a lack of funds. The project's aim had been to harness the high range of tides in Passamaquoddy Bay to generate electric power. Quickly, Williams lobbied for permission to take over the abandoned plant and convert it into a residential vocational training school, which would teach a wide variety of skills. After some delay, Roosevelt agreed, and Quoddy Village became the NYA's most publicized and successful residence center. The center accommodated up to two hundred and fifty young men at a time, mainly from New England, and gave them training in a range of skills—carpentry, drafting, electrical work, and sheet-metal work were but a few of the many available. The center also conducted adult education classes and involved the enrollees in the administration of the project. Quoddy had a mayor and a youth council of ten, elected by the enrollees; it published its own newspaper; it ran its own police force. It was, in short, a self-contained NYA community.[27] The success of Quoddy encouraged Williams to press for the development of other such centers, though usually on a smaller scale. By the middle of 1938, the program had been firmly established. More than one hundred centers were in operation, often in abandoned CCC camps or on the campuses of agricultural colleges, where the youths were instructed in farm methods and home economics while helping out with the college chores. Some of these centers were male, some female, some mixed.

Given that the majority of NYA center residents were from farms, these first programs were geared toward farm living. However, the view that fitting the enrollees for life away from the farm rather than for returning to it was a more sensible approach soon prevailed, and much more eclectic training programs were devised. At the Conway, Arkansas, residence center, for example, boys worked in the city power plant, in the heating plant of the local college, and in carpentry, cabinet-making, sheet-metal, and auto mechanics shops. Some were also getting experience in landscaping and erosion control work, as well as animal husbandry. At the Weiser, Idaho, mixed residence center the girls received training in homemaking, office practice, and nurse aiding, while the boys worked in a variety of occupations, including building superintendence, steam engineering, landscaping and surveying, metal trades, mechanics, construction work, and the broad fields of agriculture, commercial foods, and business training. In Atchison, Kansas, up to thirty girls at a time from neighboring counties lived in a large home furnished by the NYA while they worked on a machine sewing project. As many of them had not completed high school, the local director arranged for them to attend classes each morning. The afternoon was spent on the project work.

As in the community-centered programs, the aim of the residence centers was to give the enrollees the widest possible work experience in an endeavor to find them a skill which they could develop and use outside the agency. Rates of pay varied from region to region, but generally residents earned between eighteen and thirty dollars monthly, of which between thirteen and twenty-five dollars went to board and related expenses. Of all the developments in the first years of NYA's existence, the residence center program involved Williams most. He paid close attention to its administration, constantly asking state directors for information as to progress, chivying them along if need be, swamping them with advice, and trying to ensure that no "busts" were made on any of the centers. "We are on trial on this thing," he explained, "and one bad bust will do very much harm." In a real sense, then, the residence center program was Williams's creation.[28]

Other aspects of NYA activities had developed a settled look by the end of 1937. The high school and college work program, ironically the most universally accepted of all its activities, yet the one which concerned NYA staff least on a day-to-day basis, was operating well; in effect, thousands of school and college administrators were running it. The Negro program, now under the control of the redoubtable and statuesque Mary McLeod Bethune, friend to Mrs. Roosevelt, was also well established; special grants were set aside each year for blacks, mainly for college and graduate aid. Between 1936 and 1943 more than four thousand blacks were helped in this way, over and above those assisted through normal NYA channels.

The Junior Placement and Guidance Division was developing satisfactorily, and by the end of 1938 had placed about two hundred and
fifty thousand youths, including many ex-enrollees, in the private
sector.[29] Certain tensions still remained. The role of the National
Advisory Committee was never satisfactorily settled; Charles Taussig continued to seek more power and influence than either Williams or the president were willing to allow him. Yet he was really
no great problem. A letter from the president every now and then
or an occasional ten-minute interview was usually sufficient to make
him feel involved and to convince him that his committee was more
than a "front."[30]

It would be fair to say that the relationship between Williams and
Brown in the NYA structure during the first two years of its existence continued somewhat akin to that between Williams and Hopkins in the WPA, although Hopkins was probably much more involved with the administration of his agency than Williams was with
the NYA. Brown had complete control of day-to-day operations.
Williams's function was that of policymaker, charter of broad policy
guidelines, problem solver, publicist, exhorter. He gave speeches,
signed press statements about NYA activities, and reviewed the
troops from time to time, praising them for what they had done in
the field and encouraging them to even greater efforts. It was Williams, too, who dealt with the politicians. He appeared at committee
and subcommittee hearings representing the NYA, and he attended
to patronage and other political concerns.

Thus, matters of broad policy, such as the establishment of the
residence center program, obviously needed Williams's approval.
He would not, however, normally concern himself with the details
of administration. It was also his job to deal with serious personnel
problems, to be a court of last resort. The director of a New York
state girls' camp, for example, dismissed because of her inability to
work with the New York state director, Mark McCloskey, whom
she considered "nothing but an Irish politician," appealed to Williams for reinstatement. She did not get it. As a publicist, he used
the press whenever he could to explain what the NYA was, describe
its activities, and urge its expansion.

His role as exhorter was used to its best advantage at the frequent
state directors conferences, where he usually gave several freewheeling, rambling, conversational talks, in which he praised the

directors for what they were doing, urged them to do even more, and, in general terms, shared with them his view of what the New Deal was about and where it was going.

In 1938 he described their efforts as a "thrilling and generous and high minded chapter" of public administration, and claimed that "this is a great hour, and the people . . . are on our side." The previous year, a time of proposed cuts in the NYA's budget, he had assured his troubled staff that "we have a tremendous friend in the President, an unyielding, ever devoted and staunch friend in Harry Hopkins and Mrs. Roosevelt is with us one hundred per cent." Those three people, he claimed, "were proud of what you have done" and, budget cuts or not, would continue to support the NYA. The credit, he went on, should go to the state directors. "All the credit we deserve here in Washington, is that we had the sense to untie your hands and let you go places. I see you out there fighting," he told them, "and I am full up of feeling, but that is all right. Whatever happens they can't take these two years away from us."

These long rambling discourses were the highlights of the state directors conferences. John Lang, formerly state director for North Carolina, recalled them as being quite inspirational in tone and effect. Williams, his long lean body more often than not perched precariously on a table, his legs crossed, would deliver them without notes in his slow Southern drawl, and somehow the state directors were made to feel that they were indeed part of a great cooperative enterprise, that the president was truly with them, and that their problems and frustrations were minor and fleeting.[31]

Lang considered Williams's role as an exhorter and as an inspirer of confidence to have been his most important contribution to the NYA during its first years. Certainly he probably spent as much time at such conferences as he did on all other NYA activities combined. Brown's pathetic comment to Mrs. Roosevelt in August 1938 that he had seen Williams for "less than five hours in the whole year so far" is eloquent evidence of just how little engaged he was in the routine administration of the agency. The WPA was where his concerns lay.[32]

Nevertheless, circumstances were combining that would force him to take a more active role in the NYA's activities. In the first place, there was Mrs. Roosevelt. The president was fond of describing the NYA as the "missus's organization," thus indicating the intensity of the first lady's concern for it. From its inception she was constantly involved with it, asking for information, attempting to have people placed within it, making suggestions as to policy. She entertained members of the advisory committee from time to time, she saw Taussig, probably more frequently than she would have preferred, and, above all, she kept up a regular correspondence with Williams. Thus, as early as November 1935, she was writing in connection with the vocational guidance program to ask why the out-of-work activities had been so delayed and to inquire about the acceptance of an Oregon library project. She wrote about Brown's radio style, suggesting that "a little coaching as to how to keep an audience on the 'qui vive' would be advisable"; she visited projects and described them to Williams; she advocated certain policy changes; and she made it her business to know as much about the NYA as possible. Because of his great regard for her and his delight in their developing relationship, Williams tried to answer all her inquiries himself in some detail and to act on as many of her suggestions as possible. The need to keep himself sufficiently well informed on NYA matters in order to deal with Mrs. Roosevelt's frequent queries and proposals, then, necessitated his increasing involvement in matters of administrative detail.[33]

Though Williams had had intermittent contact with Mrs. Roosevelt from the earliest days of the New Deal, it was through her close involvement with the NYA that they became friends, a relationship that was to last until her death in 1962. Of all the relationships that he developed during his years in Washington, this one was the most important. From 1935 on, the two worked as a team, reinforcing each other's resolve, pursuing the same egalitarian goals, investigating in the same areas of concern. "I had a great love for her," he was to write later, "not passionate but for her good sense and great know-how." He confessed to once feeling intense anger on seeing Bernard Baruch kissing her in friendship, because he believed him to be a "scoundrel and unworthy of her affection." On another occasion, he called her "the greatest person I have ever known."

Williams continued to seek her advice, support, and approbation after he left government service and never lost the sense of wonder at their friendship which he had first developed in the mid-1930s.

He did not agree with everything that she did or thought. For example, he tried unsuccessfully to persuade her to resign as a delegate to the United Nations because of his growing disgust at President Truman's foreign policy, and he was at times irritated by her propensity to find "something in every one to admire." Yet he always considered her to be the "first woman of the world" and maintained that her continued public presence provided "some grounds to hope for a better world."[34]

As well as Mrs. Roosevelt's influence, growing dissatisfaction with Brown's performance was forcing Williams to spend more time on NYA activities. The strain of running the agency virtually on his own was beginning to tell on Williams's deputy by the beginning of 1938. He withdrew, refused to see his staff, and became unable to make decisions. Eventually his health broke, and he was hospitalized for several weeks. Therefore, Williams had to attend to much of the work that Brown had been unable to do. With some reluctance, he decided that his deputy would have to go. Brown, however, was unwilling to submit his resignation, so Williams fired him. The shocked Brown, writing to Mrs. Roosevelt, professed himself "deeply hurt to be dismissed"; nevertheless, he retained "so much personal affection" for Williams, he claimed, that "I am happy if my going will lighten his burden." Mrs. Roosevelt intervened, but Williams was adamant. Brown left the agency, and Williams replaced him with the western regional director, Orren H. Lull, a former sociology teacher and FERA official.

This incident dramatically illustrates one aspect of Williams's administrative attitude. He was never reluctant to dismiss people if he considered that they were not measuring up. Considerations of friendship, compassion, or obligation were not allowed to get in the way in such situations. If a subordinate was not performing, he was out. The main reason that Williams consistently resisted the extension of civil service provisions to NYA employees was to preserve his freedom of action in that area. Williams inspired great loyalty in his staff, but he also demanded much from them. Brown was not the only close associate to be summarily dismissed. Dr. Mary H. Hayes, for example, director of the Division of Guidance and Placement since 1935 and a close friend of Williams, was fired in 1942 because Williams had become dissatisfied with her performance. He could be a very tough man to work for.[35]

The third factor bringing him closer to the NYA was, of course, his increasing political liability within the WPA organization, which culminated in the events of December 1938 and the termination of the WPA connection. He moved full-time to the youth agency at a point when, despite the trauma and tentativeness of its inception, it had evolved into a going and growing concern, full of ideas, solidly democratic in organization, decentralized in operation. Though he had provided an important aspect of leadership, much of what had been achieved was the result not so much of his efforts as of those of the people who worked under him. It now remained to be seen if, and in what way, his total involvement with the NYA would change its focus or extend the scope of its activities.

8

Aubrey Takes Charge

Even before he took over the agency full-time, Williams had begun to push the NYA in a new direction. As the war clouds darkened in Europe and Asia, the woeful state of America's defenses became a matter of increasing concern. The resultant boost in defense spending led to a revival of employment prospects for skilled and semi-skilled factory workers, particularly in the metal trades, and Williams and Roosevelt decided that the NYA could help fill that demand.

The decision to gear the NYA's activities to defense needs was not an easy one, given the appeal of the peace movement to many liberals in the 1930s and their particular dislike of associating youth agencies with anything that smacked of militarism. Throughout the decade an array of well-organized and vocal peace societies, in John Wiltz's words, "labored mightily to prevent any weakening of the national resolve to avoid war." Pacifist sentiment was particularly strong among young people, especially college and university students. About 81 percent of sixty-five thousand college students who responded to a *Literary Digest* poll in 1935, for example, stated that they would not fight for the United States abroad, while 16.5 percent said they would not fight even if America were invaded. Student rallies and demonstrations for peace were common throughout the decade, and they were given considerable support by liberals generally.

One of their particular concerns was to ensure that no paramilitary youth organizations on the German or Soviet models were established in the United States. The CCC was profoundly distrusted by the peace movement generally and by many liberals for this reason. They saw such features as the Army's involvement in its administration, the wearing of uniforms, the marching to the work site as ominous precursors of a militaristic organization. Obviously, then, many of the supporters of the NYA and, indeed, many who worked within its organization would find the decision to move the agency into the field of national defense both puzzling and profoundly disturbing.[1]

Williams was well aware of the strains that this decision could cause, and he moved quickly to ease any disquiet, particularly among the state directors. Outlining the proposed shift in emphasis to them, he explained that

> there will be needed a large number of young people as operatives and others in this whole undertaking. We are not going to turn the Youth Administration over to the Army. We are going to handle our work so that we have training arrangements that will restore employment in such opportunities as private industry, or in the Army and Navy for these young people. Most of you have the same background I have. You abhor war, you abhor anything that has to do with the killing of people, anything that has to do with guns. It's repulsive to me, . . . but I am absolutely convinced that we have an opportunity here to participate in a program affecting national defense in a manner that should be acceptable to us and to the state of feeling which is part of our bringing up and part of our whole background.

"And it's because I don't believe in the Army," he continued, "because I don't believe in the Army's way of living, the regimentation that obtains in the Army and the form of hierarchy that obtain [sic] there," that he wanted the NYA to preempt the defense field and to make a success of it. Moreover, he insisted that accompanying this new orientation would be "a re-emphasizing of all phases of work that have to do with the comprehension or meaning of democratic living in this country." He believed, like so many, that the United States was at a crisis point and that the survival of democracy was at stake. "I think we are very much in the situation the Social Democrats were in Germany seven or eight years ago," he argued, "and we are at the point where the test of whether a democratic form of government can function effectively is being almost historically applied." One key aspect of that test would be whether the United States could greatly expand its military strength without a corresponding reduction in its commitment to democracy. Williams hoped that the involvement of the NYA in defense work would help ensure that it would be able to.[2]

Once he moved full-time into the NYA, Williams vigorously began to implement the changed program. The most urgent task was to acquire machinery on which the youths could train. Quietly, he began to do so. He and his assistants explored army surplus stores, industrial plants, and even junk yards. Anything that could be refurbished and used as a training tool was pressed into service.

The task was made somewhat easier in 1939 by a substantial increase in the agency's appropriation, something which occurred despite the prevailing climate of economy that had brought the ending of a few New Deal agencies, notably the Federal Theater, and the curtailment of most others. But this did not happen to the NYA; indeed, the congressional debate over the appropriation revealed a body of support both for it and for Williams. His friend Representative Lyndon Johnson commented on this in the House of Representatives. Claiming that "among those who have habitually looked at Mr. Williams from time to time and figured Beelzebub must be back from his vacation" there had occurred a change of heart, he said, "I suppose it is because at last the National Youth Administration has touched some heart and life close to theirs and, touching it, has touched them." Williams was extremely gratified at the level of support for the NYA and for him. It led him to hope that his blunders of 1938 were receding in the public and political mind.[3]

Progressively, Williams pushed the NYA into the industrial training area. By the time President Roosevelt announced a general defense program in mid-1940, he had moved it so far from its original role that it was officially designated a defense agency and given two supplementary appropriations, in September 1940 and March 1941, specifically for defense activity. The culmination of that movement occurred in 1941, when Williams announced that a specific youth work defense program, developed and administered by the agency, would be in operation from July 1941.

This program would be in addition to the regular out-of-school and school work programs and would have the object of preparing 380,000 people for jobs in defense industries between July 1, 1941, and June 30, 1942. The trainees would be given "actual production work under conditions similar to those of private industry," principally in machine-shop work, the sheet-metal trades, welding, and the electrical industries. Young women would be trained under this scheme as well as men. NYA plants would operate on a three-shift-per-day basis, and the average turnover time would be three months. The overarching object of the scheme was to encourage each enrollee to develop a skill that would enable him or her to find work in the defense plants of the United States. Williams, it seemed, had succeeded in his aim to make the NYA a crucial adjunct of the defense effort. Alone of all the New Deal agencies, its activities were not curtailed after the Republican revival of 1938 but expanded.[4]

One result of the NYA's changed emphasis was renewed strife between Williams and the commissioner of education, John Studebaker. The issue was who would provide vocational education for the NYA youths engaged in defense work: the agency itself, or the Office of Education. As long as the NYA had been regarded primarily as a relief agency, Studebaker had not been too concerned about NYA educational programs, but once it had become a defense training agency, his view had changed. The provision of vocational and related training, he argued, was the function of his office and of the public schools. The NYA's job, he believed, was to provide employment opportunities for needy youth. NYA officials, especially Dr. Charles Judd, who was in charge of developing educational programs for out-of-school youths, bitterly disagreed. He believed that the provision of work experience and vocational training were inseparable and that both should be controlled by the agency.

Williams, for his part, was happy to let the "school people" take over the NYA's educational activities. He was concerned at the growing antagonism that some educational administrators were showing toward his agency and believed a compromise on this issue might help mollify that group. Consequently, on June 27, 1940, he and Studebaker signed an agreement, made public on August 21, which gave the state offices of education responsibility for all "off-the-job" training for NYA enrollees, unless the state office should decide that "it is not feasible to furnish such instruction" in a given instance, in which case the NYA could continue doing the job.[5]

That agreement mollified Studebaker and the school people, but it left Judd furious. He resigned immediately and wrote Williams that though he had known all along that they differed fundamentally in their views, he had hoped to persuade him to adopt policies with which he could agree. But, he continued, "my last conference with you led me to believe that you are in a frame of mind that makes it improbable that my hope can be realized."

Taussig was also worried by the agreement and wrote to Mrs. Roosevelt. She, too, was "a little disturbed," at least until Williams wrote her a long letter that stated:

> The net result of the agreement and the new arrangement as effected by Congress is that from here on our program will be a straight production program and, frankly, I don't know but that I am very glad that the whole issue has been made clear and we are definitely in a known category because I believe that in the long run we have a greater chance for usefulness in what we can work out for young people in our end of it and what we can force the schools on the other side to develop than was true previously. We did get over into related training and assume burdens that the schools should be carrying.

The new arrangement would mean some loss at first, especially with girls, "where much of the work we have been doing was of a training character and did not have any considerable amount of production," but in the long run, Williams contended, it was better for the agency to work toward a straight production focus. Moreover, the NYA would still be furnishing the most important training of all, namely on-the-job training. Finally, the agreement contained an escape clause. If state educational authorities were unable to provide instruction, then the NYA could take it over. All in all, he believed, the agreement was an excellent one which he hoped would reverse the "trend among educators to close in on us and attempt to restrict us at every possible point."

To a degree he was correct. In the short term the agreement mollified Studebaker and his allies without greatly restricting the NYA's educational activities. Nevertheless, hostilities were to break out again. The opposition of educational administrators, epitomized by the powerful National Educational Association (NEA), was something that the NYA would have to live with for the rest of its existence. As a relief agency, the NYA had been no great threat to educators, but once it entered the training field it began to represent to them the thin end of the dreaded wedge of a federal education system, which would compete with local schools. From 1940 on, the NEA, through its executive secretary, Willard E. Givens, often supported tacitly by Studebaker, attacked Williams and the NYA continuously. It accused the agency of inefficiency and of duplicating the function of vocational schools and asserted that it was the forerunner of a federal educational system. While the agreement of June 27 may have made it easier for the agency to resist such attacks, it brought but temporary relief.[6]

When he had announced the NYA's shift to a defense orientation, Williams had assured his state directors that the change would be accompanied by a reemphasis on the agency's commitment to democratic values. How to institutionalize such a commitment, however, was a problem. Eventually, Williams came to believe that the answer might be found in the advisory committee system. To strengthen it might be the best way of developing further the connections between local community and federal agency. Accordingly, he asked Taussig to reorganize the advisory committees in such a way as to stimulate that activity, and funds were authorized to appoint a full-time director of advisory committee work. The job was offered to the Ohio State director, Burns Weston, who, after some hesitation owing to his doubt that the work would "be taken seriously and as an integral part of the national defense picture," accepted it.[7]

Unfortunately, the move to Washington was a frustrating one for Weston. He did not get on with Williams, who, he believed, did not take him seriously, was unwilling to include him in policy discussions, and simply did not understand the importance of maintaining community involvement in defense planning as the best safeguard for the preservation of democracy in the United States. Williams, for his part, having provided the impetus for increased advisory council activity, did not wish to be bothered further by it. He had no intention of including Weston in policymaking sessions, and when Weston persisted in his demands, he resolved to terminate his activities. He slashed Weston's budget by 70 percent in November 1941 and stated that he was not prepared to "go ahead with work of this character" when the jobs of "people who are indispensable to the actual context of the work program" were in jeopardy. In June 1942 the advisory council program was terminated altogether. By that time the NYA had become totally involved in the war effort and increasingly centralized in operation. In the changed situation emphasis on community involvement had become somewhat irrelevant.[8]

Not all of the NYA's expansion after Williams came to it full-time, however, had to do with defense. Some of the new programs arose directly from his WPA experience and his conviction that the New Deal provided an opportunity for the federal government to improve the quality of American life in all manner of ways. A dramatic example of this was the agency's sponsorship of the American Youth Orchestra. Under the baton of the maestro Leopold Stokowski, this orchestra of young people gave several concerts in 1940 and in 1941 undertook a successful and highly publicized tour of Latin America. The NYA organized the selection of these young musicians—no mean task when an initial application list of 15,000 had to be whittled down to 109—and provided some financial backing for the Latin American tour. In return, it received much favorable publicity, one consequence of which was the NYA's development of its own music program, based on the WPA's Federal Music Project.[9]

Williams's drive and personal involvement were also crucial in the development of the NYA's health program. In cooperation with the surgeon general, and with state and local health authorities, the agency hired health consultants on a part-time basis who conducted examinations on enrollees and referred those who needed special treatment to the appropriate specialist. The cost of such treatments was met by NYA funds, and the effect on the general health level of the enrollees was remarkable. Young people who, for economic reasons, had not had proper medical care for years, if ever, now received it regularly.

Williams often tried to develop programs in cooperation with other New Deal agencies. In June 1940, for example, the agency signed a cooperative agreement with the Farm Security Administration (FSA) whereby the FSA was to lend money to farm youths who wished to take up farming on their own, and the NYA would train them in efficient farming methods. The idea came from H. L. Mitchell, formerly of the Southern Tenant Farmers Union and then on the NYA payroll, who bombarded Williams and Will Alexander of the FSA with tales of youngsters who had been well trained at NYA resident centers and who were desperate to get on to land, but had no money to do so. Alabama was selected as the state where the scheme was to be initiated. It had hardly begun, however, when Williams was forced to terminate it, as the agency began to concentrate on defense training. Yet it remains an example of the vibrancy of the NYA under his direction, its willingness to experiment and to move into fresh areas with fresh ideas.[10]

From mid-1940 the defense aspect of the NYA program was coming to dominate both the agency and Williams's time. Every activity not directly concerned with national defense was shed, until by early 1942 even the regular out-of-school program had been abandoned. Construction projects were terminated, and the high school and college programs were ended; nothing that did not contribute directly to the war effort was permitted.[11]

This was partly in response to the activities of the Joint Committee on the Reduction of Non-essential Federal Expenditures, created by Congress in 1941 in response to increasing demands for economy in all but defense spending. The committee was chaired by that redoubtable advocate of the balanced budget, Senator Harry F. Byrd, and contained such other anti–New Deal luminaries as senators Carter Glass and Walter George and Representative John Taber, as vocal an anti-Rooseveltian as there was in the whole Congress.

One of the first agencies to be investigated by this body was the NYA. In rather torrid hearings many of the committee members seemed less interested in finding out what the NYA was then doing than in uncovering instances of past extravagance. The committee eventually recommended that the agency's activities be drastically curtailed and all its nondefense functions scrapped. Well before that occurred, however, Williams had been moving in the same direction. Therefore, the committee's recommendations, and their acceptance, did not overly disturb him. He was much more bothered when the agency's appropriation for the 1942–43 fiscal year was substantially cut, to the extent that current programs would have to be severely curtailed. The NYA's contribution to the war effort, therefore, had to be correspondingly reduced.[12]

That contribution had become considerable. The agency's files were filled with letters of tribute from defense industry employers attesting to the value of NYA training and its importance in maintaining a steady labor flow, as the massive war effort soaked up those pockets of unemployment still remaining in the country. David Goldberg, a structural steel manufacturer of Uniontown, Pennsylvania, said that the NYA-trained youths that he had employed had "averaged a higher degree of skill and ability to learn than any other class of labor that we have been able to secure under the present market. This training has been thoroughly rounded, and, as a result, they are upgraded very rapidly once they come into our shop." The Houston Ship-building Company reported that of the four thousand welders in its employ 75 percent were NYA trained and that they "made better employees than the welders hired from other sources," especially the women welders who had been through the agency. Robert I. Millonzi of Ford Brothers, Inc., a small Buffalo, New York, company which manufactured aircraft landing gear, spoke of the high quality of the NYA-trained female lathe operators that he had just hired. "In many cases," he said, "these girls are out-producing men at the same type of job." There were a few less enthusiastic reports, but the bulk of the evidence pointed overwhelmingly to the conclusion that the NYA defense program was working exceptionally well.[13]

Additional confirmation of this came from the enrollees themselves, as well as from NYA administrators. Cleo L. Curtis, painfully writing to his ex-NYA supervisor from the shipyards of Richmond, California, where he was working as a welder, said, "You gave me Just what it takes to make a welding, and I want to thank you a lots. I want to be a welding, so I could help Build ship. I really want to do my part in helper win the war, in other wise I can help I am willing to do. . . . So thank to the National Youth Administration and you all so you gave me the best of training and I can prove it." Three girls, sent to Paterson, New Jersey, from Connecticut to work with Western Electric, said that they were "the only workers at the factory . . . that has radio training." NYA officials told many similar tales of successful placements. "These N.Y.A. boys from Minnesota, Iowa and Nebraska that you sent over to us are the finest-looking applicants we've had, with these words, Lieutenant Mason, USN Employment Officer, Puget Sound Navy Yard, Bremerton, Washington began a conversation with me," ran one such report. No doubt some of this testimony was exaggerated, but the number of such reports is corroborative evidence of the success of the defense program.[14]

The reference to lads from Minnesota being sent to the shipyards of Puget Sound is indicative of a new function for the agency, one which it had taken on since coming within the jurisdiction of the War Manpower Commission in September 1942 and one which Williams was particularly interested in developing. The NYA was providing shop training all over the country; yet the demand for a particular skill or variety of skills was often concentrated at a certain time in a certain state or region. It became the agency's function, therefore, to match its enrollees with that demand. Once it had trained the youths, it transported them to where the need was greatest.

Since this often meant that it was moving people into strange environments hundreds, even thousands, of miles from home, the NYA developed a number of regional "induction centers." There enrollees from one part of the country could be temporarily housed while they learned the ways of the area to which they had come and while they found jobs and more permanent accommodations.

The Nepaug Village induction center near Hartford, Connecticut, was one such regional induction center. By April 1943 more than eight thousand NYA youths had passed through it, staying, on the average, two weeks. They had come from thirty states to work in Connecticut's defense plants, but more than two thousand were from Mississippi, many of whom were black. The differences between ways of living in the Deep South and in New England in the early 1940s can hardly be overemphasized. The bewilderment that these young men and women experienced, real as it was, would have been far greater had the induction center not been there to provide some cushioning of the blow.

There was strife at Nepaug from time to time. White youths complained bitterly "that they [were] forced to live in the same buildings with Negroes, and the colored youth . . . complained of discrimination," according to one report. Yet "with close supervision and careful interpretations of New England mores to both groups, it [was] possible to avoid any open outbreaks and maintain a semblance of order."

Sometimes the gap was too great. Four Spanish-speaking girls sent from Trinidad, Colorado, to work in the Seattle shipyards had to be returned home. Despite the best efforts of the induction center officers, they could not adjust to the strange surroundings. Nevertheless, most seemed to manage. Like Albert Liddell, a young black from Jessup, Georgia, who was sent to Nepaug, they doubtless found the "things we weren't accustomed to" a bit overwhelming at first. But again like him, they also found much that was new and exciting. "Tell the fellows to have as much money as possible," he wrote back to his Jessup supervisor, for there were places they would like to go and see when they made the trip away. Given the NYA's and Williams's policy to bring into the industrial mainstream youths from the most isolated and backward parts of the nation, and given Williams's particular commitment to equality of treatment for black enrollees, the induction centers were of vital importance to the NYA's defense effort. Without them, the tasks of adjustment might well have been insuperable for many of these young workers.[15]

From 1940 on, despite its undoubted contribution to national defense, the NYA found itself increasingly under attack from members of the Congress, from powerful interest groups within the community, from the press, and from members of the public. It was, it was claimed, far too expensive; it simply duplicated what the vocational training schools were doing much better; and while it was no longer needed as a relief agency, it had developed no alternative function. Some of the attacks were directed specifically at Williams. It was alleged that he spent public money recklessly and that he did not always tell the truth, and, of course, he was suspect politically. "One of the most radical men in the country," Representative Hamilton Fish once called him, "one of the pinkest of this pink New Deal administration."[16] This was something new for the agency, though not for Williams. Refuting such charges occupied more and more of his time during 1942 and 1943.

There was no more virulent congressional critic of the agency in those years than the senior senator from Tennessee, Kenneth D. McKellar, although that had not always been the case. For most of the New Deal years he had been a fairly strong supporter of the administration and a figure of fun because of his low boiling point, his bulbous nose, and the reverence with which he approached matters of patronage. He had never given either Williams or the NYA any trouble. In fact, as late as June 1941, McKellar had successfully prevented, in a floor fight, a cut in NYA funds. That action had prompted a letter from Williams thanking him "for your efforts on our behalf" and telling him that "your interest over the years in all matters having to do with young people has been a source of inspiration and encouragement to those of us who have been engaged in this work."

That was all to change late in 1941. For so long the faithful party man, McKellar suddenly became "the President's most trouble-some heckler." The reason for the switch related to the Tennessee Valley Authority (TVA). TVA Director David Lilienthal and McKellar were bitter enemies. Late in 1941 they disagreed violently over the location of the Douglas Dam, and Roosevelt came out publicly in Lilienthal's support. That simply brought out into the open something that had been eating away at McKellar for years—his conviction, partially correct, that no one appreciated the role that he had played in getting TVA established. He had nursed his grievance for some time, and it had warped him completely. "Of course Mr. Secretary," he once wrote Harold Ickes, "the Congressional Record shows that from 1916–1945 I have been the most effective of any of those who have fought for the TVA. Senator Norris helped out of course." This pressure, then, had been building up in him, and when the president seemingly disregarded his passionately held views about the location of the Douglas Dam, he began to flail blindly away at what remained of the New Deal.[17]

One of the agencies that got in his way was the NYA, partly because its appropriation was up for renewal. In March 1942 the senator introduced a bill aimed at abolishing the NYA and its companion agency, the CCC. The bill was sent to the Senate Education and Labor Committee for hearings, which were held between March 23 and April 17. Fighting fiercely for his agency, Williams refuted the charges of McKellar and a rather bizarre procession of witnesses that the agency was "coddling young people," that it was simply duplicating the function of the vocational schools, that it was wasteful, and that it encouraged both juvenile delinquency and left-wing attitudes among the young. "They go from idleness to drinking and from there to the pen," alleged one of the witnesses, the governor of Oklahoma, Leon C. Phillips.

Williams, who had to endure a not inconsiderable amount of personal abuse from McKellar, was able to show that he had rapidly restructured the whole program in accordance with defense needs, that he had terminated or drastically reduced all nondefense work, and that because it could pay its employees and maintain them in residence centers while training them, it was reaching people that no other defense authority could touch. He was backed up by scores of businessmen, educators, and community leaders, who either appeared before the committee or wrote to it. Each testified to the vitally important role that the agency was playing in the defense effort. Indeed, the hearings on the McKellar Bill turned into a heaven-sent publicity opportunity for Williams, and he used it to the fullest. The bill died in committee, and the NYA was clearly the winner in the short term. Nevertheless, Williams had made a powerful and implacable foe in the aging senator. McKellar eventually would have his revenge.[18]

Williams welcomed the McKellar hearings as an opportunity to refute certain charges that had been raised earlier against the NYA and which had damaged it publicly. In October 1941, the comptroller general, Lindsay Warren, had released the report of an investigation that his office had made into the NYA's affairs. That report had charged the agency with a number of irregularities, the most serious of which were that employees had spent public money on personal matters, that false claims for payment had been filed, that the army had been requested not to recruit among NYA boys, and that the age limit on NYA recruitment had been lowered from eighteen to sixteen purely to keep up quotas.

Many of the charges were petty in the extreme. For example, an executive assistant was charged with using public funds illegally for thirty-seven phone calls at ten cents a call to his wife in Maryland, calls he had made to tell her he would be working late. Some were based on inadequate research. Williams had not asked the army to refrain from recruiting among NYA youth, as was alleged. He had simply requested that it cease doing so on job sites during working hours, and this the army had readily agreed to do.

A few of the charges did have substance, and in those instances Williams acted promptly, once he was satisfied that action was justified. Dr. Mary Hayes, for example, director of youth personnel, who, it was shown, had used government money for private travel, was asked to resign. Most, however, he refuted and called for a congressional inquiry into them, which was eventually to exonerate the agency of most allegations.

The damage, however, had been done once the report had been released. The anti-Roosevelt press had a field day. The *Chicago Tribune* talked of "evidence of widespread scandal." Williams was again pilloried as a dangerous and corrupt radical, and the "keep your friends in power" speech was often given another airing. "Aubrey Williams, National Youth Administrator, has attained a new

high in New Deal bureaucratic gall and impudence," thundered the
Albany (New York) *Times Union.*

> He has demonstrated his unfitness for his job and ought to
> be removed. . . . The impudent bureaucrat who is at the head
> of this wholly unnecessary and extravagant institution re-
> plied to this criticism by the comptroller general of the United
> States by describing it to the press as "obviously another smear
> story." This familiar "party line" of the New Deal becomes
> intolerable when employed by a petty little underling against
> the officer of government charged with the high responsibility
> of safeguarding the nation's expenditures through an eter-
> nal vigilance.

In the weeks after the charges were made, hundreds of people
wrote to Warren to congratulate him for what he had done. "I hope
your 'nose', of which Aubrey Williams speaks so contemptuously
will be in many another broth of the New Deal's brewing," said one
such. For his part, Warren, a former congressman from North Carolina, said that he had been a strong NYA supporter while in the
House and that all he was concerned about was that it spent its
appropriation "in accordance with law." Be that as it may, the appearance of his report, much of which was later to be refuted, had
caused the agency substantial public damage.[19]

In the same week that the comptroller general revealed his
charges, the school administrators again went on the offensive. The
Educational Policies Commission of the NEA released a report
calling for the agency's abolition and the transfer of its functions to
state and local education authorities. Once again, the specter of a
federally controlled education system was raised. "Between 1933
and 1940," read the report, "two systems of vocational and other
forms of education for unemployed youth were developed and
operated by agencies of the federal government," and this was to be
deplored. The federal government should realize, the report concluded, "that the operation and control of education programs
should rest with the state and local agencies."

This document, too, was used by the anti–New Deal press as a
stick with which to beat the NYA. From the end of 1941 until the
eventual abolition of the agency the NEA waged a constant and
vitriolic campaign against it. Indeed, even the president became involved; he asked Williams to conduct an investigation of the "school

crowd." Williams's reply indicated that although those educators who opposed the agency were small in number, they were in strategically placed positions and wielded enormous influence, especially since they had the ear of Studebaker, who "appoint[ed] them to all key committees." "These people," Williams said bitterly, "have been able to prevent what could have been a nation-wide integration in the whole field of education of the facts, the measures, the results of your administration." Certainly they had been able to weaken the NYA's public standing.[20]

Sections of the press that had been generally favorable to the agency now started to turn hostile. Stories began to appear accusing the NYA of hoarding materials, of underutilizing tools and precision instruments "urgently needed by the war industries," of boondoggling, of subverting the nation's educational system. Paul Blanshard, Jr., a reporter for the *Cleveland Plain Dealer*, was sent by his paper to enroll secretly in a defense training program. His widely syndicated report of "little work and less training," of widespread "self-pity, bitterness and cynicism," of lack of supervision, of "discontent and laziness predominant everywhere" caused further erosion of public support for the agency. Again, no doubt some of the specific charges raised by such reports were true. In an agency of the size of the NYA it would have been extraordinary if there had not been some instances like those sensationalized in the papers. But they were not general. Williams made that point time and time again, but to no avail. The treatment that the agency received in these years helps explain the general attitude of bitterness and suspicion with which he viewed the bulk of the working press.[21]

Even the high school and college program did not escape criticism. Early in January 1942, George S. Benson, president of Harding College in Searcy, Arkansas, a small, private institution, wrote to the Arkansas director of student work, Ben Williams, to request that the twenty Harding students currently receiving NYA assistance be dropped from the payroll, as "we have plenty of work about the college that we could replace every N.Y.A. job without the loss of a single student." Williams agreed, routinely informing Benson that the funds withdrawn from Harding would be "reallocated to other institutions which will use them to employ students who otherwise will be compelled to drop out of school because of lack of funds."

That routine reply prompted a "spontaneous" request from the affected Harding students to the president and the secretary of the treasury that they be dropped from the NYA payroll, but that the money "not go to some other college where the students could likely find other employment," just as they had done. "We offer this contribution to the defense of our nation," they concluded. Benson supported the request. In a letter to Ben Williams he praised his students for "demonstrating the old American spirit" and urged that they "not be disappointed by finding this money being used by students in some other community where they too could probably get along without it." When that assurance was not forthcoming, he went to the newspapers.

An investigation subsequently revealed that the students' action had hardly been voluntary and that Benson and the president of the college's board of trustees, Clifton L. Paines, a New Orleans businessman, were the leaders of an organized campaign to force the government to reduce its spending levels. Yet the picture that the press painted was of a government agency quite unwilling to cut costs, even when it had been clearly shown that continued expenditure was unwarranted. Angry editorials again denounced Williams and his agency. "For a long time we have held in utter contempt the National Youth Administration," shrilled one such. "The motives are unpatriotic; the methods are reprehensible; the propaganda is despicable; its very existence depends on the efforts of a selfish group of fat-bellied, blood-sucking leeches in Washington," of whom, presumably, the tall, spare Williams was ringleader. "These contemptible N.Y.A. swivel-chair occupants," the paper continued, gave the money to other students, a gesture which indicated, in some mysterious way, their willingness "to see America enveloped in the flames of hell itself." Citizens, too, protested. The Harding students deserved "unstinted praise," said one irate gentleman, for turning back "the largesse with which a coddling government seduces the youth of our land." Again the facts of the incident were buried in its emotive effect, and again the public image of the NYA and its head was tarnished.[22]

All this was background for the Joint Committee on Non-Essential Federal Expenditures, which held further hearings on the NYA in December 1942 and January 1943. Williams admitted that he was treated fairly by the committee and that, apart from McKellar, he was heard most courteously by its members. They made it quite clear, however, that they did not accept his contention that the NYA, already operating on a vastly reduced budget, should be continued, especially given Williams's own admission that its relief function was no longer needed in the changed employment situation. On May 24, 1943, nicely timed to coincide with hearings on the NYA's 1944 appropriation, the Byrd Committee issued a report recommending the agency's termination on June 30, 1943. According to the report, the NYA was simply duplicating the functions of other agencies and bureaus in its defense training work. Moreover, it was administratively top-heavy, it was costly, its relief function was no longer needed, and it was employing far more women than men. In making its case, the document drew heavily on the 1941 Educational Policies Commission report. There was a minority report from Senator La Follette (Wisconsin), but given that the newly elected Congress had already shown itself to be thoroughly economy-minded, the agency's future looked bleak.[23]

Williams did what he could to meet the charges. He had been reducing administrative personnel for more than a year. State offices and administration had been scrapped; the NYA was operating on a strictly regional basis. One result of that had been the dismissal of many people who had served the agency faithfully since its inception, and he certainly did not relish what he had to do. "Frankly I am literally almost sweating blood over this thing," he told one state director, who was soon to lose his job. "It is a terrible experience to see a family break apart which had stuck together so marvellously."[24]

He lobbied strongly among the politicians. The agency had always had strong support from liberals and some moderates, men like Democrats Jerry Voorhis, Lyndon Johnson, John Kerr, and Elbert Thomas and Republicans like La Follette and Frank B. Keefe of Wisconsin, and they all promised to do what they could. He asked prominent educators friendly to the NYA to lobby on its behalf, as a counterweight to the NEA. He got members and former members of the National Advisory Committee onto the job. He gave press conferences, released statistics, made speeches, all in an attempt to persuade the public and, through them, the Congress that the NYA was still important, that it had a major role to play in the defense effort, and that it might well be needed, too, when the war was over.[25]

Indeed, Williams's intense desire to preserve his agency caused him to take an action which he was to describe more than two decades later as "the most shameful thing I have ever done in my life," something he could never bear to think about. At the request of the War Relocation Authority he had agreed to open the NYA to groups of Japanese-Americans forcibly removed from their West Coast homes whose papers had been cleared by the FBI. Two camps for these enrollees were set up in Minnesota. When the news became public, there was a great outcry. Many of the agency's friends in Congress told him that the scheme would "not do the N.Y.A. any good" in the debate over the Byrd Committee report. With great reluctance, therefore, and after Mrs. Roosevelt had advised him to do so, Williams terminated the program. The 275 young Japanese-Americans already in camps were sent elsewhere. It is a measure of the man and his commitment to justice for all that this action, taken under extreme pressure, would stay with him for the rest of his life.[26]

The NEA, however, was also on the move. On May 27 its secretary, Willard E. Givens, sent a letter to all state educational associations urging "an immediate campaign of pressure upon Congress to abolish the National Youth Administration." He followed this on May 31 with a further appeal. "If you do not want a competing federally-controlled and federally-operated system of schools under the N.Y.A.," he stated, "you should send telegrams at once to both of your Senators and all of your Congressmen stating clearly and forcefully your attitude on this question. Telegrams should be sent also from other educational, political, industrial and civic leaders. Immediate action is needed." Givens's call to action certainly bore some fruit. One congressman reported receiving over eight thousand telegrams against the NYA, mainly from school officials.[27]

That was the climate as Congress began its deliberations on the NYA appropriation for the 1944 fiscal year. Appearing before a subcommittee of the House Committee on Appropriations, Williams talked of the "immense training program which must be carried on if war production is not to decline disastrously" and argued that this was no time to dismantle an agency which was helping to meet that need. Moreover, he said, charges of duplication of function with the Office of Education were greatly exaggerated, as the NYA was now operating mainly "in the smaller communities where no other training facilities have been provided." Given that it was totally federally run, it had a flexibility that the Office of Education program, with its state and local involvement, could not have. Finally, no other training program could offer the residence centers. His argument sufficiently impressed the subcommittee that it voted five to two for continuing the agency. However, in a shock reversal, the full Appropriations Committee voted seventeen to sixteen, virtually along party lines, to reject the subcommittee's recommendation. Williams was not too upset by the vote, however. Three of the NYA's closest friends had missed the vote, and anyway he believed the climate was friendlier in the upper chamber. He expected the appropriation to clear the Senate and then be returned to the House. "We are far from licked," he said, "and are going to give it everything we have."[28]

The Senate followed the House's lead. A subcommittee of the Senate Appropriations Committee voted to restore the NYA's appropriation, only to have that reversed by the full committee. This meant that the NYA's fate would be decided on the floor. Immediately after floor debate began on June 26, Senator Harry S. Truman offered an amendment restoring to the NYA an appropriation of $48 million for defense training. A keen debate followed. Those who defended the agency spoke of its contribution to the war effort, its possibilities as a postwar training agency, and its vocational education activities in areas where the Office of Education schemes had not reached. Its opponents, led by the intemperate Senator McKellar, emphasized its expense, the apparent ineptitude of its administration, and the fact that as a relief agency it had outlived its usefulness. There were some stupidities; Champ Clark of Texas called Williams a Communist. But generally the debate was sensible, and the NYA's proponents won, by forty-one votes to thirty-seven.

It was to be a brief triumph, however. The Appropriations Bill went to a conference committee, where no agreement was reached. Returned to the House of Representatives, the bill, with the Senate amendment, was rejected on a partisan vote of 197 to 176. The NYA was finished. Faced with such a decisive vote against its amendments, together with the need to clear up the bill quickly, the Senate voted to concur with the House's action, again on predominantly partisan lines. Williams and his supporters had lost their fight.[29]

Williams was bitter about the defeat, and he laid the blame squarely at Givens's doorstep. "It is well known," he wrote him angrily, "that you and a small coterie of educators here in Washington . . . have from the N.Y.A.'s inception done everything within your power to hamper, malign and destroy it." To Father Moore of the advisory committee he spoke of the people who "destroyed" the NYA as "having committed a dastardly and enduring crime against the present and future promises of American life. We fought," he said, "and you fought and thousands of others fought with everything we had and of course, we shall keep on fighting but we should not be fooled into believing that the other side will not keep fighting too. They mean to destroy everything that offers hope and happiness to a great mass of the American people."[30]

Certainly Givens and his associates had had a hand in bringing down the NYA, but probably more important were the considerable gains that the Republican party had made in the 1942 elections. Since 1939 a conservative coalition had been able to block liberal innovation. Now it was possible to sweep away the last vestiges of the New Deal relief agencies, and the NYA was one of those. Then, too, the growth of the sentiment for economy in government was perhaps too great to ignore. The federal budget was the biggest in history, taxes were at an all-time high, and the pressure for reduction was intense. Wavering congressmen, perhaps not totally convinced by Williams's argument that the NYA was now a training, not a relief, agency, found it politic to be seen casting a vote for less government spending.

Whatever the reasons, the NYA was finished. Williams could do nothing but begin winding up the operation. The agency's supporters came forward with plaudits and commiserations; these were many, and sincerely meant. His friend Mabel Costigan was certain that "the government must not lose the influence of that fine social understanding that you almost more than anyone I know possess." Margaret Griffen, formerly the Nevada state director, said that "working for you and for the attainment and development of the ideals that you made a part of the N.Y.A. has been the greatest experience of my life, and one for which I am, indeed, deeply and sincerely grateful."

Such tributes, however, provided Williams little comfort. He could not, he said, be "composed and objective." Angry at losing the fight, bitter at Givens and his allies, "a pack of wolves, nipping at the N.Y.A.'s heels," and at the Republican party, "the folk who defeated us," worried that his own reputation as a radical might have lost the agency crucial votes, and unsure about what he would do next, he began to liquidate the enterprise that he had joined only reluctantly but to which he had become passionately committed. It was a very bad time for him indeed.[31]

9

"Pinkest of the Pink"

In July 1938 the right-wing magazine *Headlines* devoted its whole issue to an attack on Aubrey Williams, allegedly the nation's most conspicuous "Red government official." Two years later, Representative Hamilton Fish told Congress that he considered "these pinks and these radicals holding high public office" to be much more dangerous than out-and-out "reds." "I think [Williams] is one of the most radical men in the country," Fish went on. "He is one of the pinkest of the pink . . . and I am fearful if he should continue to head the National Youth Administration and deal with the youth in America." That same year, Representative Edward (Gene) Cox, a conservative Georgia Democrat, placed a rider on the NYA appropriation bill that none of the money was to go to pay Williams's salary because of his Communist inclinations. He withdrew it only after Williams had convinced him in private conversation that he was not so inclined. Not long afterward, Williams had to face a meeting of the Democratic caucus, again to deny such allegations. For most of his time in Washington, and certainly after 1938, Williams was a persistent target for charges of subversive activity and Marxist adherence, which in time led to an official FBI investigation. When the bureau's report exonerated him of any activities "which might properly be characterized subversive or disloyal to our government," he made the report public. That he felt a need to do so indicated how seriously he took the charges against him.[1]

Yet, as Lowell Mellett was later to write, "Aubrey hates Communists like the devil hates holy water." Williams's political creed will be discussed elsewhere, but a man who identified his political impulses as deriving from the teachings of Jesus Christ, the writings of Thomas Jefferson, and the example of Abraham Lincoln was far from the Marxist ideologue he was so often accused of being. He may have read his Marx, though he never indicated so, but certainly it had not influenced his thoughts to any degree. Williams was a populist—a populist whose solutions, of necessity, had relevance to more than rural America, but a populist nonetheless. As such, while he spoke for many on the left wing of the New Deal, he in no sense stepped outside traditional sources to do so.

Some New Dealers, as is well-known, were brief recruits to the cause of the world Communist movement in the turbulent and confusing 1930s, something which came back to haunt most of them in the ferocity of the McCarthy years, but Williams was never one of those. He distrusted and often disliked the Communists with whom he had contact in the course of his work, and he had no time for either their ideology or their tactics. He would not knowingly employ them as administrators in either the WPA or the NYA. Once, replying to a question from Representative Malcolm Tarver, a conservative Georgia Democrat and a friend to the youth agency, he gave as his reason for this stance a conviction "that those people who take their thinking from a foreign power have [no] business in a position of authority in connection with work of our character. . . . I never have and would not now employ knowingly a Communist to be a supervisor of any project, or, for that matter on any other parts of our organization."

From time to time, people who worked for him were accused of Communist party membership. Williams always had such charges investigated, occasionally by the FBI, more often by a specially appointed panel. If they were found to be valid, and usually they were not, then the employee was dismissed. Others were simply not hired, despite previous commitments. Jerome Davis, a leftist New York educator and publicist, was called a Communist by the *Saturday Evening Post* shortly after Williams had offered him the job of education director in Connecticut. The offer was immediately withdrawn. In his reply to Representative Tarver's question, Williams was not simply "playing it safe." He really meant what he said.[2]

And yet the allegations and accusations against him not only persisted, but intensified. Part of the reason for this can perhaps be found in the qualifications he gave to Tarver in answering his question. Having stated that Communists were not knowingly employed in the NYA, he continued: "But I want to say this, Judge Tarver: That I think one has to be very careful about allowing himself to exclude people who are struggling within the democratic form of government to do the right thing by young people. Those very people often times are the butt of attacks; and I have been accused, because I have insisted that young people have a right to express themselves and have a right to say their say." And, he said, he would not want his refusal to hire Communists as supervisors to be construed "as saying that when people get up and raise a hue and cry that this man is a Communist, that I am willing to fire him right off because somebody calls him a communist; because I am not, for this is a term that has been bandied about generally. . . . That responsibility, in my mind, rests upon us in terms of the best traditions of American life and living; it rests in the terms of Jefferson and of Lincoln and of all of those other men who have tried to teach us what real democracy means."

A year earlier, he had defended the extension of relief provisions to known Communists on the grounds that "under our form of Government we have consistently refused to make, as a condition of receiving public assistance, adherence to any political philosophies or beliefs, or religious beliefs, I think that is right and fundamental. . . . I think it would be dangerous to the country if we ever went into the matter of a man's political belief, when you are dealing with him on an entirely different basis; that is a basis of need." Such a basic, traditional defense of freedom of belief was too much for a growing number of Americans to accept in the late 1930s, as Martin Dies's House Un-American Activities Committee began indirectly to constrict the terms of acceptable adherence. It was enough to confirm, in the minds of some at least, the growing doubts about Williams's political position.[3]

Those doubts, of course, had already been fueled by Williams's public utterances of 1938, in particular the two remarks "keep your friends in power" and "class struggle is all right." While to some they indicated the depths of political corruption to which the New Deal had sunk, to others they also showed how far it had gone down an alien road. Referring to them nearly two years later, a small Pennsylvania newspaper branded Williams as "one of the scores of Soviet fellow-travellers in Washington" who was subverting defense industries. His outspokenness, as well as his sometimes thoughtless and tactless remarks to groups identified as left wing in support of positions considered to be radical, helps explain the growing perception of him as a man very far to the left.[4]

In some minds, at least, Williams was closely identified with two organizations in particular with which he had to deal during his time with the WPA and the NYA. They were the American Youth Congress (AYC) and the Workers Alliance of America. The American Youth Congress was created in 1934 by Violet Ilma, a young writer. Its aim was to become a coordinating body for the numerous youth agencies in the country to try to exert pressure on the national leadership. Ilma did not envisage the congress as having any particular political coloration, but it had hardly been established before Communist-controlled student groups took it over, organized the election of their own candidates to key posts, and ousted those, including Ilma, who opposed them. From late 1936 to 1940 it was probably the most important and certainly the most vociferous body speaking for American young people. Its leadership comprised members of the Communist party and others who were perhaps not members but who, in George Rawick's words, nevertheless "followed every twist and turn of the Communist line from 1935–36 through 1942."

The youth congress achieved much more importance and respectability than it would have otherwise because Mrs. Roosevelt became associated with it, a natural though perhaps naive outgrowth of her concern for the plight of America's young. She addressed the organization as early as 1936 and from 1938 to 1940 worked closely with its leadership. In 1938, when the AYC hosted a world youth congress at Vassar College, Mrs. Roosevelt was in attendance. In 1939 she saw the leaders of the group regularly, she arranged for the president to meet with them on one occasion, she allowed the congress to name a fellowship after her, and when the Dies Committee held hearings into the AYC's activities, she not only advised their leaders on tactics but attended the session and sat with the AYC members in order to show support. She did all this in the face of constant warnings that the AYC was under Communist control because, as she wrote in her column, "My Day," "it is quite obvious that a group with such varied organizations in it could hardly be called a branch of the Communist Party."

Mrs. Roosevelt loosened and finally broke her ties with the AYC in 1940, as she began to understand that what people had been telling her was true, that she had been used and deceived by those young people. In February 1940 the AYC held a Citizenship Institute in Washington, at the commencement of which there was a march to the White House. On a wet afternoon, waving banners with such slogans on them as "Jobs, Not Guns" or "Keep America out of War" and placards denouncing loans to Finland and supporting explicitly pro-Soviet positions and criticizing the New Deal, five thousand young people arrived on the White House lawn to hear the president address them. Instead of praising them, as they had expected, he told them a few home truths about their various stances, warned them against expecting "Utopia overnight," and called their view on Finland "unadulterated twaddle." It was, Williams recalled, "pretty rough, he had slapped them pretty hard."

Mrs. Roosevelt was upset at the president's tone, but also by the response of the young people. The unexpected chastisement prompted a boorish reaction—the president was hissed and booed. "How dare you insult the President of the United States," she angrily asked their leaders later. From then on, her relationship with the AYC cooled, the more so as she realized how she had been lied to regarding its political affiliation. She encouraged non-Communist liberals within the congress to organize resistance to the Communists, but by the end of 1940, hurt and bitter, she had severed her connection with it, and the AYC soon slipped into oblivion.

She was always to remember the experience. As Joseph Lash has pointed out, she claimed that her time with these young Communists helped her to deal more effectively with the Communist bloc at the United Nations when she became a delegate there because she could never be taken in again. Almost twenty years later, while in Williams's company at a reception, she met accidently with one of the youth congress's former leaders. She refused to talk to him, and left shortly afterward.[5]

Williams's experience with the youth congress rather paralleled Mrs. Roosevelt's. Given his position as administrator of the NYA, he would no doubt have had to have had dealings with it in any case; Mrs. Roosevelt's involvement with it ensured that he would be involved also. Earlier than she, he realized the nature of its leadership, partly because he had felt the sting of the AYC's criticism. As soon as the defense program began, the youth congress attacked him, arguing that he was converting the agency into a militarist arm of an imperialist war. In late 1939 he warned AYC leaders not to let Mrs. Roosevelt down. "It will break her heart," he said, yet he knew that they surely would.

In February 1940, during the same meeting at which the president administered his verbal spanking, Williams was booed off the stage as he tried to defend the NYA's defense program to the young delegates. Yet, just two years earlier, he had been both fulsome and public in his support of the AYC. In July 1938, speaking at a congress seminar, he exhorted the delegates to "organize to get power into the hands of the workers." In September he told his state directors that he hoped to bring into the NYA "some of the people that have been prominent in the development of the Youth Congress of America. I want some of these young people. I want them as part of this organization. . . . This is a great hour, and the people that are on our side are the people that make up such things as the World Youth Congress." He addressed the World Youth Congress meeting in August of that year, and he assigned NYA workers to projects sponsored by the AYC, terminating that activity only after the publicity attendant on the 1940 Citizenship Institute and the presidential scolding.

Williams often protested that to list him as a supporter of the discredited youth congress was unfair. He pointed out that in his official capacity he was forced to negotiate with its representatives and that they in fact came to regard him as the enemy. While that is true, it is also true that, partly because of Mrs. Roosevelt but also because of his own inclinations, he had initially allowed himself to get rather closer to them than was politically wise, an association that he was later to regret. His concern for freedom of belief and association, his liberalism, and his natural affinity for people espousing what he considered to be progressive, democratic ideals clouded his judgment for a time.[6]

Similarly, Williams got too close to the Workers Alliance of America to remain politically unscathed. The alliance was a labor union of the unemployed. Almost all of its members were WPA workers; indeed, Williams had recognized it in 1936 as the official WPA bargaining agency. Organized on a national basis, with nearly fifteen hundred locals in 1939 and a membership of only 280,482, it was not a major force in the land. Nevertheless, it performed some useful services, in particular, negotiating with local WPA supervisors about general working conditions.

Its president, David Lasser, was a graduate of the Massachusetts Institute of Technology and a former editor of the *Technocracy Review*. Though an avowed Marxist, he was not a Communist, but his second in command, Herbert Benjamin, was admittedly one, as were a number of the alliance's other top officials. As deputy head of the WPA, Williams often had to deal with alliance representatives, usually to negotiate conditions of employment. He came to know Lasser reasonably well as a result of those sessions, grew to like him, and sometimes invited him home for meals. Indeed, he was always to claim that his main interest in the alliance was to try to prevent the non-Communist Lasser from being ousted by his Moscow-oriented political enemies. Lasser was thrown out of the alliance, and in 1941 Williams used his influence to have him appointed to the WPA's administrative staff. Legislation was enacted, however, to prevent the payment of his salary from the WPA's appropriation, and he therefore resigned.

Williams's claim that his involvement with the alliance was little more than strictly professional ignores the fact that up until Lasser's expulsion and the Communist takeover he had always spoken of the union in the most positive of tones. The people who made up the alliance were "fighting our fight," he once told his state directors, and the NYA should support them. At an alliance dinner in 1938, where he was guest speaker, he praised Lasser publicly, calling him "a very fine person who had worked with him very well." In a later article he not only again spoke highly of Lasser—"a real leader and a man who has fulfilled a very difficult job very ably"—but even added "a word of commendation for his side-kick"—the admitted Communist party member, Benjamin. In June he told alliance members that "all my life, I have believed in the organization of workers, . . . and I expect to continue that. . . . I hope the Workers Alliance will grow, that it will expand. I hope that the organization of the unemployed people in America will include all of the unemployed people of America." It was in that same speech that Williams urged his audience to "keep your friends in power."[7]

Williams's support for the alliance arose from feelings that were similar to those that led him to support the youth congress—his genuine liberalism, his commitment to the unemployed and to the principles of labor organization, his reluctance to turn his back on anyone expressing progressive ideas, even though he risked being labeled "red," and his friendship with Lasser. When the Communists finally took over, he severed all connections with the body. Like Mrs. Roosevelt, he garnered from his relations with such people as Herbert Benjamin and the youth congress leaders a bitter distrust of Communists in general. "The Communists played dirty pool in those days," he recalled. "Still do, I suppose." Years later, he accepted the presidency of the Alabama branch of the Southern Conference for Human Welfare only on the condition that no Communists be permitted to join.

Yet, the taint was already on him in the eyes of many. Nothing seemed to place him more squarely in the enemy's camp than his public praise for Lasser and his organization. It was something his political foes in Congress could constantly return to, and they did so. "The Workers Alliance is a well-known communistic organization," said one opponent, Representative John Taber of New York, in 1940. "The principal officer, David Lasser, has been to Moscow at the expense of the Workers Alliance. . . . Now Williams is reported to have said that he counted the hours spent in conference with Lasser, Benjamin etc. 'as the high spot of my life in Washington.'" What sort of man was that, asked Taber, to place in charge of a youth program? "He has yielded to influences which make him a menace to the youth of the country." No matter how much Williams protested, how much he pointed out that the Communists in the youth congress hated him, how much he defended freedom of belief and association, he was always vulnerable to that sort of attack. His hasty public commitment to leftist institutions had seen to that.[8]

For some, another of Williams's commitments was further evidence of his dangerous left-wing tendencies; that was the cause of black Americans. As a young boy in Birmingham, he had grown up with Negroes and developed, as was common, a warm relationship with a few, including Mary, the woman who helped his mother with the housework, and compassion for many as a result of his travels with Brother Bryan. Yet he took no special interest in the Negro problem until he came to Washington in 1933. Not until then, he later wrote, did he become "fully conscious of and committed to the cause of the Negro."

That commitment, as has been noted, took several forms. In the first place he tried to ensure that as far as possible the agencies over which he held some power were fair in their treatment of black applicants. He appointed blacks to positions of responsibility within those agencies whenever he could, either as special officers in charge of Negro matters or simply to the general staff. In that regard, he was most successful with the NYA. Bethune's Negro Division, the appointment of black directors of Negro work to most state offices, the special Negro education program, the insistence that there be absolutely no discrimination in enrollment policies are but signposts of Williams's commitment to giving blacks a fair deal. In acting on that belief, he was not afraid of treading on toes, of bucking local custom or ordinances, of unpopularity. Once invited to a luncheon in his honor in Birmingham by the Alabama state director, he found that no black enrollees had been invited to meet him. Immediately, he told the state director, John Bryan, that he would simply refuse to appear unless blacks were allowed to participate. Bryan agreed, though with obvious reluctance.

That was not to be the end of the story, however. When Williams entered the hall where the luncheon was to be served, he found the following scene.

> I saw the negroes standing at the sides and at the rear of the room. I looked to see if any were seated, but none were, and so I said to John, "John, God Damn it, you are determined to mistreat these Negro Youth. Well, you won't do it while I am here. You have tables brought in here and chairs for these Negroes to sit down and eat." Flushed and sweating, poor, big six foot six and handsome John said, "They have already eaten." I said, "O! they have already eaten, nevertheless you have tables and chairs put here for them and serve them, just as though they had not eaten and don't serve anybody until they are seated."

In Oklahoma, late in the agency's existence, NYA staff members tore up his picture after he had insisted on the immediate integration of all projects and residence centers. It was not easy to set up desegregated NYA projects in many parts of the country, despite official policy. Normally, direct official action was necessary to achieve any movement at all. It is a measure of his commitment that from time to time he would take such a dramatic stand in order to make his moral point. Blacks recognized his sincerity, and no agency was better regarded in the black community than the NYA. As the *Chicago Sunday Bee*, a black newspaper, once said:

> No Federal agencies have been fairer to colored Americans than the N.Y.A., none as tolerant. It is the N.Y.A. that has distinguished itself by placing negroes in policy-making positions. The N.Y.A. is ahead of all the Federal agencies in working towards the full integration of colored people in the defense program and in American democracy. Aubrey Williams has been to the N.Y.A. what the Prince of Denmark has been to Shakespeare's Hamlet—he gave it life, substance and direction.

It was fair comment.[9]

Like many transplanted southerners, Williams enjoyed the company of blacks. Mary McLeod Bethune was a frequent visitor to the Williams home, normally resplendent in a vast cape and carrying a heavy cane. The Williams boys stood in awe of her, believing her to be some sort of African princess. Walter White of the NAACP was a close friend; the two men often met in O'Donnell's Fish House just off Pennsylvania Avenue to assuage a common craving for oyster stew. In segregated Washington they were only able to do so because the light-skinned White could easily pass for white.

Through contacts such as those, as well as through his agency, Williams's understanding of black deprivation and his passionate desire to help alleviate it deepened throughout the decade. In that, too, he joined forces with Mrs. Roosevelt. He was at her side when she defied the local segregation ordinances at the first meeting of the Southern Conference for Human Welfare, an act which is symbolic of their shared concern to do away with all vestiges of racism in the United States. One of the aspects of the NYA's work of which Mrs. Roosevelt was most proud was its unwillingness to compromise on the race issue.[10]

From time to time, recognizing the special regard that blacks had for Williams, President Roosevelt used him as a troubleshooter with the black community. In the winter of 1939, for example, sharecroppers in southeast Missouri staged a roadside demonstration under the auspices of members of the Southern Tenant Farmers Union (STFU), though without direct STFU involvement, against the misery of their daily lives. The majority of the participants were blacks. The demonstration lasted only a few days, but gained sufficient national prominence to cause the president to request a report on general conditions in the district. Because of his connections with the black community, his sympathy for the black cause, and his friendship with H. L. Mitchell, the STFU's secretary, it was Williams whom he asked to do the job. After receiving his report, Roosevelt ordered the National Guard to provide the shelterless campers with tents and field kitchens, though the demonstration ended before those supplies could arrive.[11]

Much more important was his involvement in the negotiations that led to the creation of the Fair Employment Practices Committee in 1941. A constant problem for the NYA was the placement of Negro trainees, a situation which the switch to a defense program served only to exacerbate. There was, after all, little use in training black youths for employment in the skilled trades if prejudice kept employers from hiring them for all but unskilled work. And this was the experience, time after time. The NYA found that the skills of black youths, no matter how well trained, were not marketable, despite all the pressure that Williams could muster. Moreover, blacks found it harder to find accommodations in areas with defense industry. The NYA was often forced to be responsible for housing their black trainees even after they had officially left the agency.

For much of 1941, this problem occupied more of Williams's energy than any other as he toured the country pleading for a change in policy. It was a disillusioning experience. Time after time it was labor, not management, which proved the stumbling block. The managers "were glad to get another tool or die worker, or a lathe operator or molder no matter what his color was," he later reported, "but not labor. They held out against them. We had trouble everywhere." In Seattle, San Francisco, and Los Angeles, as well as in the traditional areas of prejudice, well-trained black young people were being denied the chance to work at what they could do well because of their race.[12]

After a particularly moving incident, Williams resolved to do something about the situation. In early 1941 one hundred male trainees were sent from Quoddy Village to work in an aircraft factory near Buffalo, New York. One of those was black, and only he was not hired, even though he had the best grades of the group. The reason was opposition from organized labor. To a man, therefore, the trainees voted to return to Quoddy. Faced with this threat at a time of labor shortage, the management managed to persuade the union to moderate its stand, and the lad was finally taken on. Williams was most impressed with this display of strength and wondered why similar pressure could not be exerted on a national scale.[13]

He approached Mrs. Roosevelt with the problem and found that she felt as keenly as he did. Walter White of the NAACP had only recently talked to her about the same complaint. In particular, he alleged that Sidney Hillman, head of the Labor Division of the Office of Production Management, the agency responsible for coordinating defense production, was doing nothing about the inequities despite repeated protests. She resolved therefore to host a luncheon at which prominent black leaders and others who sympathized with their position would have a chance to confront those responsible for defense planning, and she asked Williams to draw up the guest list.

Hillman was invited, as was Walter White. Will Alexander was there, along with Dr. Robert Weaver of the Interior Department, unofficial head of the "Black Cabinet," a group of young and active blacks working in various New Deal agencies. Isadore Lubin came, as did Federal Security Administrator Paul McNutt. The group numbered about thirty in all, including, of course, Aubrey Williams.

Mrs. Roosevelt finished eating quickly, and then raised the issue. Williams described the situation as far as the NYA was concerned, and general discussion followed. Gradually, the view prevailed that the only way to improve things was for the president to issue a strong executive order banning discrimination in defense industries. Not everyone agreed—Hillman, for one, thought that it "would work itself out" without such drastic measures—but the consensus that Mrs. Roosevelt agreed to report to the president was a call for action.[14]

The black community now injected a real sense of urgency into this situation. A number of their leaders, notably White and A. Philip Randolph, the socialist leader of the Brotherhood of Sleeping Car Porters, the nation's most powerful black labor union, were incensed at both the exclusion of blacks from defense industries and discrimination in the armed forces and determined that blacks should take action on their own behalf. Thus, they resolved to exert mass pressure on the government, and Randolph announced that he planned to lead a march of thousands of blacks on Washington later in the year against the twin discriminations. He formed the March on Washington Movement (MOWM) to implement the decision and set a date of July 1, 1941, for the march. By June, profoundly bothered by the proposed march and fearing rioting and bloodshed, Roosevelt tried to persuade Randolph to call it off and even asked his wife to use her influence to try and have it stopped. In a letter to Randolph, she stated that although she agreed with the MOWM's goals, she was convinced that to march at that time would be counterproductive, given the tensions in Washington. Randolph disagreed. Failing vigorous action from the administration to end discrimination in defense industries, he said, the march would go ahead as planned.

As a last resort, the president summoned Williams, the man whom, more than anyone else in his administration, the black community trusted. "When I got into the President's office," he recollected, "I saw that he was tired and irritable. I said nothing waiting for him to speak, which in fact I always did—he rubbed his eyes and leaned over towards me . . . and said, 'Aubrey, I want you to go to New York and get Walter White and Phil Randolph to call off this march. . . . They are only going to make it more difficult for us who are trying to get labor and industry to hire Negroes. The missus is up there, and you get in touch with her.'" Williams immediately left for New York. At least one of the president's aides did not approve of his chief's choice of emissary. "Hell," "Pa" Watson is reported to have said on hearing the news, "Williams will join them."[15]

Williams caught the fast train to New York, breakfasted with Mrs. Roosevelt, and then went with her to City Hall, where they were to meet with Randolph and White in Mayor Fiorello La Guardia's office. They found the two black leaders intransigent. They would not call off the march unless Roosevelt issued an executive order prohibiting discrimination, and they also wanted to discuss the issues with him.

Mrs. Roosevelt agreed to arrange a meeting immediately, and although the president took some persuading, a meeting was set for June 18. Besides the president, White, and Randolph, that meeting included Secretary of War Henry Stimson, Secretary of the Navy Frank Knox, William S. Knudsen, joint head of the Office of Production Management Board, Hillman, Anna Rosenberg of the Office of Production Management, and Aubrey Williams. As Williams recalled it, the president made it clear from the outset that he favored an order stopping discrimination, but was concerned that to force the issue at that time might slow war production and that that was his paramount consideration. Turning to Randolph, whom he liked very much, he then asked, "Philip, what do you think?" Randolph, reported Williams, rose and "gave one of the most moving replies it has ever been my privilege to hear. 'We came here today,' he concluded, 'to ask you to say to the white workers and to management that we are American citizens and should be treated as equals. We ask no special privileges, all we ask is that we be given equal opportunity with all other Americans for employment in those industries who are doing work for the Government, we ask that you make it a requirement of any holder of a government contract that he hire his workers without regard to race, creed or color.'" With that, he handed Roosevelt a written statement of black demands, including desegregation of the armed forces. Williams said that the president was "visibly moved" by Randolph's plea. He may well have been, although any such display of support no doubt also had a strong political component. Moreover, he had already decided that desegregation of the armed forces was not a possibility.

The meeting concluded shortly afterward with a firm commitment from Roosevelt to issue an order and a request to La Guardia, Williams, and Anna Rosenberg to draw it up. They set to work immediately and submitted the next day a draft text. The proposed order barred racial discrimination either by management or labor in industries holding defense contracts and recommended the appointment of a grievance committee—to become the Fair Employment Practices Committee in the final draft—to police the situation. No mention was made of the armed forces issue.[16] The black leaders insisted that all their demands be met, and the order lay on Roosevelt's desk for almost a week unsigned while Randolph continued to plan his march. Desperate at the impasse, Williams contacted Mrs. Roosevelt, who was spending a few days at Campobello, to urge her to apply some pressure on Randolph.

Perhaps Mrs. Roosevelt's intercession proved the difference, for on June 24, with the march only a week away, the civil rights leaders agreed to accept the draft order, with the addition of a clause prohibiting discrimination in government as well as in defense industries. The next day, in the presence of, among others, Williams and Anna Rosenberg—indeed Williams reported that Rosenberg spread the draft out on the president's desk, thrust the pen in his hand, and literally screamed at him, "Sign it, Mr. President, sign it"—Roosevelt issued Executive Order 8802 creating the FEPC. The march on Washington was canceled.

It was with real satisfaction that Williams cabled Mrs. Roosevelt immediately to tell her the details. Randolph later wrote to him to thank him for "the fine and constructive role you played in helping to bring about this Executive Order for the advancement and well being of the Negro people" and consulted with him closely about the proposed membership of the new committee, surely a further measure of the general regard with which he was held by the black community. For his part, Williams was genuinely proud of what he had helped to accomplish and that the president had placed such trust in him.[17]

Williams was never as close to the president as he was to Mrs. Roosevelt. For the first few years of the New Deal he saw him rather infrequently, and then nearly always to discuss matters of relief policy. However, as the friendship with Mrs. Roosevelt deepened, he found himself more often in Roosevelt's company on social occasions, usually at Mrs. Roosevelt's invitation. Less frequently, he was consulted on matters not specifically connected with the NYA. His role in the crisis over the Washington march was a case in point. Williams always regarded the president with awe. "I really rather worship the man," he once wrote of him. "He had about everything—good looks, a photogenic face, an engaging warm smile, . . . an uncanny sensitive response mechanism as to what was going on inside of people. He was just about what I wished I was, . . . a truly great and good man. . . . The most personally winsome human being I was ever privileged to know."

The two men frequently disagreed on specifics. Williams found the president less than sensitive on the race issue at times, for example, and he was often astounded and appalled by some of Roosevelt's more unusual suggestions for relief projects—a pro-

gram to cut and stack all the grass along railway lines and a proposal
to set up a national scheme of field kitchens that would dispense a
"wholesome stew" daily to those in need were two particularly
bizarre examples. Yet he never lost his faith in Roosevelt. Williams
never seems to have doubted for a moment that they shared the
same social goals and had the same dream of what America could
become. For him, unlike for some other New Deal liberals, the
president never lost his charisma and was always true to his sense of
purpose. Roosevelt was always a shining liberal to him. He was not
the brilliant improviser, the man shifting principles, that so many
have discerned, but a man with whom he shared a common social
vision. Given that view, the creation of the FEPC was, for Williams,
not, as some have claimed, the result of a political president conced-
ing under pressure to something he had resisted doing for months
but a further example of his innate liberalism and strength of purpose. His faith in the president was unshakable.[18]

The FEPC scarcely proved to be either the equalizing force its
proponents so urgently desired or "the beginning of a communistic
dictatorship" that men like Mississippi congressman John Rankin
feared. Its only power to enforce its directives was to recommend
the cancellation of defense contracts held by firms shown to persist
in discriminatory hiring policies, and that it was most reluctant to
do. Employers and unions, rarely bothered by moral censure, continued to defy it. Blacks did make employment gains during World
War II, but that was probably more as a result of increased demand
for labor than from government direction. Yet the FEPC did have
some effect. Williams found the problem of placing Negro NYA
trainees somewhat easier, particularly in the shipyards and aircraft
factories. Though he did not credit that improvement to the creation of the FEPC, he nevertheless considered that the struggle had
been a worthwhile one.[19]

Williams's unswerving commitment to the cause of black equality
was, to some, further evidence of his dangerously leftist views. It
made him a number of bitter and powerful enemies, who would
combine to remove him permanently from government service in
1945. Yet, like his general belief system, that commitment derived
from no alien ideology but from traditional American ideals and
idealists—from Jefferson, from Lincoln, and, of course, from Jesus
Christ.

Williams had enormous sympathy for the weak and dispossessed and anger at the malfunctionings of the socioeconomic system which caused their plight. "I made up my mind long ago," he said in 1938, "to use my power to help those at the bottom of the social and economic ladder in America. I have and will continue to play that part. I don't care who knows it. I want it." Sometimes this passion, this distress, took him briefly into the company of people who wished to build an alternative society in the United States, but he never shared their ultimate perspectives, and he profoundly distrusted their motives. Although he spoke for the social democratic left wing of the New Deal and was, in the context of his times, a radical, his radicalism took well-worn paths. Very much in the reformist mainstream, he simply wanted to push his country closer to what he thought was its wellspring.

He believed implicitly in the "American Dream" and saw as its fulfillment not something derived from revolutionary ideology but a "more far reaching and more fundamental New Deal." He believed that "there were certain things that government can do better than private industry can do" and that it should continue to do them. But he did not wish to end private industry. He believed in a "wider distribution of opportunity" within a capitalist economic structure, not replacement of it. Despite the powerful emotions he aroused, despite the fears of Hamilton Fish, John Taber, and their ilk, Williams really went no further to the left than to call for a fully developed, essentially American welfare state. He was always a reformer, never a revolutionary.[20]

10
The REA Nomination

Both Roosevelts had hoped to retain Williams in government service, but desperately unhappy at the congressional action in ending NYA and sickened by the way the attacks had been made, he was determined to get out of Washington. His first hope was to join his sons overseas in the fight to save democracy; on August 5, 1943, at the age of fifty-three, he made application to enter the army as a private. This, predictably, was refused.[1]

However, he had another alternative. His friend James Patton, president of the National Farmers Union, an organization of small farmers which George Tindall has aptly described as "carrying the populist spirit into the twentieth century," and a member of the NYA's advisory committee, had become convinced that it was time for aggressive action to increase the membership of the group. The farmers union originated in Texas in 1902, with a membership largely drawn from former members of the Southern Alliance and the National Grange, and spread rapidly through the South in the first decade of the twentieth century. Theodore Saloutos has called it "an agricultural counterpart of the progressive movement that swept the nation," at that time, and certainly its demands—more efficient methods of marketing and production, acreage reduction, cheaper and more abundant credit facilities, the establishment of cooperatives—had both a familiar and a reforming ring about them.

After 1912 the center of strength for the union passed from the South to the Midwest, where for the next two decades it maintained a precarious and at times stormy existence as an authentic voice of small-farmer radicalism against entrenched agricultural interests, especially the American Farm Bureau. Milo Reno, for example, leader of the Farm Holiday Association boycott attempt in 1932, was president of the Iowa Farmers Union, and the type of radicalism that he exemplified was strong in most midwestern branches throughout the Depression era. During the New Deal the union formed strong links with labor organizations, and especially with the CIO. Indeed, the success of CIO organizing drives convinced Patton that his union should mount a similar effort among the nation's small farmers. Therefore, he wanted to increase his field staff, and he wanted Williams to join him.

Aubrey was sympathetic to the idea, though less than sanguine about its feasibility. He was, however, desperate to get out of Washington. Presiding over the dismantling of the NYA was a harrowing experience, and he resigned in early September. Upon his resignation he received a letter from the president praising the NYA and telling him that he had "a right to pride and America a reason for appreciation at the accomplishments" and an entreaty from his friend Mrs. Roosevelt to keep in touch and a statement that she had "always felt that you and those who worked with you did a magnificent job which will bear fruit in the years to come."[2]

Shortly afterward, he announced that he was joining the National Farmers Union as its director of organization "because its purpose and work is concerned with the welfare and betterment of people. I feel I can do more there than any other place. . . . I am more than ever impressed with the economic and social soundness of organized co-operatives. I feel their spread can only result in good on all fronts." His annual salary was to be $3,875, a huge drop from his income during his years at the NYA, and his main task was to be the organization of union locals in all the states east of the Mississippi River, concentrating at first on the South.[3]

He was very quickly on the road, where he lived with small farmers, talked with them about their hopes and their fears, and began to appreciate the dimensions of their plight. "What you and I know as one of the finest products of American life," he wrote one friend, "will be swept under by the oceans of bigness. This time it will be the family farm. . . . It is not a pretty picture." Something had to be done about this situation, and, he believed, the farmers union could be crucial to determining the future course of government policy toward small farmers. He went at his new task with a will and initially gave every indication of enjoying it thoroughly.[4]

Gradually, however, his enthusiasm palled. He disliked the incessant traveling, the cheap hotels or the uncomfortable beds in unsewered farm homes, and the time away from Anita. He knew how lonely she was and how she worried about the boys, and he wanted to be with her much more than the dictates of the new situation permitted. Furthermore, progress in the job was slow. Small farmers, he found, were often bitterly resistant to the concept of unionization, and their individualism caused them to balk at the idea of cooperatives as well. Finally, the issue of race was a constant stumbling block.

Essential in his thinking about organization in the South was the necessity for rebuilding the old black-white alliance, based on the common experience of poverty, which he saw as having been the strength of Southern Populism in the 1890s. At times he convinced himself that the possibility of reviving that alliance was at hand, that a new liberal spirit was stirring in the South. "There seems to be a bottom deep awakening," he wrote in the *Farmers Union Journal* of 1944, "a breaking up of the thick shell that has for decades covered the South; a stirring, or to use a good Southern term of 50 years ago, a refreshing. An unmistakable assertion of decency, and a turning on people who live by exploiting hatred, religious bigotry by trading in people's prejudices and fears."[5]

But those glimpses were often overshadowed by the realization that those prejudices and fears were often held most strongly among the people with whom he was trying to work. For example, in response to a call in the journal for racial decency in the South, one small farmer wrote asking him "if he were a white man or negro if he had any White Daughter and if so how would He like for one of those Daughter to return home Some night from the picture Show or Church and rush into His home and exclaim Oh—Look Father. What a lovely Husband I have. And he would be a big thick lip flat nose Negro." Experiences with that sort of sentiment caused him later to describe his time with the union as a "dismal period" and his efforts at organization "futile." Indeed, the brightest spot for him in 1944 seems to have been the presidential election campaign, when he was able to link up his efforts with those of the CIO's Political Action Committee.[6]

Perhaps the main reason for his discontent, however, was that he missed Washington desperately. He missed the excitement and the sense of purpose, he missed his friends, and he missed the Roosevelts. He wanted to be part of the drive to remake America that he was convinced would occur at the end of the war, and he knew that he would not be able to make much of a contribution from his position with the union. Henry Wallace had told him early in 1944 that "the cause is not dead, even though at times it may seem to be sleeping. When it awakes its vigor will be greater than ever," and Williams wanted to be there at its awakening. He and Anita kept in touch with the Roosevelts and even dined with them on one occasion in 1944, and he wrote the president often during the course of his travels to try to give him the feel of the people and to propose policies. In September 1944, for example, he advised the president, among other things, that there was "no love lost for Mr. Churchill," that people were "worried about jobs," and that they would "support a strong peace." He urged the president, therefore, to "announce a post-war program that will employ sixty-five million people" and to "put your cards on the table with reference to the kind of peace you want. The only element you can trust are the people. Put it out doors and let the people do some fighting for you."[7] Williams was still very much a part of the New Deal mainstream. Temporarily exiled to the provinces, he ached to be back at the center again, to continue the fight.

The chance to do so came somewhat unexpectedly. Early in 1944 the president had suggested that he consider accepting the position of executive director of the War Refugee Board, but he had declined, feeling that he owed the farmers union a bit more time. Late in the year, however, Harry M. Slattery, the colorful and combative administrator of the Rural Electrification Administration (REA), abruptly resigned. When Williams heard of this, he immediately wrote to the president to inform him that "should you feel that you would like to appoint me, . . . I should be happy to accept such an appointment." Roosevelt was delighted. "He knows the country far better than almost anybody else," he told his less than enthusiastic secretary of agriculture, Claude Wickard, who had wanted the job himself. However, Williams's radical reputation was a problem. "I do not know whether he could be confirmed by the Senate or not," Roosevelt wrote Wickard, but the president resolved to try.[8]

The REA had been established in May 1935 to provide low-interest loans for the construction of power and light lines in rural areas. Because the private utility companies had been unwilling to perform that task, the new agency had worked principally through nonprofit cooperatives established by farmers in local districts. The early history of the REA had scarcely been tranquil. Private power interests had fought its development every step of the way. The REA had also caused strife within the administration. In 1939, as part of the executive reorganization of that year, it had been placed within the Department of Agriculture, a decision that had angered both Slattery and Ickes, who had wanted it placed in the Department of the Interior. Indeed, one of the reasons for Slattery's angry resignation was constant conflict with Wickard, while at the time that the nomination was being considered, Ickes was waging a bitter behind-the-scenes battle to effect the transfer to his department.[9]

Despite the passions it aroused in the breasts of utility magnates and high government officials, by 1945 the REA had achieved a solid record of accomplishment. Through its efforts the gap between city and country had steadily narrowed, as electric power had begun to brighten rural living patterns. As William Leuchtenburg has written, "Perhaps no single act of the Roosevelt years changed more directly the way people lived than the President's creation of the Rural Electrification Administration."[10] The REA had brought profound social change, and its potential was far from exhausted. For his own views and dreams, Williams could hardly have chosen a better instrument through which to "get back in the battle" than this agency.

The president sent Williams's name to the Senate on January 22, 1945. It was not the first controversial recommendation of his fourth administration. At the time of the Williams nomination the Senate was already locked in a bitter, partisan debate over the suitability of former vice-president Henry Wallace's replacing Jesse Jones as secretary of commerce, a controversy which had aroused tensions at the grass-roots level. The Wallace nomination was generally seen as indicating that Roosevelt intended to follow his "left-of-center" course at the war's end, and people supported or opposed the nomination according to their feelings toward that course. Eventually, enough Democrats reluctantly supported the president to achieve confirmation, but in the horse trading that accompanied that confirmation the big lending agencies, especially the RFC, were removed from the Department of Commerce's control. The Williams nomination would certainly encounter similar reactions.[11]

Because of the intensity of the Wallace battle, the immediate reaction to the Williams nomination was somewhat low key. Predictably, he received the enthusiastic support of the liberal coalition.

The NAACP sent telegrams to all its branches urging every effort to secure confirmation because the nominee was "absolutely straight on our question." The president of a Mississippi-based railroad union cabled that the appointment "gives me a thrill of satisfaction, anticipation and hope." The CIO announced that it was backing him to the hilt.

Equally predictably, conservatives were totally affronted. The old-line farm organizations bitterly opposed him because of his connections with the farmers union. The *Chicago Tribune* called the nomination a "victory for radical groups in the Administration" and warned that, following hard as it did on the Wallace nomination, it gave the clearest indication that Roosevelt was once more "swinging to the left." The paper urged an all-out fight to prevent confirmation.[12]

Conservatives and liberals agreed that a bitter struggle was inevitable. The *New York Herald Tribune* believed that "the 'armed truce' under which Democrats suspended their civil war over Wallace" was likely to be shattered over Williams because "to many of the Southern Democrats Mr. Williams stands as a symbol of what they call the Left Wing element of the party headed by Mr. Wallace." The *St. Louis Post Dispatch* remarked that Williams was "likely to be accused of everything from atheism to housemaid's knee, but should come through the ordeal well, for he takes blows as he deals them, with a disarming smile." The paper believed he would "do well with R.E.A.—if Congress lets him come."[13]

One man who was determined to prevent his "coming" was his old adversary Senator McKellar, the man who had played such an important part in the fight to end the NYA. Then serving his fifth full term, this paunchy, erratic, evil-tempered old man was a figure of great power in the Senate. Because of the permanent absence of Carter Glass, he was effectively both the dean of the Senate and chairman of the Post Office Committee, which gave him control of considerable patronage. Still flailing away at the New Deal, he had not forgotten the bruising NYA fight, and he prepared to do battle with Williams once more.[14]

Again he had the support of his constituents, hundreds of whom wrote to deplore the nomination. Some protested the nominee's racial views. Others, like the man who talked of "Rosenfelt" and called the Southern Presbyterian Williams a "Jewish Communist," were somewhat unbalanced. The vast majority, however, were simply small-town conservative people who were bitterly opposed to any extension of the New Deal and who wanted no more of the Wallaces and Williamses. "His social and economic philosophy seem to be the same line of thought as that of Henry Wallace," wrote one such. "The best thing to do with Williams is to throw him into the trash pile and cover him up so thoroughly that he cannot make a comeback." To all his supplicants, McKellar gave the same comforting, combative answer. The Wallace nomination had "taken most of his time," but nevertheless he was "going after Mr. Williams strong."[15]

"Going after him strong" meant, initially, appearing as a witness against Williams at the hearings on the nomination before the Senate Committee on Agriculture, which began on February 2. The hearings opened fairly quietly, despite the angry intervention of Senator Harlan J. Bushfield, a North Dakota Republican. Bushfield, who looked, according to T. R. B. of the *New Republic*, "like a cross between a temperance reformer and Andrew Jackson" and whose campaign chest in the 1942 election had been generously lined by Colonel Robert McCormick, Irenee du Pont, Alfred Sloan, the Mellons, and the Pews, used the occasion to review a number of Williams's less discreet utterances and dubious relationships in an effort to raise the old Communist bogey. "Keep our friends in power" was trotted out yet once more, various allegations of Communist involvement made by the Dies Committee were revived, and his political leanings were closely scrutinized. Williams specifically denied any Communist connections, and the resolute defense of him by such senatorial stalwarts as Allen Ellender of Louisiana, John Bankhead of Alabama, and Burton Wheeler of Montana, all Democrats, began to give his supporters reason for cautious optimism. The *Washington Post* believed that he had "given a good account of himself," that the hearing was likely to run only another day or so, and that the committee would recommend confirmation, though the vote would be close.[16]

McKellar's appearance occupied most of February 8 and 9 and had a somewhat tempering effect on that optimism. "Nodding genially to one and all," he alternately questioned the nominee "in almost sepulchral tones" and shouted at him "like a bulldog growling down annoying puppies," his bulbous nose reddening as he did so. Drawing on all his skills of vilification, he attacked Williams with a fine disregard for fact, consistency, or elementary decency. He harried the nominee on many counts, accusing him of mishandling public funds while he headed the NYA and of making the agency a haven for draft dodgers. Citing Williams's inexperience in the field of public electrification, he stated: "In my opinion Mr. Williams may qualify as a social-work expert, but how in the name of heaven even Mr. Williams himself, as delightful and as ingratiating and as seductive a man as he is, could think he could run successfully the rural electrification business is something beyond me. So far his record indicates he knows nothing about rural matters and certainly he knows nothing about electricity."[17]

The main burden of McKellar's charges, however, was that Williams was thoroughly tainted with Communism and was thus clearly unfit for further government employment. The "hardy annuals" already worked over by Bushfield were yet again produced as evidence and discussed. "Mr. Williams was noted in the report of the Attorney General as being a member of either four or five of the Communist-front organizations," McKellar asserted. "He admitted making speeches all over the country that indicated he was quite interested, to my mind, quite as much interested in the Communist organization as he was in the National Youth Administration, it seems to me probably quite as much."[18]

In his angry desire to destroy Williams, McKellar overreached himself a little. Appearing before the committee, Comptroller General Lindsay Warren explicitly denied that Williams had in any way mismanaged public funds, and Ellender, George Aiken (Republican, Vermont), Scott Lucas (Democrat, Illinois), and the nominee himself again painstakingly and cogently refuted the Communist smear. Ellender introduced an affidavit stating that the FBI had thoroughly investigated Williams and had given him an entirely clean bill of political health.

For his part, the nominee defied "anybody to produce one single iota of evidence that I ever had one single thing to do with anything committed to the Communist Party, that I have ever been connected with it or even favorable regarding it. I was anathema to the Communistic element from the very beginning of my stay in Washington for the simple reason that apparently they didn't like the way I thought or the way I acted or the way I spoke."[19]

Williams and those who supported him recognized that it had not helped his cause to have a senator of McKellar's power working so passionately against him, yet they remained moderately optimistic. They took great heart from the impression that the old man had been treated by his colleagues as a bit of joke and had obviously been rattled by the willingness of his fellow southerners Ellender, Bankhead, and Lindsay Warren to undercut his arguments. "Unless Senator McKellar has something besides his usual maledictions," said the *St. Louis Post Dispatch*, "Williams has a good chance to be confirmed."[20]

The old senator had one card left to play, however. At the end of two days of testimony he introduced a telegram from none other than Dr. Joseph Broady, the Birmingham pastor with whom Williams had clashed as an adolescent. He was now in retirement, and a good friend of Senator Bankhead's. "Aubrey Williams grew up in the Sixth Avenue Presbyterian Church of Birmingham," read the message, "where I was pastor for 30 years. . . . The Presbyterian Church paid his college expenses. He denied the divinity of Christ after the Church educated him for the ministry. He is utterly unworthy of any official place in our government."[21]

There was no need for McKellar to spell out the implications too succinctly. In his view, this was conclusive proof that Williams was both an apostate and a man who did not pay his debts, not the sort of person who should be appointed to high government office. With that, he rested his case. The hearing was adjourned until February 14, its outcome still very much in doubt.

When it resumed, it was the turn of Mississippi's ferociously racist Theodore G. Bilbo to harry the nominee. During the recess he had come across some of Williams's recent articles on Southern life, and they had appalled him. One, in particular, roused him to a fury. In it, Williams had attacked the region's traditional political leadership—"the Roosevelt-hating political clique who set themselves up as the self-appointed spokesman of the voters of the South." The rank-and-file southerners, he said, would shortly repudiate them in the same way they had repudiated Martin Dies, Joe Starnes, and "Cotton Ed" Smith in 1944, and he called for an end to "white supremacy" politics. Angrily, Bilbo inserted the article into the record, shouting that he would "be glad to hear anything he [Williams] has to say. I do not know that he could make it any worse."

Williams had plenty to say, as might have been expected. He was not going to equivocate. "I am a Southerner," he replied, his drawl making that self-evident. "I was born in the South and I have been proud of the fact that I was born in the South, but I have been saddened that the South has not progressed as the other sections of the country have progressed. . . . One of the reasons for that is due to the fact that in its economic life it has allowed a condition to continue wherein the working people of the South had to compete against the Negroes of the South."

That was the pattern of all his replies to the Mississippian—strong, uncompromising statements of belief. When Bilbo accused him of favoring a situation in which "whites are forced to use toilets with the blacks," the inevitable end product of equal employment, Williams agreed. "I subscribe to the principle of doing away with discrimination in getting a job," he said. "I do not believe a person should be denied employment because of a man's race, creed or color. I hold that the sole basis of giving or refusing employment should be whether a man is able to do the work which he is hired to do." If one consequence of equal employment was toilet sharing, so be it.[22]

Williams was similarly blunt on the religious issue, which he simply refused to discuss with Bilbo. Quietly, looking straight at the little Mississippian, he told him:

> The matter of my not going into the ministry was a question
> of my own conscience. I frankly do not feel that is any concern
> of this committee. That is a matter between myself and my
> God, and I am happy to say that the Constitution of the United
> States definitely prohibits that any religious test being made
> of man [sic], and I do not ever wish to be a party to it by even
> condoning it to the point of discussing it.[23]

That was the way the hearing ended, amid a flurry of charges and countercharges, accusations and denials. Senator Bilbo kept at him about race and religion; Senators Bushfield and Raymond E. Willis (Republican, Indiana) went over the "Communist sympathizer" ground yet again; and senators Ellender, Aitken, and Lucas repeated their defense of the nominee. The whole hearing, in fact, reflected very little credit on most of the men involved, the nominee excepted. He, after all, had at least kept his temper, often in spite of extreme provocation, and had stuck to the business in hand. In-

deed, Senator Lucas was moved at the close to make a short statement declaring that

> in my ten years in Congress I have never seen a witness
> seeking confirmation upon [*sic*] an important agency as this,
> so abused and so maligned. Ninety-eight per cent of the evi-
> dence presented before this committee would not stand the
> test if it were offered before a court of competent jurisdic-
> tion. If you could convict this man of anything it would be that
> he is a humanitarian. . . . It has been apparent that smear is
> the chief weapon being used against Mr. Williams and some
> opposed against him seek to convict him of communism.[24]

The liberal press shared that view. The *Washington Post* angrily
asserted that the committee's treatment of Williams "has been offensive to every principle of the American society"; T. R. B. said in
the *New Republic* that Williams had "never looked finer" to his
friends than during the hearings. However, it was generally conceded that his chances of confirmation had lessened materially.
Robert C. Albright of the *Washington Post* predicted that the vote
would go eleven to nine against him. He was one off; the committee
eventually voted twelve to eight to recommend the rejection of the
nomination.[25]

It seems likely that of all the charges raised against him the
question of his racial attitudes did Williams the most damage. Certainly it cost him the support of two key southern committee members. Alabama's Senator Bankhead, originally a supporter, switched
after Bilbo had blown open the race issue. Angrily, he told Williams
privately that "this is too much, Mr. Williams. I am withdrawing my
promise to support your appointment. I did not know all this at the
time I made you the promise." Senator Richard Russell of Georgia,
who had also planned to vote for Williams and had told him so,
wrote to him after the raising of the racial issue that the people of
Georgia were outraged by his views, and that the users of REA
electricity in his state were particularly opposed to the nomination.
It was "with deep regret," said Russell, "I am therefore compelled
to advise you that I cannot support your confirmation. I hope that
you will understand my position."[26]

Without those defections, the committee vote would have been tied. If that had occurred, Senator Hendrick Shipstead (Republican, Minnesota), who favored Williams personally but preferred to vote against any nominee until the REA had been made an independent agency, would certainly have switched his ballot, and the recommendation would have been favorable. Once again, Williams's refusal to equivocate or to yield on a matter of principle had hurt him.

Yet the fight was far from over. The hearings, the attendant publicity, and the reports of the way that Williams had been treated had transformed the struggle into one of considerable importance, particularly as the Wallace fight drew to a close. The nomination would still have to be debated by the full Senate, as neither Williams nor Roosevelt had any intention of withdrawing it. Accordingly, the liberal coalition began to organize, Vice-President Truman made a ringing declaration of support for the nominee; pressure groups began to cable senators, write newspapers, make public statements, and hold rallies. Organized labor, especially the CIO, was strongly behind Williams, as were the National Farmers Union and the NAACP. Clergymen attacked McKellar and Bilbo for raising the religious issue. Senator Ellender made public a telegram from the Presbyterian Loan Fund stating that Williams owed the church no money at all.

The liberal press kept up its support. In a stinging editorial, "The South's Worst Foes," the *St. Louis Post Dispatch* bitterly criticized the five southern Democrats on the Agriculture Committee who had voted against Williams:

> These were Alabama's Bankhead, whom Williams had once termed a Tory; Mississippi's Bilbo, whose demagoguery is supreme; Connally of Texas, whose democracy often begins at the water's line; Russell of Georgia, whose views are reminiscent of John C. Calhoun's and Stewart of Tennessee, for whom K. D. McKellar is a guiding pillar of light. . . . The plight of millions on the misery margin moves the Wallaces and the Williamses, but it leaves these Democrats-in-name-only cold. Such men are the worst foes of the South today.[27]

Finally, Williams had the support of hundreds of ordinary citizens who shared his liberal vision, disliked intensely the pressures to which he had been subjected, and wanted to help in the confirmation fight. Natalie Moorman, a black Washington housewife, wrote that she "felt so strongly" about the issue that she was willing to work one day a week without pay doing "the odd clerical jobs that are part of this pressure effort." Lieutenant John Barr Foster told him, "There's a helluva lotta guys coming back from this thing with a new concept of Democracy—and it doesn't exactly agree with Mr. McKellar's. Until that time may the Aubrey Williamses and the Henry Wallaces keep the home fires burning."[28]

In an effort to coordinate and direct the growing propaganda activities on his behalf, certain of Williams's most influential supporters announced on March 9 the formation of the "Friends of Aubrey Williams Committee." The chairman was New Haven industrialist Eliot D. Pratt, and among the more important members were labor leaders William Green, Philip Murray, and A. F. Whitney and publishers Anita McCormick Blaine, Marshall Field, Mark Ethridge, and Jonathan Daniels, as well as prominent manufacturers, social workers, minority-group representatives, and advocates of public power. One of the committee's first efforts was to sponsor a newspaper advertisement headed "Who will stand with Bilbo?" It concentrated directly on the race issue, and asked, "Can political reactionaries decree that no presidential appointee shall take office if he opposes racial discrimination? . . . The Senate will answer these questions, yes or no, when they vote on Aubrey Williams."[29] The Committee also released polls that purported to show Williams slightly ahead in the Senate count, cabled publicly uncommitted senators on his behalf, and generally directed the pro-Williams forces.

Enthused by all this activity, the nominee succumbed to moderate optimism as to the outcome, at least publicly. Immediately after the hearings, he had believed his confirmation chances to be very slim. "I may be washed out in this fight," he had written his friend Myles Horton. "I personally do not care. I think I would really be most happy to stay on with the Farmers Union." Of course he did care; he cared desperately. Two weeks later, he sounded much more positive. Again writing to Horton, he said:

I have a notion we may win on the final go-round here, especially if we can have a little more time. I think the opposition has shot its wad, and, having built its case upon a structure of misrepresentation, prejudice and so forth, they are necessarily going to have an awful lot of trouble holding it up, for time alone will aid in its crumbling as we know, for evil begets evil, as our friend Tolstoi was wont to say, and finally destroys itself.[30]

But the opposition had not "shot its wad." It was far from destroyed, as it, too, mobilized its forces. Senator McKellar lobbied fiercely among his colleagues, cajoling, threatening, promising, and stating that he would use his seniority on the Appropriations Committee to block REA's money if Williams were confirmed. The American Farm Bureau campaigned heavily against him, and thousands of people from all over the country wrote their senators to urge them to rid the land once and for all of New Dealism and the New Dealers. "We want America for America," wrote one, "not for Moscow. Good congressmen and senators will fight to the finish to keep Communists out of power and put Americans in power."[31] The pressure was particularly effective on those few southern senators known to be leaning Williams's way. The young senator William Fulbright of Arkansas, for example, counted as a firm supporter of the nominee, began to waver as a result of the flood of hostile letters from the "folks down home," and there were fears that Senator Clyde Hoey of North Carolina would also defect.[32]

Both Williams and McKellar kept "prediction cards," lists of senators with their likely positions indicated and their degrees of commitment estimated. By mid-March both men had the anti-Williams forces in the lead. However, the pro-Williams people were convinced that the pressure being applied on his behalf was moving some moderate Republicans toward him. If the vote could be delayed and the pressure increased, they believed he still had a chance.[33]

Barring the way to Senate action on the nomination was a proposed treaty with Mexico on water rights. Because the issues involved were contentious and a lengthy debate was expected, Williams's opponents were eager to have it laid aside until after the vote on the nomination. Confident that they had the numbers to beat him but worried by the increasing activity on his behalf, they wanted no delay on the vote. For precisely the same reasons, Williams's supporters aimed at preventing swift action and opposed any interruption in the order of business.

On March 16, Senator Bankhead moved that the Mexican treaty

be laid aside. Majority Leader Alben Barkley prevented an immediate vote by quickly recessing the Senate. McKellar also moved that the treaty be laid aside, but he was blocked by another parliamentary maneuver. Bankhead, now firmly ranged against the nominee, did not give up. Chiding Williams's supporters for "battling for time while they carry their case to the country," he tried again on March 19, and this time was successful. By a vote of fifty-two to thirty-three, the Senate decided to lay aside temporarily the Mexican treaty and to make action on the nomination the pending business. The size of the majority dismayed the Williams forces profoundly; they seemed only to be postponing the inevitable.[34]

Nevertheless, the liberals did not give up. They staged a minor filibuster to delay the vote as long as possible while maximum pressure was applied to those few senators who had not yet declared themselves publicly. The debate was a repetition of the hearing. McKellar, Bilbo, Bushfield, Willis, and others went over the familiar charges of Communist sympathy, incompetence, racial radicalism, and religious defection. Ellender, Aiken, Lucas, Claude Pepper, and Lister Hill led the defense. Most of the time they spoke to a nearly empty chamber; but two senators, both pro-Williams, heard Ellender's long, passionate speech in which he once again took up the charge of Communist leanings, painstakingly reviewed the evidence, and took it apart mercilessly.

Only senators Aiken and Hill introduced anything new into the discussion. Both claimed that powerful business interests had moved into the fight against Williams, particularly the Copperweld Company, which had received the lion's share of orders for REA construction materials, something Williams had publicly deplored and intended to end. Thus the opposition of the monopolists, it was alleged, was added to the forces of "politics prejudice [and] animosity" ranged against the nominee. "Whatever the decision may be on this matter," said Hill, "the record will stand, because Aubrey Williams's entire life, and all his service testifies that he is and has been all his life a humanitarian."[35]

Described by the *New Republic* as "one of the most scandalous chapters in recent Senate history," the debate changed few minds. Williams was rejected by fifty-two votes to thirty-six, the only surprise being the size of the majority against him. In the end, liberal Republicans like Joseph Ball and Ralph Brewster and southerners like Fulbright succumbed to pressure from home and went against him. Nineteen Democrats voted against the nominee, all but two from the South. This mass defection was decisive; only five southern Democrats had voted against Wallace.[36]

Conservatives greeted the result with undisguised glee. The *Chicago Tribune* thought that it showed there was "still hope for the preservation of the Republic. It is not going to be surrendered lightly to crackpots, wastrels and enemies of the Constitution." Senator McKellar talked of the "new epoch" dawning for America, as the New Dealers were rooted out and destroyed. "I think the defeat of Mr. Williams was a great victory for democratic government," he declared, modestly asserting that he had "had but one desire and that was to do the right thing."[37]

Liberals were bitter, but far from demoralized. They took great heart from the level of support that Williams had received in the country, especially in the South, where even the fiery Frederick Sullens, of the *Jackson* (Mississippi) *Daily News*, with whom he had had words in those far-off days of late 1932, had come out in his favor. Sullens pointed out that "Bilbo's criticism of Williams for failing to pay his debts is hilariously funny to all who know Bilbo's record. There was a time, when he also laid his Bible down, having found that preaching was not highly profitable." The *St. Louis Post Dispatch* predicted "a day of reckoning" ahead for those "bourbons" who had voted against him, and Jim Patton announced after the vote the formation of a Political Information Bureau which would operate in the rural South against such reactionaries. "Thus good may come out of evil, . . . the good of thrusting them from public office and preventing their counterparts from slipping in."[38]

At a "victory dinner" held in Williams's honor on March 28 and attended by old friends like Mrs. Roosevelt, Wallace, senators Ebert Thomas, Aiken, and Barkley, and, of course, Lyndon B. Johnson, the atmosphere was anything but defeatist. Mrs. Roosevelt said she believed the struggle had helped people "know what the facts are and what they want, then there is nothing that will hold them back." Barkley declared that Williams personified "the finest efforts of human society to achieve equality of opportunity for all men at a time when concentration of power in the hands of the few has caused the most destructive war in history," and believed that the hour of people like him was at hand. Stating that "Aubrey's great sin has been that he believed human erosion was just as important as soil erosion," Wallace called on the group to combine "liberal ideals with the determination of conservatives," and thus make America over.[39]

Williams himself was much less carried away. His bitter disappointment showed. "I have never been one of those who took very much comfort out of defeats," he said, "and I am very frank to say . . . that I take no pleasure out of the fact that we were defeated this time." Yet even he talked about the progress that liberals had made and would continue to make now that peace was so near and President Roosevelt could return to the unfinished business of the 1930s. "Mrs. Roosevelt, I want to say this to you," he concluded, "I honor your great husband. I think he is the greatest man at the head of any state in the world today. To have known him is one of the greatest privileges of my life. . . . I am sure we're going to keep on fighting the fight." Williams said much the same thing in a letter to the president on April 8.[40]

Undeniably, many personal factors had been involved in the nomination fight. Williams had never been a popular figure with Congress; he was regarded as too outspoken, too direct, and too committed, and his activities since leaving government had simply reinforced that view. And then there was the all-important question of race. The defection of such key figures as Bankhead, Russell and Fulbright can clearly be attributed to Williams's racial views. Lister Hill told him later that had he been more equivocal when facing Bilbo's charges he would have won narrowly. The large southern vote against him must be explained partly in these terms, especially because he himself was a southerner. Finally, there was the misfortune in timing. Williams was the victim of a backlash from the fierce Wallace confirmation battle. A number of Republicans who had supported Wallace and were consequently under attack from their constituents and their party leaders tried to offset the effect of the earlier vote by rejecting Williams. He was sure that this need for compensation cost him at least the support of Ball, who had supported Roosevelt's election in 1944, Leverett Saltonstall, Brewster, and probably several more.[41]

Yet the defeat had brought home to Williams and his liberal friends just what they would be up against in their commitment to carry on the New Deal tradition in postwar America. Williams, characteristically, oversimplified when he talked about the clarity of the issues involved, but he was at least partly right. "The lines were beautifully drawn," he said. "Those standing for a life in which everybody should share spoke their piece simply. Those who stand for control by the few, fearing an economy in which everybody would share, said their piece in no uncertain terms. That is the deepest reason for my defeat."

This was, at one level, an ideological fight. Like the Wallace encounter, it was a battle about the past, about the direction in which America had moved since 1933, and about the future, whether that particular movement would continue. As the protagonists and their supporters recognized, it was a struggle over the New Deal and New Dealism. Those who wrote to McKellar expressed themselves particularly urgently. "We want no Williamses, no Wallaces nor any other of the type that is bent on perverting our historical democracy in a Democratic-Roosevelt Communism," asserted one. "This dishonorable plot against America is bigger than any party, and I hope sincerely that you and all other good Democrats will see the necessity of uniting whenever and however possible with our old enemies the Republicans, to form a coalition that may rededicate this nation to a restored freedom."[42]

Those on the liberal side were no less determined—and were perhaps equally simplistic in the details of their arguments. Excoriating McKellar for his intransigence, one irate woman talked of "the tide of liberalism" that was sweeping the globe as the war for democracy drew to a close. "What do you suppose F.D.R.'s election for a fourth term means?" she demanded, and she bade him farewell "because we won't be seeing you after 1946," when next he would face the voters of Tennessee. She was, of course, wrong. The fourth term had only days to run, McKellar lasted until 1952, and in postwar America it was the liberals who had the hard time.[43]

Despite his bold public front, Williams was bitterly disappointed by the defeat. He knew that his career as a public servant was finished; there would be no more nominations. Moreover, though he drew strength from "the number of people who had been willing to stand up and be counted on our side in this fight," he could read the signs. The next years, he feared, would be cold ones for the liberals. Also, there were immediate personal problems to be dealt with. The National Farmers Union had been in real financial trouble for years, and it had been agreed that when Aubrey left for the

REA, he would not be replaced. Instead, the division of organization which he had headed would be eliminated. The senators' action, therefore, caused acute embarrassment, but did not change the basic decision. Williams resigned from the organization as of July 1, 1945.[44]

He would not, however, be going out into the cold; rather, he would be going home. Marshall Field, the immensely wealthy and liberal Chicago publisher, had long wished to start a magazine in the South, one which would provide a counterweight to the prevalent conservative opinion in the region. In 1945 he purchased a moribund farm monthly, the *Southern Farmer*, which at the time was little more than a collection of trade news and advertisements for patent medicines, published out of Montgomery, Alabama. Through this vehicle he planned to influence southern grass-roots opinion, and he chose his friend and fellow liberal Aubrey Williams to publish it. In August 1945, therefore, rather to his surprise, Williams found himself a resident of Alabama for the first time since 1911 and, at the age of fifty-five, about to embark on a new career—that of a businessman. It was a rapid transformation.[45]

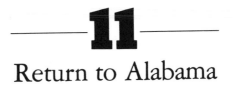

11

Return to Alabama

Aubrey Williams returned to his native Alabama at a time of political transition. Though challenged by traditional Alabama conservatism, the liberal forces generated by the New Deal, and by wartime prosperity and industrial growth, were nevertheless shortly to triumph at the state level. In late 1945 a tall, hulking politician from Coffee County in the southeast corner of the state, James E. Folsom, was becoming the symbol of those forces.

Narrowly defeated in the gubernatorial election of 1942, Folsom, a man whose political views reflected the persistence of Populism in Alabama politics, and whose "bountiful empathy for the little man, the downtrodden, the oppressed, the exploited, carried over to the Negro," was a political type quite different from those who had dominated recent politics in the region. His attitude toward the black man alone was enough to ensure that. Folsom vowed never to use the race issue for political gain, and he kept that vow. Like the Populists of the 1890s, he believed that the issue of race had been used by conservatives to keep poor whites and poor blacks apart, when their common economic interests should have ensured the opposite. That such a man was shortly to lead a successful crusade of the downtrodden against the "Big Mules" was one measure of the changes that were occurring in Alabama at the time that Williams went back home.[1]

The city of Montgomery reflected those changes to some degree. Capital of the state, proud of its reputation as "the cradle of the Confederacy," it was sometimes pictured as the epitome of an unreconstructed southern community. In 1945, as it had done for decades and, indeed, as it still does, the flag of the old Confederacy flew proudly above the state capitol. Yet Montgomery was changing, for the war had brought more industrial growth, and with it an influx of people, both black and white. More important, large military installations established and developed nearby were becoming increasingly important to the town's economic life. Though Maxwell Field, the huge airbase on its outskirts, had not yet reached the position that it achieved in the mid 1950s, when one in seven of Montgomery's families depended on it for their livelihoods, it was well on the way there. In that sense Montgomery had been "nationalized" by the war. Yet much remained the same. War and the social change that it engendered had not altered Montgomery's living patterns. It was, when Williams arrived, one of the most segregated cities in the entire South, and had been so for decades.[2]

Williams returned to Alabama with high hopes. He was optimistic about the political climate and the potential of his magazine to influence it for the good. "The power of things on our side is unusual," he wrote Myles Horton of the Highlander Folk School. "There is more than one way to skin a cat, and you know that I am going to devote it [the magazine] to strengthening the small farmer in all the relationships we want." Despite the March defeat he was in as positive a frame of mind as he had been since the end of the NYA. "I am content," he wrote Horton on another occasion. "The truth is that with the ending of the war I could be content anywhere with anything. It is all easy now, with the boys coming home, or in little danger." His sons, all of whom had served overseas, were safe, and with millions of other parents, he gave thanks.[3]

His first task was to change the *Southern Farmer*'s direction. The agreement with Field had stipulated that Williams was to head the operation as publisher, with general control over both the magazine and the printing works, which Field hoped to expand, while Gould Beech was to be the editor of the *Southern Farmer*. Beech, a former editorial writer for the *Birmingham News* and the *Montgomery Advertiser*, was a native Alabamian, a protégé of both Field's and Senator Lister Hill's, a friend of Folsom's, and a man of uncompromisingly liberal views. Grover Hall, editor of the *Montgomery Advertiser*, once claimed that he had never seen "a man with a more earnest and reasoned solicitude for the underdog than Beech." Williams had never met him, but looked forward to working with him. He sounded like a kindred spirit. In August 1945, Beech, a major in the army, was still on active service, so Williams had to begin the enterprise alone.[4]

The new direction was soon apparent. Readers of the *Southern Farmer*, long accustomed to articles and editorials fulminating against liberalism in all its guises, soon found things very different. The first issue for which Williams was responsible was that of October 1945. By then, he had changed the layout, introduced an editorial page—the first editorial in the revamped magazine was entitled "Who Started the War"—and injected an overtly liberal political tone into the *Southern Farmer*. His first article was a rebuke of Senator James Eastland of Mississippi, a man with whom he would frequently cross swords in the years ahead, for disparaging remarks that the senator had made about the performance of black troops in the war. The November issue included an article in favor of President Truman's reconversion program. The December issue featured a profile of Senator Estes Kefauver, the Tennessee liberal, and included a letter of congratulations from Senator Harley Kilgore of West Virginia, who agreed that "the rural population of the South certainly needs some facts presented with the progressive viewpoint." The January 1946 issue highlighted "the South's first need: a 65 cent minimum wage," and defended CIO organization policy in the region. By the time that Beech arrived in mid-January to take up his appointment as editor, Williams had already set the magazine on a liberal course.[5]

Beech quickly settled into the same groove. His first editorial, "How the South Can Get Rid of Syphilis," raised many a regional eyebrow; his next, "Church Leaders Join in Fighting Bilbo, Sower of Hate," returned to a more mainstream political theme. Throughout 1946 the *Southern Farmer* uncompromisingly supported a liberal populist position on state and national issues. Thus, the magazine rejoiced in the election of Folsom as Alabama's Democratic gubernatorial nominee. "The common people have elected themselves a Governor," exalted Beech. "All over the South, farmers, working people, veterans and women voters are ready for a change in politics. They want real leaders who are free to serve the people. Big Jim's victory in Alabama shows it can be done." On the other hand the Republican sweep in the November congressional elections was seen as "a black day for the common man."

During this time, Williams gave Beech a relatively free hand in the production of the magazine, though he did contribute a monthly column entitled "Publishers Notes," which was, in effect, a second editorial page. Williams himself wrote the editorial for the April 1946 issue, an issue commemorating the death of Roosevelt one

year earlier. This nostalgic tribute to his former chief, entitled
"Franklin D. Roosevelt Lives On in the Hearts and Minds of Men
and Women," was full of stories drawn from his own New Deal
experiences and redolent of his conviction that the Rooseveltian
approach to public policy had far from run its course, that the
reform agenda of the 1930s still had real relevance for the postwar
world.[6]

As well as changing the *Southern Farmer*'s editorial policy, Beech
and Williams drastically altered its format. The peculiar collection
of small advertisements for trusses, patent medicines, Bibles, and
hair blacking stayed, but those ads were joined by expanded sections for agricultural and farm news, by a women's section which
included serials such as "rolling Romance," and by features for
children and adolescents. A real attempt was made to combine a
folksy family magazine and a liberal political journal, and by the end
of 1946 there were some signs that they were succeeding. Circulation was up, partly as a result of a series of circulation-boosting
contests masterminded by Williams, and though many people were
hostile to the magazine's new stance and wrote telling Williams so,
just as many wrote praising him for it.[7] Williams and his backers
faced the new year with cautious optimism.

In 1947 the *Southern Farmer*'s strident liberalism became even
more pronounced, as it was forced onto the defensive by the shape
of national and international events, as the reality of the postwar
world began to part company with the hopes and the dreams of
Williams and Beech. They were bothered by aspects of American
foreign policy and by the growing hostility between Russia and the
West, and they bitterly opposed the terms of Truman's uncondi-
tional extension of aid to Greece and Turkey, which were confronted with a threat of Soviet intervention. America should ensure
that a properly democratic regime was established in Greece before
providing aid, argued the magazine. "If we really want to make
democracy strong in Greece we will not spend one dollar in Greece
until Butcher George [King George of the Hellenes] gets out. If
Greece needs an army to defend democracy we will not buy a
uniform for any of the 228 former Nazi supporters who are today
leaders in King George's army." Subsequent editorials and articles
developed that theme, advocating a type of New Deal for Greece
as the essential condition for the advancement of aid. The *Southern*

Farmer supported the Marshall Plan, but wished for greater United Nations, rather than United States, control of its administration.

Later in the year, the editors first took up a theme which would recur in the years ahead. They protested against the creation of a climate of suspicion and fear which had already resulted in security checks on many government officials and the dismissal of a few and which would reach its culmination in the activities of Senator Joseph McCarthy. "The men in Washington are throwing the Constitution out the window," argued Beech. "This fight has behind it men who want to take away every gain the common people have made in America in fifteen years."

For Williams the issue was equally simple. "American Freedom Being Stomped On" was the banner headline over a signed editorial that he wrote attacking the House Un-American Activities Committee (HUAC) in the November issue. Though the magazine still supported President Truman, both Williams and Beech were profoundly disturbed by what they considered to be his departure from New Deal precedents. Along with others on the liberal left, they were at least considering the possibility of a new liberal party, ideally one led by former secretary of agriculture and vice-president Henry Wallace. Thus the paper became more uncompromising in its political stands during 1947. Even the serial reflected that hardening in attitude. "Rolling Romance" gave way to "Bill and the Court House Ring," a breathless drama in which a fearless young progressive challenged entrenched power, in the person of one Judge Simpkin, in a small southern town.[8]

As the Wallace protest movement hardened into a third-party challenge, Beech's criticisms of the president became more strident and his support for the new Progressive party more obvious. Williams was unhappy with this. He had known and liked Truman in the New Deal years; the president had been one of the NYA's staunchest supporters in 1943 and led the fight to save the agency on the Senate floor. The two men still corresponded on occasion. In 1948, for example, Williams wrote to advise the president to call Congress back into session, "sticking the Republican planks under these same Republican noses." Truman responded stating that he was "glad to have had your approval of what I intended to do anyway." Disagreement over the magazine's policy toward the Democratic party in 1948 was one reason why Beech and Williams were finding it increasingly difficult to work together.

In addition, Beech had been under great strain throughout most of 1947 as a result of the rejection of his nomination to the board of directors of Auburn University by anti-Folsom forces in the Alabama state legislature. The accompanying attack on his character had profoundly unsettled him. He began to behave erratically, running up some huge bills which he charged to the company. When Williams remonstrated with him, Beech threatened legal action. The men had other differences, too, usually pertaining either to money or Beech's status within the *Southern Farmer* company. Eventually, though he recognized the precarious nature of Beech's health, Williams literally forced him to resign, an act which displayed the same ruthlessness in dealing with subordinates that he had shown during his New Deal days. Though the two men were later reconciled, Beech never worked for him again, and from May 1948, Williams was editor as well as publisher of the *Southern Farmer*.[9]

After Beech departed, the magazine stuck with the Democrats during the 1948 election campaign, all the more so after the national convention's adoption of a strong civil rights plank in the party platform. In his editorials, Williams strongly attacked the Dixiecrats who left the party in protest over that plank and made his first full-scale attack on segregation since taking over the paper. "The central evil in the South is segregation," he wrote in July 1948. "Until decent Southerners face this fact, little progress will be made toward solving the racial problem or any other problem in the South." The editorial prompted some violent reactions, but only fifty people actually cancelled their subscriptions. It was the first blow in what was to be his, and the magazine's, most persistent struggle.[10]

Williams's most significant contribution to the politics of 1948, however, was the editorial in the October issue. Entitled "Come on Back Home, Henry," it was a plea to Wallace to give up his third-party crusade, to leave "that New York crowd of sharpers," and to return to the Democratic fold. There was a need for a progressive party, he agreed, but not one "built around the communist-dominated clique which sits at the center of the Wallace movement." The Democratic party, he argued, was still the best base on which to build such an organization. Roosevelt had shown that it could be done, and the party at its recent convention had "proved . . . that it still believes in the progressive principles" that he had stood for.

This editorial was reprinted and widely distributed by the Democrats as campaign material. It represented a fair distillation of Williams's own political creed, a reaffirmation of progressive ideals
within a traditional American framework. In making such a reaffirmation, Williams parted company briefly in 1948 with many of his
closest friends and political associates. Virginia Durr, herself a Progressive party senatorial candidate, felt betrayed by him, and his
beloved Wicky was most upset by his position. His son Aubrey, Jr.,
a Wallace field-worker, simply could not fathom his father. But
Williams stuck to his view.

The election result gave him the greatest satisfaction. Once again
he was optimistic for the future. "As the astonishing returns kept
coming in," he wrote, "a whole new America began to rise up.
There was a sort of personal shame that one had such little faith in
the American people. But there was a wonderful feeling too. A
feeling that the American people couldn't be tricked, that they
couldn't be bamboozled by a bunch of poll-takers, newspaper and
magazine headlines."[11]

The New Deal, he still believed, was alive and well. Neither the
onset of the Cold War nor the experience of living in the segregated
South for three years had permanently soured his spirit. That optimism pervaded his magazine for most of 1949. He approved of
the bulk of Truman's domestic legislative proposals, social security,
compulsory health insurance, and of course the administration's
farm program, known, after Secretary Charles A. Brannan, as the
Brannan Plan. This program, aimed at stabilizing food prices and
raising farm incomes, especially for small producers, was "hailed as
a double-edge farm program which promises cheaper prices for
food for the consumer while at the same time providing parity of
income for farmers," and was enthusiastically supported in issue
after issue. Civil rights, too, was discussed with increasing fre-
quency. The magazine continued to expand its nonpolitical side
as well. There were more features, more handy hints, and more
romances.[12]

By November 1949, Williams seemed well on the way to making
a success of the enterprise. Circulation was a healthy 1,052,821,
almost triple what it had been when Williams took over. In an interview with *Time* magazine, he waxed almost expansive about his
somewhat surprising success as a businessman. Pointing out that

circulation had been built up in a variety of ways, but principally through contests for prizes ranging from Bibles to tractors, he said rather disparagingly, "I don't think very many people down here buy magazines because they want the magazine. They get a monkey wrench or something and the magazine is thrown in. . . . I don't know what they do with the *Farmer*—stick it down the toilet maybe —but they continue to buy it." "Making money," he continued, "is the easiest thing I ever tried to do." The *Time* interviewer concluded that since becoming a businessman himself, Williams had developed a kindlier attitude toward business in general.[13]

In this spirit of optimism, Williams decided to expand his enterprise. In the hope of developing the job-printing side of the business, he built a new plant and purchased the most modern of presses. The problem was that his optimism was not really justified. Despite the increased circulation, and despite Williams's casual assertion to the contrary, the *Southern Farmer* was not making money.

James Warburg, the New York financier and former Roosevelt adviser who was backing the venture with Field, was furious at the tone of the *Time* interview. "Did you really say that thing about stuffing it down the toilet?" he wrote angrily. "Why belittle your own product? And why pretend that making money is easy? Do you think your readers will like it? Or your advertisers? . . . I don't think that sort of thing does you any good. Especially when you want credit?"

As Warburg knew, the expansion of circulation did not mean increased revenues unless advertising could be correspondingly increased, and that did not happen. The *Southern Farmer* never used more than the small block-type advertisement. Since it was sold mainly to the very poor, to the vanishing breed of small farmers, the big farm implement and fertilizer companies did not use it, nor did those selling consumer goods to the middle classes. The major advertisers scarcely needed it. Williams always believed that potential advertisers were deterred by his reputation and the paper's liberal tone, and indeed some may have been; but it is more likely that the dictates of the marketplace rather than ideological preference explained its lack of advertising revenues. Moreover, given the income of its readers, it would have been fatal to raise its price.

From 1950, therefore, the magazine began retrenching, and by 1952, Field and Warburg were suggesting liquidation, both for economic reasons and because they were not altogether happy about the paper's editorial content. "We went into this thing with you in order to help you do a necessary job in the South," said Warburg on one occasion, but he expressed doubts that the paper was performing it effectively. In response, Williams argued that there were limits on what any magazine could do in the hardening southern climate and that "it has meant something for the *Southern Farmer*, standing for what it has come to stand for in the minds of political leaders down here, to just stay alive." Warburg took the point. For the time being, the paper was not to be sold, he informed his editor, given Williams's conviction that it was a worthwhile operation. "Being and surviving as the voice of freedom in the South is, I grant you, an accomplishment to be proud of in itself," he wrote. "Perhaps it is all we can hope for. I just wonder, though, if we cannot also be a more effective voice."

Nevertheless the paper remained under a cloud and continued to lose money, despite various attempts to reverse that trend. A change in name to *Southern Farm and Home* in 1951 in an attempt to broaden the circulation base to include southern cities, and thus attract more advertising, had little effect; nor did pruning the subscription list in order to reduce sales improve the situation. By November 1954, Williams himself had decided that the only sensible thing to do was to get rid of it and to concentrate on his job-printing enterprise, which was doing reasonably well. No buyers could be found, however, and in March 1955 the magazine ceased publication as a monthly. It became, instead, a quarterly almanac, full of mail order advertisements, farm news, advice to the lovelorn, and sewing patterns. It was no longer a journal of liberal political opinion. The experiment on which Williams and his backers had embarked with such high hopes had failed.[14]

Williams was depressed by the magazine's effective demise partly because, as he saw it, it left the southern plain folk with no alternative to the increasing stridence of the region's controlled press and other media outlets. As the Cold War worsened and as the climate of McCarthyism steadily constricted debate, his editorial policy remained uncompromisingly liberal. Increasingly, he found himself in disagreement with Truman's foreign policy. Though he believed that the president had been right to act when he did in Korea, he nevertheless thought that the United States's "negative, fear-inspired and largely Moscow-made foreign policy is leading us to disaster." Why should the Russians "be the ones to cut up big estates into family-type farms . . . , while we back regimes of landlords?" he asked. "Why should they be the ones to back independence movements, while we back colonialism? . . . How long are we going to befuddle our own minds by letting our own reactionaries convince us that any reform—any idea which gives a better life to more people is communistic?" The magazine supported Adlai Stevenson in 1951 largely because of what Williams perceived as his grasp of the need to reverse the trend of giving blanket support to any regime deemed anti-Communist, no matter how repressive it was. Moreover, he admired Stevenson's running mate, Alabama's Senator John Sparkman, whom he saw as representing Folsom-type populism on the national scene.

In stating his growing disquiet with the course of American foreign policy, Williams was in no sense an apologist for the Soviet Union, as were, for example, some who had flocked to the Wallace banner in 1948. Rather, he was pointing to the gap between what he considered to have been Roosevelt's dream of the postwar world and the reality of Cold War polarization. Williams's view of the world, and America's role in it, was entirely consistent with his general political philosophy. Instead of bolstering illiberal regimes for fear of the course that change might take, the United States should seize the initiative in directing that course toward progressive ends. In short, America should aim at providing a "New Deal" for the whole world. Only in that way, he thought, could Soviet influence be countered effectively. It was, perhaps, a simplistic view, but it was also an authentically American one.

Domestically, Williams began to concentrate on two issues, issues that had become and would remain central to his own belief system and his conception of what the United States should stand for. These were freedom of belief and equality for black Americans. In issue after issue he attacked the prevailing climate of fear and repression. "Are we setting up a police state?" he asked in October 1950. "When men are subject to arrest and punishment for what they say and believe, then we have gone back to the days of King George III, back to the days of the Inquisition." He assailed Senator McCarthy constantly, reproducing many of Herblock's expressive anti-McCarthy *Washington Post* cartoons as well as editorializing against him, and he also attacked the House Un-American Activities Committee. His stand on civil liberties issues during this period of danger to them was uncompromising and unpopular.

He was similarly firm on civil rights, bluntly telling his readers, most of whom would doubtless be violently opposed to his views, that "segregation by law no longer fits today's world. For our part, we have never believed in segregation. From childhood, it has been a spoiling thing. It has spoiled our enjoyment of so many of the good things, such as pride in being an American, or joy in being a follower of the teachings of Jesus—so much so that we have grown to regard it as the ARCH SPOILER! And we shall welcome the day when it is no more."

Such statements inevitably provoked reaction from the little people who formed the bulk of his readership. "I have six children," wrote one such, in canceling her subscription, "and they all hate Negroes, and they don't want to go to school with them. In the town where I live there are four or five negroes to each white, as you know that is very bad for white people. The next thing the President will try to pass will be to let Negroes eat and sleep with white people. . . . I would rather be dead." Williams well understood the background that led to that sort of thinking; he came from it. He had compassion for the poor whites of the South as well as for the blacks. But he could not compromise his convictions. In the climate of the early 1950s, that a magazine as uncompromising in its liberalism as the *Southern Farmer* could continue to exist, albeit under increasing duress, for so long is remarkable. If Williams failed, the failure was an honorable one.[15]

The *Southern Farmer*'s relative lack of success could be traced to a number of factors, most of which were outside Williams's control. One contributory cause, however, could have been his tendency to involve himself less and less in the running of the company. According to his printing manager and long-time friend, Paul Woolley, Williams was not really interested in the business, especially after 1950. He wrote the editorial page, but left most of the rest for other people to manage. Increasingly, his time was taken up with organizations and outside business interests. Of these the most important was the Southern Conference Educational Fund, which will be discussed later, but other activities, too, occupied his concern.[16]

One such activity was American Family Homes, Inc. Appalled by the living conditions of most blacks in Alabama, particularly those in the cities of Birmingham and Montgomery, "with black rotting houses jammed against each other like chicken coops in a truck," he resolved to do something about them. An inquiry to the Federal Housing Authority (FHA) elicited the information that while twenty-nine thousand homes had been built in Alabama under its auspices for whites, only sixty-one had been built for blacks. Williams was determined to change that ratio if he could. "I felt that if I could make a demonstration that there were Negroes who were able to purchase homes if they were available," he said later, "and that there was a profitable area for private enterprise, I would do something that obviously greatly needed to be done." Accordingly, he mortgaged his own house for five thousand dollars, borrowed fifteen thousand dollars from friends Jane Foster, Mary Anderson Bain, former NYA director for Illinois, and Gould Beech, and formed American Family Homes. In mid-1947 he commenced building on a tract of seventy-eight lots in Birmingham.

Right from the start there was trouble. Insurance companies were reluctant to take the FHA-guaranteed mortgages because the houses were being built for black occupancy; the FHA itself would allow only a $5,100 guarantee on an $8,000 home, compared with the $6,300 it was willing to give on an identical house in a white neighborhood, and no Birmingham bank would make construction loans. Eventually, a Jackson, Mississippi, company, Lamar Life, took the mortgages, a Virginia bank provided construction money, and the venture went ahead. By mid-1948 American Family Homes had built fifty-nine units and had sold all but two of them. They were neat, economical five- and six-room constructions, which cost between $7,700 and $8,400 to build and sold for between $8,000 and $8,750. In one year, Williams had shown that a market for such housing existed among Birmingham's blacks, and he had begun to break through the conservative financial structure that had had much to do with restricting such developments in the past. He had also made a slight profit.

Nevertheless, the company was in trouble in 1948, unable to expand because the bulk of its capital was tied up in second mortgages made necessary by the low FHA guarantee figure. He appealed, therefore, to Marshall Field and to the Meyers, a family of philanthropic liberals in New York, for help in establishing a re-

volving fund to finance the necessary second mortgages, thus freeing the company's capital for further building. They agreed to provide that help under certain conditions, and construction was able
to continue.

Things were a little easier after that. Impressed by the initial
success, Birmingham's banks and other lending agencies began to
show more enthusiasm for the project. By February 1950 the company had built over two hundred houses, and they had almost all
been sold. More important, only a handful of blacks had missed any
mortgage payments. "This has made a tremendous impression on
financial and real estate circles in the city," Williams wrote his friend
Nathan Levin. In that sense, he had already accomplished one of his
aims. The company was also making some money for its backers.
The August 1951 balance sheet showed a profit of just over $96,000,
which enabled Williams to pay both Field and the Meyer family
back in full. American Family Homes was a modest success.

Nevertheless, the company's directors decided in 1951 to wind
up its affairs. There were several reasons for this: the profit margin
was too low to justify the effort being put in; despite the easier
financial climate there was still constant trouble in placing mortgages, the Bains and Jane Foster all wanted their money out, and,
finally, the project manager on whom they depended for the day-to-
day running of the operation proved to be embezzling company
funds and had to be sacked. No more houses were built after 1952,
and though the company was not formally dissolved for several
years, its effective operation ceased then.

During its existence it had built 450 houses, mainly in Birmingham. It had sold them all to blacks and had had only five defaulters,
a far better record than that of whites on the same economic level.
Williams had shown that blacks did not default on their mortgages
when given a chance to hold them, and he had convinced several of
Birmingham's leading bankers that black housing could be a sound
investment. In that sense, American Family Homes permanently
raised the level of black housing in the city: besides providing those
who bought the homes with better accommodation than they had
ever known, the venture, by its success, had ensured that others
would continue where he had pioneered.

Williams had also made a modest profit, but that was not nearly
as important to him as the less tangible achievements. "We all have

a sort of memorial to the things we believe in," he wrote to the Bains, upon taking the decision to terminate the project. "That is of course the best thing about it all." From time to time, Williams dabbled in business ventures, mainly of the "get-rich-quick" variety. Most failed. American Family Homes was not one of those, however. Moreover, it showed that a real need could be filled with the proper amount of faith, trust, and respect. Of all his business schemes, this was the one which gave him most pride.[17]

Williams did not sever his connection with his old employer, the National Farmers Union, upon his return to Alabama. Indeed, by 1946 he had become state president of the Alabama branch of the union. His position as editor of a journal speaking principally to small farmers, his support for Jim Folsom, and his public reputation as a New Dealer among folk who still loved Roosevelt virtually catapulted him into the office. He hoped to use his position to cement further the old Populist bond between poor white and poor black farmers which he saw the Folsom movement as encouraging. To that end he began organizing a system of farmer cooperatives. Initially these co-ops would provide fertilizer, feed, and insurance, but later they could be expanded to supply a whole range of farm materials. The aim was to free the small farmer from the domination of the big farm supply companies; moreover, the experience of working together in those ventures would, he believed, further blur racial distinctions among those involved.

Again he turned to Marshall Field for finance, and in February 1947, Field provided $30,000 for the project and formed a company, Allied Ventures, Ltd., with Williams as president, to disburse the money. With that injection of funds, five small cooperatives were started in Alabama and Tennessee. Between 1947 and 1951, when it was dissolved, Allied Ventures spent $29,458 on cooperative work, the bulk of it on organization and operating expenses.

As always, Williams was optimistic at the first that they were succeeding. "I wish Mr. Field and all you who have helped in this," he wrote Howard Seitz, Field's lawyer, early in 1949, "could have been with me a few Saturdays past at a meeting of the South Alabama Cooperative. There were about 400 members present, 125 of them Negroes. It was an unforgettable sight. This is but one occasion of similar meetings now held monthly." Moreover, co-op managers and local organizers for the farmers union reported high interest in them. Although Williams's views on civil rights, which were anathema to most white rural Alabamians, were becoming well-known and were being used by the union's enemies, membership in the cooperatives continued to hold up. There were a number of reports of blacks coming to union picnics and of black and white stockholders working together on cooperative business. "We are accomplishing something down here as far as the race issue is concerned," enthused Tom Ludwig, manager of the Andalusia, Alabama, cooperative in 1948.

That optimism, which Williams shared, proved to be misplaced. By September 1949 the Georgiana, Alabama, cooperative was reporting a drop in membership, partly because of Williams's civil rights stand. One local had disintegrated completely over the issue. The trend continued. By the end of 1950 all the cooperatives had virtually ceased functioning. By that time, Williams had become thoroughly disillusioned with the whole enterprise and the attitude of Alabama's farmers. They "would stick to the cooperative only if the price was below that of the town merchant," he bitterly told one inquirer. If the merchant cut his prices, they returned to him, with the result that "these cooperative efforts failed and the whole organizational structure fell apart. There was not sufficient strength or intelligence to make it possible to have a strong organization. There was a continual demand that something be done for them. They could not get it into their heads that they had to do something for themselves." It was "not very encouraging nor a pretty picture," he concluded sadly.[18]

The failure of the Alabama cooperative movement mirrored the failure of the Alabama Farmers Union generally under his leadership. Membership declined steadily, until in March 1951 the national board of directors revoked the charter of the Alabama Farmers Union because of a lack of members, and the state organization henceforth ceased to exist. In announcing that decision, Williams also announced that he would accept no further position within the organization. Shortly afterward, the national executive decided virtually to cease operating in the South.

Williams blamed several factors for the failure, but thought the main one to be the irrelevance of national policies to the peculiar situation in the South. "I don't think anything such as a small farmer movement for such farmers living in Alabama, Mississippi, Georgia or any other states outside the Northwest can be directed by a group living in Denver or St. Paul or Jamestown," he told Ludwig. The concept of the family farm held by the national leadership was just "not right for the South."

There was much truth in this. Comprising people whose experience and traditions were far removed from those of the Deep South, the union's national leadership no doubt did not always appreciate the singularity of the region and the need to accommodate national policies to the particular situation of a profoundly different region. Yet there was a particular reason for the failure of the Alabama Farmers Union, and that was the character of its president. Williams's attempt to force a biracial union on white farmers who were well imbued with the region's prejudices at a time of hardening racial attitudes was bound to fail. His reputation as a political radical made this only more certain.

As early as 1948 there had been a challenge to his reelection as state president because of his political views. From then on those views were a constant subject of controversy and undoubtedly cost the union many members. Frequently, he had to contact individual members to refute charges such as those of the farmers of Springhill, Alabama, that he was "one of the biggest Communists in the country, and that he had denied God," a legacy of the REA hearings. As people became more intransigent in their social and political attitudes, the incongruity of a political and racial liberal leading an organization of small southern farmers became more obvious. Williams himself recognized this. Writing to Fanny Meyer Korn, another of his philanthropist friends, who had helped the Alabama union financially, he explained its failure as a result, in large part, of his insistence that "there be no Jim-Crowism in the organization." "It is all very sad," he concluded.[19]

His sadness and disillusion at the failure of the Alabama Farmers Union was compounded by his growing and profound differences with the union's national leadership, including his friend Jim Patton. Those differences would eventually cause him to sever all connections with the organization. First, Williams was concerned at what seemed to be the policy of Patton and the national leadership to support unquestioningly the administration's foreign policy. He was particularly disturbed by their action in revoking the charter of the New York branch of the union because its president, Archie Wright, had been outspoken in his criticism of certain of Truman's actions. Given Williams's dedication to the principle of freedom of speech and belief, he could hardly have been expected to have reacted otherwise.

The experience of his friends Clifford and Virginia Durr drove a second wedge between Williams and the organization. Clifford, who had resigned his position on the Federal Communications Commission in 1948 rather than take a loyalty oath, had been appointed counsel to the farmers union in 1950 and had moved to Denver. There the feisty and committed Virginia quickly got into trouble. She signed a petition, sponsored by the leftist Independent Action Committee of Denver, which advocated bringing troops home from Korea and negotiating a peace with China. The press made a considerable fuss about her involvement, and the leadership of the union demanded that she repudiate her signature and indicate that she had been duped into signing. This she was not prepared to do, though she agreed to withdraw from the organization, and her husband supported her stand. Patton, therefore, immediately fired him. Williams was outraged. Writing to Patton to urge Durr's reinstatement, he accused the farm leader of failing "to live up to your own ideals and the ideals of Roosevelt or any of the rest of us who have admired you and held you in great affection. I think you have given way to fear. I am saddened and I am disappointed. We have been through many things together. Whether we shall continue, I feel, depends more upon you than on me."[20]

The final breach came a year later, when Patton decided to hold the National Farmers Union convention in Dallas, even though it was a segregated city, and blacks, therefore, would be effectively precluded from attending. For Williams, that was the final straw. "It will destroy the only thing that was achieved down here, namely the recognition of the Negro as a farmer, just the same as the white man," he wrote in fury. "Nothing much else had come from the long hours put in by some of us, at our own expense, or the calumny we have endured. I don't think you often fight as hard as the situation demands."

Williams refused to attend the Dallas convention. His connection with the farmers union, and with Patton, ended there and then in an atmosphere of bitterness, cynicism, and disillusion, attitudes which, as he grew older and the postwar world departed more and more

from Roosevelt's dream of 1945, were tending to replace his optimism and his liberal-populist faith in human goodness and the inevitable triumph of right action. The decade of the 1950s was not a
happy one for him, as he grew older in a world that, increasingly, he
did not care for.[21]

What general political influence he had had as a result of his New
Deal connections had also dwindled away. On the local scene, he
enjoyed a certain stature, prestige, and even affection, as the town
oddball. Grover Hall, editor of the *Montgomery Advertiser*, once
wrote that he was "one of the few authentic radicals we have known
who was not a solemn, humorless ass. He is genially genteel, a
thoroughly companionable man who laughs all the way down to his
transverse colon," and went on to describe his courage in wearing
shorts in public, but he credited Williams with no real influence.
On the state level what political importance he might have had was
closely tied to that of Folsom, and that star was very firmly in the
descendant by the mid-1950s. Nationally, though he remained on
friendly terms with a number of powerful Democrats, such as Lyndon Johnson and Alabama's senators, Lister Hill and John Sparkman, his influence with the Truman administration or within the
Democratic party was negligible.

Initially, he had been a staunch ally of Truman's and, as has been
noted, had supported him strongly in the 1948 election. "Your civil
rights stand has been the greatest single happening in decent leadership since the Civil War," he had written him after his victory. "I had
the greatest satisfaction when you licked the bastards of having
been with you from the very start. When you get through with the
inauguration I'm going to ask you to let me come in at some time
when we can have an opportunity to talk. I'd like to do it quietly as
I want to help and not cause you any trouble." The president had
replied that he would very much like to see Williams again, but the
two men never did meet.

By 1950, however, they were drifting apart on a number of
issues. "I don't know what gets into the heads of you 'liberals,'" the
president wrote him testily after a Williams rebuke, "who think that
the man who sets the policies is going to change his mind with
every change of the moon." The course of American foreign policy
in the early 1950s accentuated that break. At first, Williams had
supported Truman's intervention in Korea. "There cannot be the

slightest doubt but what that the attack on Korea was mounted by the Russians," he had written his old friend C. B. "Beanie" Baldwin, once Roosevelt's farm security administrator, but now an outspoken critic of the administration. "We may not have done what we should have to lift and unify the Korean people, but we have not been liars and aggressors."

However, as the war dragged on he began to have real doubts. By the end of 1951 he had become an active critic of Truman's foreign policy, of the constriction of dissent at home, and of those liberals who still supported the president. Groups like the Americans for Democratic Action had to bear some of the responsibility for such things as loyalty oaths, he contended. "Had liberals stood four-square against limiting the basic rights, none of these things would have been able to wrap themselves in the respectability they enjoyed. Liberals gave them that respectability."[22]

Williams went to the national Democratic party convention in 1952 to support, as he had done in 1948, a strong civil rights platform, an action which, I. F. Stone commented, was "something no other white Southern liberal had the nerve to do. His appearance in Chicago was part of a consistent and hazardous pattern. Williams is living what he believes." His appeal went practically unnoticed. The Democratic party had moved on by 1952, and Williams was increasingly a lonely and forgotten figure, a relic within its ranks of an aspect of the recent past which, to some, was becoming a rather uncomfortable memory. He knew this, and was profoundly depressed. As he wrote in the *Southern Farm and Home* at this time, "We have turned our backs on the things which in the past have given us our strengths and made us the most trusted of nations." Appropriately, that article was accompanied by a picture of Roosevelt, captioned, "The only thing we have to fear is fear itself."[23]

Yet all was not universally "dark and dismal," to use another of his phrases. The return to Montgomery had had some beneficial effects on him personally. He saw much more of his family than he had for years. Aubrey, Jr., had been appointed circulation manager of the magazine, and lived in Montgomery, while Morrison, a student at the University of Alabama, was a frequent visitor home. Williams loved being back in the South, and though Anita, who had never lived there before, was not as happy, she hid her distress well. They had a few close friends, like the Durrs and the Woolleys, with whom they both were able to relax, and Williams was sufficiently tolerated as the town radical to be invited to join the occasional bull session, poker school, or golf game with people like Grover Hall or Ray Jenkins of the *Alabama Journal*. He always enjoyed the company of newspaper people, and Jenkins recalled the rounds of golf that they played as being exceedingly lengthy ones, for Williams insisted on discussing the issues of the day as they moved around the course. Moreover, when the grandchildren—Morrison's two girls and Aubrey, Jr.'s son and daughter—came to visit, as they often did, all was wonderful. Both Anita and Aubrey were devoted grandparents. Aubrey even had rows of safety pins attached to his overcoat, corresponding to their heights. He doted on them, especially the girls.[24]

In November 1950, Williams and the Bains purchased as an investment 2835 acres of mixed farmland in Autauga County, about forty miles from Montgomery, which they called Peace Farm. Later, Jane Foster and James Dombrowski, the executive director of the Southern Conference Educational Fund, and Williams's son Morrison, who from 1951 managed the property, and his wife Vivian were brought into the partnership. They hoped both to provide a rural retreat which all the partners could use from time to time and to make some money. The deed of partnership, drawn up on July 23, 1951, gave Williams authority to make decisions for the rest of them, if need be. He was, then, the senior partner, and certainly he got by far the most use out of the investment.

Sadly, Peace Farm made its owners very little money. Indeed, in 1953, when cattle prices fell drastically, the Williamses had to mortgage their home yet again in order to keep it barely afloat. By 1955 the venture had turned from cattle to corn, yet it was still losing money, partly owing to several wrong managerial decisions, and the partners began to put pressure on Williams to sell. Moreover, the man from whom Williams had borrowed money to purchase the property originally, and to whom he still owed $10,000, was threatening legal action and had every prospect of a successful judgment. Thus, it was decided to part with the property, even though Peace Farm had gotten into pig production and was at last beginning to show a profit. It was sold for $148,000 in April 1958, to the profound relief of the partners—Williams excepted. It had proved a financial disaster for them all. Like his other schemes to get rich quick, it had had rather the opposite effect. Once more, his long-suffering friends lost money on a project that he had initiated and with which he was most closely connected.[25]

Despite the financial worry that Peace Farm caused him—and he ended up putting over $40,000 into it from an original investment of $9,800, most of which he lost—Williams considered it all to have been worthwhile. He visited the property as often as he could and was never happier than when he was there, driving around the hills in a battered old Buick, his grandchildren by his side, all of them shrieking with delight at one of his jokes or singing lustily; working in the fields with his son Morrison, or on his own; getting up early in the morning just to smell the dew on the grass; cheerily presiding over family barbecues in the warm spring evenings. His friend E. D. Nixon, the chairman of the Montgomery chapter of the NAACP and "the only black allowed to hunt on Peace Farm," recalled that when Williams was on the property, he seemed oblivious to the increasing pressures of his existence as an outspoken liberal in an increasingly illiberal and conformist society.[26]

Without doubt the main reason for those pressures was his public stance on the racial issue. Williams had become president of the Southern Conference Educational Fund, the heir to the old Southern Conference for Human Welfare and the most militant anti-segregationist institution in the South in the immediate postwar years. It was to that organization that he was to give, eventually, the bulk of his time and his commitment.

12

The Southern Conference
Educational Fund

Established with high hopes in 1938, the Southern Conference for Human Welfare (SCHW) had passed the peak of its influence by 1946. Initially, it had been a coalition of various interest groups, educators, unionists, businessmen, and blacks united principally by their adherence to the principles of New Deal liberalism, their conviction that the South's salvation lay in the application of those principles to particular situations, and their desire to educate southerners in that philosophy and thus increase the likelihood of its being adopted.

It had become, however, a body geared more specifically to electoral politics and to opposing Jim Crow laws and practices. Moreover, although the organization was never dominated by Communists, members of the party did work within it. These changes in policy and the presence of Communists had caused many of the region's moderates, people like influential St. Louis publisher Mark Ethridge or journalist Barry Bingham, to leave its ranks. Never able to develop a mass base in the South and under constant attack because of its unorthodox racial stand, the SCHW had become heavily dependent on the CIO for financial support. In 1946, concerned that the taint of Communism attached to the SCHW was hindering "Operation Dixie," its ambitious organizing plan for the South, the CIO abruptly withdrew its aid, thus dealing the organization a mortal blow.

In January 1946, principally because its electoral activities were endangering its tax exempt status, the SCHW decided to separate its educational and political functions. The Southern Conference Educational Fund (SCEF) was created to direct all educational activities; henceforth the SCHW became purely a political action organization, working primarily through state committees. Clarke

Foreman, one-time special adviser to Harold L. Ickes on racial matters and president of the SCHW since 1942, headed the new body as well, but, despite this, the two were, to all intents and purposes, entirely separate.[1]

Though he had attended the SCHW's inaugural meeting in Birmingham in 1938, was close friends with many of its members, and undoubtedly shared its goals, Williams had had relatively little to do with the organization before his return to Alabama in 1945. While a public servant, he had deemed it unwise to be closely involved with such a pressure group, and during his period on the road for the National Farmers Union, he had had little time for such work. However, his reputation, his position, and his conviction ensured that that would change after his return to Montgomery. By 1946 he had accepted the position of Alabama state chairman and had also been elected to the conference's board of directors. Characteristically, he had taken those positions only after an assurance that no Communists were involved in the Alabama conference.[2]

Williams's election to the board coincided with the outbreak of a bitter dispute within the conference, in itself another reason for the rapid decline in its membership and influence. Since 1942 the conference had been administered by James A. Dombrowski. The son of a Tampa jeweler, Dombrowski had been educated at Emory, Berkeley, and Harvard before taking a doctorate under Reinhold Niebuhr at Union Theological Seminary. His dissertation, "The Early Days of Christian Socialism in America," was later published. A convinced Christian socialist himself, he had decided to devote his life to working for peaceful change in the South. He was staff director of the Highlander Folk School for ten years and in 1942 moved to the conference as its first full-time administrator, at the same time that Foreman took over as president.

The quiet, self-effacing, cautious Dombrowski was quite different in personality from the aggressive, decisive Foreman, and in time those differences began to affect the work of the conference. Foreman was irritated by what he considered to be Dombrowski's lack of initiative. Moreover, he considered his administrative inefficiency to have been partly responsible for the financial crisis that the conference found itself in in 1946. Accordingly, using the creation of the SCEF as a pretext and arguing that no man could be expected to administer both organizations, he persuaded the board of directors to remove Dombrowski from his position as administrator of the SCHW and transfer him full-time to the SCEF.[3]

Dombrowski was bitterly hurt by the decision, which had been taken without his knowledge or consent, though Foreman had managed to suggest otherwise to the board members. He refused to accept the transfer and eventually persuaded most of the board members that the matter should be reconsidered. Williams, however, was one who was not so persuaded. He urged Dombrowski to accept the new arrangement "and stop all this internal conflict." "I hope you will forgive me if I say I have had somewhat of deep experiences of the character you are doubtless going through," he wrote him. "When the President took me out of W.P.A. I felt let down and bitter but he was right. I saw it, happily after a few months, and came to look upon what he did as the finest of the many great things he did for me. I would not have swapped the N.Y.A. job for any job in the world, but I and my friends were very angry at first at what had been done."

Dombrowski remained unconvinced. He pointed out to Williams that as he had "only served on the Board a short time," he could not possibly be fully aware of either the background of Foreman's action or the ramifications of the decision. He would not, he said rather coldly, accept the board's decision without a fight. Thus, in this chilled climate began a relationship which was to develop into one of extreme warmth. Dombrowski and Williams eventually became the closest of colleagues and the best of friends.[4]

Eventually, Dombrowski was reinstated as conference administrator, but he remained there only a few months before moving voluntarily to the SCEF, on the condition that the *Southern Patriot*, the conference's newspaper, move with him. That was agreed to, and from then on, Dombrowski worked hard to disassociate the SCEF from the conference. The bitterness and distrust that the whole issue had caused had serious ramifications for the beleaguered SCHW. Throughout 1947 there was internal bickering and feuding. Prominent and long-term members, such as Mary McLeod Bethune and Roscoe Dunjee, head of the Oklahoma NAACP, resigned, several state branches suspended operations either officially or in fact and others were rendered ineffective by serious splits over the Cold War and Communist issues, and the conference's general financial position was grave. A report by HUAC on the conference, which, rather predictably, concluded that it was "a deviously camouflaged Communist-front organization," displaying "consistent anti-

American bias and pro-Soviet bias, despite professions, in generalities, of love for America," simply compounded its woes. By the end of 1947, it was on its last legs.[5]

As Alabama state president and a member of the national executive, Williams did what he could to stop the decline. The Alabama committee remained active. It strongly supported Folsom's political program and took steps to increase membership by establishing chapters in every part of the state. "We will do everything possible to organize grass roots support behind the Roosevelt Democrats who now hold three major political offices in the state," said Williams in announcing the move. In 1947 the committee published a pamphlet, "Building Together," in which it stated that its aim was "to promote the general welfare and to improve the economic, social, political, cultural and spiritual conditions of the people of Alabama without regard to race, creed, color or national origin." Under Williams the Alabama committee became the liveliest in the entire South, yet to little avail. Membership continued to slide; by September there were only 137 paid-up members in the whole state, despite all the publicity.[6]

On the national level, Williams attempted to prevent the conference getting too close to the Communists. For example, he opposed, though unsuccessfully, a decision to sponsor a series of concerts by the famous Negro bass Paul Robeson on those grounds. Meanwhile, he led the SCHW's defense against the HUAC allegations. A letter over his signature went out to ten thousand members, former members, and friends affirming his support for the body. He was appointed by the board to mediate in certain disputes with state committees, and he also chaired a subcommittee which investigated the conference's administrative structure and made certain recommendations.[7]

The task, however, was too great. The Wallace third-party candidacy simply hastened the inevitable. Foreman was a committed Wallace supporter, and his attempts to swing the conference officially behind the Wallace campaign caused a number of Truman liberals to leave the organization. When those attempts failed, other members left to work full-time for Wallace. Foreman himself resigned as president of the SCHW and the SCEF over the issue.

By May 1948, therefore, the SCHW was left virtually leaderless and without a function. Its demise was formalized at a board meet-

ing held in Richmond in November 1948, when Williams seconded
the motion that it be disbanded as being no longer necessary. Thus,
the conference died, as Thomas Krueger put it, "in obscurity and
neglected, forgotten both by its friends and its enemies."[8]

The SCEF still remained. The child had survived the parent, and
Williams had become its president after Foreman's resignation. Together with Dombrowski, he worked at disengaging it effectively
from the conference and narrowing its function to the elimination
"by educational means of racial discrimination and segregation, and
to promote in all possible ways greater understanding and friendship between people of diverse cultural backgrounds, to the end
that all may function as free members of a democratic society."

The SCEF had no members. Its activities were financed by the
donations of about three thousand contributors, all of whom received in return a subscription to the *Southern Patriot*. Policy was
decided by a board of directors and executed by Dombrowski
and Williams. The directors were a shifting group, distinguished
southerners in the main, both black and white, with educators and
clergymen predominating. Frank Porter Graham, president of the
University of North Carolina and later a United States senator,
Mary McLeod Bethune, Williams's friend from New Deal days,
Charles G. Gomillion, dean of the Tuskegee Institute graduate
school, and John Wesley Dobbs, one of Georgia's most influential
black politicians, were all SCEF directors at one time or another.
Williams would devote much of his time for almost the rest of his
days to this body, and he would make it into the most militantly
antisegregationist force in southern life in the late 1940s and early
1950s.[9]

The SCEF challenged segregation not through political activity
but through education, through the publicizing of the evils of the
system, through the advocacy of alternatives, through the encouragement of any breaches of the walls, and through constant and direct confrontation with those who held to the old ways. It attacked
Jim Crow on all fronts, in the schools, in the hospitals, in the work-
place. The *Southern Patriot* was the main vehicle through which its
views were disseminated, but it was open to the use of any method
that would advance the cause. Certain that the attitudes of the
South's political elites were about a generation behind those of the
ordinary people, Williams and Dombrowski were convinced that

constant publicity, together with the provision of alternatives, could and would bring change.

The two men worked well together and grew to like each other enormously. Williams, indeed, considered Dombrowski to be somewhat of a saint. "His honesty and integrity is so simon pure that it gets to be a bore at times," he once commented. They saw each other frequently, although Williams sometimes complained that he was unable to get to New Orleans, where the SCEF office was located, as often as he would have preferred, and they were in contact either by telephone or by letter virtually daily. It was not long before the SCEF became the most important aspect of Williams's life and Dombrowski one of his closest friends.[10]

One of the first things that they did together was to sponsor an interracial conference on civil rights at the University of Virginia on November 20, 1948. There nearly two hundred southerners signed the "Declaration of Civil Rights," which began, "We still believe that all men are created equal" and which advocated the repeal of all segregation ordinances. In a symbolic gesture, Williams led forty of the delegates on a pilgrimage to Monticello to announce the adoption of the statement. It was good theater and ensured wide press coverage of the conference, one of the first of its kind. There would be others. The organization of such meetings was always an important SCEF activity.[11]

It was in 1948 that the SCEF began what was to become a continuing campaign against segregation in education. In November, Dombrowski released the results of a poll concerning graduate education that the SCEF had carried out among southern educators. Ballots had been sent to every faculty member in eleven southern state universities, and although only a small number were returned, the result was seen as cause for some optimism. Of those who responded, 69 percent favored dropping segregation in graduate and professional school facilities, 28 percent preferred segregated regional schools, and only 3 percent wanted the continuance of the present segregated graduate school system. Williams believed that this result was strong evidence of changes in southern thinking about education and could be built upon.[12]

This concern to end segregation in graduate education was what led the SCEF to oppose the southern governors' plan to regionalize graduate education in the South. The product of a special governors' conference on education held early in 1948, the plan envisaged a regional system of specialist graduate schools accepting out-of-state students on a quid pro quo basis. It was presented as a means of providing quality education in the South at manageable cost. To Williams and the SCEF, however, it was seen as a device to circumvent Supreme Court decisions ordering the desegregation of graduate and professional schools in certain states because of inequality of facilities. Instead, blacks could be sent out of state, to a segregated regional institution.

The SCEF issued a press statement opposing the plan, and Williams spoke against it often and bitterly criticized it in private. The depth of his feeling on the issue can be seen in the tone of a letter that he wrote to John Ivey, director of the Board of Control for Southern Regional Education, on behalf of the SCEF. "I am sure that I am very unreasonable, and will probably succeed only in isolating myself from all good people," he admitted, but "I am fed up with the milk and water stuff and I can't take it any longer. It is not that I have too great a feeling of criticism for those brave souls who still are able to stomach the fight at half humane stages. It's just that I can't stomach it." Ivey resented being attacked in this way and accused Williams of "stereotyped thinking."

In one way this was true. By 1950, Williams's commitment to ending segregation in the South had become total. No matter what incidental merits the plan may have had, and it had some, the fact that it could be used to circumvent court decisions was enough to damn it utterly in his eyes. As he grew older, his views became, if anything, more uncompromising. People like Ivey, whom he saw as equivocating on the race issue, were the objects of increasingly bitter attack, while those few southerners who showed signs of opposing Jim Crow were enthusiastically praised. Dr. Clay Chennault, for example, dean of the University of Arkansas Medical School, which in 1948 desegregated its facilities, received a warm letter of commendation from Williams. His address "The Failure of Gradualism," which he delivered at Atlanta University in December 1949 and in which he attacked the whole philosophy behind gradual integration, was widely reprinted and, as much as anything else, established him as one of the South's most uncompromising critics.[13]

The SCEF's campaign against segregation in education gathered pace in the 1950s, as the Supreme Court continued to chip away at

Jim Crow's defenses. In 1950 it sponsored a South-wide conference on discrimination in higher education, again held at Atlanta University, which was attended by faculty members from fifty southern colleges and universities; in 1952 it organized an interracial youth conference at Allen University, in Columbia, South Carolina, which petitioned the Supreme Court, among other things, "to eliminate segregation in education." Williams was one of the featured speakers at that conference. In his address he argued that Jim Crow was dying. "Segregation is the one thing in our way of life that simply doesn't make sense to the majority of the world's people who are colored," he asserted. "It makes us appear as hypocrites."

In 1953 his position as a leading southern critic of the region's prevailing institutions was recognized when he was invited to debate the issue of public school desegregation on national television with Georgia's arch-segregationist governor, Herman Talmadge. Williams was extremely nervous before the debate, and later thought he had not done particularly well in it. "I let him out-talk me," he wrote. Nevertheless, the event gained him and the SCEF some national attention. As the crucial school desegregation cases moved through the court system, and as attitudes hardened, the SCEF was probably the most outspoken southern proponent of peaceful compliance. From 1953 it focused almost exclusively on that issue.[14]

Prior to that concentration, however, the SCEF had spent a considerable amount of time and money urging the desegregation of other public facilities. After a poll of southern hospital administrators had indicated some support for the abandonment of Jim Crow practices in medicine "if they thought the community was ready," the organization distributed the booklet "The Untouchables: The Meaning of Segregation in Hospitals." Beautifully produced and graphically illustrated by Ben Shahn, the pamphlet starkly documented the cost to the South in resources and, more important, in human lives of the maintenance of a dual hospital system. The SCEF continued to publicize incidents that illustrated the inequities of segregated medicine.[15]

In 1949 the SCEF's militant attack on the segregated South cost it its tax exempt status as an educational institution. The Internal Revenue Service ruled that its activities could in no way be considered apolitical and objective. Williams appealed, but the decision was upheld, probably correctly. Though the SCEF operated through publicity and persuasion rather than direct action, its focus was specific. Its only aim was to cleanse the South of its unjust social system, and in that respect it reflected completely the views of its president.

Indeed, his inability to act on these views in one situation caused him to submit his resignation as SCEF's president to Dombrowski. As was to be expected given Williams's views, the *Southern Farmer* was a union shop. As such, it was a lily-white shop; printers, like many southern labor unions, held to a strict segregationist stance. Williams tried in 1952 to hire a black printer, but opposition was so intense that he was forced to back down, and he contemplated resigning his post in the SCEF. He had no right, he wrote Dombrowski, to chair the SCEF until he could integrate his own business. "This whole thing has brought me up very sharply," he said, "and it poses for me a problem which I must solve." Dombrowski persuaded him to carry on, but he was never able to solve that particular problem. The opposition on the shop floor was too great. Williams, the friend of labor, was prevented by labor from an action that he earnestly wanted to take. The fact that he even contemplated resignation from the SCEF, given his commitment to it, is a further indication of how deeply his principles bit and of the high standards that he set for himself. Paul Woolley recalled that his inability to integrate the *Southern Farmer* caused him acute pain. Shortly after the incident one of the printers hung a cardboard "white only" sign over a drinking fountain on the shop floor. Williams's extreme anger as he tore it up, Woolley thought, was as much directed toward himself as toward the offending workman.[16]

By 1954 the SCEF had established itself as a militant critic of segregation at a time when most southerners were manning the barricades in defense of their way of life and viciously attacking those who dared oppose them. For this reason, a determined effort was made in that year to discredit and destroy the organization, as part of Senator James Eastland's "Great Southern Commie Hunt," to use a phrase from the *Montgomery Advertiser*. In many ways that attack would decisively shape Williams's economic, social, and even psychological condition for what remained of his life.

David Caute has referred to the anti-Communist hysteria that gripped the United States between 1947 and 1955 as producing perhaps the greatest crisis that America has ever suffered in its liberal and democratic values. During those years, for a complex of reasons—the rise of Marxist societies after World War II and their challenge to American power, the reaction to twenty years of reform at home and the determination of some to increase the pace of social change and others to reverse it, and the persistent belief that such changes, strains, and stresses could not have occurred without aid from traitors within—some groups made a massive attack on those values in the name of rooting out subversion.

The purges have been so closely associated with the man who most effectively rode the spirit of the age to national prominence and who gave it its name, Senator Joseph McCarthy of Wisconsin, that it is often forgotten that the fear did not begin with him and that he was simply its best-known beneficiary. President Truman and the liberals first introduced the loyalty tests, the loyalty oaths, and the committees of inquiry that characterized the period. Their avowed purpose was to find Communists, former Communists, and fellow-travelers who were working for the federal government, and they did find a few. Given the numbers who drifted in and out of the Communist party in the 1930s, it would have been surprising if that had not been the case. The question of their loyalty a decade or so later, however, was another issue, one that their inquisitors were often not disposed to pursue. Employees found to have tainted backgrounds were invariably summarily dismissed and sometimes prosecuted. As the fear spread, the inquiry broadened into many other areas: the arts, the professions, the education system, the unions. Thousands of people, usually of liberal sympathies, were accused of subversion, generally without evidence, and their lives were often shattered as a result. It was an irrational and bitter time.

Other politicians soon found that it was possible to use the climate of fear for their own ends. For some southerners it represented a chance to reverse the unwelcome pace of social change in their region. In a series of decisions the United States Supreme Court had begun to breach the walls of segregation, particularly in public education, and southerners feared that a general ruling against segregated schooling might soon come. Moreover, pressure groups such as the SCEF were becoming increasingly insistent in their demands for change. The temptation, therefore, was to link such groups with subversion and thus discredit them. If it could be shown that behind their insistence on equality was a determination to further the Communist cause, any influence they might have had would be destroyed. In the columns of the *Southern Farmer*, Williams had often attacked the assault on basic freedoms that the Communist witch-hunt represented. Now he and the SCEF were to become its victims.[17]

On March 6, 1954, as he was "exterminating pestiferous big red ants on Peace Farm," a United States marshal arrived to serve him a subpoena. The document summoned him to New Orleans to appear before the Subcommittee on Internal Security of the Committee on the Judiciary, United States Senate, at a hearing to be held from March 16, "there to testify what you may know relative to the subject matters under consideration by said committee."

The Subcommittee on Internal Security was formed in 1950 under the provisions of the Internal Security Act, and the conservative Nevada Democrat Patrick McCarran was its first chairman. Reconstituted in 1953 after the Republicans took control of the Senate under the chairmanship of Indiana senator Williams E. Jenner, it was charged with the broad task of investigating "communism in government." Jenner, an ardent admirer of Senator McCarthy, could, in the words of Robert E. Griffith, "be trusted to pummel the Democrats without embarrassing the Republicans as well."[18]

The arrival of the subpoena did not totally surprise Williams, for he had been half-expecting it since late January, when the Senate appropriated $228,000 for the Internal Security Subcommittee. At that time, Senator Jenner had announced plans to investigate alleged subversion in a number of bodies. "We haven't caught up with the leadership of the Communist underground in these United States," he had declared at the time, "but we are still on its trail." One of the groups scheduled for scrutiny was the SCEF.[19]

Williams's reaction to that announcement was characteristically combative. He immediately wired Jenner, calling the announcement

> as dishonest as it is contemptible. You well know that in the present state of fear and hysteria the words you use stand for subversion and disloyalty to the United States. . . . For my part if you have any charges against me, I suggest you refer them to a grand jury in order that the truth of the matter may be arrived at in the American way by trial in an impartial court . . . on the basis of evidence and not of gossip, and with

the right to be confronted by my accusers. . . . The only
activity in which SCEF has been engaged has been its fight for
the abolition of discrimination. . . . You may regard this as
Un-American, but it is unthinkable that an American jury will
agree with you.[20]

He released this telegram to fifty newspapers and followed it up
with letters to a number of his friends in the Senate in which he
appealed to them to try and stop the investigation and charged
Jenner with waging war on liberals generally. His friends, too, lobbied on his behalf. Myles Horton asked Senator Estes Kefauver to
help Williams, "who is under attack because he has consistently
backed the more liberal candidates and opposed the Dixiecrats,"
while a number of black leaders angrily protested the projected
probe. At a special meeting the SCEF board of directors endorsed
the Williams telegram and petitioned Jenner to call off the inquiry,
but it agreed that, should the hearing proceed, each person summoned should answer the committee as guided "by his conscience
and integrity." So encouraged was Williams by the expressions of
support that he wrote to Dombrowski in some triumph to express
his doubt, on the basis of what he had heard from Washington, that
the hearing would ever get off the ground.[21]

He should not have been so sanguine. His friends were full of
anger, sympathy, and offers of moral support. They deplored, in the
words of one of them, Senator James E. Murray of Montana, "this
new example of the depths which certain of our politicians are
willing to stoop in their greed for power." Promises of hard action,
however, were few. The bulk of the responses, in fact, indicated
how powerless most liberals had allowed themselves to become
during the McCarthy era. As his old friend Harley Kilgore wrote,
"You know how difficult it is to do anything at present, due to fa-
naticism." From columnist Joseph Alsop, another friend, he received
support and a wish that he could do more. "But what?" wrote
Alsop. "It is so often like this." Moral support, sympathy, heart-
sickness—these were not enough. The subpoena duly arrived.[22]

The serving of the document prompted an immediate, and characteristic, Williams counterattack. He issued a press statement deploring "the climate of politics" that now made him "an Internal
Security risk" even though all his activities had been carried out "in

plain view of the public and for many years," and he renewed his private appeals for support. To Mary McLeod Bethune he wrote to urge that she mobilize black opinion on his behalf. As he pointed out, the inquiry had resulted, in his view, from an agreement between Jenner and several southern politicians, including Herman Talmadge, to destroy the SCEF because of its prointegration statements and sympathies. He had already approached several black papers for support, he told her, with the overlay of bitterness that crept into his statements in the last years of his life, but very little had been forthcoming so far. "It begins to seem that when certain people want something," he asserted, "they are very free about asking some of us for help, but when I want something they do mighty little. I don't mind saying I'm pretty burned up about it."

He appealed to John Popham, southern correspondent of the *New York Times*, to attend the hearing personally, so that "it would receive fair press coverage" from the nation's leading newspaper. To Mary Anderson Bain he wrote, rather flamboyantly, that in some ways he was glad he had been so summoned: "I have longed to have a sling at some of those destroyers. . . . I have worked hard to merit this selection by this evil force. . . . This is the way the fight has always had to be made. Thank our stars we can have a small part in it." Besides, there was some good in everything. He had not had the opportunity to visit the New Orleans racetrack for some time. The enforced trip would at least give him a chance to rectify that.[23]

The actual public announcement of the hearing was made not by Jenner but by the subcommittee's ranking Democrat, Senator James O. Eastland, of Mississippi. Eastland, from Sunflower County in the Mississippi Delta, had entered the Senate in 1941 on the death of Senator Pat Harrison and had quickly become one of its most vocal proponents of segregation. Senator Herbert H. Lehman of New York, in fact, once called him a "symbol of racism." Eastland was a Dixiecrat in 1948, and at the time of the hearing was one of Senator McCarthy's strongest supporters.

His announcement came at a dinner held in his honor in Memphis, Tennessee, on March 8, where he received four awards for fighting Communism. He stated that he would be accompanied to New Orleans only by his Democratic colleagues senators McCarran and John L. McClellan of Arkansas. No Republicans were to be present. Besides Williams, Dombrowski, Professor Alva Taylor, formerly of the University of Tennessee's divinity school and then secretary-treasurer of the SCEF, and one white SCEF director, Myles Horton, were subpoenaed. No blacks were to be questioned, despite their numerical majority on SCEF's board. Three other subpoenas were served. Two were to men of whom Williams had never heard and who had had no formal connection with the SCEF, Leo Sheiner, an attorney, and Max Shlafrock, a contractor, both of Miami. They had once worked with Dombrowski on a committee investigating anti-Semitism in that city. The third was to Williams's friend Virginia Durr, once again of Montgomery.[24]

Virginia Durr had been an outspoken proponent of the black cause for many years. Born in Birmingham, the daughter of a prominent clergyman, she had grown up in a genteel, upper-middle-class southern way. During her period in Washington, however, she moved quite far to the left and became active politically in her own right. As a member of the SCHW, she had led its struggle against the poll tax. In 1948 she was a candidate for the Senate on the Progressive party ticket. Though one of the most prominent and outspoken of southern liberals, she had had no formal connection with the SCEF since 1950, when she resigned as a director upon her husband's appointment as counsel to the National Farmers Union and their attendant and ill-fated move to Colorado. She also happened to be the sister-in-law of Justice Hugo Black, not a favorite with southern conservatives.[25]

Those subpoenaed all issued formal press statements that asserted that neither they nor the SCEF had any Communist connections, claimed that Jenner and Eastland were motivated, at least in part, by a desire to "smear" the memory of the Roosevelt administration, and deplored the general attempt to "destroy all liberal thought and action in the U.S." They accelerated, too, their private counterattack.

In that campaign, Virginia Durr was particularly effective. Like Williams, she still had powerful friends in Washington. One they had in common was the Senate minority leader, Lyndon Johnson, a friend of Williams's since the early days of the NYA and a longtime admirer of Virginia Durr's. Very late on March 10, she phoned him to demand that he do what he could to curb his colleagues' anticipated excesses. Senator Johnson sleepily—his wife had had to waken him—professed ignorance of the forthcoming hearings, deplored them, doubted, given the climate of the times, that he could halt them altogether, but indicated that he would try and persuade senators McClellan and McCarran to stay in Washington. Knowing Williams and Durr as he did, particularly their propensity for giving as good as they got, he thought that Eastland on his own could do them comparatively little damage.

Johnson's powers of persuasion were effective. Eastland arrived in New Orleans on March 17, later than expected and without his two colleagues. Ominously, however, he was accompanied by Paul Crouch, an ex–Communist organizer turned paid government informer, who had been a key witness at a number of important trials involving the Smith Act, as well as several internal security hearings, including that of J. Robert Oppenheimer. Indeed, it was Crouch's memorandum "Communist Infiltration in the American Armed Forces" that had sparked the Army-McCarthy hearings, which had begun to dominate the nation's news media. His arrival gave the probe, due to open the next day, a new dimension.[26]

The hearing began at ten o'clock in the morning. Assisting Eastland were the subcommittee's special counsel, Richard Arens, and two staff members. The first testimony came from two members of the Anti-Subversive Committee of the Young Men's Business Club of New Orleans. These young men claimed that the SCHW had been a Communist front and that the SCEF was its direct descendant, with the name changed "to confuse the people." Dombrowski, they alleged, had "a record of continually supporting the Communist Party line" and a long history of identification with Communist causes. During their testimony Dombrowski's lawyer, Benjamin E. Smith, who had been denied permission by Eastland to cross-examine, asked that the rules of procedure be outlined. The senator's reply—"I will announce them when I desire"—indicated that witnesses could well expect to be grilled on almost anything and that they would not necessarily be able to dispute any adverse testimony.[27]

And so it proved. The next witness, Leo Sheiner, was never asked about the SCEF, but was instead interrogated repeatedly concerning his alleged Communist party membership. After several angry exchanges with Eastland over the propriety of such a line of questioning, he took the Fifth Amendment.

Paul Crouch then made his first appearance. He identified himself as having been for seventeen years a Communist party activist in the South and then identified Sheiner as being "an important undercover member in the Communist Party." He further testified that, in his certain knowledge, the sole function of the SCHW and the SCEF, its lineal descendant, was "to promote Communism" in the South. "It was intended to lead to class hatred," he stated, "to race hatred, dividing class against class and race against race as its real objectives despite the words that were put on paper, some of them by myself."[28]

Sheiner returned to the stand and again refused to answer any questions concerning his activities or associations, except to deny that he was currently a Communist party member. He was eventually excused, but not before Senator Eastland had excoriated him as "a disgrace to the United States." Max Shlafrock had a similar experience. Again Eastland showed little interest in his supposed SCEF relationship, but questioned him about general connections with the Communist party. Like Sheiner, Shlafrock refused to answer on constitutional grounds and was quickly excused.[29]

Next Eastland called Dombrowski. Immediately the two men became locked in a bitter dispute concerning the SCEF's records, which Dombrowski had been instructed to bring with him. He provided the names of all officeholders and directors, but refused to hand over a list of the organization's three thousand contributors. He insisted that the subpoena had not called for those, a position that even subcommittee counsel Arens confirmed. Senator Eastland, however, disagreed and warned Dombrowski that failure to provide the names could lead to contempt charges against him. The interrogation then followed the same pattern as those of Sheiner and Shlafrock. Although they asked a few questions about the SCEF's membership and activities, both Eastland and Arens concentrated much more on probing Communist influence in the old SCHW and identifying Dombrowski as closely as possible with alleged Communist and Communist-front groups. He answered all questions except those to do with SCEF contributors, after denying that he had ever been a party member or "under Communist discipline." Crouch was again called, as was another former Communist turned government witness, John Butler. Both testified that they had met Dombrowski at party meetings in the 1940s, and both identified him as a party member. Crouch, indeed, stated that Dombrowski had always been considered one of the "topflight operators."

Dombrowski vehemently denied their allegations and claimed that he had never seen Butler before. He did admit to having once known Crouch slightly, but not in connection with SCHW or SCEF activities, and insisted that he had never suspected him of being a member of the Communist party. The first day of hearings concluded with Dombrowski still on the stand, still being questioned about his alleged associations with known Communists. Senator Eastland seemed sure that he had already uncovered a subversive of the first rank.[30]

While the opening day of the hearing was doubtless difficult and distressing for those under investigation, it was not by any means the focus of national attention. The United States had had a plethora of investigations in the past few years, and the noisy preliminaries to the Army-McCarthy drama currently held the national interest. Few were concerned about the tribulations or treachery of an obscure southern group. Major newspapers like the *Washington Post* or the *New York Times* carried no reports at all of the investigation, while in the South only the *New Orleans Times Picayune* gave it extended coverage. That was to change, however. The drama of days two and three, the allegations made, the charges and counter-charges, the reactions of accuser and accused, the character and background of the personalities involved—all would ensure the brief diversion of at least some national attention.

Dombrowski returned to the stand the next morning. Again he was asked for a list of SCEF contributors, and again he refused. Eastland then dismissed him, after refusing him permission to "discuss the activity of the fund [SCEF] for a brief minute," an odd ruling given the hearing's supposed purpose. The next witness was Virginia Durr.[31]

The appearance of this striking southern lady was a turning point in the proceedings. She was accompanied to the stand by her lawyer, John P. Kohn of Montgomery, who immediately counseled her to remain silent. He then advised Eastland that for a number of reasons, but specifically excluding the Fifth Amendment, his client refused to answer any questions at all, but did wish to explain why she had decided to adopt this course. The request was rather promptly denied her, and the questioning began. It was a one-sided interrogation. Durr identified herself, agreed that she was married to Clifford Durr, and denied that she was under Communist discipline, but to all other questions she either did not respond or simply stated that she stood "mute."[32]

Somewhat discomfited, Eastland warned her that she was in contempt and brought back Crouch and Butler. Butler claimed that she had been closely identified with Communist groups and causes in the 1930s and 1940s, although he would not state definitely that she was a party member. Crouch was more specific. Claiming to have known the Durrs during his Communist party days, he charged that Virginia Durr had used her kinship with Justice Black and her friendship with Mrs. Roosevelt to introduce top Communists into White House circles during the days of the New Deal. By so doing, he averred, she had made the Roosevelts the unwitting accomplices of Soviet espionage activity. Not only was she under Communist party discipline throughout the New Deal years, he charged, but "she went beyond that; she plotted with the Communist leaders to exploit her relationship as a sister-in-law of a Justice of the Supreme Court in the interests of the World Communist conspiracy and interest of overthrowing our Government."

With that, she was excused, and she promptly and ostentatiously began powdering her nose, to the delight of the press photographers. Their reporter colleagues were still digesting the startling statement that Hugo Black's sister-in-law had been instrumental in enabling Soviet agents to penetrate the White House social scene.[33]

It was now Williams's turn to appear. He, too, had brought his lawyer, Clifford Durr, who immediately objected to the whole proceedings, and was promptly overruled. Eastland and Williams had first met in 1932, during Williams's stint in Mississippi with the Reconstruction Finance Corporation, and they had had intermittent contact since then. They cordially disliked each other; however, Eastland had sufficient respect for Williams's past prominence and continuing connections to treat him with much more courtesy than he had the previous witnesses. Williams was asked a series of questions about the SCEF's function, all of which he answered fully. Like Dombrowski, he refused to provide a list of contributors. He was then allowed, without any harassment, to make several statements disavowing any Communist involvement in the organization. He was also questioned about his New Deal activities and some of his past personal associations. When asked if he recognized Crouch, he denied ever having known the man, ever having been a member of the Communist party, and ever having knowingly associated with Communists.[34]

Back came Butler and Crouch. Butler testified that he had been introduced to Williams in 1942 as "Comrade Williams, who is a party member," and that he had also attended a closed party meeting with him. At that point, Williams, furious with rage, interrupted the testimony. "I feel it a personal privilege to say that I challenge this man to go out into the hall and make that statement in the presence of newspapermen," he roared. "I'll sue him the minute he does it." Butler agreed to comply later, and the hearings continued. Crouch was equally explicit. Claiming to have met Williams several times in the 1930s and 1940s, he insisted that Williams had reported on aspects of party work in the South and that his "activities always coincided with the work and the interests of the Communist party." Moreover, Crouch assured the senator that "I would not have made the statements I made to him to anyone, unless I had been privately informed as I had been by Rob Hall that he was a secret member of the Communist party."[35]

Then occurred one of the more bizarre aspects of this rather unusual hearing. After Crouch's identification of Williams as a party member, Senator Eastland gave Clifford Durr permission to cross-examine, though that had been denied the previous witnesses, and the lawyer took full advantage of the opportunity. He elicited from Crouch considerable detail on his activities as a Communist and repeatedly suggested that he had been "trained in deception." He was also able to show that Crouch's recollections of past meetings and conversations, on which the government had relied so heavily at this and earlier hearings, seemed disturbingly imprecise. Crouch was unsure of just when he had left the Communist party, for example; nor could he answer with any specificity questions relating to his allegedly frequent meetings with Williams.

Crouch showed such signs of discomfort that, in an attempt to take the heat off him, Arens intervened to ask him if he thought Durr was a Communist. He was not sure if he was still one, the witness replied, but he knew that he had been once. The committee room erupted with laughter, in which, according to Williams, even Eastland joined, as he moved to have Crouch's reply stricken from the record. Durr, however, did not laugh. "This testimony is under oath," he shouted. "Let's leave it in, under oath." Reluctantly, the senator agreed. Shortly afterward, Williams returned to the stand again to deny that he had ever met Butler or Crouch previously and to repudiate categorically the notion that the SCEF was simply the old SCHW with the name changed, though he admitted that there was some "overlapping." "The Southern Conference Educational Board," he asserted, "is made up of a considerable number of people who were never in the Conference for Human Welfare." With that he was excused.

What followed was without doubt unscheduled. Clifford Durr was granted the right to question Crouch about the assertion that he, Durr, had once been a Communist. Crouch then claimed that he had met the lawyer several times at closed party meetings between 1938 and 1941, but he was unable to provide any details of Durr's activities there. Crouch did charge, however, that the party had used both Durrs from time to time as transmission belts to Justice Black.

Then the lawyer became witness. Insisting that he be given the chance to testify under oath, Durr asserted flatly that "the statement that Mr. Crouch saw me in Communist Party meetings in New York during the years 1938 to 1941 or at any other time is a complete and absolute falsehood. I have never been a member of the Communist Party. I have no intention of being a member of the Communist Party. I have never taken the Communist discipline and this statement is completely and absolutely false. One or the other of us should be indicted for perjury." He left the hearing in no doubt as to his view on who that should be. Arens then asked him a few questions, mainly about his term as president of the National Lawyers Guild, and with that the second day concluded.

It had produced sufficient fireworks—the assertions that the sister-in-law of a Supreme Court justice had introduced Communists to the White House, that a New Deal administrator as important as Aubrey Williams had been a secret party member, Virginia Durr's standing "mute," her husband's demand for a perjury indictment—to ensure national attention. The major newspapers featured the proceedings, usually accompanied by the photograph of Virginia Durr powdering her nose. The *New York Times* described the hearing as "stormy," while the *New York Herald Tribune* suggested that contempt charges would probably be brought against Virginia Durr, Dombrowski, and Williams because of their refusals to answer questions or provide certain information.[36]

The next day brought more drama. Williams's friend Myles Horton, director of the Highlander Folk School in Monteagle, Tennessee, and an SCEF board member, was the first to be called. Highlander was a community school; its principal aim was to educate southern "rural and industrial leaders for democratic living and activity." Its political cast was leftward, and its survival was always problematic; yet it had existed since 1932, mainly providing short courses for labor leaders. It was also a center for interracial activity and propaganda. As such, it had long been regarded with extreme hostility by southern conservatives, while most of the region's social radicals had at one time or another been connected with it. Dombrowski had once taught there, Williams was on its board of governors, and the Durrs had both participated in its courses. All had been questioned at the hearing about their Highlander connections.

It was Highlander's activities, not his SCEF involvement, that Eastland wished to explore with Horton. He did not get very far. Horton, always a tempestuous man, soon showed a distaste for the senator's line of questioning and attempted to make a statement of principle. When refused leave to do so, he kept speaking anyway, and at Eastland's order he was forcibly ejected from the room. As he was dragged through the doors, he shouted, "They're treating me like a criminal."

Crouch returned briefly and named the alleged Communists whom Virginia Durr had assisted in breaching the White House walls. One of those happened to be Joseph P. Lash, Mrs. Roosevelt's protégé from New Deal days and the leader of the opposition to the Communist takeover of the American Youth Congress. The hearing concluded with a disquisition from another government witness, a Richard English, on the nature of Communist fronts. In his concluding remarks, Eastland stated that the hearings were part of "a general investigation over the South of the Communist Party, of Communist front organizations," that more would certainly be scheduled, and that the subcommittee would soon "convene again in the city of Birmingham for some hearings in that town."[37]

Testimony had concluded, but not the drama. As the committee room cleared, Crouch and Clifford Durr found themselves face to face. The frail, normally mild-mannered lawyer lost control. "You dirty dog," he cried, lunging at the witness. "I'll kill you for lying about my wife." Federal marshals quickly bundled Crouch away, but Durr, who was not in good health, suffered a mild heart attack and was rushed to the hospital. The incident provided good copy, and an even better photograph for the nation's newspapers; it was also a good indication of the tensions aroused by the events of the preceding three days.[38]

In a press conference just after the incident, Senator Eastland seemed somewhat shaken by what had occurred, and he admitted that Crouch had not convinced him that either Durr or Williams was a Communist. The journalists who had covered the hearings went further than that. When polled by the *Montgomery Advertiser* as to who in the hearings posed the greatest threat to American ideals, half the journalists pointed to Eastland, and most of the remainder chose Crouch. No one voted for Williams or the Durrs.

In general, newspapers that commented editorially on the proceedings, and most of those were in the South, echoed that opinion. A few, like the *New Orleans Times Picayune*, though unsympathetic to the SCEF, considered the hearing to be "messy" and a discredit to all concerned. Most were more outspoken. In a widely reprinted column, "Eastland Follows McCarthy," the editor of the *St. Petersburg Times* commented that the hearing showed that "McCarthyism is a virus not confined to any one Senator or any one party" and called on "responsible Southern Senators" to do something drastic about Eastland. The *Montgomery Advertiser* was even more critical. "There is a matter of Southern honor involved here. A Southern gentleman and lady have been publicly branded with the most opprobrious term of the hour. They have denied it under oath. . . . This is a type of character lynching which Southern Senators should deeply resent."[39]

Allan F. Rankin, the *Montgomery Advertiser*'s liberal columnist, branded the whole investigation a "tragi-farce," spoke of "political witch-hunting and citizen-baiting," and called Eastland "a demagogue out for political glory." He believed, however, "that demagogues who try to capitalize on such persecutions as this are on the way out." Two days later the *St. Louis Post Dispatch* labeled the treatment of the witnesses "cause for anger and shame" and urged that thought be taken "of the honor of Congress and of the free citizens of a free land."

The few nonsouthern newspapers that commented editorially

generally held similar views. The *Lyttleton Independent* (Colorado) talked of "the smashing of four spirits." Describing the Durrs, Dombrowski, and Williams as "liberals fighting for a new day in the South," the paper asked, "Is it necessary for Eastland to break the backs and spirits of outstanding citizens who have devoted their lives to their country? Does the Senator realize that it is the liberals who have given the common man a new life and made him reject Communism?" That paper also equated Eastland and McCarthy. "It is no wonder Eastland and McCarthy have never caught a single spy," mocked the editor. "They can't do it under Kleig lights."

In her widely syndicated "My Day," Eleanor Roosevelt defended her old friend Williams and Virginia Durr. "We had better understand," she wrote, "what Communism really is. . . . Those who hold liberal views which may go a little further than their most conservative neighbors are still not Communists." She also denied that Durr would ever have had the chance, "even if she wanted to," of getting information from the White House. Both the black press and the liberal newsmagazines deplored the hearing and the manner in which it was conducted. Given the tensions of the times, the generally sympathetic press reaction, especially that of the southern press, was both surprising and heartening to Williams and his friends.[40]

Probably buoyed by this press sympathy and by the hundreds of letters of support that he and the Durrs received—many expressing the wish that Durr had either "socked the bastard" or committed other equally violent action on Crouch's person—Williams again approached his Washington friends. There were still possible contempt citations to be dealt with. Moreover, Williams did not relish the prospect of a repeat performance in June, when Eastland had proposed to bring the subcommittee to Birmingham. In any case he had been outraged by the whole affair. He wanted such things stopped, and he wanted some redress.[41]

To his friends he wrote long accounts of what had happened. To Senator Paul Douglas he stated that "if you have never taken the time to attend one of these Senate investigating committee hearings you can't possibly believe what actually happens is taking place in the United States. . . . You had a feeling that you had absolutely no rights whatsoever, which in fact you didn't have in so far as the hearing was concerned." He begged his senatorial friends to help "stop this thing" and concluded, "Nothing else that is happening to us it seems to me is to be compared in importance to what these investigating committees are doing to destroy the fundamental safeguards of the people."[42]

His friends duly replied. Senator Hubert Humphrey declared himself very troubled by Williams's letter and by other reports he had heard. "I hope you don't mind," he asked, "if I use your letter in discussions with some of my colleagues. . . . There is involved a very serious violation of civil liberties. We must do something about it." Douglas, too, promised to help. "I have little confidence in the professional witness [Crouch] you mention. . . . He may be another Titus Oates. We shall keep pressing for the essential Congressional reforms. In the meantime, I feel deeply for all you are going through. But I am confident your reputation will stand."[43]

But promises of possible reforms, while cheering, did not help much with contempt citations and the projected hearings. Quick action was needed. Early in April, Williams lunched in Washington with his two closest senatorial friends, Lister Hill and Lyndon Johnson. Both told him not to worry; they guaranteed to sort the matter out. Williams returned from Washington a somewhat relieved man. Thus, the announcement on May 9, 1954, that Eastland's proposed Birmingham probe of Communism in Alabama would not take place because of "the press of Senate business" and press suggestions that Williams had "been assured by Senate Democratic leaders he would not be cited for contempt, and was given a pledge the Durrs would likewise be absolved" came as no surprise to him. Johnson had told him all that two weeks earlier.[44]

So the great southern "Commie hunt" came to an abrupt end. The Subcommittee on Internal Security made no further sorties into Dixie, and Senator Eastland turned to other things. If, as was suggested, he had been hoping to advance his national political career by uncovering regional subversives, he must have been disappointed at the result. The three days in New Orleans had brought him more adverse publicity than good.

Yet the hearing had left its mark on those involved. For the minor players Sheiner and Shlafrock, it meant the end of their professional lives in Miami. The Florida Bar Association moved to disbar Sheiner in retaliation for his taking the Fifth Amendment, while Shlafrock found there was no future in that city for a contractor suspected of Communism. For both men the accusation of subversion was sufficient to ruin them. The Durrs were not ruined, but Clifford Durr found that his opportunities to make a living as a lawyer in Montgomery, which had always been precarious, were even further restricted. To be branded a Communist was, in the eyes of many of his fellow citizens, tantamount to proof. Moreover, what little social contact they had had with whites outside their small liberal circle was terminated.[45]

Ironically, Paul Crouch, the professional witness, also lost as a result of those March days in New Orleans. He never testified for the government again. Joseph Alsop, who had not known how to assist his friend Williams when the hearings were first scheduled, certainly went into action upon their completion. In a series of widely syndicated columns, the result of a detailed investigation of Crouch's evidence at a number of trials and hearings over the years, he and his brother Stewart exposed so many glaring inconsistencies in his testimonies that the attorney general, Herbert Brownell, at a press conference with Alsop at his side, announced that Crouch would no longer be used as a witness and that, possibly, perjury charges would be preferred against him.[46]

Crouch fought back. He demanded that the Alsops, Brownell, and Deputy Attorney General William P. Rogers be investigated for possible Communist sympathies. Somewhat ironically, he appealed to the ACLU for assistance in mounting his defense. Senator Jenner was quick to term Crouch's charges "absurd." The committees and congressmen for whom he had provided so much that they wanted to hear now wished to have no more to do with him. He died of lung cancer in November 1955, almost unnoticed. There were very few obituaries; perhaps the kindest came from one of those whom he had accused, Clifford Durr. Writing in *I. F. Stone's Weekly*, Durr called him "not the source of the evil, but its mere conduit. Crouch did what he was hired to do. . . . He died a lonely and despised man by those who used him, but those who hired him remain in respectable and powerful positions. They used him, and when he was of no further use to them they threw him aside." After Crouch's death his widow, left penniless, wrote to Williams asking for money. In compassion, he sent her some.[47]

For the SCEF, Dombrowski, and Williams, the aftermath of the hearing was more complex. Dombrowski thought that the SCEF benefited from the exposure, and this may have been true in the short term. There was a host of inquiries as to its activities, and in May 1954 twenty-five new directors, most of whom were white, were added to the board. The organization continued its fight for an integrated South, its relative strength apparently undiminished by the experience. Yet, in the long run, the SCEF was hurt by New Orleans. As the civil rights movement grew in strength and respectability, a number of the more important new groups, especially those with predominantly Negro leadership, wanted little to do with it because of the Communist taint left by the investigation. Roy Wilkins, for example, chairman of the Leadership Conference on Civil Rights, a body formed to coordinate civil rights activity, refused, ostensibly on technical grounds, the SCEF's application to join. Such treatment was a prime reason for the organization's decline in importance toward the end of the 1950s, and, incidentally, for much of Williams's bitterness in the last years of his life. He felt betrayed and rejected by his friends and by the people whom he had fought so hard to help.[48]

Williams's business was hurt somewhat by the publicity surrounding the New Orleans hearing, as he lost some advertising. Yet the hearing was eventually to have a profound effect on his life. In May 1955 the American Legion monthly publication *Firing Line* devoted its whole issue to "Communism in Agriculture"; largely based on his New Orleans testimony, most of the issue was an attack on Williams and on the *Southern Farm and Home*. The July issue contained an attack on the SCEF, also largely based on what was alleged at the hearing.

Williams was outraged. As the official transcript of the hearing had not yet been published, there had, in his view, been collusion between the subcommittee and *Firing Line*. He began to consider a lawsuit, and also approached an old New Deal acquaintance, Louis Johnson, formerly assistant secretary of war and then the legion's national commander. Johnson promised to prevent any further attacks, and he did so, but by that time the damage had been done.

Firing Line had a large circulation in the South. After the two articles, Williams's business lost printing contracts, and there was a further, and this time serious, drop in advertising revenues. Indeed, in 1955 he was not even allowed to bid on a state Department of Agriculture publication. He protested to his friend Governor Folsom that that was "a pretty damn sorry way to treat any person who has on all occasions stood up for you and tried to be as helpful as possible," but to no avail. In the current climate, there was nothing the governor felt disposed to do. Williams's business, always precarious, was now doomed. The unsubstantiated accusations had materially affected his livelihood. They also meant increased loneliness. Williams wrote that "you can't do very much about the black mark such a thing puts into the minds of people. I like to play poker and golf, meeting with other men for bull sessions." There would be less of that now.[49]

The committee's report, along with the transcript of the hearing, was published in September 1955. The report was brief and concluded that "the Southern Conference Education Fund Inc. is operating with substantially the same leadership and purposes as its predecessor organization, the Southern Conference for Human Welfare." That organization, it asserted, "was conceived, financed and set up by the Communist Party in 1938 as a mass organization to promote Communism throughout the Southern States." The report recommended an investigation by the attorney general and the Subversive Control Board.[50]

However, no such investigation was forthcoming. The report was quietly filed away and forgotten, except by those who had been hurt. This strengthened even further Williams's conviction that such investigating committees had no place in a democratic society. As late as 1958 he was still thinking of petitioning the Senate "for the redress of grievances done to him by the Internal Security Subcommittee. . . . I could have one hell of a lot of fun." It was a direct result of this that his last public office was chairman of the National Committee to Abolish the House Un-American Activities Committee.[51]

The investigation of the SCEF, one of many examples during the McCarthy era of the harrying of domestic dissenters in the supposed pursuit of subversion, was probably the turning point in the organization's existence. From then on, no matter how unjustly, it bore a certain stigma in the eyes of many, and its work and influence suffered as a result. For Williams, too, the experience was crucial. The treatment that he had received left him embittered; what last vestiges of optimism he had had about the South's capacity for change had gone. His business had been badly affected; his social and private life had been further constricted; and he was increasingly subject to harassment and vilification, lonely and without influence in a milieu which oppressed him. The last years in Montgomery were not happy ones, the more so when the onset of serious illness added weakness and intense physical pain to his other concerns.

13

The Struggle Continues

By 1954 the liberal awakening that Aubrey Williams had confidently discerned in the postwar South had proved to be a chimera. The South of the mid-fifties was an increasingly illiberal place. Gaining strength after the Supreme Court's decision on desegregation in public schools, the forces of "massive resistance" closed in on those who stood against the prevailing view, and Williams became more and more an isolated and lonely figure.

Williams's business continued to lose money and to take up less of his time. The magazine, he told Rexford Tugwell, had become a "dwindling publication which the national advertisers won't touch." From 1955 until it ceased publication in 1959 the *Southern Farm and Home Almanac* was little more than a mail-order catalog, full of small advertisements interspersed with agricultural information. Appearing quarterly, its circulation having dropped from a peak of 1,300,000 to a paltry 350,000, it was a poor apology for the influential journal of liberal opinion that Warburg and Williams had hoped to create, and Williams was deeply ashamed of its decline.

Occasionally, though, he still used it as a vehicle to state his views on what was wrong with the South, and what was required to right it. Fittingly, his last editorial was a characteristically uncompromising attack on segregation. Called "The Man with the Hammer," it blamed the ills of the region on "the work of a few people." "It is still my belief," Williams declared, "that most people in these deep South States are loyal to the United States, they are really and truly Christians, and if it weren't for the leadership of a wrong headed few, they would act much as people in other parts of this great land of freedom act. As it is, the life of the average Southerner is one long apology for the basic American institutions of human rights, equality and freedom."

So some of the old optimism remained, alongside the newer bitterness and disillusion. This editorial provoked the usual rash of invective and cancelled subscriptions. "I would love to recommend that you stick your heart in a hollow log and ask God to forgive you and help you tell some truth," wrote Rev. H. T. Isgitt of Converse, Louisiana. Another Louisianian considered the piece proof that Williams was "a communist inspired nigger lover." Experience must have prepared Williams to expect such a response, though it could not remove the hurt that such invective still caused. He had few regrets when the magazine finally ceased publication.[1]

The job-printing side of his business was also failing, in large part owing to his liberal reputation. After 1955 he lost contract upon contract, and he was not permitted even to bid on any government publications. Late in 1957 he lost his largest account, one which comprised 40 percent of his job work, all the printing for a large Memphis-based mail-order house. This occurred immediately after he had telegraphed President Eisenhower to support the sending of federal troops to Little Rock, Arkansas, during the desegregation crisis there and at a time when the Communist charge had once again been raised against him in the region's press. To Williams, the timing of these events seemed more than coincidental. "I can't get the straight of it," he wrote Dombrowski. "I do not want to believe that it is due to the *Birmingham News* articles, and/or my stand on the Little Rock debacle, but it comes from Memphis and at just this time."[2]

In 1958, Warburg determined that the Field Foundation should quit the enterprise as soon as a buyer could be found, the more so since Marshall Field had died in 1956, thus breaking the personal connection. At one stage, Williams decided to bid for the company himself, provided satisfactory repayments could be arranged, and made the foundation a formal offer. Soon, however, he had second thoughts. "I have come to feel that what is involved is more than I wish to undertake at my age," he told the foundation's vice-president in formally withdrawing the offer.

Instead, he decided to break his ties with Montgomery and return to Washington. His sons were now "either up that way or far from here," and he missed his beloved grandchildren. Furthermore, with no ties of birth or kinship in the South and unable to come to terms with the prevailing social climate, Anita was desperately keen to leave. Accordingly, he sold his property, and, with the help of a loan from Dombrowski, purchased a comfortable little house on N

Street, into which they planned to move just as soon as the Southern Farmer company was sold, for Williams had undertaken to remain with the company until a suitable buyer could be found. Sadly, none was forthcoming. The N Street house had to be sold, at a small profit, and the move north postponed.

The company was to remain his and the foundation's burden for a few more years yet, for he would not break his word. Anita was angry and bitterly disappointed. She felt she could bear the South no longer, and in 1960 moved briefly to Brooklyn to a small property purchased with the proceeds of the sale of the N Street house. It was not that she wanted to live apart from her husband. She just could not stand Montgomery, the constriction of their lives, and the effect it was having on their relationship any longer. She longed for the culture she had enjoyed so much in Washington, and for a life apart from tension and harassment. After six months she returned to Aubrey, but the fact that she felt it necessary to have made the break at all is some indication of the desperation she felt.[3]

Given the dwindling output of the Southern Farmer business, there was time for other ventures. Williams dabbled in real estate, for once successfully, and also embarked on another get-rich-quick scheme, this time with Gould Beech, with whom he had become reconciled. Together they invested in a wildcat mining project in Texas, and together they lost their money. Always intent on beating the capitalists at their own game, Williams was never quite able to do so. Though he had achieved a standard of modest affluence by the end of the decade through real estate investments, he never ever made his "killing."[4]

His business ventures, like his gambling on the horses, were little more than hobbies, however. He still devoted the bulk of his time after 1955 to the SCEF and the cause of black equality. In a climate unremittingly hostile to its advocacy, the organization continued to urge compliance with the Supreme Court decision on public schools and deplored the hardening of white attitudes on the issue and the reluctance of the Eisenhower administration to speak out against defiance of the law. The SCEF could do little, however, to influence the course of events, as the policy of "massive resistance" held the field. When President Eisenhower was forced to send troops to Little Rock in 1957 in order to ensure the desegregation of the city's high schools in the face of mob violence, Williams cabled him on behalf of the SCEF to tell him that "you are finding out what many of us in the South have known for a long time, that the only time States rights are used is to obstruct the rights of minorities which are powerless and have practically no rights or protection under so called states rights. . . . As a Southerner whose people lost everything they had in the 1860's, I wish to thank you and to express my deepest gratitude to you for the firm stand you have taken."

But such messages of support were the most the SCEF could do in the battle for desegregated schools.[5] Williams and his board had concluded that political power was essential to real change and that the condition of blacks would improve only when they achieved that power. Accordingly, the SCEF began to concentrate its activities on the right to vote. It attacked restrictive voting practices, encouraged voter registration drives, and publicized the inequities of the southern political structure. This involved much more grassroots activity and a closer attention to local organization than ever before, and Carl and Anne Braden were added to the permanent staff as field secretaries, with particular responsibility for the voting rights drive.

The Bradens were a singular couple. From widely different backgrounds—Anne was an upper-middle-class girl from Mississippi, Carl a working-class boy from Louisville, Kentucky, with strong socialist leanings—they had both become committed to the black cause. In 1954, acting on that commitment, they arranged to sell a house in a white neighborhood in Louisville, where Carl worked as a journalist, to a young black couple. The reaction to that action was predictable and violent. The Bradens were subjected to constant harassment, and Carl was eventually imprisoned for eight months for allegedly contravening Kentucky's sedition laws. He was released in 1956 after the Supreme Court had ruled such state laws to be unconstitutional.

Williams had taken a keen interest in their case. When he heard in 1957 that they were planning to move to Chicago, he wrote immediately, with characteristically mixed metaphors, to urge them to remain in the South. "I don't think you should throw away all that you have done there," he argued, "all the seed that you've sown, all the fine example you have lived, all the suffering you have undergone—they should not take you away from where you have sown your very blood in the streets and in the courts." Shortly afterward, the Bradens accepted his offer of the field secretaryships. Their joining the SCEF was in many ways a shot in the arm for the organization. Their energy and dedication saw to that. It did, however, change the SCEF's character somewhat. No longer was it responsive mainly to the views of Williams and Dombrowski. The Bradens soon came to wield considerable influence in its councils, not always to Williams's satisfaction. His influence in the organization, though still profound, was no longer predominant.[6]

One of the Bradens' first successes was the organization of a conference on voting restrictions in the southern states, held in Asbury Methodist Church in Washington, D.C., on April 27, 1958. There, after Martin Luther King had refused an invitation to do so, Williams gave the keynote address, his "Report from the South." In it he exhorted the local black communities to support the efforts of the SCEF and other groups working in the South. "There is disquieting evidence that Negroes do not always take advantage of the opportunities which are offered them," he charged. "We must recognize the Negroes' struggle for what it is—the spearhead which is challenging the hypocrisy of American political party alignments and which, if it succeeds can clear the ground of creeping fascism and totalitarianism which is inherent in the thinking of the power elite and their supporters, the conservatives and reactionaries of both parties."

As speaker after speaker detailed examples of the systematic denial of basic political rights to southern blacks, there were sighs and exclamations throughout the crowded church. Though few of the friends from Capitol Hill whom he had invited attended the sessions—the absent included people like Lister Hill, John Sparkman, and Allen Ellender, who he knew "wouldn't want to be caught dead with me" there—Williams was pleased with the conference. It received a good press, and its findings were eventually presented to the United States Civil Rights Commission.

It was the type of activity that he hoped the Bradens would continue to stimulate, and from time to time they did so. In January 1960 a mock hearing, "The Voteless Speak," also held in the Asbury Methodist Church under SCEF auspices, detailed what progress, if any, had occurred over the past two years. Williams spoke on this occasion as well, the press were present, and again he was pleased with the enterprise. He was always much more convinced than the

Bradens of the utility of this type of activity. For their part, they were certain that the organization of grass-roots voter registration drives brought much better results, and this remained a point of difference between them.[7]

Much of Williams's work for civil rights after 1955 occurred outside the SCEF. A prime case in point was his involvement in the Montgomery bus boycott of 1955 and 1956. That December day in 1955, when Rosa Parks refused to give up her seat on the Cleveland Avenue bus for a white passenger, is often regarded as the symbolic beginning of the civil rights revolution. Out of the year-long boycott, southern blacks acquired their most charismatic and effective leader in the young pastor Martin Luther King, a tactic of revolution in passive resistance to segregation, and, almost for the first time, a sense of their collective power.

Given Williams's own commitment, it was inconceivable that he should not have become deeply involved in the struggle. Williams was inclined to downplay his role in the event. "I was only an onlooker and a well-wisher," he subsequently wrote. Like most who have studied the event, he claimed that it was his friend E. D. Nixon, then president of the Alabama chapter of the NAACP, who galvanized Montgomery's blacks into action, who persuaded King to lead the protest, and who continued to influence events behind the scenes. He, Williams, did little more than provide moral support at all times, and financial assistance when required.

Nixon, however, had a different view. "You know if it hadn't been for Aubrey Williams," he said later, talking of the boycott, "I don't believe we could've ever mustered up courage to do it. You don't know what it means to have a white man that negroes can trust and we do trust Aubrey Williams. That man has so much self respect that it rubs off on you." That was Williams's importance. He provided those blacks who were challenging the white power structure directly for the first time with both an endless fund of advice and support and a constant reminder that not all white people were against them, that at least one man was always willing to speak on their behalf, to post bond for them if need be, to raise money when it was required. His role was far more than that of an onlooker. He was an active source of support and inspiration throughout the struggle.

He became absorbed in the boycott. At one point, a planned trip to Europe was postponed because of it, and Anita pronounced herself heartily "sick of it." Yet Williams drew great strength and inspiration from what had happened. To Mrs. Roosevelt he described it as "really a wonderful thing to see, this coming alive of a whole race of people and fighting to gain their freedom. I suppose no one man should ask more than to see that and to have the chance to help a bit here and there." He told his son Aubrey, Jr., with characteristic hyperbole, that he believed it to be "the most important thing to happen in the nation's history," all the more so because of the nonviolent nature of the protest.[8]

Only one dark cloud marred this otherwise brilliant sky. E. D. Nixon and Martin Luther King had a falling-out over the disposition of funds sent to the Montgomery Improvement Association (MIA), the organization formed to represent the boycotting blacks and to coordinate all activities. King was the MIA's president, and Nixon its treasurer. Claiming that King was misusing money, Nixon resigned his office and resisted all efforts by Williams to bring the two men together. To some extent, Williams shared Nixon's concern.

Rooted in this disagreement, William's view of King was never a totally positive one. When King had some tax trouble in 1960, for example, Williams was inclined to believe the Internal Revenue Service's version. "I think he has no one to blame but himself for the fact that there appears to be large discrepancies in the accounts of M.I.A.," he told Dombrowski. "E. D. Nixon as you know resigned because of the looseness of the M.I.A. and that meant King. Nixon isn't so sure there isn't a lot of truth in what they are charging about the disappearance of M.I.A. money. . . . I will have to say Jim I am pretty well fed up with the personal leadership of King. I personally have very little confidence in the man's judgement." Williams's distrust of the man who was to become the symbol of black resistance to segregation meant that the SCEF was not always able to cooperate with the other civil rights groups beginning to work in the South, for King's influence on the whole movement was pervasive and he was personally involved in many of those bodies. This was to become a point of strong disagreement between the Bradens and Williams, one of a number which were to develop as the 1950s drew to a close.[9]

Williams continued to try to influence events in Washington. He acted not so much as the leader of the SCEF but as an old Washington hand himself, who still had some friends in positions of power. One frequent recipient of encouragement, advice, and, from time to time, vigorous protests was Lyndon Johnson, the Senate majority leader. Begun in the New Deal days when Williams had appointed the young Texan to be state NYA director, the friendship between the two men lasted throughout their lives. Williams never held the common view that Johnson was a man of shifting principles, a pragmatist and power broker. To him, he was always a committed liberal who shared his own populist perspectives, despite, at times, considerable evidence to the contrary. Indeed, Ray Jenkins, editor of the *Alabama Journal*, once claimed that Williams would "bend over backwards to excuse L.B.J."

Nevertheless, at times even Johnson felt Williams's bitter displeasure. In 1957 Congress was debating the first civil rights act to be introduced since the days of Reconstruction. Johnson was in charge of its passage through the Senate and, in an attempt to achieve a broader base of support, had agreed to an amendment permitting the right to trial by jury in civil rights cases. To Williams, this was enough to render the bill useless because no southern jury, he believed, would ever vote to convict in such circumstances, and he wrote and told Johnson what he thought of him in no uncertain terms.

In his reply, after referring to their "many years" of friendship, the majority leader disclaimed any intention of passing legislation "that would 'abolish' any legitimate power of the courts. . . . I tell you quite frankly that I cannot find it in my conscience to juggle with the concept of equity in order to bypass one of the fundamental concepts of our liberties. Furthermore, I cannot agree with you that we must do so in order to secure an effective guarantee of voting rights. I do not believe that the jury trial and the right to vote are incompatible and, speaking again as a friend who wishes you well, I believe if you examine all of the facts carefully you will come to the same conclusion." The bill became law with the jury trial provision included. Experience, however, showed that it was Williams's fears rather than Johnson's hopes which were more in accordance with reality. Convictions under its provisions were very few and far between.[10]

In 1958 another friend from New Deal days, Congressman Emmanuel Celler, was the recipient of a strong letter of protest. Celler had recently testified before a House Judiciary subcommittee against the mounting tide of racial violence in the South. While applauding that, Williams wanted to know why he had not similarly protested against the activities of HUAC, which had scheduled hearings in Atlanta in July 1958 to investigate Communism in the civil rights movement. "It is apparently the open aim of Arens [now counsel to HUAC] and the Walters Committee," he cabled the congressman, "to publicly pillory any white person, Jew or Gentile, who openly favors and works for the implementation of the Court's mandates with respect to the rights of minorities. . . . This thing down here makes some of you fellows look rather foolish. In the 'hearings' in Atlanta the Federal Government will clearly be used to harass and destroy those who are trying to uphold the rights of people as set forth by Congress and the Supreme Court."

Carl Braden, and through him the SCEF, were to be scrutinized by the committee, and that no doubt added to his sense of urgency. But for Williams, the issues of civil rights and civil liberties were inextricably entwined. Attack one and the other was inevitably in jeopardy. Therefore, all attempts to erode either had to be vigorously opposed. In this particular case his forebodings were amply justified. Braden appeared before the committee and, like Virginia Durr in 1954, refused to answer questions about his political beliefs but did not invoke the Fifth Amendment. He was eventually found guilty of contempt of Congress and sent to prison, an event which further reinforced Williams's conviction that such investigatory bodies had absolutely no place in a democratic society, and which helped convince him to join those who were working through organized pressure groups for their abolition.[11]

Another issue in which civil rights and civil liberties intersected was the attempt by some legislators, notably Senator Eastland, to return to state courts some jurisdiction over sedition cases. Such a law would void the Supreme Court decision of 1956 on the Braden case, the Nelson decision, as it was called, which gave federal courts sole jurisdiction in that area. Legislation to that end was first introduced in the 1958 congressional session.

Williams was highly agitated, especially when he read press reports that a number of liberal senators, including Johnson, supported the bill. He feared—and the example of Carl Braden gave his fears some justification—that in the increasingly illiberal and conformist South state sedition laws would be used to silence all who criticized Jim Crow. Once again, Johnson bore the brunt of his protest. "What in heavens name has gotten into you that you are urging the overthrow of the Nelson decision and other decisions of the Supreme Court," he cabled the majority leader. "Lyndon, if you pass the Nelson decision bill they will put people like me in jail for advocating the right of Negroes to vote. Please do not support this bill. I am asking you personally." "Take the advice of an old friend and keep your shirt on," Johnson cabled back. "The Senate in my judgement is not going to do anything that will wind up by throwing innocent people into jail." He was right. On August 21, 1958, the Senate, by one vote, sent the bill back to the Judiciary Committee. Johnson was among those who voted to recommit.[12]

The immediate scare was thus averted, but the bill, known as S.3, was reintroduced in the 1959 session. Again Williams went on the warpath, spurred by Johnson's pessimism about the prospects of preventing its passage. He wrote long letters to key senators outlining the reasons for his opposition to the measure, and he visited Washington to put personal pressure on some of his friends. To Senator Ellender, a supporter of the legislation, he said:

> If the Nelson decision is set aside, the Legislature of each state can make its own definition of the word sedition. . . . I also like to think of myself as a Jeffersonian Democrat, but when one takes a look at his Virginia Bill of Religious Liberties, it is pretty obvious that his opposition to the Alien and Sedition Laws was based on much more than a belief in States Rights. His pledge of eternal hostility to all forms of tyranny over the mind of man is one we should keep in mind, more than we are inclined to do in these excited times. . . . With the shift in the political climate, we can well become the victims of our attempt to silence the other fellow.

Again he sought out Johnson and found his opposition to the bill firm. To Mrs. Roosevelt, who was emphatically not a Johnson supporter, he wrote telling her of his efforts, and, in particular, lauding the majority leader. "I spent several days in Washington this week and it would have done your heart good to see how many of the old crowd responded to the efforts to defeat the bills aimed at the

Supreme Court," he told her. "It was really thrilling to see how many of our old New Dealers are still around and in positions where they can be useful. . . . I saw Lyndon and he is fully aware of what is behind bills like S.3. . . . He spoke out strongly against any legislation which would weaken the court. I am completely confident he is sincere in this. . . . If these bills are again defeated, it will be Lyndon who accomplishes it. . . . Without his leadership I fear they will be enacted into law."

Johnson pulled out every stop in his fight against the legislation, and was eventually successful. Although the bill passed the House fairly comfortably, it again foundered in the Senate, and was dropped. Johnson's vehement opposition was in large part responsible for that outcome. Williams was naturally delighted with the result, both because it vindicated his own efforts and because it justified his faith in the majority leader. As early as 1958 he had urged Johnson to run for the presidency, and Johnson's stance in 1959 only confirmed his opinion that his friend was the best prospect for the liberal wing of the Democratic party in 1960.[13]

The successful fight against S.3 was one of the precious few good points of the years after 1955. The harassment of Williams and the SCEF, which had grown in intensity throughout the decade, continued. The Communist label was constantly raised, and little could be done to prevent the inevitable distortions.

One such attack took place in 1957, shortly after he had attended the Highlander Folk School's twenty-fifth anniversary, held on Labor Day. There, in the company of such notables as Martin Luther King, his deputy Ralph Abernethy, folk singer Pete Seeger, and Rosa Parks, he had taken part in various festivities, including folk dancing, and had also addressed the assembly. In his speech he warned that the South was "playing with fire" and "doing again what was done 100 years ago." Some senators, he said, were advocating the same sort of defiance that had brought destruction a century ago, and that if they persisted, such a conflict was inevitable "because there can be no turning back on this one because of world opinion." He concluded by talking rather bitterly of the ostracism that white liberals like himself suffered from their fellow southerners, while being "treated as an untouchable by the organizations of the North who are fighting for the same things nationally that he is fighting for as a Southerner."[14]

This speech, typical of many that Williams made, would probably have occasioned no comment at all had not two uninvited guests infiltrated the gathering. One was Abner Berry, a black reporter for the Communist party newspaper, the *Daily Worker*; the other was an aide to the segregationist governor of Georgia, Marvin Griffin, who was attending the conference disguised as an employee of the Georgia Water Pollution Department. Neither would have been admitted if their true identities had been known.

Both published accounts of their attendance. Berry's was laudatory, but gave the strong impression that he had played a crucial role in the event. The one from Governor Griffin's employee was somewhat different. In early October the Georgia Commission on Education, a state body created in the wake of the Brown decision in order to coordinate the fight to preserve a segregated school system, released an illustrated paper in which Highlander was branded as a Communist training school. Berry's presence at the gathering was taken as proof positive of this. The paper was full of photographs of scenes from the Labor Day celebration, particularly scenes that showed the interracial dancing. One picture, of King, Myles Horton, and Williams, with Berry in the foreground—Williams claimed Berry had inserted himself there when he saw the camera pointing his way—was labeled "the four horsemen of racial agitation." Williams came in for special attack. "Few people have aided the Communist Party more in its conspiracy against peace between the races in the Southern part of the United States" than he, claimed the commission, and the article listed no fewer than forty-eight front organizations of which he was allegedly a member and reproduced much of Crouch's New Orleans testimony as supporting evidence.[15]

The charges made by the commission were taken up by a number of southern newspapers, particularly the *Birmingham News*. A series of articles on "Red Fronts" by *News* reporter Edwin Strickland went over the same ground in great detail, again using the New Orleans testimony as evidence. "His association, often in the role of leadership in Communist fronts is a long one," said Strickland, "and extends over a period of twenty years." Furious, Williams demanded a retraction and an apology. To Clarence Hanson, publisher of the *Birmingham News*, he wrote:

> If you had attacked me for standing for equality for Ne-
> groes I would have been surprised for until last week I had a

high opinion of your integrity, but when you got into bed
with the Griffins and the Ace Carters and called me a Communist, that was hitting below the belt. . . . The saddest part
of incriminating another person's character is that in the hate-
ridden climate of the Deep South, and nowhere more than
Birmingham you are perfectly safe in doing so. You need have
no fear that your victim will be able to redress the wrong
done to him by court action. So you do not even have to be
brave to do what you did.

To R. F. Hudson, of the *Montgomery Advertiser*, which had repeated
the charges, he wrote more in sorrow than in anger, for he had
considered him a friend. "You have been kind and courteous to me
since my arrival here twelve years ago, and I have deeply appreciated it." But the "vile slander" had ended all that. "Your paper
should be hauled into court and made to answer" for it. First,
however, he wanted to "express my shock and indignation to you,
the person with whom I have always had my dealings."[16]

Williams was correct in asserting that in the prevailing climate
charges such as these could be made with impunity. By 1957 members of the southern power structure, indeed, white southerners
generally, had closed ranks solidly in defense of what they considered to be their traditional form of social organization, and in
such a climate there was to be no court action, and no retraction or
apology. Instead the charges became part of segregationist folklore,
to be used whenever necessary. A 1958 Georgia Commission on
Education pamphlet *Communists and the NAACP* repeated them, as
did a 1961 effort, *CORE and Its Communist Connections*, which also
reproduced the "four horsemen" picture. In fact the photograph
became quite famous. *American Opinion*, the official publication of
the right-wing John Birch Society, produced it as a postcard, help-
fully identifying each of the persons depicted as "well-known Communists." It was also turned into a billboard which was displayed
prominently on southern freeways. In 1963, testifying against President John F. Kennedy's civil rights bill before the Senate Commerce Committee, Governor Ross Barnett of Mississippi referred
to the Georgia commission's 1957 publication as proof that the civil
rights movement was Communist-led. Berry, the Communist in-
filtrator, had written to Horton apologizing if his unauthorized
presence at the meeting, and his subsequent article, had caused
anyone any trouble. He did not know the half of it. For Williams, at

least, it had resulted in more harassment, more tension, and more loneliness.[17]

The next year brought harassment of a different kind, at the SCEF-sponsored Washington conference on voting restrictions in the South, held on April 27. Williams, accompanied by Anita and his son Morrison, arrived at the Asbury Methodist Church rather late and was unable to find a parking place. Because they all wanted to be present at the conference's opening, they decided to risk leaving their car parked illegally at a bus stop for a few minutes. After the formal words of welcome, Morrison slipped out to move the vehicle. When he did not return, Anita went to look for him and, after a few increasingly frantic hours, found him in a cell at the local police station. A policeman standing by the illegally parked car had promptly arrested him and taken him away, without even permitting him to let anyone know what had happened. Anita posted bond, and Morrison was duly summoned to a hearing the following Monday. They then returned to the Asbury Church, perplexed that a relatively minor traffic offense could have provoked such a serious response. The car remained impounded.

The hearing the following Monday was a nonevent. The court officer moved to dismiss the charges and stated that although he had been told that "the F.B.I. has an interest in the case," he could nevertheless find no reason for prolonging the affair. Morrison paid the impoundment charges, and they reclaimed their car and set off for home. It was then that Williams discovered that his address book, which included a list of all the SCEF contributors, had been removed from the glove compartment during the impoundment. He was furious. "Such is the present condition of this country that a group of citizens can't meet in open conference under the roof of a church without being harassed by the police and the F.B.I.," he thundered in an open letter to all who had participated in the forum, but there was nothing he could do. The police denied all knowledge of the missing book.[18]

Having to live constantly with harassment and slander was obviously distressing to Williams, particularly because of its effect on Anita. But the attacks would have been much easier to bear if he could have been sure that most liberals recognized the calumnies for what they were and were unwavering in their support for him. Unfortunately, that was not always the case. After New Orleans, in his view, far too many former friends and acquaintances wished to put distance between themselves and Williams and the SCEF. This left him sick at heart, increasingly isolated, and increasingly bitter. "I get so damned mad at that bunch of liberals in Washington," he once confessed to Dombrowski. "My whole world begins to boil and I want to somehow get at them."

To Senator Paul Douglas, who had written to a constituent agreeing that the SCEF was a Communist front, he poured out his anger and his sadness. "Paul, this burns me up," he wrote. "When you say these things about the Southern Conference Educational Fund you are saying them about me. For I am and have been its president for its entire life. . . . If this organization isn't worthy of the confidence of decent people then I am either a crook or a fool. And while I know I am not the former I don't think I am the latter. . . . No, Paul, you were never more wrong in your life."

One of the reasons he remained so committed to Lyndon Johnson was that Johnson never listened to the "red-baiters." Early in 1959, when Williams led a delegation to Washington in opposition to S.3, all of the Senate's leading liberals refused to see them. Johnson, however, gave them "well on to an hour." Thus encouraged, they visited several conservative senators, "none of whom seemed to be afraid of us." He became distanced from many of his former liberal friends in Congress and in the labor movement. As he told Dombrowski, he believed that "these people are simply not interested in the little handful of us that are down here. We just [sic] as well make up our minds to that for once and for all."[19]

Williams came to feel the same way about a number of black leaders and organizations, which were gaining in power and purpose in the wake of the Brown decision, the Montgomery bus boycott, and the other events that signaled the start of the "Second Reconstruction." The SCEF had expected to work closely with such bodies, but that proved not to be the case. In 1956 the SCEF tried to join the Leadership Conference on Civil Rights, an NAACP-controlled body which coordinated civil rights activity in the South. The application was refused by the leadership conference's chairman, Roy Wilkins, ostensibly because the organization "decided not to increase the membership of the Conference at the present time," but Williams was convinced that the real reason was the reluctance of many civil rights bodies to come too close to people who had been "smeared by the Eastland Committee."

There is probably much truth in his assertion. The years after 1956 were years of growth and consolidation for the black-led civil rights groups. Goals were charted, tactics developed, and alliances forged. Sometimes political caution and the need to achieve respectability dictated responses to certain people and groups, and the SCEF, with its reputation soiled by the New Orleans hearings and their aftermath, was regarded by some as an organization to be avoided. Martin Luther King certainly thought so. In 1960 he backed off, at the eleventh hour, from appearing at an SCEF-sponsored function because, in his biographer's words, of "the possibility of a taint." Wilkins, a canny and pragmatic man, probably felt the same way.

Williams reacted angrily to such treatment, and with great bitterness. "It burns me up," he complained to his friend Justine Wise Polier, "to have a bunch of hypocrites parading their patriotism at the expense of some of us down here who are besieged on all sides for standing for what we do. It is hard enough to fight on one front, but then to be attacked from behind by a crowd of underlings who live in a safe region and stab those in the back who dare to fight for what they believe, at literally the risk of their lives daily," that was just too hard to take. He told another friend that the SCEF was still the only interracial civil rights body working in the South, as the "N.A.A.C.P. doesn't want the only kind of white people they can get, those who are smeared by the Eastland Committee, so they have practically none."[20]

Williams never forgave Roy Wilkins for his action. "It is a waste of time talking to him," he told Dombrowski in 1959, after a suggestion that perhaps another approach for membership should be made. The AFL-CIO, the NAACP, the "northern Civil Rights groups"—they had "thrown all such as WE to the lions," he claimed. One of the reasons why he did not warm to Martin Luther King, apart from the matter of the Montgomery Improvement Association funds and his alleged tendency to grab for headlines, was Williams's conviction that he was far too close to the NAACP. "King is playing a crafty game," he stated on one occasion. "He is taking his advice from National N.A.A.C.P. and Benny Mays. Neither of these sources have any place for S.C.E.F. in their work. I think we had better stick to Negro leaders like Nixon, Gomillion, Simpkins, etc." The incident referred to above simply confirmed him in that belief. Williams's increasingly bitter attitude toward many of the new civil rights leaders helps explain the SCEF's relative isolation as the movement developed in the years after 1955. In a sense, it was left behind in the crowd.[21]

At times his sense of having been betrayed by the black leadership seemed to stretch over to include Negroes generally. Writing of the "suffering" of the southern white liberal, he once remarked that blacks were not always sufficiently supportive of their efforts. "He must live as a stranger amongst his own people," he complained, "and the Negroes often give him little backing or none at all." He himself had never received any Negro business; yet some black companies had always been in a position to help him if they had wanted to. "If the white liberal is smeared then the Negro community has a tendency to try and disassociate themselves from him or her," he charged. Liberal whites could not change the South without black help, and they were not getting enough of it. Educated blacks had to make a "joint and valiant effort to lift up the mass of the Negroes. . . . A Negro has got to carry his race with him as he rises, he cannot rise alone." The need for more black self-help became a frequent theme with him, as old age, weariness, and a tincture of cynicism tempered the optimism that had so characterized his first years back home. "In the final analysis," he wrote on another occasion, "the Negro must prove his ability to add to the social whole and not detract from it. I have no doubt that he will do that, but he must never forget that this can be the greatest contribution to his acceptance."[22]

Williams's increasing isolation from liberals outside the SCEF was compounded by policy and personality disagreements within it. He had originally welcomed the addition of the Bradens to the SCEF staff. "I keep hoping that somebody will be able to turn the trick. . . . If any two people can make a dent in the sordid, scheming devil-ridden South I believe you two can," he had told them on their appointment, and soon he had developed a warm friendship with Anne. But he found working with Carl very difficult indeed. "We have a problem in this boy," he told Dombrowski in 1958. "He has a chip on his shoulder and is suffering from hallucinations of moral superiority. . . . If he gets too difficult you will just have to let him go."

One of the reasons for their disagreements was political. Williams, the populist-liberal, could not always fathom Braden's socialism, his conviction that the South's racial problems were simply one manifestation of the general class struggle. But mainly their differences were personal. Braden was aggressive, even "pushy," full of ideas for the SCEF's development, impatient with delays in their implementation. Getting older and more tired and used to having things his own way, Williams resented the younger man's attitudes and what he construed as interference; no doubt he sometimes imagined slights where none was intended. The result was an increasingly difficult work situation.[23]

There were serious differences over policy as well. The Bradens pressed for closer cooperation with King, for example, and this Williams opposed. One disagreement which had long-range implications concerned fund raising. The Bradens wanted to establish a permanent fund-raising organization in New York, which would take advantage of the wealthy liberal element there, as well as more actively involve such prestigious supporters as Mrs. Roosevelt. Accordingly, they made preparations to form such a body. When he heard about it, Williams was bitterly opposed. "You can get one effort out of them a year," he said of the New York people. "They are willing to make that, and I think that is all you should ask of them. Do not push them. Take what they are willing to give you." The Bradens carried the day, however. The SCEF board decided to set up a New York committee and to appoint a paid fund raiser there, despite Williams's objections. He was most unhappy at the decision.[24]

The appointment of a person to the fund-raising job caused further disagreement. The Bradens wanted to offer it to the Reverend William Howard Melish, an Episcopal priest from New York who had been active for many years in interracial work there, and they persuaded Dombrowski that Melish was the man for the job. Williams, however, was strongly opposed. Chairman of the Council on American-Soviet Friendship since 1942 and a member of the American Labor party, Melish was far too closely identified with left-wing causes and groups, he believed, and would frighten off as many contributors as he attracted. His involvement in a bitter intra-diocese controversy was a further handicap. Besides, Mrs. Roosevelt had warned him against making the appointment. "People won't see him," she had said. Nevertheless, Williams lost this fight as well. Melish was offered the position.

He proved to be a good fund raiser, and the SCEF's coffers swelled as a result of his efforts. Nevertheless, Williams's fears proved justified. A number of prominent liberals severed their connections with the conference, including, in 1960, Mrs. Roosevelt herself. At an SCEF fund-raising dinner in New York, Mrs. Roosevelt and Williams were chatting when Joe Cadden, one of the members of the American Youth Congress whom she had trusted and by whom she had been betrayed in the days of the New Deal, came up and introduced himself. Mrs. Roosevelt was cool to him, and he soon made his excuses. After he had gone, she turned to Williams and said, "I am told there are a good many like him attached to the conference." Williams replied that such folk "have a way of attaching themselves to movements such as this," but assured her that they had no influence on the SCEF's policy or work. Mrs. Roosevelt then changed the conversation, but shortly afterward a letter arrived from her severing her affiliation with the SCEF and requesting that no more material be sent to her. Williams was desolated by her action, but there was nothing to be done. "There is nothing one can say," he told Dombrowski. "She is slow to act, and firm when she does. I shall not ask her to reconsider." Moreover, Mrs. Roosevelt had made it quite clear that their personal relationship was not at risk.

That incident was symbolic of the differences between Williams and the Bradens. He did not always approve of the direction in which they were pointing the organization. For some time he had resolved to give up the SCEF's presidency as soon as a successor could be found, and the loss of Mrs. Roosevelt, for whom he still retained the greatest love and respect, made him all the more determined to do so.[25]

Not everything about Montgomery life in his last years, however, was gloomy and negative. He still had his family, especially the beloved grandchildren; they were spread out a bit now, but were still frequent visitors home. He had the farm, the occasional visits to the New Orleans racetracks—"What an unregenerate I am, completely incorrigible," he had told Dombrowski after one such—and the golf, most often with Paul Woolley. Montgomery had a minor league baseball team, and Williams never missed a game; he sat in the bleachers and yelled himself hoarse. So life was not all bad. "I like pleasures," he had written a friend in 1958. "I like horseracing, playing poker, listening to good music, loving my granddaughters." There was yet some time for all of that, despite the grimness of his public existence.[26]

Moreover, he had finally become serious about writing his auto-biography. For years people had been trying to help him write one, completely unsuccessfully. Houghton Mifflin had even given him an advance in order to encourage production, but nothing had been forthcoming. Now, however, with Virginia Durr to help him, it was finally going to be done. For several months they worked away diligently before Virginia, like the rest, gave up in despair. Such a book would have to be written independently, not with Williams. She wrote to Anne Braden to try to persuade her to take over where she left off. "He is simply hopeless as he will not use himself as the hinge for the story and goes off in tangents about other people being more important and he really is of such a nature that he can't write about himself. If you know Aubrey better as time goes on, you will realise that he is so male and so Southern! It is because of your being an Alabamian and being a Southerner your-self that makes you such a person because you can understand him and the struggle he has gone through. . . . He personifies in his person the 'whole southerner,' as opposed to the Shizophrenic [sic] variety we have at present. I see so much of him and really know him too well to write about him, if such a thing can be."

Anne was unable to accept the commission, and Williams was left to soldier on alone with his book. Predictably, it was never finished. He presumably never knew of Virginia's characterization of him as the "whole southerner." If he had, he doubtless would have been pleased, for southern he certainly felt himself to be, even in those troubled years. "Top of the morning to you, and a beautiful morn-ing it is," he wrote a friend in 1959. "Nowhere on this earth is it possible to find more beautiful mornings than can be found here in this Southland of ours." Life certainly still had its joys.[27]

Both joy and sorrow, however, nearly ended for him in 1959. For some time he had been feeling uncharacteristically tired and listless. At first he tried to cure himself, through food faddism and the type of patent medicines he advertised in his magazines. Writing to Adele Davis, author of *Let's Eat Right to Keep Fit*, to request a "schedule of nutrition that will give me maximum health," he complained of "cramps in the legs, dark spots all over me," and a "lack of sexual vigor." He had never been one of those "so called sex athletes," he confessed, "but during the past year my ability to function has all but disappeared." To add insult to injury, he concluded, Anita kept complaining about his odor. "She is right I know, but nothing I do seems to eliminate it."[28]

Davis tried to help, but eventually, as pain increased, Williams took his problems to more conventional medical practitioners. Serious stomach cancer was diagnosed, and in early October he underwent major surgery. He was not expected to live; indeed, the SCEF had his obituary prepared and ready to run. However, he surprised everyone by pulling through—and making a very rapid recovery. At sixty-nine, his constitution was so remarkably strong that by the end of November, not noticeably the worse for wear, he was out on the golf links with Woolley.

Sickness was a great shock to him emotionally, of course. "It was about the most harrowing business I ever went thru [sic]," he confessed to his sister Myrtice. "I guess I simply wasn't prepared to know what being sick was never having really been sick." Yet he was immensely buoyed by the messages of cheer and goodwill that poured in from all over the country. Lyndon Johnson wrote to tell him that he was "one of the best friends I have," and that pleased him. What absolutely delighted him, however, were the scores of messages from people he did not know—ex-NYA enrollees, old WPA folk, southerners who sympathized with his position on race. "I remember well, Mr. Williams, the thirties and the steadfast role you played in bringing life to the reforms of the New Deal," wrote one such. "For a good twenty-five years the name Aubrey Williams has meant to me that which was inspiring, progressive and clean in the movements of the South," said another, and there were literally hundreds more. The realization that people had not forgotten him, that for some, at least, his life had meaning and purpose was tremendously important to him. He himself counted it a crucial factor in his rapid recovery.[29]

By January 1960, Williams was almost his old self again. He campaigned enthusiastically for Johnson in the preliminaries to the Democratic party convention and even attempted to persuade Mrs. Roosevelt to switch her allegiance from Adlai Stevenson to the majority leader. He failed, but had some success with E. D. Nixon, who initially had not been as convinced as Williams that Johnson was sound on civil rights. Eventually, however, he agreed to go with Williams to the Democratic convention in Los Angeles as part of the Johnson bandwagon.

Williams had little time for the other main candidates, Hubert Humphrey or Stevenson, but preferred either to the eventual nominee, John F. Kennedy. He had detested his father in the 1930s and believed the son to be a nasty chip off the old block. The religious issue also entered into his dislike for Kennedy. Williams, so profoundly southern in so many ways, was at one with much of his region in that too. He had a distinctly anti-Catholic streak in him, and knew it. "If I have a blind-spot it is with respect to Catholics," he once wrote his friend, author Irving Brant; "I have the greatest trouble in not being prejudiced on that score. I have an inherent distrust of them."

He was bitterly disappointed at the convention's choice, and sat out the 1960 campaign, making gloomy pronouncements about the moral bankruptcy of the nation which it seemed to highlight. "And where to turn is the problem," he complained. "The two alternatives seem to be the Rightist Catholicism or leftist Communism, and I want nothing of either of them. Ah me, woe is me." Despite the gloom, however, he seemed physically sound.[30]

Then the illness struck again, and this time recovery was far from swift. Williams began to feel unwell in April 1961, but it was not until August that he had further surgery. He was out of the hospital by September, but was still very seriously ill, sedated most of the time, and forced to undergo frequent chemotherapy treatments. For Anita, it was almost too much to bear. "To see a man waste away under your eyes gets you where it hurts," she wrote Dombrowski. "He is fighting so hard and has amazing strength. . . . B'gosh I believe he's going to make it at least for a while." She was right in her prognosis, but even partial recovery was a painfully slow process. Under the circumstances he decided to give up the SCEF presidency. "I have at long last come to the decision that I am unwilling to be responsible for leading an organization while I am in no way discharging that responsibility," he cabled Dombrowski. "Nor is there any possibility that I shall be able to do so in the foreseeable future. I am seriously ill and cannot do anything but try to get well. Please accept this. To plead with me will do no good and will make it more difficult for me." The SCEF board accepted Williams's resignation on October 28, 1961, with great regret. Naming him president emeritus, the board recorded its "deep affection and appreciation for his long years of invaluable contribution to the cause of justice and freedom." He never attended another SCEF board meeting. His long involvement with the organization was over.[31]

14

A Struggle Ends

Williams's "contribution to the cause of justice and freedom" was not quite finished. His recovery was very slow and would never be complete, but he did get better. In early 1960, Williams had become head of another organization, one to which he had devoted a considerable amount of his energies between his two bouts of illness. That organization was the National Committee to Abolish the House Un-American Activities Committee.

From its inception the House Un-American Activities Committee had been opposed by individuals and groups concerned with the threat to constitutionally guaranteed liberties, and often to themselves, that its procedures and practices seemed to entail. In the 1950s much of that opposition was centered in California, a state where the committee had been active and where some erosion of civil liberties had occurred. Two of the most important anti-HUAC pressure groups that developed there were the Emergency Civil Liberties Committee (ECLC) and the Citizens Committee to Preserve American Freedoms.

Deeply involved with both these organizations was Frank Wilkinson. Once a slum clearance expert with the Los Angeles City Housing Authority, Wilkinson had been removed from his position in 1952 at the height of the McCarthy period for refusing to list, at the request of the city council, all the organizations to which he had belonged since 1935. Since then he had worked full-time in the civil liberties area. In 1958, Dombrowski asked him to attend the HUAC hearing scheduled for Atlanta, where the SCEF was to be under investigation, in order to assist Carl Braden, the only SCEF official summoned to attend. He did so, and was promptly subpoenaed himself. When, like Braden, he refused to answer questions, invoking the First Amendment, not the Fifth, as his grounds, he was held in contempt of Congress and sentenced to prison. As his appeal against the conviction proceeded through the court system, he worked harder than ever to mobilize opinion against the evils of a process of which he had become a victim.[1]

One of the people with whom he came in contact was Williams. His message that, for maximum effectiveness, the many anti-HUAC pressure groups should coordinate their activities was one with which Williams strongly agreed. Moreover, Williams shared Wilkinson's conviction that such committees were antipathetic to the democratic way of life. His own experiences at their hands had amply taught him that; those of people like Carl Braden simply reinforced the view. For Williams, the causes of civil rights and civil liberties were entwined; one was not possible without the other. As early as 1958 he had talked of organizing "something to fight the Un-American Activities Committee," and throughout 1959 his resolution to do so hardened. In August 1960, "as a result of mounting national interest," the formation of the National Committee to Abolish the House Un-American Activities Committee was announced, and Williams was named its first chairman. Wilkinson was to be field representative, its one paid official. The other members of the new committee's executive were mainly people with solid liberal connections, especially members of the ACLU.

The immediate program was to distribute anti-HUAC literature in order to secure maximum support for a motion for HUAC's abolition, which was to be presented by Representative James Roosevelt to Congress at the beginning of the 1961 session. Williams scoffed at charges that at least six officials of the new body had been identified as Communist party members. "The woods are full of people who are not Communists who have been identified as Communists by people who have been proven over and over again to be liars and perjurers," he claimed, no doubt with the New Orleans hearings in mind. The group hoped to organize local committees in fourteen major cities.

Williams was delighted with this chance to have a crack at the people who had so circumscribed his life. As his involvement with the SCEF had dwindled, he saw the committee as a good direction for his energy. Indeed, he told Dombrowski he wanted to be relieved of the SCEF presidency as soon as possible so that he could devote himself full-time to the anti-HUAC struggle. "I don't think I should get the S.C.E.F. involved in that fight, which I will do if I continued as president," he said. Besides, "I feel that many of my reactions are due to my having been at this same post too long. I think the Fund and I will both do a better job, so far as this particular job is concerned. I ask you to please respect my wishes in this." At seventy, he threw himself into the new task with vigor and enthusiasm.[2]

Initially everything went well. The work of the committee was given both impetus and urgency by the Supreme Court's decision, on a five-to-four vote, to affirm the convictions of both Braden and Wilkinson. They eventually went to prison in May 1961. Branches of the committee were quickly established in a number of cities, pamphlets arguing the case for abolition were produced and distributed, and Williams was soon busy working on plans for developing "a broad grass roots organization on behalf of the abolition of H.U.A.C." He was hopeful of involving church groups and labor unions in the fight. Nothing much came of these and other schemes, however. Williams was never able to provide the aggressive, national leadership that the committee needed if it was to become an effective pressure group, for he was slowed by the recurrence of the cancer in 1961. Precisely at the time that his influence was most needed, he was unable to make any contribution at all. Wilkinson was in jail at the time, and there was no one left to organize the national effort.[3]

Even before illness had rendered him ineffective, however, the work of the national committee had been hampered by Williams's insistence that the committee be seen as representative of a broad spectrum of liberal opinion, and not simply as the creature of the far left. His distrust of possible Communist influence led him to insist that Russ Nixon, the cochairman of the largest state branch of the organization, the New York Council, resign as the price for his own continued involvement in the work.

An executive of the United Electrical, Radio and Machine Workers of America, a union with a strong leftist tradition, Nixon had been closely associated with left-wing causes for a long period of time and had taken the Fifth Amendment before HUAC in 1956. Williams believed that his presence in the organization was preventing liberals from joining, that he was contemptuous of those considered to be "middle-of-the-road," like Williams himself, and that he was turning the New York Council into a pro-Soviet cell. Thus, he demanded Nixon's resignation. If Nixon did not go, then he,

Williams, would. Nixon eventually resigned under pressure from, among others, Anne Braden, but the New York Council was bitterly critical of Williams's "behind the back attacks" and virtually stopped functioning. In the atmosphere of bitterness and mutual recriminations that Williams's so-called "purge" engendered, the prospects for effective national cooperation were far from good.[4]

Williams recognized the anger that his action had caused and began to move to conciliate the disaffected groups. Scarcely had he begun to do so, however, when illness struck again. Unable to provide any leadership, and with Wilkinson in jail, the national committee simply ceased to function. The movement was in an "impossible situation," wrote Anne Braden in 1961. There was no central organization, and Williams was "too sick to pull things together as he had planned. Someone else must do it," without consulting Williams, if need be. Thus, Richard Criley, president of a Chicago-based civil liberties group, the Committee to Defend the Bill of Rights, agreed to coordinate the committee's activities pending Wilkinson's release from prison and Williams's recovery.

Williams never recovered sufficiently, however, to resume active work with the committee. Though he agreed, reluctantly, to remain as chairman, so that the group could continue to use his name, he was little more than a figurehead thereafter. As he wrote his old Wisconsin colleague, philosopher Alexander Meiklejohn, famous for his defenses of the First Amendment, with "most of [his] lower insides taken out" he could not do very much. Moreover, the illness had left him in a precarious emotional state as well. Williams, the great public speaker, could no longer talk on the subjects most dear to him, "without breaking down and finding it impossible to continue. This is a very sad situation for me, for I wish to continue to participate in these endeavors."

He was never really able to do so again, and he formally resigned the chairmanship of the anti-HUAC committee in 1963, becoming, as he had with the SCEF, its first chairman emeritus. In that capacity he continued to do what he could to aid the cause. His last public-speaking appearance, in 1964, was at a rally at the American University sponsored by the committee. There, frail and ill, he was jostled and abused by George Lincoln Rockwell and other representatives of the American Nazi Party. Characteristically, he stood his ground, supported by his son. Nevertheless, what effectiveness he had had as the committee's leader had ended with the recurrence of cancer in 1961.[5]

Williams's period of involvement with the national anti-HUAC committee, truncated as it was, was probably the time of his closest institutional association with the far left. Men like Russ Nixon, Otto Nathan, Nixon's New York cochairman, and even Frank Wilkinson himself had long-term connections with leftist organizations and groups, including, in some cases, the Communist party and its various fronts. Williams recognized the dangers this presented and, as he did in New York, moved decisively to check any sign of what he considered to be party domination. Yet, his long-term hostility to working with Communists and their associates did seem to be moderating slightly. "I feel that it really boils down to this," he wrote historian Irving Brant, who had earlier questioned his developing association with Wilkinson: "We must judge people by their conduct and not by their beliefs. . . . In this time of storm and stress . . . we must accept or reject associations on the basis of what persons do in relation to us and the objects we are seeking." Thus, if toward the end of his life he began gingerly to work with people whom he formerly would have shunned, it was not that he had been duped, as some alleged. More likely, his views on the legitimacy of such cooperation had changed.[6]

Throughout 1962, however, his prime concern was with matters far removed from politics: his illness and the consequent problems of what was to happen to the business and where he would spend what were obviously going to be the last few years of his life. On both of those matters he vacillated constantly. The business continued to lose money. Its biggest remaining account was that of Sears and Roebuck's Atlanta store, and when the company decided in mid-1962 to do its own printing, Williams was sure that that would mean the end of his business. "I fear it is only a matter of weeks until we have to close down," he said. Nevertheless, in December, he changed his mind and made an offer to the Field Foundation for the plant, which it accepted. He was finally the owner of the company that he had controlled for so long. He planned to hang on to it, he told Dombrowski, and even put some new plant in. By February, however, his plans had again altered drastically. He decided to quit the Southern Farmer company for good, and he arranged to sell it, on the same terms as those that he had received from the foundation, to his production manager and friend, Paul Woolley. Woolley took over the enterprise at once and promptly changed its name to avoid the stigma associated with the plant because of its previous owner. Williams prepared, finally, to leave Alabama.[7]

The reasons for the sudden change in plans were various. He had had further surgery in February 1963. Though not as serious as that of 1961, it was serious enough to make him realize that he could never work again, let alone think of expanding his activities. The grandchildren were no longer close by, there was little to keep him in Montgomery. Anita desperately wanted to move, and he himself wanted a quiet atmosphere in which, once more, to try and write. Finally, Alabama's political climate was becoming even more hostile. Governor George Wallace was planning to establish his own state anti-American affairs body, and Williams believed he would certainly be one of the first to be investigated. In his current physical and emotional state, he knew he "just couldn't take it." He feared he would break down on the witness stand, and that he could not have borne.

The decision was made to leave as soon as possible. Where to go was no problem. Morrison and his family were in York, Pennsylvania, and they wanted to be close to them. They decided, therefore, to look for a property in either southeastern Maryland or southeastern Pennsylvania, and in the meantime they would relocate in Washington, D.C.

On May 15, 1963, Williams left the South for the last time. The *Montgomery Advertiser* commented on his departure. Hailing him as the "city's leading liberal" and one of its "most colorful and controversial citizens," it paid grudging tribute to the strength of his convictions and to his willingness to "state his beliefs publicly, no matter how controversial." "He is a genial, genteel and thoroughly companionable man," continued the editorial, repeating Grover Hall's comment, "who laughs all the way down to his transverse colon." It had been a long time since a southern newspaper was so kind to him.[8]

Williams was deeply depressed about the move and about going to Washington. He felt like a quitter, he said. Besides, "I had rather be a big fish in a small hole, even tho is [*sic*] be a stink hole, than to be buried in a bog hole like DC." Other matters had greatly affected him as well. Mrs. Roosevelt's death in November 1962 had shocked him profoundly. He had dined with her a few months previously, where they had discussed the hereafter with an earnest young Episcopalian minister. Recounting the details of his latest surgery, Williams remarked that he had been supposedly clinically dead on the operating table for a moment or two, and asked the cleric where he had been during that time, "how long before St. Peter let me in or the Devil stuck his fork in my behind and threw me into the cauldron." Mrs. Roosevelt "screamed with laughter," and said she had never given much thought to the afterlife; "what will be will be." Now she was dead, and Williams was desolated by her passing. Though ill himself, he had journeyed north to her funeral, which he found "sadder than I ever thought it could be." "I felt," he said, "as they lowered her into the grave that it was the saddest moment I have ever lived." Months later, he was still unable to talk about her death without breaking down. Despair and sadness were increasingly his companions, he said, as his own life drew to its end.[9]

His depression intensified once he had arrived in Washington and had taken up temporary residence in a small apartment near the cathedral. "I am unhappy here," he told Dombrowski, and "find everyone here afraid to associate with me." Still, they would move as soon as a suitable farm could be found in Maryland or Pennsylvania, and things would look up. That dream was to be soon shattered. A visit to a surgeon, himself an old NYA boy, confirmed that the cancer had reached the stage where an operation "would do no good." It was just a question, then, of waiting for the end, which could be very soon.

There was no point, therefore, in looking further for the little farm. Washington was where he would finish his days. At first, his reaction was angry and bitter. He lashed out at the city and those who lived in it. "It is a faceless, voiceless, terror-ridden wasteland of people sitting at desks, eating, going back and forth in automobiles, fornicating and keeping their mouths shut and seeing nothing, hearing nothing," he railed to Clifford Durr. "I don't care, I don't want to spend time with most people anyway, and the more they leave you alone the better I like it. . . . There is so little to live for. Only a few people that I love and admire, and my sons and grandchildren."[10]

Gradually, however, as he became used to the certitude that soon he would "simply slip into the long endless sleep from an awareness that I have never nor can never understand," some of the bitterness dissipated. He settled himself into a routine of working at his memoirs several hours a day, trying desperately, now that he was "old and near the end," to "put something down in writing." He particularly wanted to cover the New Deal years "and my puny efforts to help the Negro," but he also wrote on the contemporary scene and on the forces that had given his own life meaning.[11]

His comments on his country's future were usually dark with foreboding. Events, including the president's refusal to pardon Braden and Wilkinson in 1961, had, it seemed to him, amply justified his low opinion of Kennedy—"the most dangerous man in our lifetime to occupy the White House," he called him at this time. He was bitterly opposed to the young president's foreign policy, which he considered to be hopelessly reactionary, a continuation of the Cold War attitudes that had been proven bankrupt, in his view, in the previous decade, and which had led to so much repression and injustice. "We are a stupid people," he stated. "We have put the hard-nosed boys . . . in charge of foreign policy instead of the liberals and [they] do not really believe in freedom for the common people." "What we need to do is to begin to rely upon our way of life, rather than upon Armies and the C.I.A. . . . The world has gotten so rotten that I have no joy in it any more. What are we doing in Viet Nam, our being in bed with Chang Kai Shek [sic], Willie Brandt, Franco?" "When I was growing up," he recalled, "I was happy, of course I was young and full of vinegar. But we were proud of being the greatest democracy. The Statue of Liberty was our symbol. I loved the Stars and Stripes and tears rolled down my cheeks when they played Irving Berlin's 'I Love America.'" Not any more. America was a changed and, in some cases, terrifying place, and as he once told Lyndon Johnson, he was "frightened to my very core" for his grandchildren, who had to grow up in it.[12]

When he turned to writing about himself, as opposed to the events and movements in which he had played some part, Williams was concerned to make clear what it was that had shaped him, that had made him act in the ways he had. Again, as he had done all his life, he referred to quite traditional sources and value systems when attempting to explain himself to himself. He wrote about his Protestant heritage and its impulsion "to make life better, more just, to help make people more considerate of other people, kinder, and

more regardful of others. It's not that this heritage urges poking
ones nose into the affairs of others, though many think that is what
it amounts to. . . . It is based on anger that rises up in you when you
see a person or any living thing hurt by another person and are unable to do anything about it."

The code that this heritage inculcated was the one he had tried to
live by all his life, and the men whom he admired most were those
who seemed to personify its provisions. "All my life I have cata-
logued people by these values," he wrote. "I guess I put Jefferson at
the very top. Then early in life I decided I wanted to be like
Lincoln, his freeing the slaves made a great impression on me. His
sad, compassionate face, he became a pride and an example." Williams's intense feeling for Lincoln was doubtless unusual for a southerner, but ran deep. "A deathless heritage to all who shall fight for
freedom," he once called him.

He was often compared to Lincoln physically—both had the
same lanky, rather awkward frame and similarly gaunt features—
and he considered this to be vaguely irreverent. Once, during the
New Deal days, Jonathan Mitchell of the *New Republic* wrote an
article on Williams comparing his compassionate concern for the
underdog with Lincoln's. Thanking him, Williams wrote, "Curiously
he [Lincoln] always represented the Presidency of the United States.
I do not think I ever felt that anyone else really occupied the White
House, and also somewhat curiously I feel that no matter who is
there, Lincoln is always there. Others seem to me to have departed,
but he still remains."

He never articulated his debt to Jefferson as specifically. Perhaps
since he was a southerner, a liberal, and a defender of the "common
man," he felt the parallels were too obvious to require extended
comment.[13]

Finally, he admired Jesus. Williams had not been a practicing
Christian since his Cincinnati days, and he had little sympathy for
most doctrinal tenets. "I was never able to swallow this immaculate
conception doctrine," he confessed. "I had a feeling Mary, this is
sacrereligious [*sic*] I know might have strayed into the woods when
Joseph was working, many good women have. I thought of Jesus as
a good pure Man that so loved the world, but this business being
the son of God I have trouble with from the start." But at times,
Williams wrote as though he saw himself and Christ as having had

similar life experiences. "I saw Jesus as an outcast, a Pariah," he wrote, "whom every organization man was afraid to have anything to do with. All acquaintances of Joseph and Mary keeping out of sight when he was around, clubs refusing to have him as a speaker —a subversive, a first amendment case, in contempt of the official committees of his day."

Jesus Christ was always for him an example to follow, "the great Moralist, maybe the greatest" that had ever been. Throughout his life he turned to the gospels, not for spiritual solace, but for guidance on how to live. The only purpose Williams could find for "being born and living three score and ten years" was "to try to ease the hardships of myself and other living animals including human," and Jesus helped him with that. It is significant that even in these writings, the private thoughts of a dying man, there was no mention of Marx. The "pinkest of the pink" was cast very much in a traditional mold.

If Jesus had always been important to him, the institutional church was not. Some of the sharpest barbs in his last writings were reserved for organized religion. He was particularly severe on Catholics: they "give their people a lot of good theater, they cater to the lighter sides of human nature." Southern Baptists were to him "the most powerful force upholding segregation and the brutalizing treatment of the colored race" in the contemporary South. "If Jesus should rise and walk into any of the Southern Baptist Churches today," he alleged, "you could be sure that they would at least ask him to leave, and at the worst, they would hang him." The Presbyterians, "behaving as all well brought up young ladies should," also came under attack. Only the Methodists received even qualified praise. "With all its evil elements," Williams still thought that the Methodist church was "the most powerful force in the South today for equality, for democracy, for the inviolability of the rights of the individual." Generally, though, his view of the church was still as jaundiced in 1963 as it had been in 1921, when he made the decision to leave it.

Williams also wrote about his native region and its people. He was, as he had been all his life, bitterly critical of much of southern life, but through it all his compassion for the South and southerners, even for those who had most bitterly reviled him, was evident. Talking of "the poor white Southerner," for example, he described him as "worked to death on the land, worked to death in the mine or the mill or the factory, once again he got rid of his anger and his frustrations and fear and panic by taking after the Niggers." His problems had not been understood, he charged; "he has not been understood, he has been despised and insulted over and over, and he has been cheated and he has been gulled and he has been exploited. But the cause of the Negro cannot be won, the South cannot be saved until he too is saved." This attempt to explain, as much to himself as to anyone else, why his life had taken the course it had, what it was that had shaped his responses, provided some solace and comfort in those last years as he waited for death.[14]

There were moments of happiness, too, both public and private. The historic summer of 1963, when the southern black revolution reached its climax, filled him with joy and a profound sense of vindication. In that year, after Martin Luther King's assault on the city of Birmingham had broadened the essentially student-dominated protest movement of sit-ins and freedom rides into one with a genuine mass base among southern black people, the Kennedy administration was finally moved to propose the most sweeping civil rights legislation since Reconstruction. "How glorious everything is, breaking wide open for the Negro," Williams exulted to Dombrowski. "I read with disbelief place after place desegregation [sic]. My friend, you had more to do with bringing this about than any other white man. . . . I don't want to die of course, but I do thank whatever Powers there be that I have live [sic] long enough to see this happen."

There was some bitterness as well "at the way everyone now wants to climb on the Civil Rights bandwagon" and some criticism for Martin Luther King's "choice of white allies." He was disgusted at his involvement with Ralph McGill and Lillian Smith, for example, who, Williams claimed, no doubt unjustly, "would have spit on him five years ago." Exultant as "the present flood-tide" made him, he could not forget "those fearless ones who stood alone for many years," and he had hoped that they, not the McGills and the Smiths, "fair weather liberals," as he regarded them, might have gained some recognition in this hour of triumph. "Ah me," he mused, "but that is the way it has ever been. We were 'expendibles' [sic]." Nevertheless, the events themselves were dramatic vindication of their courage and their sacrifice.[15]

King's plan to lead a mass march on Washington in August 1963 in support of President Kennedy's omnibus civil rights bill fascinated him. He recalled his involvement with the proposed 1941 march and wrote to King about it. He urged the black leader to go through with the march: "Now that you have the ball rolling you must demonstrate more than ever," he said. He recounted the events of the meeting in La Guardia's office to King and told him that he should stand as firm now as Phillip Randolph had done in 1941. "Remember," he said, "you get nothing for free."

As the day of the march approached, he made plans to participate. Dombrowski, too, decided to attend, even though he was by now so crippled with arthritis that he could scarcely walk, and a wheelchair had to be hired for him. On August 28, along with a quarter of a million other Americans, black and white, Williams— pushing Dombrowski's wheelchair part of the way—marched with Martin Luther King to the Lincoln Memorial, there to stand, probably unrecognized, as King outlined his dream. All differences with the black leader were temporarily forgotten, as the two old warriors became caught up in the emotion of the moment, for it was a dream they shared, a dream they too had battled for. For Williams, August 28, 1963, was a wonderful day. Standing in that crowd, holding hands with a young woman named Donna, "a beauteous gal from Ohio," who had helped him with the chair, and singing with her the symbolic songs of freedom, he felt that perhaps it had all been worthwhile. If he was soon to return to earth, if he was soon to declare that marching was all very well but that the job was now to prevent King "from going over to the Urban League–N.A.A.C.P.– Core crowd," he still had this day to savor.[16]

The frequent visits to and from the family, particularly Morrison, Vivian, and the children, and the occasional talks with old friends from New Deal days also gave him pleasure. One of his first visitors on his return to Washington was the vice-president, Lyndon Johnson, who had read about the move north in a Baltimore paper. Mrs. Williams recalled that he spent most of the visit complaining about the powerlessness of his new job and about the insults he endured at the hands of the Kennedys, stamping around the small apartment, making such a racket that she was sure the neighbors would complain. The Williamses later returned the call, and Johnson came again to see him shortly after Kennedy was shot. Williams gave the new president, or "boy," as he normally addressed Johnson, the benefit of his counsel on various matters of state. Thus their friendship endured to the end, even though Williams profoundly disagreed with the escalating American involvement in Vietnam, and told the president so. Incidentally, in his kindness toward and concern for the old man, Johnson displayed a warm, human, generous side of his character which many of his biographers ignore.[17]

Occasionally, Williams traveled outside Washington, usually to attend dinners or other social events in his honor. A function held by the Chicago Committee to Defend the Bill of Rights in April 1963 prompted a tribute in the *Chicago Sunday American* from liberal columnist Irving Dillard. In a piece entitled "Salute to a Great Southerner" he asserted that "what Alabamian Hugo L. Black has been to the Bill of Rights on the Supreme Court, Aubrey W. Williams has been at the grass roots in the South. There is hardly a major phase of the life of the South that Aubrey Williams has not influenced for good."

In April 1964, several hundred persons whose lives he had touched honored him at a luncheon in Washington. One of these, Ruth France, writing to him about it, spoke of the young men and women all over the country who "had their chance because of the National Youth Administration" and had not forgotten him. "You might have thought that this was accomplishment enough," she continued, "but I suspect your greatest contribution by far will be what you did by going back to Alabama, and doing what had to be done there. You must take great satisfaction now, as you see your lost causes become great causes." Indeed he did. He gave thanks that he had lived long enough to see at least some of his personal concerns become national ones.[18]

The cancer, however, was growing worse. The Williamses had moved to a small, comfortable two-story house in northwest Washington, and it was there that Williams spent his last months, increasingly bedridden and often in great pain. He discouraged callers apart from his family. "I see as few people as possible," he told Myles Horton, who had asked for a visit, "and am not able to do anything, but if you wish—call me and if it is one of my good days I will see you." Before long, he had given up his daily writing and was simply waiting for the end.

In typical Williams fashion, though, he used his remaining

strength to compose farewell letters to his friends. These were often long, rambling, and disconnected affairs, obviously the work of a man who was failing fast. Yet much of his commitment, and his humor, remained to the very last. He hated the idea of going to hell, where he would assuredly end up, he told Avrahim Mezerik, the liberal author and editor, because "it will be full of Republicans and I can't talk to them." To Frank Wilkinson he offered advice on how to "get a budget" and an exhortation to carry on the struggle. "Remember always that you are fighting for the most precious thing there is," he urged, "the freedom of the individual. Bring in all nations and races of men, for they count this the most precious thing, just as you and I do. My sincere respect and love for you." Wilkinson, deeply moved, told him in reply that "your greatest contribution has been the contagion of your own commitment— that one must always struggle for the rights of man. And so I allow my memory to drink long upon our happiest hours. I hear your laughter and see your tears as you recount your reading of Twain: I hear you as the 'grandfather to end all grandfathers' . . . , and again you have entrapped me through your call for an appointment on an 'urgent matter'—only to find that we're just in time for the first race at Santa Anita. Oh Aubrey, we pledge to you and for you: *We shall overcome.*" There were many such tributes.[19]

By November, Williams was totally bedridden, unable to move and in terrible pain, conscious of the burden he was placing on Anita, and hoping that death would come soon. "Anita sleeps on top of the sheet in fear that I will kill myself," he told Mezerik. "Where did man get this idea that putting yourself out of pain was such an opprobrious thing—I think it should be encouraged by at least half of the population." He was still alive enough, however, to take great pleasure at Johnson's triumph over right-wing senator Barry Goldwater in the presidential election of that year. "Johnson I thought made a good campaign," he wrote, but "what he will do with this tremendous mandate nobody (I don't think he does) knows."[20]

Johnson's great victory, however, was one of his last memories. Toward the end of the year he slipped into a semicoma; the periods of lucidity became fewer and further between and eventually ceased altogether. His remaining strength kept him going for a few weeks more, but in the early hours of March 5, 1965, he died in his sleep.

Tributes and messages of sympathy poured in from all over the country. The president sent flowers, as did the first lady. "We are sad today," wrote Lady Bird Johnson. "Aubrey was part of our 'young days'—how we loved the work we did together in the N.Y.A. He was a valiant soldier in helping the young folks of our country." Anna Roosevelt Halstead recalled how much her parents had loved Aubrey, while Martin Luther King, their differences again forgotten, called him "a giant of a man." "His genuine goodwill," the black leader said, "broad humanitarian concern and unswerving commitment to the cause of freedom and justice will remain an inspiration to generations yet unborn." Equally impressive were the hundreds of messages from ordinary folk, people who had worked for the WPA and the NYA or who had read *Southern Farmer* and stood with him in their hearts.[21]

The liberal press mourned his passing. I. F. Stone talked of his Alabama populist heritage and claimed that he was "ruined politically by the streak of humanity in his genes. . . . Nothing in our time has been harder than to be a truly Christian white man in today's South. Aubrey was." The *Nation* called him "a great and good man who in his lifetime embodied the conscience of the white South." Perhaps the most moving tribute, however, was that paid by the *Washington Post*. His courage, the paper said, "was wrapped in extraordinary gentleness. . . . In all he did he was impelled by the same warm humanity and social concern. Of Aubrey Williams it could truly be said, above all else he loved his fellow man." It was a fitting epitaph.[22]

Conclusion
In Search of Aubrey Williams

When the great Progressive senator Robert La Follette of Wisconsin died in 1925, Senator William E. Borah reportedly said of him, "It is hard to say the right thing about Bob La Follette. You know he lived 150 years."[1] Any attempt to sum up the meaning of Aubrey Williams's life faces a similar sort of problem, for his public career stretched over more than four decades through periods of rapid social and political change and involved work in different regions, fields, and causes.

Yet his life did have a unity. Perhaps Frank Wilkinson expressed it best when he praised him for "the contagion of your own commitment—that one must always struggle for the rights of man." Whether as social worker, government official, publisher, civil rights activist, or crusader for civil liberties, that is what Williams always tried to do. His whole public life was a working out of his commitment to a need "to make life better, more just to help make people more considerate of people, kinder and more regardful of others." It was that commitment, and his refusal to compromise his ideals, that led him both to great triumphs, his rapid acceleration in the FERA and WPA hierarchies, for example, and to great defeats, the most important being his loss of the REA nomination in 1945.

The intensity with which he held his attitudes led at times to fierce self-excoriation, as when he acquiesced in the termination of the NYA camps for relocated Japanese-Americans during the fight to preserve the youth agency, for he felt he had fallen far short of his ideals. It led, too, to a bitter impatience with those who seemed to be compromising with the enemy, as, for example, he considered southern moderates like Lillian Smith and Ralph McGill to be doing, and even to dissension within his family circle. Aubrey, Jr., once remarked that his "ethics and integrity were hard for us lesser mortals to live with at times." His eldest son, Winston, who never finished high school and, unlike his brothers, showed little interest or involvement in the concerns of his father, was, according to Virginia Durr, treated unfairly for a while because of these supposed shortcomings. The high standards that he set himself he expected from others, and, obviously, not everyone could measure up.[2]

In Williams's last years he devoted much of his time to trying to explain to himself what it was that "made me tick," that fed his continuing passion for social and economic justice. His own answers to those questions—the importance of Jesus and the influence of the social gospel, his veneration of traditionally American heroes like Jefferson and Lincoln, his early absorption of southern populist egalitarianism—have already been discussed, and should be taken seriously. Williams believed he was shaped by these men and their ideas, and there is more than enough evidence in his public life of their influence to substantiate his claim.

As for those influences that he himself could not discern, and there were doubtless many, the evidence is, inevitably, rather silent. Williams himself seldom mentioned his mother, for example. Virginia Durr said that he was devoted to her, though he saw her very rarely after his departure from Birmingham in 1911, and certainly it was she, rather than his weak drifter of a father, who was important to him as a boy. She introduced him to Jesus, helped him as best she could to get the education that she so desired for him, fed his early commitment, the one that stayed with him throughout his life, to helping the less fortunate. Her influence on him must have been profound; yet the evidence is not there to draw any more specific conclusions. His relationships with his brothers and sisters were unexceptional. Again, he saw relatively little of them once he had left the South, and he had little in common with his brothers anyway, though he maintained a perfectly amicable relationship with them. He was closest to his elder sister Myrtice, who was a social worker in New Orleans and who shared many of his attitudes, including his position on race. They corresponded frequently, he visited her often, especially after his return to Montgomery, and they had a warm, loving involvement with each other.[3]

One point probably worth noting, and this may have some connection with his feeling for his mother and sister, is that throughout his life Williams enjoyed the company of, and was particularly influenced by, women older than himself, more often than not of high social station, women like Mrs. Steele, the pastor's wife in Birmingham, Mrs. Witter and Marie Kohler in Madison, and, above all, Mrs. Roosevelt. Their public partnership, their common concern for the problems of the young people of America, of the blacks, and of the unemployed, has already been discussed. It was without doubt the most important relationship of his public life.

The influence on him of Franklin Roosevelt was also profound. As has been pointed out, Williams was never as close to Roosevelt as he was to his wife; he always stood somewhat in awe of the president. Yet he never lost his faith in him, never doubted the extent and the sincerity of his liberal commitment. Even in crisis periods of his own life, that faith never wavered. In the painful interview preceding his departure from the WPA, Williams told Roosevelt that he understood why he was being passed over, apologized for his indiscretions, and pledged continued and total loyalty.

He believed that the 1944 election campaign was the clarion call for a renewed and widened New Deal offensive, and his nomination as REA administrator seemed to confirm that to him. Forced to work with reactionary forces during the war, Roosevelt had decided to break free as peace approached. Williams had been given the job, he believed, because the president wanted someone who shared his convictions, someone who would not compromise one iota with reactionary southern political leaders. Perhaps he was wrong in that faith, perhaps he was dazzled by the Roosevelt charm, but perhaps not. Certainly, he never thought so.[4]

The South, Jesus, Jefferson, Lincoln, the Roosevelts—according to Williams, these were the forces and people that helped make him what he was. There were many others, some recognized— John L. Lewis, Harry Hopkins, and, of course, James Dombrowski —some not. Southern poverty and injustice instilled in him a sense of anger and need, and great public figures gave him a sense of higher possibilities. Together they formed his driving dream, a dream which many of his adversaries found so startling that they traced its origins to alien philosophies. Yet when its outlines are examined no radical doctrines emerge.

Given such essentially American sources of inspiration, it is not surprising that Williams's dream was a variation on familiar themes. Perhaps he gave it its clearest articulation in those tortured weeks following March 1945 when he lost a job he wanted desperately and then the president he revered and loved. In a long, often moving document written for his files, he tried to set down an explanation of, and a justification for, his political beliefs because "these beliefs and attitudes have been the subjects of a debate in our highest legislative body." Williams's document revealed, for example, that he believed in free enterprise, but with equal opportunity for all—no monopolies or giant corporations. He believed in strong labor unions, public housing, public health, public education. He believed in the right of all Americans to earn their own livings, and that it was a duty of government to provide for those unable to do so. He believed that the New Deal had, basically, been traversing the correct paths, if not as far or as fast as was necessary. He also believed, however, that the momentum that it had engendered could not be checked, that a "new day was dawning," and that the "wider distribution of opportunity" would be a fact of postwar American life.

Much of his later bitterness is explained by the puncturing of this dream. Williams was a social democrat and, in some ways, a radical; yet his radicalism was entirely traditional. He was very much in the reformist mainstream; he simply wanted to push his country closer to what he thought was its wellspring. Never a revolutionary, Williams saw at the end of the dream only a fully developed, essentially American, welfare state, one in which traditionally egalitarian and humanistic ideals would at last be realized.[5]

This traditional egalitarianism informed his struggle on behalf of America's blacks and set him apart from many of his fellow southern liberals. Opening a Negro youth center in Birmingham in 1938, Williams said, as has already been mentioned, "I made up my mind long ago to use my power to help those at the bottom of the social and economic ladder in America. I have and will continue to play that part. I don't care who knows it. I want it. . . . I want to say as a Southerner I covenant that the black man shall have his share in that better life." For the rest of his life, Williams strove to keep that covenant despite all the vilification and loneliness that it caused him. It was his key concern after 1945.

Why he, a southerner, should have believed in the cause of black equality so passionately cannot be known with certainty. Obviously, his deep-seated belief in equality of opportunity for all had much to do with it, while his long sojourn outside the South doubtless helped him shed any racism that his southern boyhood may have bred in him. Williams, who wore few convictions lightly, took none more seriously than this commitment to securing racial justice in America. At times pessimistic about the efficiency of his "puny efforts," as he once called them, in the end he lived long enough to see his position vindicated. Finally, his sacrifices seemed worthwhile.[6]

As has been pointed out, Williams was never a first-rank New Deal figure; yet he was probably the most important spokesman for its social democratic left wing. As such, he was a distinctive New Deal type. Thousands like him worked in local NYA and Farm Security Administration offices, on the Federal Writers Project and the WPA educational program, and in the REA, the FHA, and the FCC. They did a host of different jobs, but all thought of themselves in some degree as being part of a sweeping social movement, saw themselves as the local agents of a general social change, and believed implicitly in its value. Williams was one of the most visible of this group and, as such, became an important symbol of their hopes. Those like him recognized this—and loved him for it. Moreover, at few other times in American history have men of his particular social vision been as close to power and been able to influence important events as they were then, if only for a time. The New Deal gave wider credence to the social democratic tradition than it has had at any other time in America, and Williams was among the most important of the thousands who were able to contribute because of this.

Similarly, though not a major figure in the constellation of brave men who changed the shape of the American South, Williams was nevertheless representative of a group of people whose role in that great drama should not be forgotten. He was one of the most important of the lonely band of white liberals who in the years of segregation stood against the prevailing mores; the conscience of the white South, they reminded their white fellow citizens that there was another way to glory and enabled black southerners to realize that not all white faces were enemy faces. They were few and were much reviled; yet "they too," as Morton Sosna has written so movingly, "had a dream." If that dream is now at least part reality, men like Williams played a vital role in making it all possible.[7]

When Williams died, Hubert Humphrey, then vice-president, mourned that "America has lost a great fighter for human rights." I. F. Stone spoke of Williams's loneliness as being "the price of living in full accord with a tender conscience." Such a conscience impelled this tall, passionate, decent man to become what he was, to do what he did, to refuse to compromise his ideals, to fight doggedly for what he thought was right. Paying tribute to him after his death, his friend Sylvia Crane remarked that these efforts had enlarged "the scope of human dignity everywhere." The judgment was apt.[8]

Notes

This book was written to appeal to the general reader as well as to the historian. Accordingly, the scholarly apparatus has been kept to a minimum, and the documentation is presented as simply as possible. To keep the text uncluttered, the sources for quotations and other items are often summarized in notes covering one or more paragraphs. Sources in each note are generally given in the order in which the information appears in the text; by matching text and notes the reader should be able to discern the source for any particular item.

Chapter 1

1. For Alabama politics see Sheldon Hackney, *From Populism to Progressivism in Alabama*, and William D. Barnard, *Dixiecrats and Democrats*, especially chap. 1. Aubrey Williams left two collections of papers, that held by the Franklin Delano Roosevelt Library and hereafter cited as Williams Papers, and a smaller collection held privately by his widow, Mrs. Anita Williams of Washington, D.C., when I used it (hereafter cited as Williams, Private Material). The latter collection was subsequently sent to Hyde Park to be assimilated into the main collection. It includes extensive autobiographical material written by Williams during the last years of his life. I would like to thank Mrs. Williams for allowing me to use this collection. The above quotation can be found in folder B.1.

2. Williams, Private Material, folder B.1. See also biographical details in Williams Papers, boxes 37, 42, and 47. These are principally clippings from newspapers, mainly written on the occasion of his nomination to be rural electrification administrator in 1945. See also *Washington Post*, December 26, 1938.

3. Williams, Private Material, folder B.1.

4. C. Vann Woodward, *The Origins of the New South*, pp. 136–37, 227.

5. Williams Papers, box 37, biographical material. Williams, Private Material, folder B.1.

6. Williams, Private Material, folder B.1.

7. Ibid.

8. Ibid.

9. Ibid. See also Williams to Joe and Lee Slaughter, July 24, 1935, Williams Papers, box 4.

10. Williams, Private Material, folder B.1. See also biographical data in Williams Papers, box 37.

11. Williams, Private Material, folder B.1.

12. Ibid.

13. Woodward, *Origins of the New South*, pp. 212–15, 232–34.

14. Williams, Private Material, folder B.1.

15. Ibid. See also Williams Papers, box 37.

16. Williams, Private Material, folder B.1.

17. Ibid.

18. Ibid.

Chapter 2

1. Williams, Private Material, folder B.16. James Cass and Max Birnbaum, eds., *Comparative Guide to American Colleges*, p. 341.

2. Williams, Private Material, "Maryville." Williams to A. W. Calhoun, February 16, 1959, Williams Papers, box 30.

3. Williams, Private Material, "Maryville."

4. Ibid.

5. Judge Wiley Rutledge to Williams, June 17, 1940, Williams Papers, box 4.

6. Williams to Judy Papier, January 7, 1956, Williams Papers, box 32; Williams to Charles L. (Turkey) Smith, July 16, 1935, Williams Papers, box 4. Williams, Private Material, "Maryville."

7. Williams to "Turkey" Smith, July 16, 1935, Williams Papers, box 4; Grace Jewell Mounce to Williams, January 12, 1936, Williams Papers, box 2.

8. Williams, Private Material, folder B.9.

9. Williams, Private Material, "Maryville."

10. Ibid.

11. Ibid.

12. Zane L. Miller, *Boss Cox's Cincinnati*, pp. 3, 5, 98–99, 155–57.

13. O. W. Thomas to Williams, December 7, 1936, Williams Papers, box 4; Williams to Wayne Coy, February 25, 1937, ibid. Williams, Private Material, "Army Stitch."

14. Williams, Private Material, "Army Stitch." See also biographical material in Williams Papers, box 37.

15. Williams, Private Material, "Army Stitch." Louis E. Nohl to Williams, July 6, 1936, Williams Papers, box 3. Adjutant General to Williams, November 11, 1937, Williams, Private Material, clippings and letters.

16. Adjutant General to Williams, November 11, 1937, Williams, Private Material, "Army Stitch."

17. Williams, Private Material, "Army Stitch."

18. Adjutant General to Williams, November 11, 1937, Williams, Private Material, clippings and letters, folder B.3, "Return from France."

19. Williams, Private Material, "At War's End."

20. Ibid. See also Williams to Professor Talbert, September 8, 1958, November 20, 1958, Williams Papers, box 32.

21. Williams, Private Material, "At War's End." See also Williams Papers, boxes 1 and 52.

22. Williams, Private Material, "At War's End." Williams to Anita Schreck, April 6, 1920, December 18, 1920, Williams Papers, Box 1.

23. Williams, Private Material, folder B.3, "Return from France." Rev. J. M. Broady to Williams, February 22, 1922, Williams Papers, box 1.

24. Williams, Private Material, "At War's End."

Chapter 3

1. The Records of the Wisconsin Welfare Council Papers, 1919–58 (formerly the Wisconsin Conferences of Social Work) are held at the State Historical Society, Madison, Wisconsin. They will be referred to henceforth as WCSW Records. Material for the foregoing section is drawn particularly from box 1, folder 15 (Report of the Business Meeting, WCSW, October 12, 1922), and box 4, folder 15 (*A Statement of Purpose, Work and Organization of the Wisconsin Conference of Social Work*, May 1926). See also Williams Papers, box 44, "The New Deal—A Dead Battery," and Lubove, *The Professional Altruist*.

2. Williams, Private Material, folder B.2. WCSW Records, box 1, folder 15 (Business Meeting Report, October 12, 1922; Report of Executive Secretary, October 13, 1922).

3. Williams, Private Material, folder B.2. Interview with Mrs. Anita Williams, (henceforth Anita Williams interview), Washington, D.C., April 4, 1976.

4. WCSW Records, box 1, folder 15 (Board of Directors, May 31, November 13, 1923, April 17, 1924). Ibid., box 7, folders 1 and 2 (Scoring Schedules for Better Cities Contest).

5. WCSW Records, box 1, folder 15 (Board of Directors, January 21, 1925–January 7, 1926).

6. Mrs. Areson was soon to be replaced by Edith "Jane" Foster who was later to work with Williams on the FERA and the WPA and with whom he maintained a life-long friendship. WCSW Records, box 1, folder 16 (Report to Board of Directors, October 5, 1926, February 18, 1927, October 3, 1928).

7. Williams, Private Material, folder B.2. WCSW Records, box 2, folder 1 (copies of speeches made on behalf of the Children's Code). Marvin B. Rosenberry to Walter K. Morley (Madison, Wisconsin), June 17, 1925, in Marvin B. Rosenberry Papers, State Historical Society of Wisconsin (henceforth Rosenberry Papers), box 9.

8. WCSW Records, box 1, folders 25 and 26 (proposed legislation, 1928), folder 16 (Report to annual meeting, October 7, 1929).

9. Williams, Private Material, folder B.2. Anita Williams interview.

10. WSCW Records, box 1, folder 16 (Board of Directors, January 23, April 24, October 2, 1931, March 10, 1932).

11. Ibid., box 1, folder 16 (Board of Directors, March 21, 1930, October 2, November 20, 1931).

12. Ibid., box 1, folder 16 (Board of Directors, May 6, 1931; Executive Committee March 6, 1931). For a discussion of the debate over work relief see Chambers, *Seedtime of Reform*, particularly pp. 188, 205–7.

13. WCSW Records, box 1, folder 16 (Executive Committee, March 6, 1931). Williams, Private Material, folder B.2.

14. Mr. Irving Seaman to Mrs. Florence Buckstaff, January 8, 11, 1932, Board of Directors, June 17, 1932, all in WCSW Records, box 1, folder 16. Mrs. Buckstaff was the conference's president, Miss Kohler having resigned in 1930.

15. Williams, Private Material, folder B.2. Williams to Marie Kohler, May 20, 1930, Williams Papers, box 1.

16. WCSW Records, box 1, folder 16 (Board of Directors, October 8, 1930). Williams to J. B. Huenink, Holland Fox Fur Company, January 15, 1932, Williams Papers, box 1. Williams, Private Material, folder B.2.

17. Williams to Elmer Scott, executive secretary, Civic Federation of Dallas, October 6, 1931, Williams Papers, box 1. Regents of the University of Wisconsin to Williams, July 20, 1932, ibid. File of lecture notes, reading lists, etc., in Williams Papers, box 5. Williams, Private Material, folder B.2. Anita Williams interview.

18. "The New Deal—A Dead Battery" in "A Southern Rebel," Williams Papers, box 44.

19. Records of the Federal Emergency Relief Administration (henceforth FERA Records), record group 69, National Archives, Washington, D.C. *Reports of Reconstruction Finance Corporation Field Representatives re the Relief Situation in States, 1932–33.* See Pierce Williams to Fred Croxton, November 2, 1932, "It occurred to me that you could get the benefit of Aubrey Williams's services as a special cooperating representative through the American Public Welfare Association." Tindall, *The Emergence of the New South*, p. 374. Hoover, *The Memoirs of Herbert Hoover*, Vol. 3. *The Great Depression*, p. 174.

20. "The New Deal—A Dead Battery," in "A Southern Rebel," Williams Papers, box 44. Williams, Private Material, folder B.17.

21. "The New Deal—A Dead Battery," in "A Southern Rebel," Williams Papers, box 44. Williams, Private Material, folder B.17.

22. Tindall, *Emergence of the New South*, p. 374. "The New Deal—A Dead Battery," Williams Papers, box 44. Williams, Private Material, folder B.5.

23. "The New Deal—A Dead Battery," Williams Papers, box 44. Williams, Private Material, folder B.5.

24. Tindall, *Emergence of the New South*, pp. 27–28, 233, 648.

25. Tindall, *Emergence of the New South*, p. 422. "The New Deal—A Dead Battery," Williams Papers, box 44. Williams, Private Material, folder B.17.

26. Rose Nathanson to Williams, November 19, December 8, 1932, Williams Papers, box 1. Professor John L. Gillin to Williams, November 14, 1932, ibid. Anita Williams interview, April 4, 1976.

27. "The New Deal—A Dead Battery," Williams Papers, box 44. Williams, Private Material, folder B.5.

Chapter 4

1. For a description of the creation of the FERA see Charles, *Minister of Relief*, pp. 1–44, and Burns and Williams, *Federal Work, Security and Relief Programs*, pp. 21–28.

2. WCSW Records, box 1, folder 16 (Board of Directors, January 20, 1933, June 19, 1933; Executive Committee, May 12, 1933).

3. Williams, Private Material, folder B.5.

4. Ibid. See also Tindall, *The Emergence of the New South*, p. 475.

5. Williams to Harry Hopkins, July 2, 12, August 6, 1933, Records of the Federal Emergency Relief Administration (henceforth FERA Records), State Series, 1933–36, Arkansas. Williams, Private Material, folder B.5.

6. Williams to Harry Hopkins, August 6, 12, 1933, FERA Records, State Series, 1933–36, Arkansas. Hopkins to Williams, August 16, 1933, ibid.

7. Williams to Harry Hopkins, July 16, August 14, 16, 1933, FERA Records, State Series, 1933–36, Mississippi.

8. Williams to Harry Hopkins, July 24, September 13, October 13, 1933, FERA Records, State Series, 1933–36, Alabama.

9. Williams, Private Material, folder B.5. Williams to Harry Hopkins, August 10, 16, 1933, FERA Records, State Series, 1933–36, Texas. Report of FERA conference, September 5–8, 1933, Hopkins Papers, box 25, conferences.

10. Report of FERA conference, September 5–8, 1933, Hopkins Papers, box 25, conferences. Williams, Private Material, folder B.5. Charles, *Minister of Relief*, pp. 46–48. Adams, *Harry Hopkins* pp. 56–57. Schlesinger, *Coming of the New Deal*, pp. 268–69.

11. Williams to Hopkins, August 10, September 20, 21, 1933, FERA Records, State Series, 1933–36, Texas. *Dallas Morning News*, September 20, 1933. Both Westbrook and Marie Dresden were shortly to come to Washington, Westbrook initially as head of the FERA's Division of Rural Rehabilitation and Stranded Populations, and Marie Dresden in a variety of capacities, including a stint with the NYA. They both became firm friends of Williams.

12. Williams to Hopkins, October 11, November 9, 1933, FERA Records, State Series, 1933–36, Texas. Schlesinger, *Coming of the New Deal*, pp. 274–76.

13. Williams to Hopkins, October 19, 1933, FERA Records, State Series, 1933–36, Louisiana.

14. Williams to Hopkins, October 30, 1933, Williams Papers, box 27.

15. Adams, *Harry Hopkins*, p. 57. Williams to Searle F. Charles, October 16, 1952, Williams Papers, box 30.

16. Charles, *Minister of Relief*, p. 48. Williams to Anita Williams, November 7, 1933, Williams Papers, box 27.

17. Williams, Private Material, folder B.5. Hopkins to Aubrey Williams, November 8, 1933, Williams Papers, box 27.

Chapter 5

1. Minutes of conference of State Governors and Mayors, November 15, 1933, Hopkins Papers, box 25, conferences. Charles, *Minister of Relief*, pp. 48–52. Burns and Williams, *Federal Work, Security and Relief Programs*, pp. 29–37.

2. Hopkins to Roosevelt, December 12, 1933, Williams Papers, box 3. Charles, *Minister of Relief*, pp. 51–52. Adams, *Harry Hopkins*, p. 58.

3. Charles, *Minister of Relief*, p. 59.

4. Ibid, p. 65.

5. Rep. John Dockweiler to Hopkins, January 9, 1934, Records of the Civil Works Administration (henceforth CWA Records) National Archives, Washington D.C., State Series, 1933–34. Williams to Dockweiler, January 10, 1934, ibid.

6. John C. Lindsay to Williams, January 26, 1934, CWA Records, administrative correspondence, State Series, 1933–34. Hopkins to Hubert Fairall, January 29, 1934, ibid.

7. Williams to Hopkins, January 13, 1934, Williams to Algernon Blair, January 11, 1934, Williams to Rep. Lister Hill, February 23, 1934, all in CWA Records, State Series, 1933–34.

8. Two recent studies which discuss both "race liberalism" in the 1930s and black responses to it are Kirby, *Black Americans in the Roosevelt Era*, and Sitkoff, *A New Deal for Blacks*. On blacks in the CCC, see Salmond, *The Civilian Conservation Corps*, pp. 88–101.

9. Williams to George B. Power, December 29, 1933, to T. Arnold Hill, January 30, 1934, to Robert L. Vann, January 26, 1934, all in CWA Records, interracial correspondence.

10. Williams to Hopkins, January 16, 1934, Hopkins to Williams, January 23, 1934, Williams to Will Alexander, January 29, 1934, all in CWA Records, interracial correspondence. Williams to Eugene Jones, adviser on negro affairs, Department of Commerce, August 17, 1934, FERA Records, Old Subject File, interracial relations. On Washington, see Kirby, *Black Americans*, pp. 58, 139–45.

11. Williams to Mrs. Roosevelt, undated 1934, FERA Records, Old Subject File, interracial relations.

12. Charles, *Minister of Relief*, p. 65.

13. Williams, Private Material, "The C.W.A."

14. Charles, *Minister of Relief*, pp. 66–67. *New York Times*, April 1, 1934.

15. Charles, *Minister of Relief*, p. 31. Malcolm Miller to Williams, November 30, 1934, FERA Records, State Series, 1933–36, Arkansas.

16. Williams, Private Material, folder B.8.

17. Ibid. Adams, *Harry Hopkins*, pp. 63–65. *New York Times*, August 9, 10, 14, 1934. Williams to Hopkins, July 24, 1934, Hopkins Papers, box 100. George S. Wilson to Williams, April 2, 1934, FERA Records, New Subject File, personal correspondence of Aubrey Williams. Williams to George S. Wilson, April 11, 1934, ibid.

18. Williams, Private Material, folder B.8. Macmahon, Millett, and Ogden, *The Administration of Federal Work Relief*, pp. 25–26.

19. Anita Williams interview. Interview with Virginia Foster Durr, Wetumpka, Alabama (henceforth Durr interview), May 29, 31, 1976. Williams to Harrison Garner (Madison, Wisconsin), January 27, 1934, Williams Papers, box 53. Williams to Paul E. Stark (Madison, Wisconsin), August 20, 1934, ibid.

20. Williams, Private Material, folder B.8. Anita Williams interview.

21. Williams, Private Material, "Groups in the New Deal."

22. Ibid.

23. Ibid.

24. *New York Times*, April 1, August 10, 1934.

25. Charles, *Minister of Relief*, pp. 44–48.

26. Sherwood, *Roosevelt and Hopkins*, p. 65. Williams confirms this account in Williams, Private Material, "Harry Hopkins."

27. *New York Times*, November 30, 1934. Williams to Mrs. Isaac Witter, October 1, 1934, Williams Papers, box 5. Williams, Private Material, folder B.6. Charles, *Minister of Relief*, p. 94.

28. *New York Times*, May 7, 1934.

29. Rawick, "The New Deal and Youth," pp. 18–35. See also Davis, *The Lost Generation*, pp. 168–69; Lorwin, *Youth Work Programs*; and Lindley and Lindley, *A New Deal for Youth*, pp. 6–11.

30. Davis, *The Lost Generation*, p. 105. Chamberlain, "Our Jobless Youth," pp. 579–82. Melvin, *Youth, Millions Too Many?* p. 155.

31. For the CCC, see Salmond, *The Civilian Conservation Corps*.

32. "A Work Program for American Youth" (typescript), in records of the National Youth Administration (henceforth NYA Records) in National Archives, Washington, D.C., file 75, working and data files on an NYA history project. See also Lindley and Lindley, *A New Deal for Youth*, p. 11; Rawick, "The New Deal and Youth," pp. 172–73. U.S. Federal Security Agency, *NYA Final Report*, pp. 47–48.

33. U.S. Federal Security Agency, *NYA Final Report*. See also Ella Ketchin, "Report on Camps for 1936 Fiscal Year," NYA Records, file 325, correspondence of the director of Division of Educational Camps. For transient youth see NYA Records, file 38, quasi-official correspondence and data file of the deputy executive director, 1935–38.

34. Rawick, "The New Deal and Youth," p. 175.

35. Eunice Fuller Barnard, "Youth Cries Out for a Salvaging Hand," *New York Times*, July 1, 1934. John A. Lang to Roosevelt, October 27, 1934, Williams Papers, box 13.

36. Hopkins to FERA State Administrators, October 3, 1934, Williams Papers, box 13. Memo for files, December 1934, Williams Papers, box 13. Williams to Tilla Durr, May 7, 1957, Williams Papers, box 32. See also "The NYA," in Williams, Private Material.

37. Memo for files, December 1934, Williams Papers, box 13. Fred J. Kelly to Williams, November 7, 1934, ibid. "The NYA," in Williams, Private Material. Rawick, "The New Deal and Youth" p. 176.

Chapter 6

1. Charles, *Minister of Relief*, pp. 100–101. Adams, *Harry Hopkins*, pp. 72–73. Leuchtenburg, *F.D.R. and the New Deal*, pp. 124–25.

2. Leuchtenburg, *F.D.R. and the New Deal*, pp. 124–25. Charles, *Minister of Relief*, pp. 104–5, Adams, *Harry Hopkins*, pp. 76–77. Williams, Private Material, folder B.8.

3. Williams, Private Material, folder B.7. Charles, *Minister of Relief*, pp. 108–20. Adams, *Harry Hopkins*, pp. 78–81.

4. Williams, Private Material, folder B.7. *New York Times*, November 24, 1935. Adams, *Harry Hopkins*, pp. 83–84.

5. Hopkins to Roosevelt, April 11, 1935, Williams Papers, box 13. See also

Rawick, "The New Deal and Youth," pp. 177–78.

6. See the file on Studebaker's program in Williams Papers, box 13. See also Rawick, "The New Deal and Youth," pp. 182–84.

7. Frances Perkins to Harold L. Ickes, May 6, 1935, Williams Papers, box 13.

8. Marvin McIntyre to Taussig, April 23, Papers of Franklin D. Roosevelt (henceforth Roosevelt Papers), official file 444-D. Charles Taussig to David Sarnoff, April 18, 1935, Papers of Charles W. Taussig (henceforth Taussig Papers), box 8. Taussig to Owen D. Young, April 23, 1935, Taussig Papers, box 16. Taussig to Aubrey Williams, May 13, 1935, ibid., box 19. Taussig to Roosevelt, May 1935, Roosevelt Papers, OF 444-D.

9. Roosevelt to Hopkins, May 28, 1935, draft proposal labeled "Early June," both in Williams Papers, box 13. Rawick "The New Deal and Youth," p. 182–85.

10. Studebaker to Hopkins, June 8, 1935, Williams Papers, box 13. Steve Early to Hopkins, June 14, 1935, Roosevelt Papers, OF 444-D.

11. Williams, Private Material, "The NYA" Williams to Tilla Durr, May 7, 1957, Williams Papers, box 32. Roosevelt to Early, June 10, 1935, Early to Hopkins, June 14, 1935, both in Roosevelt Papers, OF 444-D. Eleanor Roosevelt, *This I Remember*, pp. 162–63. Lash, *Eleanor and Franklin*, pp. 539–40. Kearney, *Anna Eleanor Roosevelt*, pp. 23–26.

12. Early to Hopkins, June 14, 18, 1935, Roosevelt Papers, OF 444-D. *New York Times*, June 27, 1935.

13. Williams, Private Material, folder B.7.

14. Williams, Private Material, folder B.7. *New York Times*, November 24, 1935, February 16, 1936. Charles, *Minister of Relief*, pp. 128–32.

15. Charles, *Minister of Relief*. For a full description of the way the WPA operated see Macmahon, Millett, and Ogden, *The Administration of Federal Work Relief*.

16. Charles, *Minister of Relief*, pp. 134–36. Macmahon, Millett, and Ogden, *The Administration of Federal Work Relief*. See also WPA Records, State Series, field reports.

17. Williams, Private Material, folder B.7.

18. *New York Times*, July 7, 1936. Adams, *Harry Hopkins*, pp. 92–94, 113–14.

19. *New York Times*, August 23, October 6, 1935, February 16, 1936. Adams, *Harry Hopkins*, pp. 86–87.

20. Williams, Private Material, "Groups in the New Deal."

21. *New York Times*, June 12, 14, July 25, 1936.

22. Williams to Rep. John Dockweiler (Democrat, California), October 29, 1938, WPA Records, State Series. Williams to W. G. Henderson, July 6, 1938, ibid.

23. Williams to Senator Morris Sheppard, November 6, 1938, ibid.

24. J. Banks Hudson to Williams, October 5, December 8, 1938, ibid.

25. *New York Times*, October 13, 1935.

26. *New York Times*, July 25, August 9, 1936.

27. Williams, Private Material, folder B.8. Senator Josh Lee to Williams, July 30, year missing, Williams Papers, box 28. Salmond, *The Civilian Conservation Corps*, pp. 102–6.

28. Williams to Robert V. Hinckley, November 24, 1938, Ray Crow (Alabama) to Williams, February 17, 1936, Williams to Thad Holt (Alabama), April 22, 1937, Williams to A. P. Morgan (Alabama), January 30, 1937, all in WPA Records, State Series.

29. Williams to Ray Branion, January 18, 1936, WPA Records, General Subject Series.

30. Williams to John Rankin (Philadelphia), January 30, 1936, WPA Records, State Series.

31. Williams, Private Material, folders B.7 and B.9.

32. Williams, Private Material, "Groups in the New Deal." Interview, Mary Anderson Bain, Washington D.C., April 6, 1976. *New York Times*, December 6, 1936.

33. Leuchtenburg, *F.D.R. and the New Deal*, p. 328. Williams, Private Material, folder B.7.

34. Adams, *Harry Hopkins*, pp. 123–35. *New York Times*, October 17, 20, November 7, 1937, March 27, 1938.

35. *New York Times*, June 5, 1938.

36. Williams, Private Material, "Some New Dealers." Anita Williams interview. Aubrey Williams, Jr., interview. Virginia Durr interview.

37. *New York Times*, June 28, 1938.

38. *Chicago Tribune*, June 29, 1938. *Washington Post*, June 29, 1938. *St. Louis Post Dispatch*, June 28, 1938.

39. *New York Times*, June 29, 1938. C. S. Boothby to Williams, June 28, 1938, Williams Papers, box 3. R. B. Altridge to Williams, July 1, 1938, ibid.

40. *New York Times*, June 29, 30, 1938.

41. Williams, Private Material, "Some New Dealers."

42. *New York Times*, July 3, 4, 5, 1938. *Chicago Tribune*, July 10, 1938.

43. *New York Times*, July 7, 1938.

44. Williams, Private Material, "Some New Dealers." *Chicago Tribune*, November 24, 1938. *New York Times*, November 23, 1938.

45. Williams, Private Material, "Some New Dealers."

46. *Time*, January 2, 1939. *New York Times*, December 26, 1939. Williams, Private Material, folder B.9 and "Some New Dealers."

47. Adams, *Harry Hopkins*, p. 145. Williams, Private Material, "Some New Dealers." *St. Louis Post Dispatch*, December 22, 1938. *Washington Post*, December 22, 1938.

48. *Washington Post*, December 22, 23, 26, 1938. *Time*, January 2, 30, 1939.

49. Williams to Leo Schreck, January 9, 1939, Williams Papers, box 13. Williams to Jane Foster, January 7, 1939, ibid.

50. Williams to Mrs. W. K. Clements, April 19, 1939, ibid.

Chapter 7

1. NYA Records, group 33, Minutes of State Directors Conference, August 20, 1935, "Thumbnail Sketches of State Directors of N.Y.A. as of August 12, 1935."

NYA Records, group 38. For examples of pressure from young people wanting assistance see NYA Records, group 40, miscellaneous alphabetical correspondence, 1935–41.

2. See press release, in Williams Papers, box 16. NYA Records, group 95, biographical sketches of NYA officials.

3. NYA Records, group 33. "Thumbnail sketches."

4. Marvin McIntyre to Williams, July 16, 1935, Roosevelt Papers, OF 444-D. NYA Records, group 2, records of the chairman of the National Advisory Committee, biographical notes on members of the National Advisory Board of the NYA.

5. NYA Records, group 75, Minutes of the National Advisory Committee Meeting, August 15, 1935.

6. NYA Records, group 33, Conference of State Youth Directors, August 20–21, 1935. *New York Times*, August 21, 1935.

7. Burns Weston to Taussig, October 19, November 9, 1935, Isaac Sutton to Taussig, October 31, 1935, all in Taussig Papers, box 17. Mrs. Roosevelt to Williams, October 31, 1935, Williams Papers, box 4.

8. *New York Times*, October 17, 1935.

9. Ibid. See also transcript of a telephone conversation between Williams and Osborne, November 18, 1935, Williams Papers, box 28.

10. Williams-Osborne telephone conversation, November 18, 1935, Williams Papers, box 28. For McCarl see Williams to Hopkins, October 10, 1935, Hopkins Papers, box 81.

11. Williams-Osborne phone conversation, November 18, 1935, transcript of telephone conversation between Taussig and Osborne, November 18, 1935, both in Williams Papers, box 28. See Mrs. Roosevelt to Williams, October 31, November 30, 1935, Williams to Mrs. Roosevelt, October 10, December 19, 1935, January 15, 1936, both in Papers of Eleanor Roosevelt (henceforth Eleanor Roosevelt Papers). Selection pertaining to the NYA and to Aubrey Williams microfilmed by the library staff for the author and is in his possession. *New York Times*, August 27, November 15, 1935, January 9, 1936. *New Republic* 86, no. 1118 (May 6, 1936): 366–7.

12. NYA Records, group 75, Minutes of the National Advisory Committee, August 15, 1935. Rawick, "The New Deal and Youth," p. 20. Salmond, *The Civilian Conservation Corps*, pp. 88–101. Poynton, "The Negro Division of the N.Y.A." I am indebted to Ms. Poynton's work for much of what follows on blacks in the NYA.

13. Ambrose Caliver to Dr. L. R. Gilderman and Mr. John L. Corson, July 27, 1935, Minutes of Conference of Negro Leaders, August 1935, in NYA Records, group 116, Records of the Officer of Negro Affairs, file of early "inactive" correspondence, 1935–38. Ibid., 118, Final Report of the Director of the Office of Negro Affairs (1943).

14. NYA Records, group 116, Minutes of Conference of Negro Leaders, August 8, 1935. Mary McLeod Bethune to Corson, August 24, 1935, NYA Records, group 1, Proceedings and Correspondence of the National Advisory Committee. press release, December 2, 1935, Williams Papers, box 16. Saddler

held the position only until mid-1936, when it was abolished and an Office of Negro Affairs created in its place with Mary McLeod Bethune as its head.

15. Corson to William J. Campbell (Illinois), September 17, 26, 1935, Brown to Bruce Overton (Tennessee), December 17, 1935, both in NYA Records, group 2, Records of the Chairman of the National Advisory Committee.

16. Williams to Mrs. Roosevelt, December 23, 1935, January 15, 1936, *Report on Educational Camps for Young Women*, February 10, 1936, all in Eleanor Roosevelt Papers, microfilm selection. Charles Taussig, "Youth and Democracy," typescript of an address given to a meeting of the Parents League of Greenwich, Connecticut, February 18, 1936, Taussig Papers, box 14. Taussig to Judd, November 29, 1935, F.D.R. to Secretary of the Treasury, December 11, 1935, both in Taussig Papers, box 4. *Report on National Advisory Committee Activities*, Eleanor Roosevelt Papers, microfilm selection.

17. Williams, Private Material, "The N.Y.A." Judd to Studebaker, April 21, 1936, Taussig Papers, box 4. Selma Borchard to William H. Hinckley, March 17, 1936, ibid., box 1.

18. *Report on Educational Aid*, February 10, 1936, Eleanor Roosevelt Papers, microfilm selection. Minutes of NAC Meetings, April 28 and 29, 1936 (henceforth 1936, NAC Minutes), NYA Records, group 75.

19. *Report on N.Y.A. Publicity* and *Report on N.Y.A. Work Projects*, both February 10, 1936, Eleanor Roosevelt Papers, microfilm selection.

20. 1936, NAC Minutes, NYA Records, group 75.

21. Aubrey Williams, "Youth and Government," *Progressive Education* 12, no. 8 (December 1936): 501–7. Minutes of the Conference of State Directors, May 19–21, 1936, NYA Records, group 15, Agenda, Stenographic Transcripts and Proceedings of Conferences called by the Executive Director and the Administrator 1935–39. See also material on the first NYA projects in NYA Records, group 38.

22. Transcript of Regional Conference (Western Region) of NYA Staff, May 19, 1936, in NYA Records, group 50, Transcripts of Telephone Conversations, etc. 1936–38. Roosevelt to Williams, June 26, 1936, Williams Papers, box 4.

23. Press Release in NYA Records, group 38. NYA Handbook of Procedures in NYA Records, group 75.

24. Hal G. Blue, An Analysis of the Work Project Program in Colorado (November 1936), NYA Records, group 38. C. B. Lund to Brown, July 14, 1937, NYA Records, group 75. Report on Smackover, Union County, Arkansas, in NYA Records, group 250, Reports Concerning Outstanding Work Project Units by State, 1938. National Advisory Committee Press Release, February 8, 1938, in Taussig Papers, box 10. Lindley and Lindley, *A New Deal for Youth*, pp. 22–23, 47, 54.

25. NYA Records, group 93, miscellaneous file of case histories, 1937–42.

26. Minutes of Meeting of NYA State Directors, October 26–28, 1937, NYA Records, group 38. Memo by Colonel Harrington on NYA Construction Projects, September 27, 1937, NYA Records, group 75.

27. Report, "The Operation of Quoddy," NYA Records, group 75. *New York Times*, September 5, 1936, March 18, 1937.

28. Minutes of Conference on Resident Projects, December 16, 1937, NYA Records, group 15, File of Agenda, Stenographic Transcripts and Proceedings of Conferences called by the Executive Director and the Administrator, 1935–39. Paul B. Jacobson, "Youth at Work," *Bulletin of the National Association of Secondary School Principals* (May 1941), pp. 114–19. Lindley and Lindley, *A New Deal for Youth*, p. 92.

29. Poynton, "The Negro Division of the N.Y.A." See also NYA Records, group 118, Final Report, National Youth Administration, Division of Negro Affairs (1943). Rawick, "The New Deal and Youth," p. 221.

30. Taussig to Mrs. Mae K. Sargent, December 21, 1936, Taussig Papers, box 15. Taussig to Roosevelt, February 14, 1938, Roosevelt Papers, PPF 3647. Roosevelt to Marvin McIntyre, March 1, 1937, Roosevelt Papers, PPF 1644.

31. Williams to Eleanor Roosevelt, January 15, 1936, Eleanor Roosevelt Papers, microfilm selection. *New York Times*, May 12, 1937. *Atlanta Journal*, November 27, 1938. Minutes of Conference of State Directors, September 9, 1938, October 26, 1937, NYA Records, group 75. Interview with John A. Lang, Washington, D.C., September 17, 1970.

32. Eleanor Roosevelt to Aubrey Williams, August 6, 1938, Eleanor Roosevelt Papers, microfilm selection.

33. Williams, Private Material, "Mrs. Roosevelt." Eleanor Roosevelt to Aubrey Williams, November 30, 1935, March 7, August 13, 1936, Eleanor Roosevelt Papers, microfilm section.

34. Williams, Private Material, folder B.10.

35. Interview with Mary Anderson Bain. Richard Brown to Eleanor Roosevelt, undated, Eleanor Roosevelt to Williams, August 6, 1938, both in Eleanor Roosevelt Papers, microfilm selection. Press release, undated, Williams Papers, box 12. Williams, Private Material, folder B.7.

Chapter 8

1. Wiltz, *From Isolation to War*, pp. 11–14, Chatfield, *For Peace and Justice*, pp. 259–63, 271–73, Salmond, *The Civilian Conservation Corps*, pp. 115–20.

2. Minutes of Conference of State Directors, November 11, 1938, NYA Records, group 15.

3. U.S. Congress House, *Congressional Record*, vol. 84, 76th Cong., 1st sess., 1939, pp. 7320–33, 8117–8120. Ibid., vol. 85, 76th Cong., 2nd sess., 1939, p. 260. NYA Records, groups 50 and 75.

4. U.S. Congress, House, *Congressional Record*, vol. 86, part 11, 76th Cong., 3rd sess., 1940, pp. 12484–13111. Ibid., vol. 87, part 2, 77th Cong., 1st sess. 1941, pp. 2009–29. Ibid., part 3, pp. 2411–14. Press release, July 1, 1941, Williams Papers, box 18.

5. Williams to Studebaker, July 23, 1940, draft of agreement, June 27, 1940, both in Williams Papers, box 24. Williams to Judd, June 8, 1940, Williams Papers, box 12. Press release, August 21, 1940, Williams Papers, box 18.

6. Eleanor Roosevelt to Williams, September 12, 1940, Williams Papers, box 4.

Judd to Williams, August 15, 21, 1940, Williams to Judd, September 28, 1940, all in Williams Papers, box 12. Williams to Mrs. Roosevelt, October 3, 1940, Williams Papers, box 8. Taussig to Judd, October 27, 1940, Taussig Papers, box 4. Taussig to Eleanor Roosevelt, October 4, 14, 1940, Eleanor Roosevelt to Taussig, September 22, 1940, both Eleanor Roosevelt Papers, microfilm selection. Report of Education Policies Commission of the National Education Association, October 1941, Williams Papers, box 25.

7. Taussig to Weston, August 20, 1940, Weston to Taussig, September 28, October 22, 1940, both in Taussig Papers, box 17.

8. Weston to Taussig, July 11, October 10, 1941, April 24, 1942, Weston to Williams, June 22, 1942, Williams to Taussig, November 17, 1941, all in Taussig Papers, box 17.

9. Williams to Stokowski, December 22, 1939, transcript of telephone call, Orren Lull to Williams, January 2, 1940, both in Williams Papers, box 25.

10. NYA Records, group 112, Reports Concerning Operations of State NYA Health Programs, 1941–42. H. L. Mitchell to Aubrey Williams, February 20, June 12, 1940, Mitchell to Will Alexander, February 16, 1940, all in NYA Records, group 41, General Office File of the Deputy Administrator, 1939–43. Williams to H. L. Mitchell, June 8, 1940, Williams Papers, box 12.

11. Williams to all state directors, March 3, May 23, 1945, NYA Records, group 75.

12. U.S. Congress, *Reduction of Non-Essential Federal Expenditures*, 77th Cong., 1st Sess., 1941, pp. 177–262. U.S. Congress, *Preliminary Report of the Joint Committee on the Reduction of Non-Essential Federal Expenditures*, doc. 152, part 2, 77th Cong., 2nd sess., 1942. U.S. Congress, House, *Congressional Record*, vol. 88, part 3, 77th Cong., 2nd sess., 1941, pp. 353–54.

13. Robert I. Millonzi, Buffalo, New York, to NYA, Buffalo, January 5, 1943, David Goldberg to Fred Cowing, superintendent, NYA Training Program, Bailey Park, Pennsylvania, February 8, 1943, 1943 report of the Houston Ship Building Company, all in NYA Records, group 75. See also the file of such letters in Williams Papers, box 6.

14. Cleo L. Curtis to Mr. Walter, January 28, 1943, NYA Records, group 75. Cleo, Juanita, and Vern to Mr. Wilson, May 28, 1943, Richard F. Gorman, resident youth personnel officer, Seattle, to Ray Sandegren, state director, Division of Youth Personnel, Tacoma, Washington, March 7, 1942, both in NYA Records, group 210, letters from director, Division of Youth Personnel, to state youth personnel directors, 1941–42.

15. Report on Nepaug Village, April 1943, excerpts of letters written by former enrollees of a shop project for Negroes at Jessup, Georgia, 1943, both in NYA Records, group 75. John M. Foskett, acting director of youth personnel, region 11, to Mrs. Marie D. Lane, February 27, 1943, NYA Records, group 226, copies of letters received from NYA youths and their parents, 1942–43.

16. U.S. Congress, House, *Congressional Record*, vol. 87, part 3, 76th Cong., 3rd sess., 1940.

17. Williams, *Huey Long*, pp. 680–81. Williams to McKellar, June 20, 1941, Williams Papers, box 7. Kenneth D. McKellar to Ickes, February 13, 1945,

McKellar to Belle Fryer, February 17, 1945, both in Papers of Senator Kenneth D. McKellar (henceforth McKellar Papers), miscellaneous, 1945–51.

18. U.S. Congress, Senate, *Termination of Civilian Conservation Corps and National Youth Administration*, 1942.

19. *Washington Post*, October 2, 3, 6, 1941. *Chicago Tribune*, October 2, 12, 1941. *Albany Times Union*, October 9, 1941. Mrs. George B. Steele, Greensboro, North Carolina, to Warren, October 2, 1941, Warren to Mrs. Steele, October 6, 1941, both in Papers of Lindsay Carter Warren (henceforth Warren Papers), box 26. Williams to Hayes, June 24, 1942, Williams Papers, box 12.

20. "The Civilian Conservation Corps, the National Youth Administration and the Public Schools," report of the Educational Policies Commission, National Education Association of the United States and the American Association of School Administrators (Washington, 1941), NYA Records, group 75. *Chicago Tribune*, October 12, 1941. Williams to Roosevelt, April 30, 1942, Williams Papers, box 4.

21. See *Washington Post*, March 22, 1942. *Baltimore Evening Sun*, July 8, October 2, 1941. *Memphis Press-Scimitar*, December 2, 1941.

22. George Benson to Ben Williams, January 10, 26, 1942, Ben Williams to Benson, January 14, 1942, Harding College Students to Roosevelt, to Henry Morgenthau, January 24, 1942, J. W. Hull to Williams, January 28, 1942, Walter Gordon Williams to Williams, January 29, 1942, undated clipping from *Greenfield* (Tennessee) *Gazette*, all in Williams Papers, box 25.

23. U.S. Congress, *Reduction of Non-Essential Federal Expenditures*, 78th Cong., 1st sess., 1943, pp. 1970–2007. U.S. Congress, Senate, *Additional Report of the Joint Committee on the Reduction of Non-Essential Federal Expenditures*, doc. 54, 78th Cong., 1st sess., 1943. Williams to Mrs. Robert Salyers, January 19, 1943, Williams Papers, box 3.

24. Williams to Ivan Munroe, state youth administrator, Oregon, June 11, 1942, Williams Papers, box 12.

25. Williams to Representative Jerry Voorhis, March 11, 1943, Williams Papers, box 6. Williams to Roosevelt, March 17, 1943, ibid., box 24. Williams to Father Edward Moore, May 28, 1943, ibid., box 12. Senator Elbert Thomas to Elder John Widtsoe, July 5, 1943, Papers of Senator Elbert Thomas (henceforth Elbert Thomas Papers), box 60. Rep. John Kerr to E. S. Askew, Raleigh, North Carolina, January 25, 1943, Papers of John Hosea Kerr (henceforth Kerr Papers), box 21.

26. Williams to Orrin Kaye, March 29, 1943, Rep. Frank B. Keefe to Williams, May 28, 1943, transcript of phone call between Williams and Joseph Samler of the War Relocation Authority, May 31, 1943, all in Williams Papers, box 25. Williams, Private Material, folder B.10.

27. Willard E. Givens to State Education Associations, May 27, 1943, NYA Records, group 75. Willard E. Givens to State Education Associations, May 31, 1943, Williams Papers, box 25. Williams to James H. Richmond, president of Murray State Teachers College, July 6, 1943, ibid., box 4.

28. U.S. Congress, House, *Department of Labor, Federal Security Agency, Appropriation Bill for 1944: Hearings before the Sub-Committee of the Committee on Appropriations*, 78th Cong., 1st sess., 1943, pp. 22, 305–7. Williams to John Lang, June 16, 1943, Williams Papers, box 2.

29. U.S. Congress, *Congressional Record*, vol. 89, part 5, 78th Cong., 1st sess., 1943, pp. 6578–6638, 6959–69, 7085 ff.

30. Williams to Willard E. Givens, June 17, 1943, Williams Papers, box 25. Williams to Father Moore, July 22, 1943, ibid., box 2.

31. Mabel Costigan to Williams, July 9, 1943, Margaret Griffen to Williams, July 6, 1943, both in ibid., box 12. Williams to James H. Richmond, Murray, Kentucky, July 6, 1943, ibid., box 4.

Chapter 9

1. *Headlines*, vol. 1, no. 1, July 30, 1938, in Williams Papers, box 27. U.S. Congress, House, *Congressional Record*, vol. 86, part 3, 76th Cong., 3d sess., 1940, p. 3445. Paul McNutt to Aubrey Williams, Sept. 12, 1942, in Williams, Private Material. Williams, Private Material, "The Communist Front Label."

2. *Washington Star*, February 6, 1954. U.S. Congress, House, *Department of Labor, Federal Security Agency Appropriation Bill for 1941: Hearings before the Sub-Committee of the Committee on Appropriations, House of Representatives*, 76th Cong., 3d sess. (henceforth, *Appropriation Hearings*, 1941), Washington, 1940, pp. 608–9. Williams to Mrs. Roosevelt, October 27, 1940, anonymous to Mrs. Roosevelt, September 3, 1940, both in Eleanor Roosevelt Papers, microfilm selection. Williams to Mrs. Roosevelt, October 24, 1939, Williams Papers, box 26. Williams to Jerome Davis, October 2, 1939, ibid., box 53.

3. *Appropriation Hearings*, 1941, pp. 608–9. U.S. Congress, House, *Work Relief and Relief for Fiscal Year, 1940*, 1939, pp. 97–98.

4. Clipping from *Washington* (Pennsylvania) *Reporter*, October 31, 1940.

5. Rawick, "The New Deal and Youth." Lash, *Eleanor and Franklin*, pp. 597–611. Kearney, *Anna Eleanor Roosevelt*, pp. 5–53. Williams, Private Material, "Mrs. Roosevelt." Williams to James Dombrowski, April 9, 1960, Black Collection, Hollis Burke Frissell Library, Tuskegee Institute (henceforth, Black Collection).

6. *New York Times*, July 3, 1938. Conference of State and Regional Directors of NYA, September 9–10, 1938, NYA Records, group 38. *Appropriation Hearings*, 1941, pp. 158–59. Williams, Private Material, "Mrs. Roosevelt."

7. *New York Times*, June 14, 1936. Howard, *The W.P.A.*, p. 120. Conference of State and Regional Directors of NYA, September 9–10, 1938, NYA Records, group 38. High, "Communism Presses Its Pants" and "Who Organized the Unemployed?" U.S. Congress, House, *Investigation and Study of the Works Progress Administration*, 1939, pp. 37–145, 1112–15. U.S. Congress, Senate, Senate Special Committee to Investigate Campaign Expenditure and Use of Government Funds, *Investigation of Senatorial Campaign Expenditure and Use of Government Funds, Report No. 1. Part 2*, 1939, pp. 365–66.

8. Williams, Private Material, "The Communist Front Label." U.S. Congress, House, *Congressional Record*, vol. 86, part 3, 76th Cong., 3d sess., 1940, p. 3452.

9. Williams, Private Material, "The NYA." Poynton, "Negro Division of the National Youth Administration." *Chicago Sunday Bee*, November 30, 1941.

10. Kearney, *Anna Eleanor Roosevelt*, pp. 86–87. Williams, Private Material, "Mrs. Roosevelt." Anita Williams interview, April 4, 1976.

11. Cantor, *Prologue to the Protest Movement*, pp. 47–48, 70–77.

12. *Occupations among Negroes–A Survey*, September 1941, NYA Records, group 75. Memo on Training of Negroes in Texas, September 8, 1941, ibid. Williams, Private Material, "Mrs. Roosevelt."

13. Williams, Private Material, "Mrs. Roosevelt."

14. Lash, *Eleanor and Franklin*, pp. 532–35. Williams, Private Material, "Mrs. Roosevelt."

15. Lash, *Eleanor and Franklin*, pp. 532–35. Sitkoff, *New Deal for Blacks*, pp. 315–23. Williams to Mrs. Roosevelt, June 20, 1941, Williams Papers, box 26. Williams, Private Material, "Mrs. Roosevelt."

16. Lash, *Eleanor and Franklin*, pp. 534–35. Sitkoff, *New Deal for Blacks*, p. 321. La Guardia to Roosevelt, June 19, 1941, Williams Papers, box 3. Williams, Private Material, "Mrs. Roosevelt."

17. Williams to Mrs. Roosevelt, June 20, 24, 25, 1941, Williams Papers, box 26. Randolph to Williams, July 19, 1941, Williams Papers, box 3. Williams to Randolph, July 22, 1941, ibid. Williams, Private Material, "Mrs. Roosevelt."

18. Williams, Private Material, "President Roosevelt." Sitkoff, *New Deal for Blacks*, p. 322.

19. Tindall, *Emergence of the New South*, pp. 713–17. Marie Lane, director, Division of Youth Personnel, to Williams, September 8, 1942, Robert Wayne Burns to Williams, May 20, 1942, both in NYA Records, group 41, General Office file of the deputy administrator, 1939–43. Missouri Field Report, April, 1943, NYA Records, group 75.

20. Negro Division Newsletter, February 1, 1938, NYA Records, group 116, file of early "inactive" correspondence. Typescripts of "Personal Statement" and "The South," Williams Papers, box 37. "What is America," ibid., box 42.

Chapter 10

1. Colonel Robert G. Bernreuter to Williams, October 26, 1943, Williams to Bernreuter, November 1, 1943, both in Williams, Private Material, folder A.1.

2. Williams to James Patton, January 3, 1943, Patton to Williams, August 6, 1943, both in Williams Papers, box 3. Tindall, *Emergence of the New South*, pp. 130–31, 428. Roosevelt to Williams, September 6, 1943, Mrs. Roosevelt to Williams, September 27, 1943, both in Williams Papers, box 3. For the Farmers Union, see Saloutos and Hicks, *Twentieth Century Populism*, pp. 219–54; Saloutos, *Farmer Movements in the South*, pp. 184–212, from which the quotation is taken.

3. Williams, Private Material, folder A.1.

4. Williams to Henry Louvaint, November 18, 1943, Williams to Margaret Valiant, December 20, 1943, both in Williams Papers, box 3.

5. Williams to Anita Williams, April 29, 1944, Williams Papers, box 1. U.S. Congress, Senate, *Nomination of Aubrey W. Williams, 1945*, pp. 93–94 (henceforth *Williams, Nomination Hearings*).

6. F. C. Dale (Midland, Texas) to McKellar, undated, McKellar Papers, box 333 (political, 1944). Dale sent to McKellar a copy of the letter he had written to

Williams. "The New Deal—A Dead Battery," Williams Papers, box 42.

7. Wallace to Williams, February 1, 1944, Williams Papers, box 32. Williams to Roosevelt, September 6, 1944, Roosevelt Papers, OF 5394. Williams, Private Material, "Mrs. Roosevelt."

8. Roosevelt to Secretary of State, January 25, 1944, Williams to Roosevelt, December 18, 1944, Roosevelt to Claude Wickard, December 22, 1944, all in Roosevelt Papers, OF 5394. Albertson, *Roosevelt's Farmer*, pp. 390–91.

9. Schlesinger, *Politics of Upheaval*, pp. 381–84. Ickes to Roosevelt, January 10, 1945, Wickard to Roosevelt, January 29, 1945, both in Roosevelt Papers, OF 1570. Albertson, *Roosevelt's Farmer*, pp. 387, 397–98.

10. Leuchtenburg, *F.D.R. and the New Deal*, p. 157.

11. *New York Herald Tribune*, January 23, 1945. *Time*, January 29, 1945. *Wall Street Journal*, February 5, 1945. *Washington Post*, January 23, 1945. Williams, Private Material, tape 6, "The R.E.A."

12. Leslie Perry to Julian Steel, February 5, 1945, W. W. Ramsey to Williams, January 29, 1945, both in Williams Papers, box 37. *New York Herald Tribune*, February 1, 1945. *Chicago Tribune*, January 23, 25, 1945.

13. *New York Herald Tribune*, February 4, 1945. *St. Louis Post Dispatch*, January 25, 1945.

14. *St. Louis Post Dispatch*, January 25, 1945. Williams, *Huey Long*, pp. 680–82.

15. F. C. Dale to McKellar, January 1945, McKellar Papers, box 333 (political, 1944–45). Frank Bernschater to McKellar, February 26, 1945, James W. Freeze to McKellar, February 5, 1945, McKellar to R. King, Jr., January 31, 1945, McKellar to Forrest Q. Stanton, Jr., February 8, 1945, all in McKellar Papers, box 335 (political, A–Z).

16. *New Republic* 112 (April 2, 1945): 446. *Williams, Nomination Hearings*, pp. 46ff., 79ff. *Washington Post*, February 8, 1945.

17. *Williams, Nomination Hearings*, pp. 133–38. *St. Louis Post Dispatch*, March 25, 1945.

18. *Williams, Nomination Hearings*, p. 148.

19. Ibid., pp. 176–91, 238.

20. *St. Louis Post Dispatch*, February 8, 1945.

21. *Williams, Nomination Hearings*, pp. 168, 175.

22. Ibid., pp. 193–94, 318.

23. Ibid., p. 280. For Williams's demeanor, see *Washington Post*, February 21, 1945; *Philadelphia Record*, February 21, 1945.

24. *Williams, Nomination Hearings*, p. 312.

25. *Washington Post*, February 21, 27, March 3, 1945. *New Republic* 112 (March 5, 1945): 333.

26. Williams, Private Material, tape 6, "The R.E.A." Senator Richard Russell to Williams, February 21, 1945, Williams Papers, box 37.

27. See the hundreds of letters and telegrams of support in Williams Papers, box 37. *New York Herald Tribune*, March 7, 1945. *St. Louis Post Dispatch*, March 4, 1945.

28. Natalie Moorman to "Friends of Aubrey Williams," March 12, 1945, Lt. John Barr Foster to Williams, February 6, 1945, both in Williams Papers, box 37.

29. *Washington Post*, March 12, 1945.

30. Williams to Myles Horton, February 21, March 5, 1945, Williams Papers, box 37.

31. McKellar to J. G. Scrugham, March 17, 1945, McKellar Papers, box 335 (political, A–Z). Alice Mayberry to Senator Styles Bridges, February 23, 1945, McKellar Papers, box X-24 (misc.).

32. Williams to R. B. Smith, March 14, 1945, Williams Papers, box 37.

33. Statement of Friends of Aubrey Williams, undated, Williams Papers, box 36. McKellar Papers, box 335 (political, A–Z).

34. *Washington Post*, March 17, 18, 20, 1945.

35. U.S. Congress, Senate, *Congressional Record*, 79th Cong., 1st sess., 1945, pp. 2525–36, 2607–11, 2648–51.

36. *New Republic* 112 (April 2, 1945): 446. *Washington Post*, March 24, 1945.

37. *Chicago Tribune*, March 26, 1945. McKellar to M. L. Naramore, March 28, 1945, McKellar Papers, box 335.

38. *Jackson Daily News*. March 24, 1945. *St. Louis Post Dispatch*, March 26, 1945.

39. Transcript of "Testimonial Dinner to Aubrey Williams," March 28, 1945, pp. 10–11, 14–16, in McKellar Papers, box 338.

40. Ibid., pp. 21–35. Williams to Roosevelt, April 8, 1945, Roosevelt Papers, PPF 8939.

41. *Washington Post* March 3, 24, 1945. *St. Louis Post Dispatch*, March 24, 1945. Williams, Private Material, tape 6, "*The R.E.A.*"

42. *New York Herald Tribune*, March 24, 1945. A. R. Silvester to McKellar, February 12, 1945, McKellar Papers, box 333 (political).

43. Belle Fryer to McKellar, February 1945, McKellar Papers, box 335 (misc., 1945–51).

44. Williams to Mrs. Eddie Swanson, May 10, 1945, Williams Papers, box 37. Patton to Williams, June 4, 1945, Williams to Patton, June 11, 1945, both in ibid., box 32.

45. A copy of the agreement installing Williams as publisher of the *Southern Farmer* can be found in Williams Papers, box 32.

Chapter 11

1. Barnard, *Dixiecrats and Democrats*, pp. 1–23. The quotation is from page 14.

2. Bedford, *Trouble Downtown*, pp. 134–35.

3. Williams to Myles Horton, July 18, August 9, 18, 1945. Records of the Highlander Research and Education Center, 1917–1973 (henceforth Highlander Records), State Historical Society of Wisconsin, box 42, folder 4.

4. "Plan for Operation for *Southern Farmer*," in Williams Papers, box 32. Barnard, *Dixiecrats and Democrats*, p. 82.

5. *Southern Farmer*, October, November, December 1945, January 1946.

6. Ibid., February, March, April, July, December 1946.

7. Ibid., June, July, September 1946.

8. Ibid., March, April, May, June, November 1947.

9. Williams, Private Material, "Return to Alabama." Williams to Harry S. Truman, July 14, 1948, Truman to Williams, July 15, 1948, both in Papers of Harry S. Truman (henceforth, Truman Papers), Private Personal File 1926. Williams to James Warburg, April 27, 1948, Williams Papers, box 34. Mary Beech to Williams, April 29, 1948, Williams to Mary Beech, May 6, 1948, both in ibid., box 36. Williams to Gould Beech, undated 1948, ibid., box 35. Transcript, phone conversation, Aubrey Williams and Gould Beech, ibid., box 34. Williams to Gould Beech, November 16, 1958, ibid., box 30. Barnard, *Dixiecrats and Democrats*, pp. 80–88.

10. *Southern Farmer*, July, August 1948.

11. Virginia Durr interview. Aubrey Williams, Jr., interview. Louis Brownlow to Williams, October 20, 1948, Williams Papers, box 30. *Southern Farmer*, October, December 1948.

12. *Southern Farmer*, February, March, April, May, November 1949.

13. *Time*, November 21, 1949.

14. Becker, *Marshall Field III*, p. 377. Warburg to Williams, November 30, 1949, Williams to Warburg, June 14, 1950, Warburg to Williams, January 26, 1952, all in Williams Papers, box 34. Williams to Warburg, February 4, 13, 1952, Warburg to Williams, February 6, 1952, Williams to Warburg, November 1, 1954, Warburg to Williams, April 4, 1955, all in Williams Papers, box 32.

15. *Southern Farmer*, September, October 1950. *Southern Farm and Home*, November, 1952, January, March, April, June 1954. Mrs. M. Cherry, Orangeburg, South Carolina, to Williams, undated, Williams Papers, box 36. Hamby, *Beyond Liberalism*, p. 491.

16. Interview with Paul Woolley henceforth Woolley interview), Montgomery, Alabama, May 30, 1976.

17. Becker, *Marshall Field III*, p. 378. Williams, Private Material, "Return to Alabama." Williams to Mrs. William Korn, New York City, undated, 1948, Williams, Private Material, folder B-12. Williams to Marshall Field, August 23, 1948, Meyer Family to Williams, November 29, 1948, Williams to Nathan Levin, November 6, 1948, January 11, 1949, February 6, 1950, L. B. Cooper, Montgomery Real Estate and Insurance Co., to Williams, August 23, 1949, Herbert Bain to Williams, May 7, 1951, May 23, 28, 1952, Jane Foster to Williams, April 10, 1953, Williams to Bain, July 12, 1951, all in Williams Papers, box 34.

18. Becker, *Marshall Field III*, p. 378. Williams to Howard Seitz, November 9, 1951, Williams Papers, box 32. Williams to Howard Seitz, February 10, 1949, ibid., box 36. Orville Mastin to Williams, March 7, 1949, Thomas Ludwig to Williams, undated, 1948, both in Williams Papers, box 33. Minutes, Board of Directors, Georgiana, Alabama, Co-operative, September 24, 1949, Roland Sanders, manager, Chelton County Farmers Union Co-operative, to Board of Directors, July 8, 1950, both in ibid. Williams to David E. Conrad, June 30, 1959, Williams Papers, box 30.

19. Minutes, meeting of Alabama Farmers Union, April 12, 1951, Williams Papers, box 33. Williams to Tom Ludwig, undated, 1957, ibid., box 32. Williams to Mr. G. K. Williams, Springhill, Alabama, January 18, 1949, ibid., box 33. Williams to Fanny Meyer Korn, July 21, 1953, ibid., box 31.

20. Minutes, meeting of Alabama Farmers Union, April 12, 1951, Williams Papers, box 33. Williams to Patton, May 14, 1951, ibid. *Denver Post*, May 13, 1951. Interview with Clifford Durr, Wetumpka, Alabama, December 29, 1974 (henceforth Clifford Durr interview).

21. Williams to Patton, May 14, 1952, Williams Papers, box 32.

22. Clipping in Williams Papers, box 31. Barnard, *Dixiecrats and Democrats*, pp. 125–46. Williams to Truman, January 11, 1949, Truman to Williams, January 15, 1949, both in Truman Papers, PPF 1726. Truman to Williams, November 18, 1950, Truman Papers, OF Chronological Name File. Williams to Baldwin, August, 1950, Papers of J. Howard McGrath (henceforth McGrath Papers). Williams to Isadore Lubin, September 26, 1951, Williams Papers, box 39. Williams to Alexander Meiklejohn, September 23, 1953, Alexander Meiklejohn Papers (henceforth Meiklejohn Papers), box 31, folder 1.

23. *Daily Compass*, July 20, 1952, clipping in Williams Papers, box 32. *Southern Farm and Home*, April 1952.

24. *Southern Farm and Home*, June 1952. Anita Williams interview. Virginia Durr interview, May 29, 1976. Paul Woolley interview, May 30, 1976. Interview with Ray Jenkins, Montgomery, Alabama (henceforth Jenkins interview), May 31, 1976.

25. All the material on Peace Farm is taken from correspondence between Williams and his partners, the title deed, the deed of sale, and other legal documents pertaining to it and letters between Howard Bell and Williams found in the Carl and Anne Braden Papers (henceforth Braden Papers), box 17, folder 3. The author thanks Mrs. Anne Braden most sincerely for allowing him access to this collection.

26. Paul Woolley interview, May 30, 1976. Interview with E. D. Nixon (henceforth Nixon interview), Montgomery, Alabama, May 31, 1976. Williams to Herb Bain, June 29, 1955, Braden Papers, box 17, folder 3.

Chapter 12

1. Sosna, *In Search of the Silent South*, pp. 88–104, 140–49. Krueger, *And Promises to Keep*.

2. Williams, Private Material, "Return to Alabama." Minutes, Board of Representatives, Southern Conference for Human Welfare, September 26, 1946, Braden Papers, box 18, folder 6.

3. Krueger, *And Promises to Keep*, pp. 104–6, 155–57.

4. Williams to Dombrowski, December 26, 1946, Dombrowski to Williams, December 28, 1946, both in Braden Papers, box 18, folder 3.

5. Krueger, *And Promises to Keep*, pp. 157–81.

6. "Building Together," Minutes, Board of Representatives, Southern Conference for Human Welfare, October 16, 1947, both in Braden Papers, box 18, folder 6. Report of the administrator, Southern Conference for Human Welfare, "Some Highlights of the First Quarter," 1947, Braden Papers, box 18, folder 4.

7. Minutes, meeting of Board of Representatives, Southern Conference for Human Welfare, July 12, 1947, Braden Papers, box 18, folder 5. Meeting of Board of Representatives, October 16, 1947, ibid., folder 6.

8. Krueger, *And Promises to Keep*, pp. 187–92. Minutes of final meeting, Board of Representatives, Southern Conference for Human Welfare, November 21, 1948, Braden Papers, box 18, folder 6.

9. SCEF statement in Williams Papers, box 41. The only history of SCEF is Klibaner, "Southern Conference Educational Fund."

10. Klibaner, "Southern Conference Educational Fund," pp. 168–69. Anita Williams interview. Paul Woolley interview, May 30, 1976.

11. *Southern Patriot*, vol. 6, no. 10, December 1948. *Richmond Times Dispatch*, November 21, 1948. *New York Times*, November 21, 1948.

12. *Southern Patriot*, vol. 6, no. 9, November 1948.

13. Press release, June 26, 1949, "The Failure of Gradualism," December 28, 1949, Williams to John Ivey, March 6, 1950, Ivey to Williams, March 8, 1950, Williams to Clay Chennault, August 30, 1948, all in Williams Papers, box 39. The "Governors Plan" never really got off the ground, and was made irrelevant by various Supreme Court decisions, including the landmark Brown decision of 1954.

14. Williams to Howard McGrath, June 1950, Florence Reed to Williams, November 29, 1952, clippings from *The State*, Columbia, South Carolina, December 31, 1952, and the *Louisville Courier Journal*, January 10, 1953, all in Williams Papers, box 39. Transcript of the debate, ibid., box 35. Williams, Private Material, "Return to Alabama."

15. *Southern Patriot*, vol. 10, no. 5, May 1952. Minutes of meeting of SCEF Board of Directors, October 25, 1952, Williams Papers, box 39. Klibaner, "Southern Conference Educational Fund," pp. 97–101.

16. Williams to Howard McGrath, June 9, 1950, E. J. McLarney, deputy commissioner of internal revenue to SCEF, July 8, 1952, Williams to Dombrowski, February 11, 1952, all in Williams Papers, box 38. Paul Woolley interview.

17. *Montgomery Advertiser*, May 9, 1954. Caute, *The Great Fear*. Bedford, *Trouble Downtown*, pp. 131–35.

18. The original subpoena is in Williams Papers, box 41. For the subcommittee see Griffith, *Politics of Fear*, pp. 118–20, 208–10.

19. *New York Times*, January 28, 1954.

20. Williams to Jenner, January 31, 1954, Williams Papers, box 41.

21. Williams to Hubert H. Humphrey, to Herbert Lehman, to John J. Sparkman, and to William Fulbright, all February 5, 1954, to Dombrowski, February 23, 1954, all in Williams Papers, box 41. Minutes, special SCEF meeting, ibid., box 39.

22. Murray to Williams, February 22, 1954, Kilgore to Williams, February 11, 1954, Alsop to Williams, February 17, 1954, all in Williams Papers, box 41.

23. Press statement, March 6, 1954, Williams to Bethune, March 7, 1954, Williams to John Popham, March 7, 1954, Williams to Mary Anderson Bain, March 7, 1954, all in Williams Papers, box 41.

24. *New Orleans Times Picayune*, March 10, 1954. Virginia Durr interview. For a detailed and critical account of Senator Eastland's public life see "Jim Eastland, Child of Scorn," in Sherrill, *Gothic Politics*, pp. 189–233. Alva Taylor was eventually excused attendance on medical grounds.

25. Virginia Durr interview.

26. Virginia Durr interview. *New Orleans Times Picayune*, March 10, 18, 1954. For Crouch see Joseph and Stewart Alsop, "Information on the Informer,"

Washington Post, April 16, 1954; "Matter of Fact," *New York Herald Tribune*, May 19, 1954. *New York Times*, May 28, 1954.

27. U.S. Congress, Senate, *Southern Conference Educational Fund, Inc.* (henceforth SCEF Hearing), 1955, pp. 1–5.

28. Ibid., pp. 6–11, 14–15.

29. Ibid., pp. 16–29.

30. Ibid., pp. 30–80.

31. Ibid., *New Orleans Times Picayune*, March 19, 1954.

32. *SCEF Hearing*, pp. 83–90.

33. Ibid., pp. 93, 98–99. Virginia Durr interview.

34. *SCEF Hearing*, pp. 102–16. Williams, Private Material, folder B.19.

35. *SCEF Hearing*, pp. 117–21. Rob Hall had been secretary of the Alabama branch of the Communist party. Butler subsequently decided not to repeat his charges against Williams outside the hearing room.

36. Ibid., pp. 124–48. See also Williams's own account of the hearings, "The Red Menace," in Williams Papers, box 44. *St. Louis Post Dispatch*, March 19, 1954. *Atlanta Constitution*, *Washington Post*, *New York Times*, *New York Herald Tribune*, all March 20, 1954.

37. *SCEF Hearing*, pp. 51, 103, 150–62. *Washington Post*, March 21, 1954, Virginia Durr interview. The others so named were Howard Lee, Malcolm Cotton Dobbs, Joseph Gelders, and Gilbert L. Parks. For Highlander see Adams, with Horton, *Unearthing Seeds of Fire*.

38. *Washington Post*, *New York Times*, both March 31, 1954.

39. *Montgomery Advertiser*, March 21, 25, 1954. *New Orleans Times Picayune* March 21, 24, 1954. Eastland had recovered his confidence by the time he returned to Washington. Speaking to reporters, he described SCEF as "a particularly vicious organization," and indicated that he would recommend contempt citations against some of the witnesses.

40. *Montgomery Advertiser*, *St. Louis Post Dispatch*, both March 25, 1954. *Lyttleton Independent*, March 26, 1954. Williams thought that Mrs. Roosevelt was a bit weak in her defenses of them all. "Frankly I thought she hedged on Virginia and was none too freewheeling with regards to what she thought of me" (Williams to Mary Bain, March 27, 1954, Williams Papers, box 41). *Chicago Defender*, April 3, 1954. Alfred E. Maund, "The Battle of New Orleans," *Nation*, April 3, 1954. Jennings Perry, "The Congressional Inquisition Moves South," *I. F. Stone's Weekly*, March 29, 1954.

41. See Williams Papers, box 41. See also Allan Barth to Durr, March 20, 1954, Thomas Gravell to Durr, April 1, 1954, both in Papers of Clifford J. Durr (henceforth Clifford Durr Papers). *New York Times*, March 22, 1954. *New Orleans Times Picayune*, March 21, 1954.

42. Williams to Douglas, March 23, 1954. Similar letters went on the same day to senators Matthew Neely, Kilgore, Humphrey, and John Sherman Cooper, Williams Papers, box 36.

43. Humphrey to Williams, March 31, 1954, Williams Papers, box 36. Douglas to Williams, April 13, 1954, Williams Papers, box 41.

44. Williams to Lyndon Johnson, Williams to Lister Hill, both April 5, 1954, Williams Papers, box 36. Williams to Robert Allan, April 20, 1954, Johnson to

Williams, April 2, 1954, both in ibid., box 41. *Montgomery Advertiser*, May 9, 1954.

45. *SCEF Hearing*, appendix, "The State of Florida, on the relation of George A. Broutigam, Esquire, State Attorney of the Eleventh Judicial Circuit of Florida, Movant vs Leo Sheiner, Respondent." Virginia Durr interview.

46. See Joseph and Stewart Alsop, "Information on the Informer," *Washington Post*, April 16, 1954; "Matter of Fact," *New York Herald Tribune*, May 19, 1954; "The Powerful Imaginer," *Washington Post*, April 9, 1954; *New York Times*, May 28, 1954.

47. *New York Times*, June 9, 1954, November 19, 1955. *I. F. Stone's Weekly*, December 12, 1955. Anita Williams interview.

48. SCEF, Minutes of Board Meeting, May 8, 1954, Williams Papers, box 39. "The Red Menace," ibid., box 44. Roy Wilkins to Albert Barnes, SCEF vice-president, February 4, 1957, ibid., box 39. Williams, Private Material, "Return to Alabama."

49. "The Red Menace," Williams Papers, box 44. *Firing Line*, vol. 4, no. 11, May 1, 1955, and vol. 4, no. 13, July 1, 1955. Williams to Folsom, September 19, 1955, Williams Papers, box 30.

50. *SCEF Hearing*, committee report. *New York Times*, September 13, 1955.

51. Williams to Aubrey Williams, Jr., May 30, 1958, Williams Papers, box 32.

Chapter 13

1. Williams to Rexford Tugwell, March 25, 1958, Williams Papers, box 32. Williams to Phil Kirby, April 14, 1959, ibid., box 31. Rev. H. T. Isgitt, Converse, La., to Williams, January 29, 1957, George W. Henry, Bernice, La., to Williams, January 28, 1957, both in ibid., box 43. *Southern Farm and Home Almanac*, first quarter, 1957.

2. Williams to Dombrowski, October 24, 1957, Braden Papers, box 17, folder 5.

3. Williams to Warburg, September 9, 1958, Williams to Maxwell Hahn, June 1959, both in Black Collection. Dombrowski to Williams, November 18, 1959, Braden Papers, box 17, folder 13. Williams to Robert Asher, May 23, 1958, Williams Papers, box 30. Williams to Cary McWilliams, October 14, 1958, ibid., box 31. Anita Williams interview.

4. Williams to Will T. Sheehan, August 1, 1957, Morrison Williams to Williams, April 20, 1959, both in Williams Papers, box 32. Aubrey Williams, Jr., interview.

5. Klibaner, "Southern Conference Educational Fund," pp. 216–26. *Birmingham Post and Herald*, September 26, 1957. A copy of the telegram can be found in Williams, Private Material, folder A.4.

6. Klibaner, "Southern Conference Educational Fund," pp. 240–41, 281–83. Ann Braden to Harvey O'Connor, April 12, 1957, Braden Papers, box 58, folder 8.

7. Williams to Lister Hill, to John Sparkman, to Allen Ellender, all April 15, 1958, Braden Papers, box 63, folder 5. All the material on the conference comes from the Braden Papers, box 63, folders 2–7. For the 1960 mock hearing, see folder 8.

8. "Bus Boycott" in "A Southern Rebel," Williams Papers, box 44. Williams,

Private Material, "Return to Alabama." *National Guardian*, March 13, 1965. E. D. Nixon interview. Williams to Myrtice Clements, March 20, 1956, Williams Papers, box 30. Williams to Mrs. Roosevelt, July 26, 1956, ibid., box 32. Aubrey Williams, Jr., interview. On Nixon, see Bedford, *Trouble Downtown*, pp. 135–41. Lewis, *King*, pp. 48–57.

9. Williams to Dombrowski, February 26, 1960, Black Collection. Williams, Private Material, "Return to Alabama." E. D. Nixon interview.

10. Jenkins interview. Lyndon Johnson to Williams, July 25, 1957, Black Collection. Klibaner, "Southern Conference Educational Fund," pp. 238–39.

11. Williams to Representative Emmanuel Celler, July 1, 1958, Black Collection. Klibaner, "Southern Conference Educational Fund," pp. 258–59.

12. Williams to Johnson, August 20, 1958, Johnson to Williams, August 21, 1958, both in Black Collection.

13. Klibaner, "Southern Conference Educational Fund," pp. 273–76. Williams to Dombrowski, undated, Williams to Mrs. Roosevelt, June 6, 1959, both in Williams Papers, box 35. Johnson to Williams, May 12, 1958, ibid., box 30. Williams to Senator Allen J. Ellender, May 29, 1959, Williams to Senator Joseph O'Mahoney, June 6, 1959, both in Black Collection. Williams, Private Material, folder A.4.

14. Transcript of speech at Highlander Folk School, Labor Day, September 2, 1957, Williams Papers, box 43.

15. Statement by Myles Horton, October 5, 1957, Horton to Max Hahn, October 10, 1957, copy of paper produced by Georgia Commission on Education, all in Highlander Papers, box 29, folder 30. Williams, Private Material, folder A.4.

16. *Birmingham News*, October 5, 7, 1957. Williams to Clarence Hanson, October 17, 1957, Williams to R. F. Hudson, November 15, 1957, both in Williams, Private Material, folder A.4.

17. Berry to Horton, October 18, 1957, "Communists and the N.A.A.C.P.," "Core and Its Communist Connections," all in Highlander Papers, box 29, folder 30. *New York Times*, July 13, 1963. Williams, Private Material, folder A.4.

18. Williams to conference participants, undated, Braden Papers, box 28, folder 5. Williams to Albert Croft, May 3, 1958, Williams Papers, box 30.

19. Williams to Dombrowski, July 31, 1956, December 30, 1958, Williams to Justine Wise Polier, January 9, 1959, Williams to Senator Paul H. Douglas, January 15, 1959, all in Black Collection.

20. Albert E. Barnett, SCEF vice-president, to Roy Wilkins, December 4, 1956, February 11, 18, 1957, Wilkins to Barnett, February 4, 1957, all in Williams Papers, box 39. Williams to Dombrowski, February 18, 1957, Williams to John Bolt Culbertson, April 17, 1957, Williams to Justine Wise Polier, August 13, 1957, all in ibid., box 38. Lewis, *King*, p. 110.

21. Williams to Dombrowski, July 8, 25, 1958, August 26, 1959, February 26, 1960, Black Collection.

22. Williams to C. G. Gomillion, December 4, 1958, Braden Papers, box 17, folder 5. Williams to Arthur Lobeman, February 13, 1959, Williams Papers, box 31.

23. Williams to Bradens, July 25, 1957, Williams to Dombrowski, October 16, 21, 1958, both in Braden Papers, box 17, folder 5. Klibaner, "Southern Conference Educational Fund," pp. 288–89.

24. Williams to Ann Braden, March 31, 1958, Braden Papers, box 17, folder 5.

25. Klibaner, "Southern Conference Educational Fund," pp. 290–95. Williams to Dombrowski, April 8, 9, 13, 1960, Williams to Justine Wise Polier, May 4, 1960, Eleanor Roosevelt to Williams, April 5, 1960, Anne Braden to Williams, July 20, 1960, all in Black Collection. Williams to Albert Barnett, March 5, 1958, Braden Papers, box 17, folder 5.

26. Williams to Dombrowski, November 13, 1960, Braden Papers, box 17, folder 5. Williams to Myrtice Clements, May 13, 1959, Williams to P. D. East, undated, 1958, both in Williams Papers, box 30. Virginia Durr interview.

27. Williams to Harry Barnard, December 5, 1957, Williams Papers, box 30. Williams to Judy Papier, February 21, 1956, ibid., box 32. Virginia Durr to Ann Braden, undated, 1958, Braden Papers, box 64, folder 9. Williams to John Bolt Culbertson, April 21, 1959, Black Collection. Virginia Durr was wrong; Anne Braden was not from Alabama, but from Mississippi.

28. Williams to Mrs. Adele Davis, undated, 1959, Williams Papers, box 30.

29. Paul Woolley interview. The obituary is in Braden Papers, box 64, folder 9. Williams to Mrs. Myrtice Clements, November 11, 1959, Williams Papers, box 30. Lyndon Johnson to Williams, October 12, 1959, ibid., box 31. Robert Wood to Williams, October 27, 1959, Max Sien to Williams, November 1, 1959, Esther Auerback to Williams, October 22, 1959, all in Braden Papers, box 21, folder 6.

30. Williams to Lyndon Johnson, April 4, 1960, Williams to Irving Brant, October 10, 1958, Williams to Richard Goldman, December 13, 1960, all in Black Collection. Paul Woolley interview. E. D. Nixon interview.

31. Anita Williams to Dombrowski, September 1961, October 2, 4, 1961, Williams to Dombrowski, September 26, 1961, all in Braden Papers, box 21, folder 7. Minutes of SCEF Board of Directors, October 28, 1961, Braden Papers, box 22, folder 6.

Chapter 14

1. For material on Frank Wilkinson, the ECLC, and the Citizens Committee to Preserve American Freedoms, see Braden Papers, box 19, folder 7; box 51, folder 1; and box 53, folder 1.

2. Williams to Professor Talbert, September 28, 1958, Williams Papers, box 32. Press release, August 15, 1960, Braden Papers, box 53, folder 1. *New York Times*, August 10, 1960. Williams to Dombrowski, January 14, 1960, Black Collection.

3. See ACLU press release, February 27, 1961, Braden Papers, box 50, folder 12. Pamphlets in ibid., box 53, folder 10. Williams to James Roosevelt, June 12, 1961, ibid., box 21, folder 7.

4. Russ Nixon to Otto Nathan, July 19, 1961, Anne Braden to Nixon, July 21, 1961, Anne Braden to Williams, July 21, 1961, Otto Nathan to Richard Criley, Dorothy Marshall, and Anne Braden, July 28, 1961, Anne Braden to Sylvia Crane, July 30, 1961, Otto Nathan to Williams, August 9, 1961, all in Braden Papers, box 77, folder 13. See also Goodman, *The Committee*, pp. 450–52, and Lader, *Power on the Left*, pp. 57–63.

5. Anne Braden memorandum to National Committee members, September 9,

1961, Richard L. Criley memorandum to National Committee members, October 3, November 6, 1961, Minutes of meeting of the National Committee to Abolish the House Un-American Activities Committee, November 18, 1961, all in Braden Papers, box 77, folder 13. Wilkinson to Bradens, May 27, 1963, ibid., box 51, folder 1. Williams to James Halloway, October 10, 1962, ibid., box 21, folder 7. Williams to Alexander Meiklejohn, September 18, 1962, Meiklejohn Papers, box 31, folder 1. Interview with Anita Williams and Aubrey Williams, Jr.

6. Goodman, *The Committee*, pp. 391, 393–94, 430–33, 450–52. Williams to Irving Brant, October 10, 1958, Williams to Frank Wilkinson, October 13, 1958, both in Black Collection.

7. Williams to H. H. Matthews, August 5, 1962, Williams to Dombrowski, December 29, 1962, February 17, 1963, Williams to Mary Anderson Bain, February 10, 1963, all in Braden Papers, box 21, folder 7. Paul Woolley interview.

8. Williams to James Dombrowski, May 8, 15, 1963, Anita Williams to Dombrowski, February 26, 1963, all in Braden Papers, box 21, folder 7. Paul Woolley interview. Anita Williams interview. *Montgomery Advertiser*, February 10, 1963.

9. Williams to Dombrowski, undated, January 24, February 13, May 15, June 1963, Braden Papers, box 21, folder 7. Williams, Private Material, "At Present—1963."

10. Williams to Dombrowski, June, July 8, 1963, Braden Papers, box 21, folder 7. Williams to Clifford Durr, July 23, 1963, Williams, Private Material, folder A.3.

11. Williams to Durr, July 23, 1963, Williams, Private Material, folder A.3. Williams to Dombrowski, July 8, 1963, Braden Papers, box 21, folder 7. Williams, Private Material, "At Present—1963."

12. "Margaret" to Williams, undated, Williams, Private Material, folder A.3. Williams to Lyndon Johnson, January 29, 1962, Braden Papers, box 21, folder 7. Williams, Private Material, "At Present—1963."

13. Williams, Private Material, "At Present—1963." See also the handwritten material on Mrs. Roosevelt, and Williams to Jonathan Mitchell, January 23, 1939, Williams Papers, box 2.

14. Williams, Private Material, "At Present—1963."

15. Lewis, *King*, pp. 171–263. Williams to Dombrowski, July 8, August 15, 1963, Williams to P. D. East, August 22, 1963, all in Braden Papers, box 21, folder 7.

16. Williams to Martin Luther King, July 1, 1963, Williams to Dombrowski, August 15, 25, 1963, both in Braden Papers, box 21, folder 7. Williams to Dombrowski, September 9, 1963, ibid., box 17, folder 5.

17. Williams to Dombrowski, June 1963, Braden Papers, box 21, folder 7. Anita Williams interview. *Montgomery Advertiser*, March 20, 1964. *New York Times*, March 7, 1964.

18. Clipping in Braden Papers, box 17, folder 5. Williams, Private Material, "At Present—1963." Ruth France to Williams, April 14, 1964, Williams, Private Material, "Clippings and Letters."

19. Williams to Horton, February 20, 1964, Highlander Papers, box 42, folder 5. Williams to Avrahim Mezerik, July 20, 1964, Williams to Frank Wilkinson,

July 22, 1964, Wilkinson to Williams, July 27, 1964, all in Williams, Private Material, "Clippings and Letters."

20. Williams to Avrahim Mezerik, November 17, 1964, Williams, Private Material, "Clippings and Letters."

21. Lady Bird Johnson to Anita Williams, undated, Anna Roosevelt Halstead to Anita Williams, March 6, 1965, Martin Luther King to Anita Williams, March 19, 1965, file of letters and telegrams of condolence, all in Williams, Private Material, "Clippings and Letters."

22. *Washington Post*, March 7, 1965. *Nation*, March 22, 1965. *I. F. Stone's Weekly*, March 15, 1965.

Conclusion

1. Leuchtenburg, *Perils of Prosperity*, p. 139.

2. Wilkinson to Williams, July 22, 1964, Williams, Private Material, "Clippings and Letters." Aubrey Williams, Jr. interview. Virginia Durr interview.

3. Virginia Durr interview.

4. Williams, Private Material, "Roosevelt."

5. Typescripts of "Personal Statement" and "The South," Williams Papers, box 37. See also "What is America," ibid., box 42.

6. Negro Division Newsletter, February 1, 1938, NYA Records, group 116, records of Office of Negro Affairs (file of early "inactive" correspondence). Williams, Private Material, "At Present—1963."

7. Sosna, *In Search of the Silent South*.

8. *I. F. Stone's Weekly*, March 15, 1965. Hubert Humphrey to Anita Williams, March 8, 1965, Sylvia Crane to Frank Bane, September 27, 1965, both in Williams, Private Material, "Clippings and Letters."

Bibliography

Essay on Sources

Manuscripts

This book is based mainly on manuscript sources. The most important collection was the Aubrey Williams Papers, held at the Franklin D. Roosevelt Library. Nearly half the collection has to do with Williams's NYA work, the rest is mainly concerned with the post-1945 period of his life and particularly with the SCEF. Of particular interest are the files of correspondence with Mrs. Roosevelt on a variety of matters, including the 1941 proposal for a march on Washington, and the full collections relating to the 1945 REA nomination and the 1955 investigation of the SCEF by the Senate Internal Security Subcommittee. There is a considerable amount of material dealing with Williams's presidency of the Alabama Farmers Union and with his business affairs, including the *Southern Farmer* and American Family Homes, Inc., but nothing relating to the National Committee to Abolish the House Un-American Activities Committee. Except for quite voluminous files having to do with reaction to his controversial speeches of 1938 and his eventual removal from the agency, there is comparatively little on his work with the WPA. Some material concerning his period in Wisconsin is housed there, mainly that having to do with the model cities program, while his unpublished autobiography, "A Southern Rebel," also deposited there, was valuable for most aspects of his life. As well as correspondence concerning the SCEF, the collection contains a reasonably full set of minutes of directors meetings, pamphlets, surveys, copies of the *Southern Patriot*, and various speeches made by Williams on its behalf. There is comparatively little on his involvement with the SCHW.

Next in importance was the private collection of papers held, when I used them in 1976, by Williams's widow, Anita Williams. This collection contains a significant amount of correspondence to do with SCEF affairs, particularly the period after 1955, not held in the main collection, personal correspondence from the last years of his life, and material relating to the NCHUAC. Of most importance, however, was the huge body of Williams's unpublished writings. This includes some drafts of "A Southern Rebel," but the bulk is the result of feverish activity in the last years of his life "to set something down in writing." This material was the main source used in discussing his pre-Wisconsin days and was also invaluable for its insights into the other periods of his life—and into himself—containing, as it does, long accounts of his activities with the RFC and the New Deal agencies and of his relationships with the Roosevelts and his fellow New Dealers. Strongest on the New Deal period, it also has invaluable material on his time in Wisconsin and on the years after 1945.

Third in importance was the extensive Carl and Anne Braden collection at the State Historical Society, Madison, Wisconsin. The bulk of the SCEF records are now located there, as is a significant amount of material concerning the SCHW. Most of my discussion of Williams's role in that body is drawn from these papers. A considerable amount of personal material is also located there, including the records of the Peace Farm venture and correspondence with the Bradens and Dombrowski having to do with Williams's final illness and his resignation as SCEF president. The collection also houses full records concerning the NCHUAC and Williams's involvement in it. As far as the SCEF was concerned, the Braden collection was crucial in supplementing my understanding of its post-1955 activities, an area where the Williams Papers are less detailed. The Black Collection, Hollis Burke Frissell Library, Tuskegee Institute, contained a few items of interest, principally relating to the SCEF, but most of the material there can also be found in either the Williams or the Braden collections.

Several collections in the Hyde Park Library were of great importance. The Eleanor Roosevelt Papers contain much correspondence between Williams and Mrs. Roosevelt, mainly concerning NYA matters, but there are some interesting general letters as well, including correspondence about the projected 1941 Washington march. The Harry Hopkins Papers were of importance in expanding my understanding of Williams's role in the FERA, CWA, and WPA, though they contain comparatively little of a personal nature. The Charles W. Taussig Papers had a few items of importance having to do with the NYA and Williams's friendship with Mrs. Roosevelt, while the president's papers were mainly of interest for the lengthy letters from Williams about the hostility of the National Education Association to the NYA, letters concerning the 1944 elections and the mood of the country, and material relating to the 1945 REA nomination.

The NYA records at the National Archives contained some useful material. Of particular value were the transcripts of state directors conferences, which gave valuable insights into Williams's contribution as an exhorter of men, and the well-classified files of the director's correspondence. The WPA records were less satisfactory, and one is led to conclude, as other historians have done, that the bulk of day-to-day WPA business went unrecorded. The State Series File (610) and the General Subject Series (100) did, however, give the flavor of the everyday operations of the agency and of Williams's role within it. In particular they were valuable in explaining the nature of the Williams-Hopkins relationship and in enabling me to understand the complexities of the "politics in the WPA" issue and of Williams's importance as a troubleshooter in that area. The CWA records held some items of interest, principally the Administrative Correspondence File, which included material on race relations in the agency, which Williams handled. The State Series File provided insights into Williams's general role in the CWA. The FERA records, too, were of value. The New Subject File contains material not found elsewhere, while a file of reports from RFC field representatives sheds light on his work there. The FERA State Files contain the reports that Williams made to Hopkins when he was field representative for the southwestern region, as well as some correspondence between the two men not found elsewhere. The lengthy field reports were of particular value, both in aiding one's understanding of the FERA's mode of operation and in gaining insight into Williams's administrative and personal style. The FERA Old Subject Files, including Inter-racial Relations, gave a sense of Williams's role within the agency once he had come to Washington and of his professional and personal relationship with Hopkins.

Besides the Braden Papers several collections at the State Historical Society, Madison, Wisconsin, contain items of importance. The records of the Wisconsin Welfare Council (formerly the Wisconsin Conference of Social Work) was the prime source for unraveling Williams's public activities in that state, as well as containing a few items of personal correspondence. The papers of Marvin B. Rosenberry, once president of the conference, also helped in that regard. The Records of the Highlander Research and Education Center contain a considerable amount of correspondence between Williams and Highlander's director, Myles Horton, which shed light on certain aspects of Williams's career, particularly his period as an organizer with the National Farmer's Union and as chairman of the Alabama Farmers Union. The Alexander Meiklejohn Papers contain a few items having to do with the NCHUAC.

Other collections of value include the sprawling Kenneth D. McKellar Papers, held at the Memphis Public Library, which contain much important material to do with the end of the NYA and the REA confirmation struggle. The Clifford Durr Papers at the State Department of Archives and History, Montgomery, Alabama, also have some items of value, principally items concerning the Internal Security Subcommittee investigation of 1955. The Lindsay Carter Warren Papers were useful in connection with the end of the NYA. The Harry S. Truman Papers, Independence, Missouri, include a few personal letters of interest.

Other Sources

Though this book has been written primarily from manuscripts, it is obvious from the bibliography that I made considerable use of other sources as well. I used the *New York Times* and *Washington Post* throughout, the *St. Louis Post Dispatch*, *Chicago Tribune*, *New York Herald Tribune*, and *Baltimore Evening Sun* for the period 1933–45, and the *Montgomery Advertiser*, *New Orleans Times Picayune*, and *Atlanta Constitution* for the post-1945 years. Other newspapers and magazines were consulted selectively. I read the *Southern Farmer*, held at the Department of Agriculture Library, Beltsville, Maryland, in its entirety, as well as the *Southern Patriot*. The various government documents listed in the bibliography, principally hearings and reports, were used mainly in connection with Williams's NYA activities, the REA nomination, and the Internal Security Subcommittee hearing of 1954.

I consulted many secondary works. Some were of a general nature. Like that of a generation of historians, my knowledge of the general context of New Deal

America and of the Roosevelt administration has been enriched by Arthur Schlesinger's three-volume *Age of Roosevelt* and by William Leuchtenburg's brilliant *Franklin D. Roosevelt and the New Deal, 1932–1940*, still the best one-volume study of the period. C. Vann Woodward's magisterial *Origins of the New South, 1877–1913* is basic to an understanding of the social and intellectual climate in which Williams was formed, while George B. Tindall's *Emergence of the New South, 1913–1945* carries the story forward to the time he returned there. I used Roy Lubove's *Professional Altruist* and Clarke A. Chambers's *Seedtime of Reform* to understand the state of the social work profession, and its intellectual climate, at the time that Williams joined it.

There are no standard histories of the agencies with which Williams was associated during the New Deal era, though an understanding of their workings can be gained from such contemporary studies as Ernest and Betty Lindley's *A New Deal for Youth*, Donald S. Howard's *W.P.A. and Federal Relief Policy*, Arthur Burns and Edward A. Williams's *Federal Work, Security and Relief Programs*, and the exhaustive *Administration of Federal Work Relief* by Arthur McMahon, John Millett, and Gladys Ogden. Harry Hopkins still lacks a good biography, but Searle F. Charles's *Minister of Relief*, though superficial in its analysis of the man, is nevertheless still extremely valuable on the workings of the relief agencies, on Hopkins's position within them, and on his relationships with those he worked with, including Williams. Henry H. Adams's recent biography, *Harry Hopkins*, concentrates more on the period after Hopkins had left the WPA and adds little to Charles's discussion. For Mrs. Roosevelt, her social concerns, and her relations with Williams, I found Joseph Lash's *Eleanor and Franklin* to be of some value, but I also used a little-noticed but thoroughly worthwhile monograph, James R. Kearney's *Anna Eleanor Roosevelt: The Evolution of a Reformer*. This book is at times factually incorrect, but seems nevertheless to be much more analytically persuasive than Lash.

Three recent books have added to my understanding of blacks in New Deal America and of Williams's ideas on race. The most important in my view, Harvard Sitkoff's *A New Deal for Blacks*, supersedes Alan Kifer's 1961 Wisconsin doctoral dissertation, "The Negro under the New Deal," as the standard study of the way that the New Deal programs affected black people, but it is more than that. Sitkoff discusses the rise of black protest groups in the 1930s and includes a useful discussion of the March on Washington Movement. Less broad in scope, but equally valuable, is John B. Kirby's *Black Americans in the Roosevelt Era*, which convincingly demonstrates the linkage in the minds of some New Dealers, including Williams, between "reform liberalism" and "race liberalism," discusses their attempts to act on that conviction, and explains the black response to their actions. It helps place Williams in a specific New Deal context. More general, but equally important in setting Williams within a context, is Morton Sosna's fine study of twentieth-century southern liberalism, *In Search of the Silent South*, which is basic to an understanding of why certain southerners thought and acted in opposition to the prevailing mores of their region. Thomas A. Krueger's study of the SCHW, *And Promises to Keep*, is also helpful in that regard.

Though at times lacking in analysis, David E. Caute's *The Great Fear* is an exhaustive study of the climate of opinion that made senators McCarthy and Eastland possible. Robert E. Griffith's superb *Politics of Fear* explains, among other things, why Williams's powerful political friends were not of much use to him during the Internal Security Subcommittee's investigation. William D. Barnard's *Dixiecrats and Democrats*, though lacking social analysis, is nevertheless a good discussion of the climate of Alabama politics at the time that Williams returned there in 1945 and of the rise and fall of James E. Folsom. David L. Lewis's *King*, the best study of the black leader, contains useful material in its early chapters about the growth of the black-led civil rights movement in the 1950s, and about its relationships with such white-led groups as the SCEF. Lawrence Lader, in *Power on the Left*, helped me understand the context that created the NCHUAC.

Apart from Kifer's work, which has already been cited, the theses and dissertations that helped me most in the preparation of this study were George Rawick's pioneering work on the New Deal youth agencies, "The New Deal and Youth," which a whole generation of scholars has used with gratitude, Susan Poynton's excellent study of the Negro Division of the NYA, and Irwin Klibaner's exhaustive study of the SCEF. I found the Klibaner work indispensable to my understanding of Williams's later years.

The comparatively few works discussed above are but the most important of those that helped me understand the context of Aubrey Williams's life. Others have been cited in the text on particular occasions and are listed in the bibliography. Still others have been neither cited nor placed in the bibliography, because to do so would be to list the literally thousands of books and articles, read over a long period of time and often half-remembered but nevertheless crucially important in forming a set of ideas, that form the topography within which scholarly work occurs.

Sources Cited in Text

Manuscripts

Franklin Delano Roosevelt Library, Hyde Park, New York
   Harry L. Hopkins Papers
   Eleanor Roosevelt Papers
   Franklin D. Roosevelt Papers
   Charles W. Taussig Papers
   Senator Elbert Thomas Papers
   Aubrey W. Williams Papers
National Archives, Washington, D.C.
   Records of the Civil Works Administration
   Records of the Federal Emergency Relief Administration
   Records of the National Youth Administration
   Records of the Works Progress Administration
State Historical Society, Madison, Wisconsin
   Carl and Anne Braden Papers

Records of the Highlander Research and Education Center
Alexander Meiklejohn Papers
Marvin B. Rosenberry Papers
Records of the Wisconsin Conference of Social Work
Harry S. Truman Library, Independence, Missouri
　J. Howard McGrath Papers
　Harry S. Truman Papers
University of North Carolina Library, Chapel Hill, North Carolina
　John Hosea Kerr Papers
　Lindsay Carter Warren Papers
Other Collections
　Black Collection, Hollis Burke Frissell Library, Tuskegee Institute, Tuskegee, Alabama
　Clifford Durr Papers, State Department of Archives and History, Montgomery, Alabama
　Senator Kenneth D. McKellar Papers, Memphis Public Library, Memphis, Tennessee
　Aubrey Williams Papers, collection held privately by the family

Government Documents

U.S. Congress. *Congressional Record.* 76th Cong., 1st sess., 1939; 76th Cong., 2nd sess., 1939; 76th Cong., 3d sess., 1940; 77th Cong., 1st sess., 1941; 77th Cong., 2nd sess., 1942; 78th Cong., 1st sess., 1943; 79th Cong., 1st sess., 1945.

U.S. Congress. House. *Department of Labor, Federal Security Agency, Appropriation Bill for 1941: Hearings before the Sub-Committee of the Committee on Appropriations*, 76th Cong., 3d sess., 1940.

U.S. Congress. House. *Department of Labor, Federal Security Agency, Appropriation Bill for 1944: Hearings before the Sub-Committee of the Committee on Appropriations*, 78th Cong. 3d sess., 1944.

U.S. Congress. House. *Investigation and Study of the Works Progress Administration: Hearings before the Sub-Committee of the Committee on Appropriations*, 76th Cong., 1st sess., 1939 (acting under House Resolution 130).

U.S. Congress. House. *Work Relief and Relief for Fiscal Year 1940: Hearings before the Sub-Committee of the Committee on Appropriations*, 76th Cong., 1st sess., 1939.

U.S. Congress. *Reduction of Non-Essential Federal Expenditures: Hearings before the Joint Committee on the Reduction of Non-Essential Federal Expenditures Congress of the United States*, 77th Cong., 1st sess., 1941.

U.S. Congress. *Reduction of Non-Essential Federal Expenditures: Hearings before the Joint Committee on the Reduction of Non-Essential Federal Expenditures*, 78th Cong., 1st sess., 1943.

U.S. Congress. Senate. *Nomination of Aubrey W. Williams: Hearings before the Committee of Agriculture and Forestry*, 79th Cong., 1st sess., 1945 (on the Nomination of Aubrey W. Williams to be Administrator, Rural Electrification Administration).

U.S. Congress. Senate. *Southern Conference Educational Fund, Inc.: Hearings before the Sub-Committee to Investigate the Administration of the Internal Security Act and Other Internal Security Laws of the Committee of the Judiciary*, 83rd Cong., 2d sess., 1955 (*Subversive Influence in the Southern Conference Educational Fund, Inc.*).

U.S. Congress. Senate. Special Committee to Investigate Campaign Expenditures and Use of Government Funds. *Investigation of Senatorial Campaign Expenditures and Use of Government Funds*, 76th Cong., 1st sess., 1939, *Report Number 1* (pursuant to Senate Resolutions Number 230 and 290), part 2.

U.S. Congress. Senate. *Termination of Civilian Conservation Corps and National Youth Administration: Hearings before the Committee on Education and Labor on S 2295, A Bill to Provide for the Termination of the National Youth Administration and the Civilian Conservation Corps*, 77th Cong., 2nd sess., 1942.

U.S. Federal Security Agency. *Final Report of the National Youth Administration, 1936–1943*. Washington, D.C., 1944.

Newspapers and Periodicals

Albany (New York) *Times Union*
Atlanta Constitution
Atlanta Journal
Baltimore Evening Sun
Birmingham News
Birmingham Post and Herald
Chicago Defender
Chicago Sunday Bee
Chicago Tribune
Dallas Morning News
Denver Post
Firing Line
I. F. Stone's Weekly
Jackson (Mississippi) *Daily News*
Lyttleton (Colorado) *Independent*
Memphis Press-Scimitar

Montgomery Advertiser
Nation
National Guardian
New Orleans Times Picayune
New Republic
New York Herald Tribune
New York Times
Richmond Times Dispatch
St. Louis Post Dispatch
Southern Farmer (later *Southern Farm and Home*)
Southern Patriot
Time
Wall Street Journal
Washington Post
Washington Star

Interviews

Mary Anderson Bain, April 6, 1976.
Clifford Durr, December 29, 1974 (for Southern Oral History Program, University of North Carolina).
Virginia Foster Durr, May 29, 31, 1976.
Ray Jenkins, May 31, 1976.
John A. Lang, September 17, 1970.
E. D. Nixon, May 31, 1976.
Anita Williams, April 4, 1976.
Aubrey Williams, Jr., April 5, 1976.

Anita and Aubrey Williams, Jr., June 9, 1976.
Paul Woolley, May 30, 1976.

Theses and Dissertations

Kifer, Allan F., "The Negro under the New Deal, 1933–1941." Ph.D. dissertation, University of Wisconsin, 1961.
Poynton, Susan M. "The Negro Division of the National Youth Administration, 1935–1943." M.A. thesis, La Trobe University, 1975.
Rawick, George P. "The New Deal and Youth, the Civilian Conservation Corps, the National Youth Administration, the American Youth Congress." Ph.D. dissertation, University of Wisconsin, 1957.
Klibaner, Irwin. "The Southern Conference Educational Fund: A History." Ph.D. dissertation, University of Wisconsin, 1971.

Articles

Chamberlain, John. "Our Jobless Youth: A Warning." *Survey Graphic* 28, no. 10 (October 1939): 579–82.
High, Stanley. "Communism Presses Its Pants." *Saturday Evening Post*, July 9, 1938, pp. 5–6, 30–36.
———. "Who Organized the Unemployed?" *Saturday Evening Post*, December 10, 1938, pp. 8–9, 30–36.
Jacobson, Paul B., comp. "Youth at Work." *Bulletin of the National Association of Secondary School Principals* 25, no. 99 (May 1941): 114–19.
Maund, Alfred E. "The Battle of New Orleans." *Nation* 178, no. 14 (April 5, 1954): 281–82.
Perry, Jennings. "The Congressional Inquisition Moves South." *I. F. Stone's Weekly*, March 29, 1954.
Williams, Aubrey. "Youth and Government." *Progressive Education*, 12, no. 8, December 1936.

Books

Adams, Frank, with Horton, Myles. *Unearthing Seeds of Fire: The Idea of Highlander*. Winston-Salem: Blair, 1977.
Adams, Henry H. *Harry Hopkins: A Biography*. New York: Putnam, 1977.
Albertson, Dean. *Roosevelt's Farmer: Claude R. Wickard in the New Deal*. New York: Columbia University Press, 1961.
Barnard, William D. *Dixiecrats and Democrats: Alabama Politics, 1942–50*. University: University of Alabama Press, 1974.
Becker, Stephen B. *Marshall Field III: A Biography*. New York: Simon and Schuster, 1964.

Bedford, Henry F. *Trouble Downtown: The Local Context of Twentieth Century America*. New York: Harcourt Brace, 1978.

Burns, Arthur E., and Williams, Edward A. *Works Progress Administration. Division of Social Research. Research Monograph 24, Federal Work, Security and Relief Programs*. Washington: Government Printing Office, 1941.

Cantor, Louis. *A Prologue to the Protest Movement: The Missouri Roadside Demonstration of 1939*. Durham: Duke University Press, 1969.

Cass, James, and Birnbaum, Max, eds. *Comparative Guide to American Colleges*. New York: Harper and Row, 1965.

Caute, David E. *The Great Fear: The Anti-Communist Purge under Truman and Eisenhower*. New York: Simon and Schuster, 1978.

Chambers, Clark A. *Seedtime of Reform: American Social Service and Social Action, 1918–1933*. Minneapolis: University of Minnesota Press, 1963.

Charles, Searle F. *Minister of Relief: Harry Hopkins and the Depression*. Syracuse: Syracuse University Press, 1963.

Chatfield, Charles. *For Peace and Justice: Pacifism in America, 1918–1941*. Knoxville: University of Tennessee Press, 1971.

Davis, Maxine. *The Lost Generation: A Portrait of American Youth Today*. New York: Macmillan, 1936.

Goodman, Walter. *The Committee: The Extraordinary Career of the House Committee on Un-American Activities*. London: Secker and Warburg, 1969.

Griffith, Robert E. *The Politics of Fear: Joseph R. McCarthy and the Senate*. Lexington: University of Kentucky Press, 1970.

Hackney, Sheldon. *From Populism to Progressivism in Alabama*. Princeton: Princeton University Press, 1969.

Hamby, Alonzo L. *Beyond the New Deal: Harry S. Truman and American Liberalism*. New York: Columbia University Press, 1973.

Hoover, Herbert. *The Memoirs of Herbert Hoover*. Vol. 3, *The Great Depression*. London: Hollis and Carter, 1953.

Howard, Donald S. *The W.P.A. and Federal Relief Policy*. New York: Russell Sage Foundation, 1943.

Kearney, James R. *Anna Eleanor Roosevelt: The Evolution of a Reformer*. Boston: Houghton Mifflin, 1968.

Kirby, John B. *Black Americans in the Roosevelt Era: Liberalism and Race*. Knoxville: University of Tennessee Press, 1980.

Krueger, Thomas A. *And Promises to Keep: The Southern Conference for Human Welfare, 1938–1948*. Nashville: Vanderbilt University Press, 1967.

Lader, Lawrence. *Power on the Left: American Radical Movements since 1946*. New York: Norton, 1979.

Lash, Joseph P. *Eleanor and Franklin*. New York: Norton, 1971.

Leuchtenburg, William E. *Franklin D. Roosevelt and the New Deal, 1932–1940*. New York: Harper and Row, 1963.

_____. *The Perils of Prosperity, 1914–32*. Chicago: University of Chicago Press, 1958.

Lewis, David L. *King: A Biography*. Urbana: University of Illinois Press, 1978.

Lindley, Betty, and Lindley, Ernest K. *A New Deal for Youth: The Story of the*

National Youth Administration. New York: Viking, 1938.

Lorwin, Lewis. *Youth Work Programs: Problems and Policies*. Washington: American Youth Commission, 1941.

Lubove, Roy. *The Professional Altruist: The Emergence of Social Work as a Career, 1880–1930*. Cambridge: Harvard University Press, 1965.

Macmahon, Arthur W.; Millett, John D.; and Ogden, Gladys. *The Administration of Federal Work Relief*. Chicago: Public Administration Service, 1941.

Melvin, Bruce L. *Youth, Millions Too Many?: A Search for Youth's Place in America*. New York: Association Press, 1940.

Miller, Zane L. *Boss Cox's Cincinnati: Urban Politics in the Progressive Era*. New York: Oxford University Press, 1968.

Roosevelt, Eleanor. *This I Remember*. New York: Harper and Row, 1968.

Salmond, John A. *The Civilian Conservation Corps: A New Deal Case Study*. Durham: Duke University Press, 1967.

Saloutos, Theodore, *Farmer Movements in the South, 1865–1933*. Lincoln: University of Nebraska Press, 1960.

Saloutos, Theodore, and Hicks, John D. *Twentieth Century Populism: Agricultural Discontent in the Middle West, 1900–1939*. Lincoln: University of Nebraska Press, 1951.

Schlesinger, Arthur M., Jr. *The Age of Roosevelt*. Vol. 2, *The Coming of the New Deal*. Vol. 3, *The Politics of Upheaval*. Boston: Houghton Mifflin, 1958, 1960.

Sherrill, Robert E. *Gothic Politics in the Deep South*. New York: Ballantine Books, 1969.

Sherwood, Robert E. *Roosevelt and Hopkins: An Intimate History*. New York: Harper and Row, 1948.

Sitkoff, Harvard. *A New Deal for Blacks: The Emergence of Civil Rights as a National Issue*. Vol. 1, *The Depression Decade*. New York: Oxford University Press, 1978.

Sosna, Morton. *In Search of the Silent South: Southern Liberals and the Race Issue*. New York: Columbia University Press, 1977.

Tindall, George B. *The Emergence of the New South, 1913–1945*. Baton Rouge: Louisiana State University Press, 1967.

Williams, T. Harry. *Huey Long*. New York: Knopf, 1969.

Wiltz, Charles E. *From Isolation to War, 1931–1941*. London: Routledge and Kegan Paul, 1969.

Woodward, C. Vann. *The Origins of the New South, 1877–1913*. Baton Rouge: Louisiana State University Press, 1951.

Index

of Martin Luther King, 253; friendship
with Lyndon Johnson, 254–57, 261, 282,
284; criticizes liberals, 260–61; criticizes
black leadership, 261–63; and the Bradens, 263–65; difficulties within SCEF,
263–65; and baseball, 265–66; tries to
write autobiography, 266, 277–80; illness of, 266–69, 273, 282–83; and 1960
election, 257, 268; and Catholicism, 268;
resigns from SCEF, 268–69; and
NCHUAC, 270–74; moves to
Washington, 274–76; and Jesus, 278–79;
and white Southerners, 279–80; and
Washington March, 281; death of, 283;
influences on, 285–87
Williams, Aubrey, Jr., 27, 204, 216, 218,
286
Williams, Ben, 155–56
Williams, Charles, 4–5, 286
Williams, Eva Taylor, 4–7, 286
Williams, Frankwood E., 48
Williams, Jere, 27
Williams, John Sharp, 39
Williams, Morrison, 27, 216–17, 260, 275
Williams, Pierce, 67, 85
Williams, Roby, 5
Williams, Vivian Thomas, 217
Williams, Winston Tyndall, 14, 24–25, 286
Willis, Raymond E., 188, 193
Wilson, George S., 66
Wilson, Samuel Tyndall, 13–15, 17
Wilson, Woodrow, 22
Wisconsin Board of Control, 34
Wisconsin Conference of Social Work, 25;
origins, 26; activities, 27–34; and De-

pression, 31–34; and relief policy,
33–34; and disagreements with Williams,
34–35
Wisconsin, University of, 26, 35, 41; extension division, 26, 31
Witter, Mrs. Isaac P., 26, 29–30, 287
Wolman, Leo, 32
Woodward, C. Vann, 4
Woodward, Ellen S., 85
Woolley, Paul, 208, 216, 227, 265, 267,
275
Workers Alliance of America, 93, 97, 165,
167–69
Workers General Federation of Europe, 21
Work relief: debate over, 32–33, 71–72,
78, 95
Works Progress Administration (WPA), 35,
86, 93, 99–102, 121–22, 124–26,
128–29, 136–37, 140, 163, 167, 221,
267, 284, 287, 289, 293 (n. 6); origins of,
78–79; administrative structure, 80,
86–87, 92–94; and disaster relief, 88;
politics in, 89–91
World War I, 18–22
Wright, Archie, 213
Wright, Houston, 122

Young, Owen D., 82
Young Men's Business Club of New Or-
leans, 233
Young Men's Christian Association
(YMCA), 10, 19
Young Women's Christian Association
(YWCA), 127
Youth: and Depression, 72–76